C000140629

LAND'S END TO
– IN FIFTE

LAND'S END TO JOHN O'GROATS
– IN FIFTEEN YEARS!
Alan Plowright

Moorfield Press

First published in Great Britain
by
Moorfield Press 2002

Copyright © Alan Plowright 2002

Page Layout by
Highlight Type Bureau Ltd, Bradford, West Yorkshire
Printed in England by
The Amadeus Press, Cleckheaton, West Yorkshire

A CIP catalogue record for this book is available from the British Library

ISBN 0 9530 1194 1

The moral right of the author has been asserted

Colour photographs: Alan Plowright

mainly across country, in 1967. An inspiring record of his adventures, its vividly descriptive narrative brought to life a journey that was, at times, quite harrowing. He wrote of blundering through swirling mists whilst crossing Dartmoor's intimidating wastes and being halted by impenetrable clouds on Scotland's high tops. I marvelled at his achievement of covering a distance of 1100 miles in fifty-five days, despite his tribulations.

I was prompted to begin long-distance walking and I even cherished hopes of emulating Hillaby's remarkable achievement. Also at that time I discovered the writings of Alfred Wainwright, creator of the beautifully crafted Pictorial Guides. His *Walks in Limestone Country* caught my eye and introduced me to the unforgettable scenery of the Yorkshire Dales that lay on my doorstep. After a period of exploration of the areas he described in his Guide I decided to tackle my first long-distance walk. I chose the Pennine Way as a suitable challenge, for a section passes through the Dales thus providing the opportunity to familiarise myself with part of it before attempting the complete walk.

Despite my initial doubts about tackling such a journey I completed the 270-mile trek from Edale in Derbyshire to Kirk Yetholm, a village just to the north of the Scottish Border, in under three weeks. The first endurance test of my walking career was safely behind me.

A walk through the Scottish Borders formed the next section of my challenge to walk the length of the country. Returning to Kirk Yetholm I journeyed to the start of the West Highland Way at Milngavie on the outskirts of Glasgow. The walk included two days on the splendid Southern Upland Way that traverses Scotland from Portpatrick, near Stranraer, to Cockburnspath, situated on the coast to the east of Edinburgh.

With the aim of walking the remaining distance through Scotland I recommenced my journey at Milngavie with my sights on John O'Groats. I travelled the West Highland Way, also one of Scotland's finest long-distance footpaths, which led me to Fort William. From there I ventured through the remote, but captivating, wilderness of Wester Ross and Sutherland, to reach Durness, near Cape Wrath. A trek along the rugged north coast followed, until I finally reached my objective, the north-east tip of Britain.

Buoyed by my progress I continued to nibble away at my goal by attempting Offa's Dyke Path, an official long-distance footpath that roughly follows the line of the King of Mercia's great earthwork, constructed in 757 along the Welsh border. Unbeknown to me, I was to suffer my first failure, for I was forced to retire after covering around half its length due to a long-standing back problem. Determined not to be outdone I returned to the point where I had succumbed on my first attempt and, on this occasion I managed to complete the walk.

My next task was to link the northern end of Offa's Dyke Path, at Prestatyn, with Edale, which lies at the southern end of the Pennine Way. I discovered that such a walk existed, albeit undesignated and I managed to obtain a relevant guidebook, entitled *The Cestrian Link*. Its title is derived from the name afforded to natives of Chester, the ancient city that it passes. The detailed route instructions within the guide appeared to be just what I required but, unfortunately, during my journey I found that many of the footpaths indicated had become overgrown or disappeared, causing considerable heartache and frustrating detours. However, I persevered and eventually reached my destination.

Having covered the distance between Chepstow, the southern extremity of Offa's Dyke Path, and John O'Groats, I realised that the majority of my challenge was behind me. However, thirteen years had elapsed since I took my first faltering steps from Edale along the Pennine Way and I reckoned that I must tackle the remainder before my wind and legs became unequal to the task. With eager anticipation I checked the remaining distance, from Chepstow to Land's End, and found I had roughly 285 miles to cover along a reasonably scenic route.

The final chapter of my extensive trek was carried out in two stages and the second, a walk from Land's End to Exeter, was completed whilst Cornwall and Devon were still suffering the effects of the foot and mouth epidemic. This unfortunately necessitated considerable road-walking and resulted in sore feet, but this was a minor drawback to what proved to be a stimulating part of my 'end to end' traverse.

There were no wild celebrations when my dream was finally realised. However, there was great satisfaction in achieving a long-standing aim that had taken me through the wonderfully diverse countryside of Britain, which revealed itself, warts and all, in fair weather and foul. 1360 miles had been covered, considerably more than the 874 by road, but I considered my cross-country route infinitely more rewarding than that taken by Doctor Barbara

Moore and her fellow competitors - despite the fact that it took me nearly fifteen years longer than those stalwarts to complete!

Although the journey was undertaken in stages, for purposes of continuity it is described as a complete walk. Perhaps the following account of my travels through the length of Britain will inspire you to tackle some or all, of such a trek. If it does, I hope that you derive as much pleasure from your wanderings as I did.

Alan Plowright 2002

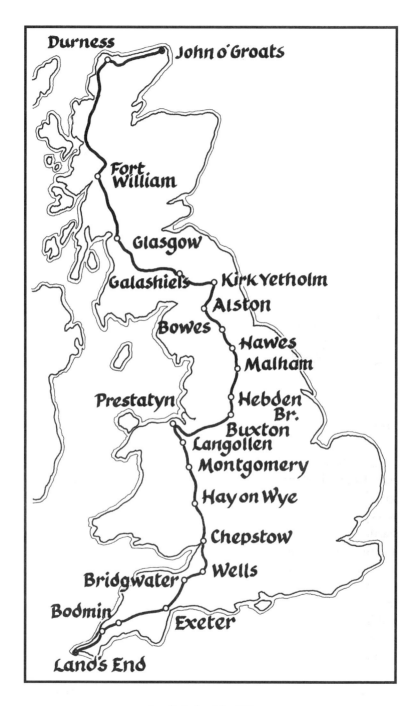

Land's End to John O'Groats

CHAPTER ONE

Land's End to Exeter

DAY ONE : LAND'S END - ST JUST

I was bathed in sunshine as I reached the entertainment complex that Land's End has become. A good omen, I reckoned. The sparkling white façade of the village entrance shimmered in the sun's glare, an oasis amidst an expanse of parked cars and sand. This startling edifice, inspired by 'Southfork,' of television's *Dallas*, hides a cluster of 'delights' that constitute Land's End Village, a modern complex claiming to provide attractions for the whole family.

I was quite unprepared for the miniature Disneyland that met my eyes as I ventured through the entrance arch. Crowds were milling around an array of white stucco buildings and an assortment of souvenir shops and bars. Diversions, such as 'The Restless Sea' and 'The Last Labyrinth' enticed visitors into their portals.

I quickly abandoned the hurly-burly of the village and headed for point itself, a sixty-foot granite cliff that descends to stub a large toe into the Atlantic, in the direction of the Longships lighthouse, standing a mile out to sea. Pausing at the famous signpost, its finger pointing towards John O'Groats, 874 miles away, I watched a smiling family being photographed beneath the sign's other finger indicating the distance to their home town. A good way to earn a fiver a time, I thought, studying the long queue of people waiting their turn in the queue for the resident photographer.

Land's End was not always as popular. According to Cairns Boston, managing director of the site for many years, it was known as the armpit of tourism before he took over its running in 1982. He described it as the 'p and p' (pee and postcard) stop of Britain and an embarrassing and dangerous place, because of erosion. David Goldstone, the owner at that time, spent a million pounds on improvements before falling foul of the district council over his £1.50 entry charge. He sold out in 1987 to the property tycoon and yachtsman Peter de Savary who was to purchase the hotel at John O'Groats two years later. Things forged ahead. The new owner hired David Bellamy as a wildlife consultant and John Taylor, who had repackaged his Littlecote estate in Berkshire, to create man-made attractions. 'The Labyrinth' was dug out of a cavern, the paths to the headland were surfaced, grass was replanted and the site was reopened in 1988.

Cairns Boston bore the brunt of criticism from those who objected to the development and gained the title of 'Mr Land's End,' for he represented the unacceptable face of change. One day he gave a greeting to an elderly lady at the local garage, which was received with stony silence. 'Are you not speaking to me?' Cairns inquired. 'No,' was the reply. 'You are the man who has ruined Land's End.'

Taken aback, Cairns retorted, 'I provide employment for a lot of people. There are good family facilities, a high-class restaurant and a comfortable hotel in an area where they are sparse. This garage makes money from it. We all do well.'

'Is that so?' she responded. 'You've ruined it. I wouldn't go near it.'

The managing director asked, 'When did you last go there?'

'Twenty-six years ago!'

Peter de Savary's ownership lasted a mere three years. Feeling the effects of a property recession he sold it to a New Zealander, Graham Ferguson Lacy, under whose tenure things progressed in the same direction.

In 1996 Kevin Leech, a former funeral director, turned multi-millionaire, purchased the site. A self-made man, he also counted the Chedder Gorge Cheese Company and the Needles caravan site amongst his numerous acquisitions. Things must have been shaky, for he obtained Land's End and John O'Groats as a job lot for a mere £6 million. His aim was to continue the upgrading of facilities at both sites. Another chapter, filled with good intentions, had begun in the continuing saga of Land's End.

It was difficult to decide if I found favour with the current version. Love it or loathe it, the place typifies the age-old battle between 'progress,' which brings development plus employment, and leaving a place of natural beauty to the mercy of erosion.

What does the future hold, I wondered as I gazed over the jagged rocks of the point, with startling white foam gnawing at its extremities?

I joined the army of tourists making their way to the white-walled First and Last Refreshment House, beckoning from the nearby cliff-top. Beyond the café a wide and eroded path begins its journey along the cliff-tops. People crawled like ants along the undulating thoroughfare but soon thinned out and I recalled reading that if you walk for ten minutes in either direction from the point you will find yourself virtually alone.

As I took my first steps towards Exeter, all my preparation was about to be put to the test. You can't go wrong on the South West Coast Path, I told myself, if you keep the sea on the correct side of you until you reach Newquay.

I had not progressed far before I encountered a mere handful of people and from thereon I met only a few hardy walkers of the coast path. The rugged coastline looked spectacular in the June sunshine. Lush grassy carpets, bristling with a host of sub-tropical plants, veered sharply down to sheer tawny cliffs that plunged into a vibrant-blue ocean.

A few miles from Land's End I came upon secluded Sennen Cove, a charming village tucked into the folds of sheltering cliffs. Typical of Cornish fishing villages depicted in films of yesteryear it appears heavily dependent on tourism, for fishing boats were scarce.

I walked along the inviting beach of the bustling, popular resort that nestles by the aptly named Whitesand Bay. Sunbathers soaked

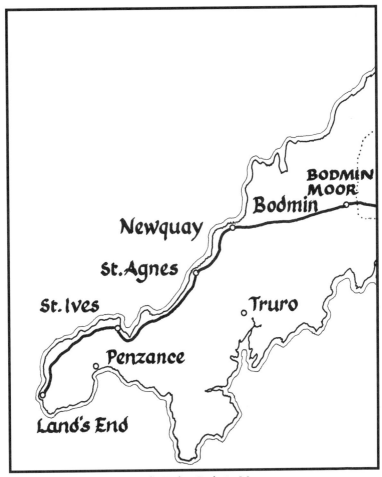

Land's End to Bodmin Moor

up the afternoon sun as I trod its mile of pliant sand, my enjoyment tempered by trudging through what seemed like grainy treacle. Surfers romped amongst the breakers spilling onto the shore and I admired the more accomplished amongst them, skillfully gliding along the wave crests.

The dramatic coastal scenery continued to enthrall on that hot, cloudless afternoon as I traversed the next two miles of coastal path. It frequently carried me away from the cliff-tops and tested my stamina with steep gradients but the landscape was never dull. Milky samphire and succulents clung to the rock faces as gulls and rock pipits soared above. Bright orange montbretia mingled with

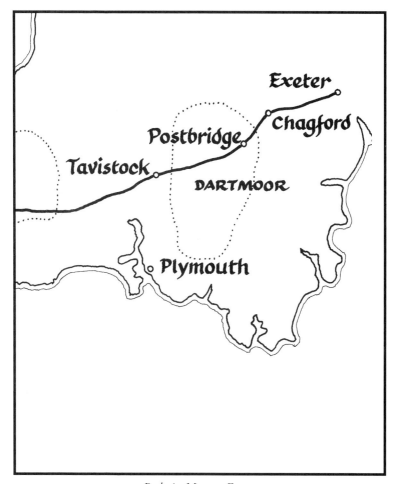

Bodmin Moor to Exeter

white cups of bindweed, adding splashes of colour to the cliff-top tangle of blown stalks and grasses.

As I rounded Gribba Point I gained my first view of the Brisons, two rocky pyramids protruding from the sea roughly one mile from Cape Cornwall. They signified it was nearly time to leave the coast path and head for my night's accommodation on the outskirts of St Just. As I approached the mouth of the Cot Valley, a deep groove in the seaboard, I could clearly define the prominent landmark of Cape Cornwall. This rocky buttress protrudes from a coastline dotted with megalithic remains and the remnants of tin mines, once the life-blood of Cornwall. When the industry was at its peak in the

1850's underground workings stretched from the cape as far as the Brisons, beneath the sea-bed.

Apart from Land's End and a few other exceptions the Cornish coast is as solitary as it was more than five thousand years ago when a curious, but peaceful race of tomb-builders arrived from Mediterranean climes. They established settlements, practiced their religion and built elaborate graves that punctuate the landscape to this day. The remarkable quoits, large gravestones and burial chambers are a residue of their megalithic cult. One such exposed chamber, sunk into the rim of the cliffs between the Cot Valley and Cape Cornwall is Carn Gloose, a ring with a round shaft at its centre, down which the dead were lowered into what was perceived as eternity.

Nearby, a lone chimney dents the skyline, a sad reminder of the demise of Cornwall's thriving tin-mining industry. It is set amongst long-abandoned mine levels dating from the eighteenth century when progression was made from the 'tin-streaming' of the surface to burrowing into cliff faces to extract directly from rich veins.

I veered into the Cot Valley, a secluded gully of charm and beauty, accentuated by the benevolent sun's rays. The exposed coastal landscape rapidly changed to one of lush vegetation. Shrubby willows and a dense covering of Japanese knotweed heralded my entrance into a rural idyll.

Sheltered from the sea breeze I descended into the depths of the valley where a narrow lane and overgrown footpaths penetrate a patchwork of verdant woods and green meadows. It took careful map-reading and a request for guidance at a sequestered cottage to set me on course for my night's resting-place.

That evening I strolled across fields to St Just, a pleasant old town, having former associations with tin-mining. It boasts an ancient church and a small amphitheatre used for the performance of medieval mystery plays until the seventeenth century. This grassy indent is now a meeting-place for the youngsters of the town.

As I enjoyed a meal that included the inevitable Cornish Pasty in a friendly café I inquired how local shops and businesses had coped since the imposition of foot and mouth restrictions the previous February. The waitress told me that some footpaths had recently re-opened and tourism was beginning to pick up after a lean few months. She also explained that the traditional test of a good pasty was to drop it down the deepest shaft of a tin mine. If, at the bottom, it remained intact, then it was 'vitty,' which I took her to mean 'tough.'

DAY TWO: ST JUST - ST IVES

The following morning I set out full of expectation. That day I planned to do a little inland walking and discover some of the ancient remains that litter the area.

All went well initially, for I soon found the prominent granite outcrop of Carn Kenidjack, known locally as the 'Hooting Carn,' with its attendant stone circle and a scattering of tumuli. However, whilst I was investigating the site the weather turned against me. It began to rain with a vengeance and I sheltered for a while in the shadow of the carn. Eventually I was forced to brave the unrelenting rain, which, lashed by a fierce wind, drove horizontally into my face for the next two hours. Water seeped into every pore and, most annoyingly, the outer pockets of my rucksack. Thankfully I had protected my belongings in the main portion of the sack with a substantial plastic bin liner for just such an occurrence but the persistent rain seeped into my map-case and reduced my carefully prepared route-maps almost to pulp. Help!

Alone in a bleak and grey wilderness, I struggled over the peculiarly named Woon Gumpus Common, unable to see more than twenty yards ahead. To compound my woes, mist had perversely joined in the fun. My planning and good intentions began to evaporate. You can keep the nearby stone circles and standing stones, I fumed. I'm not searching for them in this deluge. I even gave up on Chun quoit, preferring to keep to an easily distinguishable track leading to Bosullow Common, home to the unique Men-an-tol, probably the most famous ancient monument on the Land's End peninsula.

Determined to at least see the remarkable set of three stones, the central one resembling a cartwheel standing upright on its rim, I plodded grimly along the track that traverses Bosullow Common. Absolutely drenched and miserable I fortuitously came across a dilapidated barn whose leaking roof afforded a little shelter. Removing my sodden outer clothing I hungrily devoured some welcome sandwiches whilst I took stock of my situation.

Realisation dawned that it was foolish to blunder over open country in such harsh conditions. I decided to backtrack to the nearest road and keep to tarmac for the rest of my day's journey to St Ives. Men-an-tol would have to wait.

I left my rude shelter and eventually reached a road that winds towards the village of Trevowhan. As I did so the rain eased and the mist began to roll away. Sod's law decreed that the sky cleared and the sun came out. I cursed myself for forsaking Men-an-tol as I joined the coast road to St Ives that lay nine frustrating miles away.

The road twisted like an energetic snake as I pounded its unrelenting surface and thankfully traffic was quite sparse. I headed for Zennor, a village I was eager to see due to its association with a quoit that stands high on the hills above. I had not been lucky in my quest for quoits that day and I weighed up the possibility of making a detour of over two miles to see it.

Unfortunately, the actual mileage appeared twice that shown on the map due to the extremely sinuous road. By the time I reached Zennor the afternoon was well advanced and my feet were beginning to rebel against the tarmac. I reluctantly gave up on the detour. The village did offer compensation, however, for I was instantly drawn to the prominent tower of the Church of St Senara and the huddle of quaint granite buildings that lay in its shadow.

I hurried down a narrow lane towards the hamlet, unobtrusively nestling beneath a swelling line of ancient moorland hills patterned with a tracery of prehistoric stone-hedged field systems and isolated farmsteads. On the hills above, from Zennor quoit to Carn Kenidjack, relics of past occupation abound and I had frustratingly missed out on most of them.

Pausing at the entrance to the Wayside Folk Museum, I watched a waterwheel, its paddles lazily turning. Nearby stands a large flat stone with an indentation in its top and a notice above it, identifying the lichen encrusted edifice as the Zennor Plague Stone. It was instrumental in preventing the spread of cholera during the Cornish epidemics of 1836 and 1849. During those periods no one was allowed in or out of the village and food was left for the villagers beside the plague stone, which was sited on its perimeter. Payment for the goods was made by coins left overnight in the recess of the stone, which contained vinegar. This acted as a disinfectant and ensured that the money was germ free.

In the church I discovered a bench end depicting the Mermaid of Zennor, whose beauty and bewitching singing is said to have lured a sweet-voiced chorister to her watery lair in Pendour Cove. It is a carving that would have been familiar to D.H. Lawrence who spent eighteen months in the area with his wife Frieda, during the First World War. They stayed at the Tinner's Arms in the village before moving to a cottage at nearby Higher Tregerthen. Unfortunately, the couple was evicted on suspicion of spying for the enemy, probably due to he and his German-born wife's penchant for lustily singing her country's folk songs.

The afternoon wore on as I forsook Zennor and trudged along tarmac once more. The sun had retreated and sea and sky merged in a pool of grey that washed out the horizon. Despite the gloom the rain had thankfully not returned.

After an hour's progress I stopped at a lay by to pass the time of day with a man scouring the hills above with binoculars. He was watching the antics of a cuckoo and his accent sounded familiar. It transpired that he and his wife, who was sitting patiently in their car, hailed from Scunthorpe. 'I've travelled all over Yorkshire wi' me job as an engineer,' he told me, adding that he had once broken several bones by falling from a boiler on which he was working.

Bidding farewell to the friendly couple I began the final leg of my day's journey. Above me flew a watchful buzzard, often described as 'the poor man's eagle.' This ferocious-looking bird is remarkably passive, despite its reputation. Frequently mobbed by annoying crows, it responds with lazy indifference, but baited too much it will turn on its back and display its intimidating talons.

As visitors will know, the roadsides of Cornwall are festooned with notices advertising cream teas and the road between Land's End and St Ives is no exception. I managed to resist the temptation of scones, oozing succulent jam and clotted cream, until my pace began to slow and St Ives still seemed an eternity away. I abandoned the road at one of the signs and, forsaking my good intentions, approached a nearby farmhouse. As I entered the farm kitchen and sat down at a table I was besieged by three friendly Labradors whose black heads and cold noses rubbed themselves against my hands. Not wishing to be pushed out, a grey cat named Sheba, perched on my knee whilst I enjoyed a mouth-watering cream tea.

My clandestine interlude at the farm meant that more time had slipped by and evening was upon me as I completed the remaining miles of winding road. At last I made the long descent towards St Ives Bay, pausing to admire the quaint chapel perched high above the town, its graveyard overflowing with a forest of decorative headstones.

I had hoped to explore St Ives that evening, but nineteen miles of walking had drained my stamina and enthusiasm. Consequently, I headed straight for my accommodation situated a good distance from the centre of town. To say that my room was poky would be an understatement. It would have been difficult to accommodate Sheba, let alone swing her round in it. The bed was reasonably comfortable and I enjoyed a good night's sleep, happy that I would not be required to make any annoying detours next day. I planned to return to the more accommodating coast path.

DAY THREE : ST IVES - ST AGNES

My apologies to St Ives. I did not do the busy resort justice on the following morning as I set out on what was to be another long day's journey. There was no time to linger if I was to cover the envisaged twenty-three miles to St Agnes before evening. I fairly skipped through the town, throwing cursory glances at its inviting sea front and quaint cottages lining narrow alleyways. Mindful of shipwrecks and smugglers I hurried past the harbour and along the already crowded promenade before climbing a steep, winding hill to the upper part of town.

My first task was to skirt Carbis Bay and circle the Hayle Estuary, no easy task, for it involved a detour of over three miles. How I longed to cross the narrow mouth of the estuary but I was determined not to attempt the treacherous sands that nearly enveloped John Hillaby when he foolishly tried to wade across. Even the eminent preacher, John Wesley had to be rescued from a fast-rising tide.

It proved a long haul and nearly two hours elapsed before I reached the town of Hayle that lies on the eastern side of the estuary. I hurried along the road that bounds the estuary and joined the golden sands of St Ives Bay. The weather was much improved that morning and the sun beamed on me as I strode for two miles along the bracing beach. It seemed endless and the tribulations of the previous day were forgotten as I watched the sea washing the foreshore and the wind tossing sand around the base of the dunes. The varying strata of the cliffs could be clearly seen. Prominent veins of clay were visible, sandwiched between layers of soft buff-coloured rock that virtually crumbled at the touch.

As I neared Godrevy Point, at the northern end of the bay, I returned to the coast path and began a roller-coaster walk along the bucking thoroughfare. The miles indicated on the map appeared to expand once more with the surfeit of climbing and descending.

A strip of good walking country lay between the road and the cliffs. It is under the care of the National Trust and contains frequent car parking spots, ideally situated, overlooking the sea. As a diversion I studied the varied activities of the occupants of numerous parked cars. These included sleeping, knitting, listening to radios, reading the paper and staring at a passing lone walker. What causes people to drive to a lovely spot and never leave their car, I wondered? Someone calculated that the average distance walked from a parked car is a mere seventy-five yards. How this startling discovery was made is not clear, but I'm sure that a short and invigorating walk would greatly benefit motorists seemingly anchored to their cars. However, they should avoid the gruesome motives of certain unfortunates who, I was informed, walk to the edge of a local promontory and throw themselves off.

In the early afternoon I detoured to a nearby road, lured by a sign indicating a café, where I found several customers chatting good humouredly with the friendly proprietor who was quite a talker. With spectacles perched precariously on his nose end he cracked a string of jokes before switching to the serious plight of local farmers and the effects of foot and mouth on the area. 'The burden falls, not only on them, but also on those involved in tourism and serving the agricultural industry,' he indicated, quoting an example of a firm that supplied marquees for functions and outdoor events. Apparently, the local agricultural show had been cancelled, depriving them of £3000 of business. 'There'll be a shortage of feed next spring,' the man warned. 'The farmers are being forced to use the grass, normally stored for that purpose, to feed animals and their new-born young that can't be moved.'

I listened with interest to the knowledgeable fellow as I munched a king-sized slice of cake smothered in buttercream. Just the thing to slow a walker down!

So engrossed was I in the conversation, I barely noticed that three quarters of an hour had slipped by before I returned to the contorted coast path. An energetic and bracing few hours passed before I negotiated the steep descent to Portreath. It was already five o'clock in the evening and, according to my map I had another seven miles to cover. Concerned that I would be late for my evening meal, which I knew would be served at 7 pm, I decided to contact the guesthouse where I was staying and let them know of my delay. Being one of the deprived people who do not own a mobile phone, I located a telephone box in the centre of the village. Workmen were digging up the road outside and I couldn't hear a thing until the men obligingly switched off their juddering pneumatic drills.

The lady proprietor seemed none too pleased that I may not arrive in time for dinner and gasped in amazement when she learned I was walking from St Ives. I promised to get there as soon as possible, indicating I would be extremely grateful for any food she could provide.

I hurriedly sought the path leading up the steep incline from the village but lost many more vital minutes threading through confusing streets and lanes. Eventually the coast path and I were reunited and I took a fleeting bird's eye view of the cove in which the village huddled. White-walled cottages lined the estuary and others clung adventurously to the abrupt hillsides. A narrow road wound to the top of ragged, protective cliffs to complete a scene that was worthy of unhurried scrutiny, but in my haste I paid little heed to secluded Portreath.

The sky clouded over, the wind strengthened and it began to rain. How I regretted my earlier dalliance. Now that I was fighting against the clock nature had turned against me. I quickly put on my waterproofs and tightened the hood of my jacket against the driving rain. Unlike the earlier part of previous day, when the weather turned foul, I had at least a clear path to follow, albeit a bucking and writhing one. Buffeted by the violent wind I battled for three miles along exposed cliff-tops, continually checking my watch, which appeared to have gathered momentum. Suddenly the ground began to drop away and another cove appeared beneath me. A steep, knee-jarring descent was made to the hamlet of Porthtowan, where I found refuge from the wind and rain. Hereabouts, ruined chimneys dot the landscape, marking the remains of a long-dead copper industry, which, at one time, gave rise to richer and more numerous mines than those from which lead was extracted.

St Agnes still lay over three miles away and, with barely a second glance, I took my leave of Porthtowan, which huddled gloomily beneath leaden skies. I clambered up to the cliff-tops once more, panting with the effort and cursing an itinerary that demanded I cover twenty-three miles that day. My anxiety ensured that I kept up a good pace and also a sharp lookout for the point where I was due to leave the coast path and head for St Agnes. Thankfully, the rain began to abate but brooding clouds hampered visibility until my straining eyes spied my destination. Its white-walled buildings sat prominently on a distant hill, in the shadow of St Agnes Beacon, a rough pyramid that rises several hundred feet above the coast. I estimated that it lay about one and a half miles away and I decided to throw caution to the wind, forsake my planned route and cut directly across open country. For my sins I tripped on some rough ground and fell heavily. Fortunately, long grass cushioned my landing and I was merely shaken. Cursing my recklessness I dusted myself down and ploughed onwards, eventually reaching a road that wound towards St Agnes.

The final mile of my day's journey seemed to take an eternity and it was well past seven o'clock when I finally located my night's accommodation. Breathlessly I discarded my boots and waterproofs at the entrance and hurried to the reception desk. It was unmanned and staff flitted to and from the dining room carrying food.

'Ah, there you are!' a voice boomed behind me. I recognised it as that of the proprietor, and turned to see an elderly lady who was clearly flustered. She cast a disdainful look at my dishevelled appearance as I apologised for my late arrival. Mercifully, she made no comment on the windswept lone walker who had disrupted her timetable. I could hear the conversation of other guests, seemingly already enjoying their meal, issuing from the dining room.

'You don't mind finding your own way to your room?' the dragon almost demanded, hurrying to the reception desk and handing me a key, 'We are terribly busy.'

'Not at all.' I replied meekly.

'When you are ready, come to the dining room and I'll organise some food for you.'

I heaved a sigh of relief. She was not a bad sort after all.

A short time later I entered the dining room. Conversation abruptly ceased and all heads swung in my direction. Resisting the urge to check my flies, I realised the diners had obviously been well-briefed regarding the madman who had walked twenty-three miles from St Ives and upset 'madame's' schedule.

Sitting down as unobtrusively as possible at a corner table, I surveyed my fellow guests, none of who appeared to be under seventy years of age. They were already well into their meat and two veg but kept their eyes trained on me as I waited to be served.

My meal, when it eventually arrived, was fine, despite the service provided by a young Italian that spoke virtually no English, and a tight-lipped teenage waitress. As I ate, other guests politely questioned me concerning my day's journey and, like the proprietor, appeared amazed that anyone should walk such a distance for enjoyment. I did not divulge that I intended to walk to Exeter, for fear of stretching their credulity to the limit.

I was partway through the meal when my companions abruptly rose from their tables as one and trooped from the room leaving me to eat in silence. The lady of the house rushed in to inquire if things were satisfactory and sped out again, a look of harassment on her lined features. Grateful as I was for her concern, I was at a loss to understand why the woman should be so put out by catering for a relatively small number of guests.

When I left the dining room the proprietor beckoned me. She indicated a nearby door. 'In there!' she said before scurrying away. I took her remark to mean I was to go in the residents' lounge, which, I assumed, was another formality to be observed.

On entering the oak-panelled room, I felt I was in time warp. It reeked of a long past, sedate era. Varnish was everywhere and antimacassars lined the backs of the heavy, aging settees and armchairs that filled the room. A television, which looked incongruous in its old-fashioned surroundings and which no one appeared to be watching, lit one corner of the dim lounge. Its inhabitants huddled together and conversed in hushed tones, paying me no heed. The steady snores of a sleeping guest reverberated around the large fireplace, which contained a blazing fire, despite the time of year. Another was immersed in a book, oblivious to her companions, and never uttered a word.

Pretending to watch television I weighed up my surroundings. The house was large and impressive, but was showing signs of neglect. Its ambiance was spoilt by lapses, such as dust on the stairs, cheap paper serviettes instead of napkins and those annoying tiny bars of soap in the bathroom that refuse to produce any lather. The lady proprietor projected an air of gentility and refinement but she needed to move with the times. The place required money and a strong hand to lick it into shape. As a guesthouse it had promise but its lack of organisation was common knowledge amongst the villagers who, I later learned, considered the lady an eccentric.

However, I had no real cause for complaint. My room and bed were comfortable and the lady wished me well as I left. As I thanked her, I indicated that my stay had been an experience.

DAY FOUR : ST AGNES - NEWQUAY

Refreshed by a sound night's sleep I began my day's journey by threading through St Agnes. The northern extremity of the village borders Trevaunance Cove, an inlet ravaged by the restless sea, whose ceaseless efforts to break in on the land have wreaked havoc with attempts to build lasting harbours. Three were built during the seventeenth century but all were destroyed by storms, and the eighteenth century version was washed away in the 1900's. Winstanley, the architect of the first Eddystone lighthouse was involved in one of the attempts.

Life was also hard on the heights above the tempestuous ocean and men have toiled for tin since the first Cornishmen raised the three barrows on St Agnes Beacon. Partway up the beacon lies a deposit of sand and clay, which can only have been laid down when the sea covered it. It demonstrates the dramatic rise and fall of the Atlantic coast hereabouts.

I passed the prominent Parish Church that dominates the centre of the village. It was rebuilt in 1848 but still retains a sixteenth-century font, fashioned from local stone. Amongst other relics is a curious wooden almsbox, carved to represent a man in Elizabethan costume. The church register of births includes that of John Opie, a carpenter's son who became a renowned painter and acquired the title of 'The Cornish Wonder.' Despite never receiving any tuition, his remarkable talent eventually led to his election to the Royal Academy and his appointment as professor of painting. His work was prolific and included over 500 portraits.

On the cliffs above St Agnes stands a preserved engine house, with a tall chimney attached. It marks the site of Wheal Kitty, typical of the forest of such buildings that litter the area. The name 'Wheal,' meaning workplace, is common in these parts, for the remnants of Wheal Friendly, Wheal Music and Wheal Liberty lie hereabouts.

At its peak, in the 1850's, the Cornish mining industry utilised some 650 engines to pump water from the workings, crush the ore and lift it and the miners to the surface. The patenting of a high pressure engine by Richard Trevithick, the son of a Cornish miner, allowed mines to go deeper and facilitated the pumping of greater quantities of water from them. Following the collapse of the Cornish mining industry, many local inhabitants emigrated in an attempt to find work and mines closed in large numbers. An important part of Cornwall's heritage was slipping away until, in 1935, the Cornish Engines Preservation Society was inaugurated to protect the remaining structures. The society was renamed the Trevithick Society after the great inventor and was instrumental, alongside the National Trust, in the preservation of many crumbling sites. Wheal Kitty has survived better than most and it possesses a modern visitor centre, which outlines the development and decline of Cornwall's greatest industry, whose lasting reminders are the sprouting chimneys that decorate the windswept heights above Trevaunance Cove.

The weather was in a reasonable mood that morning as I set out on my last section of coast path walking, for I was due to strike inland at Newquay. Buffeted by a stiff wind and bolstered by periodic bursts of sunshine I maintained a good pace, determined not to dally at the outset. The roller-coaster path continued to duck and dive and, as I approached frequent indents in the coastline I could see the eroded footway tenaciously clawing its way up the far side of the valley. I peered down great gashes in the rocks, scoured by the angry waves that pounded them and thought of smugglers, booty and the luring of passing ships into those dangerous waters. Great protrusions in the coastline with evocative names, such as Cligga Head, Shag Rock and Droskyn Point underwent my inspection before I gazed down upon the compact town of Perranporth and its adjacent sweep of tawny sand, Perran Beach. Beyond the beach lay the undulating Penhale Sands, in whose folds can be found a holiday camp, golf links and Wheal Vlow, another example of the redundant mine workings that had become so familiar.

I was impressed by the pleasant resort. The good burghers of Perranporth deserve full marks for their efforts to create a colourful environment. Impressive gardens, studded with waving palm trees and flamboyant flowerbeds bordered my route to the crowded main street. The place is evidently a popular destination for holiday-makers and rightly so. They spilled onto the road and filled the shops and cafés, creating a bustling, carefree air. I was loath to leave them to their candy-floss and bargain hunting, but Newquay beckoned and the majority of my day's route lay ahead.

The all too familiar steep climb awaited me as I waved goodbye to the sea front and headed for Penhale Sands. Toiling up the sandy incline I came upon three women who seemed out for an enjoyable day. They were laughing and joking and gleefully told me they were searching for witches. I doubted if such characters inhabit Penhale Sands and there were none in evidence. One of the trio suggested they searched the exposed Perran Beach rather than the maze of dunes and she made towards a steep sandy path that descended to the shore. Her friends would have none of it and persuaded her to continue their curious search amongst the sandy hillocks. I reasoned that the going would be easier along the beach and said goodbye to the ladies, unsure if they were drunk, or the hot sun had affected them.

As I descended the path to the shore I could see the expanse of Perran Beach stretching as far as the eye could see. Three miles of firm sand beckoned, promising temporary relief from the cavorting coast path. The only disappointment was the amount of rubbish around the high watermark, some of it discarded by careless visitors and the remainder washed ashore by the breakers. Determined not to allow my enjoyment to be spoilt by unsightly litter and flotsam, I strode along the near-deserted flat ribbon of sand listening to the screeching of wheeling gulls and breathing the sweet sea air.

Suddenly, my tranquility was shattered by the sound of gunshots. Tempted to run for cover in the lee of adjacent rocks I watched open-mouthed as a group of soldiers appeared on a bluff above me and fanned out over a nearby headland to the accompaniment of more rifle fire. I glanced at the map and discovered my close proximity to Penhale Camp. The men were obviously taking part in a training exercise and, being a devout coward, I wished they would play their army games somewhere else.

Near the point where the sand ran out and towering rocks closed in I was forced to leave the comfort of the beach and climb onto grassy Ligger Point. Here, I passed several notices warning the public to keep off the Ministry of Defence land where the soldiers, who had thankfully disappeared, had been making merry.

I was soon approaching Penhale Camp where I came upon a substantial wire fence that appeared to encircle not only the camp but most of extensive Penhale Point. I scratched my head and studied the map. It clearly showed a path running through the middle of the camp, but none was visible. A notice warning me to keep out was posted beside the locked entrance. Beyond the wire I could see a team of soldiers struggling with a large wooden pole, which they were trying to place over a wide, muddy ditch. More training, I reckoned as I watched the men and women toil with the makeshift bridge. A wicked thought hit me. If I had to follow the wretched fence all the way round Penhale Point, they deserved to fall into the mud when they attempted to shin along the pole. Serve 'em right.

I was forced to follow the perimeter fence wherever it led me. Cursing the annoying disruption to my schedule I kept to the cliff-top path hoping I would not have to add another two miles to my itinerary. At least the weather was favourable. The sun was beating down from a clear blue sky and the keen wind kept me cool. Perfect walking weather

My pace quickened and, as I strained to see how far the perimeter fence extended I noticed a lone figure ahead of me. The man was striding purposely and I reckoned he must be as frustrated as I was with the detour. I kept him in my sights until the fence obligingly changed direction and was no longer heading for the tip of Penhale Point. The diversion was not proving as severe as I had anticipated and I was able to cut across the headland, adding roughly a mile to my journey.

To further boost my spirits a stunning view of Holywell Bay appeared when I reached a vantage point on the cliff-top. I caught sight of the lone walker who was admiring the seascape from a convenient seat. When I joined him I discovered he was a Cornishman who hailed from Falmouth and had walked extensively around his home county. Initially, his brogue was difficult to decipher but I warmed to the friendly man who was keen to tell me about the area and of his early years as a fisherman sailing out of Falmouth.

'Like the mining industry,' he told me, 'fishing's no longer viable and I've been forced to find other ways of earning a living.' He was currently working as a postman, which, he indicated was splendid for exercise and enjoying the countryside, except during bad weather.

When he learned I was walking to Exeter he exclaimed, 'I wish I could go with you,' adding, 'Newquay's a little over four miles away.' My spirits rose.

He smiled wickedly. 'As the crow flies. If you take the shortest route you'll have to cross the Gannel estuary.' My spirits sank.

'Is that possible?' I asked.

'There is a ferry, but I don't know the crossing times and you'll need the tide in your favour.'

'I'll hope my luck's in,' I responded.

'It's an extra two miles if you go round the estuary.'

For the second time that day I faced a detour. I thanked him for the information and began to negotiate a steep path, which descends to the tiny haven of Holywell, lying amidst a sea of sand dunes. As I ploughed across them, my boots filling with sand, I took the wrong route, as I discovered when I had gone about half a mile out of my way. Reluctant to retrace my steps I cut across an adjacent golf course, trusting I would not be struck by a stray golf ball.

Luckily I escaped unscathed and eventually found the path I was seeking. This pleasant thoroughfare led me through undulating meadows to the village of Crantock, a gem of a place. Peace permeated this tiny corner of England that time had seemingly passed. Quaint thatched cottages and neat flourishing gardens were the order of the day.

I paused for a word with an elderly resident I found sitting in a shelter overlooking the tiny village green. He told me of the saint and the sinner connected with the village. The saint is St Carantoc, after whom the settlement is named and whose story is told in the elegant modern glass of the church windows. By contrast, the sinner, portrayed by a wooden figure sitting by the stocks in the churchyard, was brought there to sit in the stocks to await justice. His name was William Tinney, a smuggler's son who robbed a poor widow and he became the last person to occupy the stocks.

Wishing the man well I left Crantock, heading for the ferry-point. When I reached the Gannel estuary the tide was out and I was forced to circle the wide inlet. It proved no easy task when I followed a path that petered out and I blundered across several fields before ending up in a caravan park. The only consoling thought was that John Hillaby decided to wade across the estuary at low tide and sank in up to his waist.

A helpful caravanner suggested I take a path to Trevemper, which lies some way from the estuary. 'From there,' he said, 'you can take the road to Newquay.' According to the map it appeared to be the most direct course, but I did not relish the two miles of road walking it indicated.

An hour later, weary and footsore in the hot sun, I trudged into Newquay, full of anticipation. The place, I knew, began life as a tiny fishing hamlet. I was about to discover it has grown into probably the largest resort in Cornwall and the one that most resembles Blackpool. As I entered its main street the first thing to catch my eye were shuttered premises with 'Sex Machine' emblazoned on their frontage. The mind boggled.

Things did not improve when I passed noisy amusement arcades and avoided groups of boisterous youngsters. Even the buildings lacked character. I hurried to a restaurant to escape.

Suitably refuelled I headed for the bay, whereupon my impression of the town mellowed. The view over Towan Beach was impressive, with the prominent 'Island,' a much-photographed rocky outcrop connected to the mainland by a suspension bridge, at the forefront. The long wall of the sheltered harbour hemmed the western fringe of the golden sands, pounded by the Atlantic breakers, for which Newquay is renowned. It is considered the best place in Britain for surfing and frequently hosts major

Land's End

St Ives

Tavistock

Dartmoor - Powder Mills

Bickleigh

Tiverton - Grand Western Canal

Wells

Bristol

Monmouth - Monnow Bridge

Offa's Dyke near Kington

Pont-Cysyllte Aqueduct

Clwydian Hills

Llanasa

Mold

Aldford

Vale of Edale

championships.

Beyond the harbour, the prominent Huer's House perches on a high promontory. In years past a look out posted on its ramparts scanned the ocean for shoals of pilchard and gave a signal to the waiting fishermen if activity was spotted.

My love-hate relationship with the town was curtailed when I sought my accommodation on its outskirts. I was looking forward to putting my feet up and enjoying a good night's rest. My room, like the one in St Ives was small and basic. Were all rooms in popular seaside resort boarding houses so cramped? Nevertheless, sleep came easily, after an eventful day.

DAY FIVE : NEWQUAY - ST WENN

Near disaster struck next morning. Whilst I was dressing I bent down to pull on my socks and aggravated a long-standing back injury. I limped to the dining room for a pre-arranged early breakfast and tried to forget my discomfort.

As I was completing my meal I noticed the remaining guests patiently waiting outside the door. At 9am precisely the lady of the house rang a bell and they filed obediently into the room, reminding me of the matriarchal proprietor of the guesthouse in St Agnes.

When the time came to leave, my back-pain persisted. I had difficulty in lifting my rucksack, but managed to hoist it onto my shoulders and stagger along the street. My situation was so dire I decided to stick to roads that day, for I could not have clambered over stiles, or struggled over rough terrain.

Before leaving Newquay I found a chemist's shop and bought some painkillers, hoping that they would at least keep me moving. Initially the pain was so bad I considered aborting my walk, but I persevered and eventually the tablets provided some relief.

Beneath leaden skies, I struggled dejectedly along a quiet road leading to the undisturbed hamlet of Colan. The most interesting of its scattering of dwellings is the 700 year-old church, which I examined as I took an opportunity to rest. Its porch retains the original roof timbers and sports an eighteenth-century sundial. Pride of place in the body of the church is given to the sixteenth-century brasses depicting two local families, older than the Spanish

Armada and large in number. In all thirty children can be found on the brasses.

I threaded slowly along narrow country roads that crept almost apologetically through the secluded hamlets of Trevithick and Tregaswith. The urge to tip-toe through these tiny, sleepy settlements was strong. As I progressed I encountered several field-paths, to which entry was denied. Notices, warning of foot and mouth restrictions were prominently displayed on gates and stiles. These did not augur well. The sobering thought struck me that I may be forced to keep to tarmac for the remainder of my trek.

Around midday I plodded into St Columb Major to be greeted by a surprising cluster of palm trees at the head of its long main street. Grey facades, interspersed with whitewashed cottages, lined my route as I sought a shop where I could buy food. The character of the town changed as I progressed. Buildings began to age and a decorative seventeenth-century coffee shop provided a fine example of the place's long history. I also found a medieval rectory overlooked by the 90-foot tower of the church, reputed to be 600 years old.

I ate sandwiches in the shadow of ancient dwellings and my setting would have been perfect were it not for the nagging pain in my back. Even an interesting conversation with a native of the town, who told me that every Shrove Tuesday the ancient game of hurling is played with a silver ball, failed to lift my spirits

A series of meandering thoroughfares led me to Reterth, Tregonetha and, eventually to the tranquility of St Wenn that presides over a landscape of green rolling hills laced with verdant hedgerows and the occasional ploughed field. Its brightly painted schoolhouse and the neighbouring church basked in glorious afternoon sunshine as I rested by the roadside, cheered by the knowledge that a mere mile and a half remained of my day's journey. That morning I had not dared to believe I would complete it. If I made it to my destination, Tregolls Farm, a night's rest would hopefully ease my back-pain.

The remaining distance to the farm was covered at a snail's pace to minimise my discomfort. Time was not at a premium and the picturesque valley positively gleamed. I walked to the accompaniment of trilling warblers and the indignant tones of wrens gliding in the sweet air, or concealing themselves in abundant hedgerows threaded with the rich purple of foxgloves. Luxuriant grass verges sparkled with colourful myrtle, ragwort and campion. Mid-Cornwall appeared an area to be savoured.

Even more satisfying was my arrival at Tregolls Farm. It provided the opportunity to shed my cumbersome rucksack and rest my aching back. The sight of the rustic-brick façade of the ancient farmhouse was enough to please even the most discerning. Set amidst rolling, well-manicured lawns, Tregolls, Cornish for 'home on the ridge' appeared very enticing.

Marilyn, the farmer's wife, was surprised when I asked if she could remove my rucksack. I explained my predicament and she was most sympathetic as she led me inside for a tour of the 300-year-old house, complete with mellow beams and slate-flagged floors. I learnt that the adjacent farm buildings had been converted into well-equipped holiday homes. These formerly redundant premises had the pleasing names of Honeysuckle, Clover and Blackberry and each contained a four-poster bed, log burners and all amenities.

My room was very tasteful and extremely comfortable, or it would have been had my back not proved troublesome. I was loath to take too many painkillers and suffered until bedtime, when I relented. Despite the medication I slept fitfully, frequently waking in pain and breaking into a cold sweat at the prospect of abandoning my journey.

DAY SIX : ST WENN - ST NEOT

I was in a quandary when I woke the next morning. It took an age to dress, for my back was extremely stiff and painful. I realised there was no way that I could carry a bulky rucksack. Somehow, I had to relieve the load on my suspect back. I hobbled down to breakfast and asked my host if she would post some of my belongings, which I needed to jettison, to my home. She helpfully agreed, but questioned my fitness to continue. I told her that if the pain became too severe I would quit and return home.

I prayed that the ruse would work and took a couple of painkillers as I departed. My pack certainly felt lighter. It contained only the bare essentials I would need for the remainder of my walk.

There was virtually no change of clothing, but being ostracised was preferable to abandoning the journey!

Would my back hold out? I tentatively shuffled along a lane that wound towards Tregustick. Mercifully after I had covered about a mile my stiffness began to ease and relief flooded through me as I increased my pace.

I began to take more notice of my surroundings and a sign denoting the Saints' Way caught my eye. This middle-distance footpath, I learnt later, is thirty miles in length and crosses Cornwall from Padstow in the north, to Fowey in the south. It links two major estuaries and passes several religious sites as it traverses the granite spine of the county. In ancient times the Way was used by Celtic saints travelling from Wales to Brittany. The modern version of the Saints' Way was formerly opened in 1986, to be enjoyed by ardent walkers.

The weather was still in my favour as I tramped through the undisturbed hamlets of Tregawne and Ruthernbridge. I noted several cottages displaying the same delicate-red stonework as Tregolls Farm and I was impressed by a tranquil, flower-fringed pool lying in the shadow of a garland of trees at Tregawne. Adjoining this pool was a larger version, providing a play area for waterfowl.

The stream issuing from these rippling waters passed beneath a rustic bridge in the sequestered hamlet of Ruthernbridge. I was impressed by the view from the bridge of a tall slender memorial standing proudly against a lush-green backdrop of dense woodland. Unfortunately, the effect was marred by the intrusion of the rusting roof of a barn that had been left to rot.

My enjoyment continued as I walked the lanes, bathed in sunshine, until I reached the uninspiring confines of Nanstallon, where I inadvertently took a wrong turn. I paid the price. Forced to walk nearly two miles along a busy trunk road into Bodmin, I eventually reached its outskirts where a sign welcomed me to the historic county town.

I found it a most pleasing place with a friendly, old-fashioned air. Its long and narrow main street, barely wide enough for single line traffic, was thronged with people. The quaint shop facades gave a feel of how Bodmin must have been a century ago. From the numerous signs indicating places of interest, the town has seemingly much to offer in the shape of viewpoints, museums, gardens and a steam railway. Even a Camel Trail was advertised. This puzzled me, for as far as I know there are no deserts in Cornwall. Happily, I learnt later it referred to the River Camel and its trail, for walkers and cyclists, which runs from Bodmin to Padstow and to Poley's Bridge on Bodmin Moor.

My back was holding up well and I was gaining in confidence with each hour that passed. I felt much better than I had during the previous fitful night and, as it was lunchtime, I reckoned I had earned some refreshment. Entering an inviting café, I saw a notice indicating a garden at the rear, where I found some ornate wrought-iron tables and chairs. I was tickled by a note on the menu, which stated, 'We do not sell fast food, we serve good food as fast as we can.' It did turn out to be good but the self-effacing proprietor who served me, in shirtsleeves and a tea towel draped over his arm, had obviously not read the latter part of his cryptic message thoroughly. Despite the long wait I enjoyed the opportunity to relax, half-expecting the strains of a string quartet to float across the garden.

During my approach to Bodmin I had noticed a prominent column on the skyline. I knew from the map it was a landmark known as The Beacon and I set out to climb to it after lunch. When I reached the town-square I stopped to admire Shire Hall, once the seat of the county court. Constructed in 1838 from local granite, it was the scene of many famous trials including that of Mathew Weeks who was convicted of the murder, on the windswept slopes of Rough Tor, on Bodmin Moor, of a local girl Charlotte Dymond. This heinous crime has intrigued ever since it was committed in 1844. Modern-day visitors to Shire Hall can participate in the 'Court Room Experience,' as a juror in the re-enactment of the trial of Mathew Weeks. At the end of these proceedings jurors are asked to cast their vote and decide the plaintiff's fate.

Bodmin houses a jail whose grandiose frontage resembles the portals of a great French chateau. Napoleonic prisoners built it in 1778 and it was the site of the last public hanging in Britain. Several thousand spectators travelled to see the event in 1909, hiring special trains to ensure they wouldn't miss the gruesome spectacle.

One of the governors of the Naval Prison, an annex of the jail, fathered a famous author who was born in the town. Cyril McNeile, writing under the pen name, 'Sapper,' was the creator of the thrilling detective yarns featuring Bulldog Drummond.

As I left the town-square I asked for directions to The Beacon from a passer-by and was surprised to hear a broad Yorkshire accent. 'You go up this hill, luv . . .' the woman began, in tones acquired in Rotherham, her birthplace. I found that she had moved to Bodmin some years ago, but still retained a deep affection for her home county.

Following a stiff climb I emerged on top of the hill upon which The Beacon stands. It offers a panoramic view of the town and the surrounding countryside. The distant contours of Bodmin Moor, clearly visible beyond a patchwork of fields and hedgerows, made my heart beat a little faster, for I hoped to reach its southern extremity before the day was out.

An inscription on The Beacon revealed that it is a memorial to Sir Walter Raleigh Gilbert, a descendent of the great explorer, and a general in the Bengal Army who fought in the Napoleonic Wars. His military exploits and devoted service to his home community encouraged the building of this conspicuous edifice in his honour.

I did not linger at the memorial and, a little way out of Bodmin, I passed the site of the town's once great earthwork, Castle Canyke. This was not visible from the road but another piece of local history soon appeared. I was obliged to cross a busy road junction and watchfully reached a large traffic island at its centre. With traffic thundering around me I came upon the ancient, weather-beaten Carminow Cross in what seemed an incongruous setting. This moss-encrusted stone cross relates to the Carminow family who held the local manor of Lanhydrock up to the early part of the seventeenth century. They were said to have settled in Cornwall before the conquest and were prominent in court circles during the reign of Henry VII and Henry VIII. They were regarded as the 'King-and-power-courting Carminows' and brides within the family were advised to 'marry for love but always to see that thou lovest where money lies.'

As soon as I was able to escape the roar of traffic I took to the country roads and headed towards Cardinham Woods, which are threaded by waymarked walks. These, I hoped, would bring relief from pounding tarmac. Annoyingly, the path I wished to take through the woods was out of bounds due to foot and mouth restrictions. Cursing the wretched disease I returned to the road and spent several hours on a winding route to St Neot, my stopping-place for the night. I noted that all the footpaths in the area were similarly affected but my annoyance at having to keep to the roads was tempered by the fact that I was still walking and my back was no longer a major concern.

The long afternoon turned to evening and it was well past six o'clock when I descended a steep hill and obtained my first glimpse of the homely village of St Neot set in the heart of the picturesque Glynn Valley. Despite the slate-grey clouds temporarily obscuring the sun, the rural hideaway looked most appealing. White-walled cottages stood out amongst the cluster of stone buildings, but pride of place belonged to the church whose tower rose majestically above a mantle of yew and maple that coats the surrounding hillsides.

As fast as my back would allow I hurried into the village where I came upon the picture postcard scene of the church, a pristine white-walled inn and the old Post Office. The sleepy settlement appeared deserted, apart from a lone figure. It turned out to be an eighty-eight-year-old lady who I could not pass without being interrogated. She had no qualms about waylaying a stranger, for she demanded to know how far I had travelled, where I was headed, what family I had and their ages. Pleased as I was to chat with the determined lady, who, I discovered, had spent her whole life in the village and had never ventured farther than Weymouth, I was anxious to find my accommodation. Eventually she indicated my destination, a charming cottage, conveniently sited only a few yards from where we were standing.

As I had when I saw Tregolls Farm for the first time, I knew I would enjoy staying in the quaint old building, its walls sparkling-white in the emerging sunshine and framed by cascades of fuchsia and laburnum. At each of its tiny windows sat tubs of fiery geraniums. Pink roses climbed its façade and clematis surrounded the front door, at which I was welcomed by the lady of the house and two dogs, named Tes and Tas. Before I had chance to size up the delightful dwelling I was obliged to follow Tas through the back garden to a tinkling stream. Apparently this was a ritual the animal performed with every newcomer. As I admired the inviting prospect Tas looked at me as if to say, 'It's splendid, isn't it?' The dog, I discovered spent hours either at this spot, or peering into various dark corners of the garden. This seemed a strange way to spend her time and, according to her owner, her barmy companion Tes had even less of a brain. They made a unique canine couple.

When I was shown around the 350 year-old cottage, it was like stepping back in time. The low oak beams gave a superb feel to the place but I had to remember to duck my head to avoid decapitation. Amongst the numerous antique fittings and ornaments were several keepsakes possessing a naval connection, including model ships and a hornpipe. These, I discovered, belonged to the husband who had spent more than twenty years at sea.

Later that evening, as I sank into the enveloping softness of an ample bed, I reflected on the day's events. After the tribulations of the previous night I could hardly believe my luck. My back was much improved, thanks to the lighter load I was carrying and I had hit upon another superb place to stay.

A visitor's book was conveniently left in the room for me to add my details and comments. I read with interest, as I frequently do, the entries of previous guests. They included several comments about escaping noisy, smelly London and the usual rapturous praise for the establishment. In this particular case they were well-deserved but I often find gushing remarks about the most mediocre accommodation and exaggerated comments such as, 'Heaven!' and 'We'll be back!' I sometimes mischievously wonder if anyone has ever written, 'Hell!' and 'We won't be back!'

Next morning, after a good night's rest, I ate a hearty breakfast, watched closely by two pairs of expectant eyes. Tes and Tas were coveting my bacon and sausages. They looked so pitiful I couldn't resist surreptitiously feeding them from time to time.

DAY SEVEN : ST NEOT - CALLINGTON.

Before leaving the village I paused to inspect the holy well, where, for 1000 years, people drew water watched over by Saint Neot as he recited the psalms. The saint is shrouded in mystery. Legend purports that he was a king of Wessex who gave up the throne for a hermit's cell. He is also believed to have had a regular diet of fish, which he obtained daily from the well.

The church is, of course, dedicated to the saint and boasts many colourful stained-glass windows. They are of fifteenth and early sixteenth-century origin and form one of the richest legacies of Cornwall. Over a century ago the damaged and faded windows were lovingly restored by a devoted parson. St Neot is depicted on them in twelve scenes. These include him taking his vow as a monk, abdicating his crown to a younger brother, and receiving fishes from the holy well.

I was sorry to leave the engaging settlement of St Neot, nestling on the southern fringe of Bodmin Moor. I blessed my luck in finding such a spot, for I had originally planned to cross the breadth of the moor, but had been discouraged from doing so by the outbreaks of foot and mouth disease in the area. Accordingly it proved to be another day of road-walking but there were some mitigating attractions. The first of these was a popular beauty spot, Golitha Falls, sequestered in ancient woodland beyond the hamlet of Draynes. It lies within a National Nature Reserve and careful coppicing has produced the multi-stemmed oak trees, which cover most of it. The woods are one of Cornwall's richest sites for lichens and mosses that thrive in the humid conditions created by the falls.

As I left the road and entered the wood I saw several butterflies fluttering in the sunny morning air. The nearby, specially managed fields are habitats for such varieties as the silver-washed fritillary and speckled wood. I followed a well-worn track for roughly a mile with sunlight dappling the abundant vegetation of the woodland floor. Cow-wheat and foxglove surrounded the mature trunks of spreading oaks, home to pied flycatchers and woodpeckers. Swooping dippers heralded the approach of the series of rapids and waterfalls that flow through the granite gorge of the River Fowey. Originally, a large boulder, known as the Golitha Stone, blocked the river and it was blasted away in the nineteenth century to allow salmon further upstream to spawn.

Squatting by the turbulent waters of Golitha Falls I watched the antics of cavorting wagtails and searched the depths for signs of otters that reputably frequent the river. Shimmering in the sunlight the falls cascaded over lichen covered boulders, creating a watery idyll. The scene was so inviting it was a wrench to stir myself and retrace my steps through the wood.

I had progressed a further half-mile when I came upon King Doniert's Stone, standing in a small walled enclosure by the roadside. Badly eroded and in two pieces, it has clearly seen better days. Its ornately carved base stands side by side with the remains of its time-ravaged column. A man was industriously mowing the grass within the enclosure and I discovered he was a local postman who maintained three ancient sites in the area. He apparently rose at 4am and did his postal round before attending to his maintenance duties. What a pleasurable way to earn a living I thought as I studied his tanned features on that gloriously sunny morning.

King Doniert, the friendly postman told me, was a ninth-century king of Cornwall, of which little seems to be known. 'He couldn't have died at this spot,' he said. 'He was drowned and his last request was for a stone to be displayed in his memory.'

When I told the man I was making for Darite and, eventually, Callington, he said I would pass near Trethevy quoit, which was one of the sites that he tended. 'It's magnificent,' he added, 'one of the finest megalithic tombs you'll find.'

I thanked him and took to the road once more, overlooked by the southernmost hills of Bodmin Moor. I gazed at them, frustrated that I was prevented from roaming the hummocks that bear the remains of ancient habitation. Hut circles, crosses and tumuli litter the landscape, in addition to stone circles. The most notable of the prehistoric circles is The Hurlers, standing near the elevated hamlet of Minions. In fact, the site consists of three circles, two of which are marked by granite uprights and the remaining one by stones that have keeled over. Local legend has it that they are rings of men turned to stone for the sinful practice of indulging in the Cornish game of hurling on the Sabbath.

I could make out the distant buildings of Minions surrounded by scrub-coated slopes, peppered with the remnants of mine-workings and presided over by gaunt chimneys. The bleakness of the exposed landscape was in stark contrast to the vibrant vegetation that hemmed the road. Soaring foxgloves protruded over hedgerows, framing the hills beyond.

In the village of Darite a sign indicated the route to Trethevy quoit, but I had more pressing needs and went in search of refreshment. As I did so I passed a row of villagers chatting on a roadside seat. They stared at the oddity walking the roads on such a hot day, sporting a rucksack. We passed the time of day and one of them directed me to the village store, which was unfortunately closed. I asked a man painting an upstairs window of the building when it would reopen. He shouted through the open window to his wife, 'Ethell, open up will you? There's a chap outside who looks in need of a cool drink.' I wiped the sweat from my forehead and thanked him. No sooner had I done this than I was ushered into the store by the pleasant woman who was eager to know where I had walked from and where I was making for.

A short time later I approached the seat once more and all heads followed me as I passed. 'Had your lunch?' inquired one.

'Yes, thanks,' I replied. 'I'm off to Trethevy quoit, but I'm heading for Callington.'

I detected murmurs of excitement and incredulity in my wake. It was probably the highlight of the week for the team of spectators.

On my way to Trethevy quoit, which lies on the outskirts of the village, I was nearly set upon by an angry dog. Its master roughly called it off without a word of apology or greeting. Perhaps the man thought I was a vagrant. Reflecting on the surliness of the dog owner I passed through a stile and was confronted by the massive structure of Trethevy quoit. The slabs of local granite, from which it is constructed, are so large it must have required endless toil to extract them from the rocks and smooth their surfaces. The wall-slabs lean against each other like playing cards and the roof comprises the largest stone of all, fourteen feet long and nine feet wide. Another slab covers the entrance, probably to prevent the spirits of the dead from escaping. I could only stare in wonderment at this megalithic burial site that has stood for thousands of years.

The remainder of the long, hot afternoon was spent pounding the roads, for again I found prohibitive notices displayed on footpaths. Beyond Darite I walked through its tiny neighbour, Crow's Nest, which sported an inviting roadside inn. The name intrigued me. Was the hamlet inhabited by sailors in years gone by?

As I trod the protracted main street of the next village, Pensilva, I realised that I had passed the 100-mile point. Downhill from now on, I thought frivolously as I surveyed the great swathe of Cornish countryside stretching before me. Somewhere in the hazy distance lay the county border, which I intended to cross on the following day.

I was obliged to give the shaded tracks of Bicton Wood a miss and continue my tarmac trail to Golberdon and, eventually, Callington, a pleasant market town lying at the foot of Kit Hill, a popular viewpoint. From that 1100-foot vantage point the winding valley of the Tamar, which forms the boundary between Devon and Cornwall, can be clearly seen. Formerly owned by Prince Charles, Kit Hill was gifted to the people of Cornwall to commemorate the birth of Prince William and is now a countryside park.

I halted overnight at Callington and that evening I strolled around the town, whose most striking feature is the unique display of colourful murals painted on the walls of various buildings by both amateur and professional artists. Callington is renowned for its on-going Mural Project, a celebration of the town's heritage, landscape and industry. A Mural Trail leads the visitor around fourteen sites, an absorbing town tour of artistic ingenuity. The one that made the deepest impression was 'The Secret Pasty Factory,' adorning Jack James's Wall in New Road. It was a humorous depiction of the manufacture of the famous Ginsters Cornish Pasty that is made in the town. Amongst others that caught my attention was the 'Return of King Arthur,' which reflects the area's strong links with the sea and shows the king arriving at a Cornish port. The most unusual site for a mural was the wall of the police station, on which was displayed a pastoral Taymar Valley scene.

I also threaded through several narrow alleyways that reveal the old character of the town. One of these thoroughfares approaches the fifteenth-century church, in which resides the tomb of Lord Willoughby de Broke who fought on Bosworth Field at the birth of the Tudor dynasty. He was appointed Marshall of the Army by Henry VII and became Steward to the Duchy of Cornwall.

DAY EIGHT : CALLINGTON - TAVISTOCK

I viewed the nine-mile journey as a rest day, compared with what had gone before. The reason I could take things easily was due to a change of route, courtesy of the foot and mouth epidemic. My original intention had been to walk to Lydford, admire its famous gorge and cross Dartmoor by footpath, incorporating part of the Lych Way. Unfortunately, the section of moor I had hoped to traverse remained closed but I discovered that the area to the south and east had been re-opened. I decided to divert to Tavistock and take the roads that traverse the moor to Two Bridges and Postbridge.

A good part of the journey was spent trying to avoid the main road that links Callington and Tavistock. I kept to minor roads where possible, by way of St Anne's Chapel and Gunnislake, where I crossed the bridge over the Tamar. In woods above the river, to the north of the bridge, formerly stood the Devon Great Consols Mine, in its time the largest copper mine in Europe and the producer of half the world's supply of arsenic. The two valuable commodities were carried by rail to the river port of Morwhellam where they finished their journey being lowered down an incline of one in three onto the quays below. Vast fortunes were made and Tavistock could be described as the 'Klondyke' of England at the height of the search for mineral wealth, with the town surrounded by mining activity. Shares in the Devon Great Consols Mine, originally bought for £1 were sold for £800. Average wages for the miners were fourteen shillings a week and female workers received one and three pence a day. It is said these poor, exploited workers sang hymns they worked.

I followed the main road for the greater part of the remaining distance to Tavistock and paid little heed to the hamlets of Gulworthy and Lumburn, for I was eager to escape the roar of passing traffic. When I finally entered the pleasing confines of the town, I felt my forced change of route had it advantages.

The ancient market town is a busy centre for those who live on the western margins of Dartmoor. Its heart, Bedford Square, is something to behold. During its long history the town was presided over by two masters. In the monastic period the Benedictine monks of Tavistock Abbey held sway, being replaced by the Russells, later to become the Dukes of Bedford. Both amassed considerable wealth, due to minerals found on their lands. The Bedfords gave their name to the town-square and the Bedford Hotel. Francis, the seventh duke, virtually rebuilt the centre of the town in the 1840's in a mixture of Gothic and Tudor styles using a green volcanic ash called Hurdwick stone that was quarried nearby. The splendid architecture he created gives the town its rich character. Buildings such as the Guildhall and the Bedford Hotel are fine examples and both are sited within the original confines of the abbey. Not only did this benefactor remodel the town he attempted to alleviate the appalling conditions of the mineworkers and those employed in the town's wool mills, foundries and tanneries, which produced smoke, dust and grime in streets already polluted by open sewers. Amongst his many good works Francis built cottages for the miners and their families and endeavoured to reduce disease and malnutrition.

I owe the great man an apology. When I first set eyes on the statue, erected in his honour, outside the Guildhall, its inscription, 'Sir Francis,' caused me wrongly to deduce it was that of the great seafarer, Sir Francis Drake who was born in the town. I learnt later that his statue stands by the Plymouth Road at the entrance to the town.

As time was plentiful I was able to explore the environs at my leisure. I wandered through the nineteenth-century Pannier Market, to which local people originally carried their produce, in panniers, to sell. Adjacent to the market stands a row of tasteful shops and a splendid pavement café where I relaxed in the, by now, obligatory sunshine. I discovered from the proprietor that Tavistock is the home of the cream tea. Apparently, they were served to abbey visitors in medieval times, long before it became a speciality of the West Country.

Having spent a lazy, but absorbing afternoon, I realised I must gather my strength for the next day's crossing of Dartmoor, which would be far more arduous. That evening I was joined by my long-standing walking friend, Roy, who was to accompany me to Exeter. We talked well into the evening about my experiences and I explained the route we would be taking. It felt good to have a companion after eight days of lone walking.

DAY NINE : TAVISTOCK - POSTBRIDGE

The morning dawned bright and sunny, which augured well for crossing the exposed landscape of the moor. Initially walking was easy and we made good progress to Moorshop, relishing the view of Dartmoor's rugged tors coming ever closer. The roadside verges were ablaze with colour and they contained several prominent signs urging motorists to drive with 'Moor Care.'

Leg muscles complained as we began the long climb to the moor's summit and habitation became sparse. Behind us the Tamar Valley and the distant undulating hills of Cornwall shimmered in the convivial morning sunshine. In the midst of this green and fertile vista huddled Tavistock, a reminder of man's influence amidst a patterned landscape that evolved over millions of years.

The lush valley was gradually transformed into a yawning landscape of sheep-cropped grassland, punctuated by gnarled granite outcrops that thrust themselves into an unblemished skyline. Leaving the comfort of modern living behind we entered uncompromising territory, peopled for 10,000 years by prehistoric tribes. At the time of man's arrival the moor was almost wholly covered by trees. The resilient newcomers made clearings in the forests and hunted wild animals. Their descendants began to use the area as a burial ground and a place of worship. Visible remains of their stone monuments and burial cairns abound, creations hewn from the indigenous granite and subjected to the most violent wind and weather. Bronze and Iron Age stone circles, hut circles and stone rows dot the moorland wastes, paying tribute to man's ancient beliefs and practices.

My reverie at entering the portals of ancient civilisation was tempered by the appearance of a large roadside car park around which visitors wandered, stretching their legs or feeding the acclaimed ponies, which roam the moor. These hardy animals are as tough as they come and have no problem relieving humans of their sandwiches. Sheep were also in attendance, ever watchful for a good meal. I noted with wry humour that they wandered across the road with little respect for the fact that the land to one side of it was out of bounds due to foot and mouth restrictions and the other had free access.

We followed the winding, unfenced road towards Merrivale with a spring in our step. When the sun is shining and an invigorating wind plays upon your face there is no finer place than Dartmoor. In its surlier mood I imagine it to be the wettest, coldest, loneliest and most alarming place. I was pleased in one way to be crossing it on tarmac, despite the lack of adventure, for its remoter environs of fens, mires and featherbeds, where half of the moor's rivers have their source, can be extremely intimidating. John Hillaby took an intrepid route across what he termed 'The Dire Moor,' and it was nearly his undoing. He was blighted by impenetrable mist on the summit of Great Kneeset and wandered off course into the extremely unappetising Cranmere Pool, which he describes thus. 'The bog stretched out as far as I could see. In the cold air the surface steamed slightly, like a pudding. I chucked a piece of turf in. It quivered.' He sank into this morass about a dozen times eventually extricating himself from what he described as a 'huge sponge.'

Above the pristine-white, seventeenth-century Dartmoor Inn and its attendant scatter of cottages that comprise Merrivale looms a great gash in the green hillside. The quarry is typical of many that fleck Dartmoor and it supplied granite for buildings nationwide. The gaunt Staple Tors overlook the scene of devastation, glowering disapprovingly at man's desecration of the landscape that is thankfully over, for the quarry closed in 1997. During the latter stages of its occupancy it was used for the cutting and polishing of granite brought from elsewhere. Some of this stone was used for the building of the memorial at Goose Green, dedicated to British servicemen who lost their lives in the Falklands War.

Within half a mile of Merrivale lies some of the best-preserved stone architecture of Dartmoor. A stone circle, stone rows and a standing stone cluster on the green sward that borders the road we were taking. It is believed that the road itself runs through the site of an ancient village, to which the ceremonial complex presumably belonged. We cannot be certain of the importance placed on these stone monuments by their builders but it is hard not to believe that they had some religious significance, or were astronomical observatories. What ceremonies were performed here is a matter of conjecture. However, the Dartmoor Exploration Committee excavated several stone circles between 1894 and 1904 and found charcoal, which implies the existence of funeral pyres or bonfires. Two stone rows run parallel to each other at the Merrivale site, with a large upright stone at their heads. Such rows often led to a burial cairn or cairns and appear to invite upward procession. The rows are sometimes referred to as the Plague Market, for it served the same function as the plague stone at Zennor. Here the farmers left their produce to be collected by the people from plague-ridden Tavistock in 1625.

A further two miles of road-walking brought us within sight of Princetown, known for its prison. Of all the developments attempting to make practical use of Dartmoor, the most extraordinary must be the building of this penal institution. It stands, at nearly 1,500 feet above sea level, exposed to the wild elements and virtually in the dead centre of the moor. The enterprise began when Thomas Tyrwhitt, an auditor to the Duchy of Cornwall, bought land at Two Bridges and began to improve the local road system. One of the roads led to a small settlement he was in the process of building, on the highest ground in the area. He called it Prince's Town, in honour of his friend the Prince of Wales.

In 1805 the government was becoming alarmed at the large numbers of French prisoners of war rotting in old hulks in Plymouth Sound. Tyrwhitt saw the opportunity of using convict labour to continue his improvements at Princetown and, in 1806 he laid the foundation stone of a prison near his house. In 1809 the building was completed. 9,000 prisoners were held there and overcrowding was such that they were continually on the verge of rioting. Despite such problems Trywhitt continued to enlarge the village of Princetown, establishing a market, a brewery, a corn mill and additional houses.

After cessation of hostilities, the French prisoners were repatriated in 1817 and the prison stood empty until 1849 when it was modernised and reopened by the government to house Britain's convicts.

In my imagination, 'Dartmoor Prison,' as it is commonly called, conjured up a picture of an eerie, brooding building, shrouded in swirling moorland mist. The reality, bathed in bright sunlight was far removed from the remote and creepy place I had envisaged. It stands roughly half a mile from the Tavistock to Two Bridges road, flanked by farm buildings and the dwellings of Princetown. The sombre-grey building looked austere but not as foreboding as I had anticipated.

There was no time to dwell on the merits of Princetown and its prison, for Roy was striding ahead of me like a greyhound released from its trap. This was his first day and his eagerness was plain. Therefore, it was full steam ahead for Two Bridges where we planned a lunch stop. The road stretched, arrow straight, before us flanked by mellow-stone walls fringed with yellow bands of buttercup. Wisps of feathery cirrus flecked the serene azure sky as the sun beat upon us.

We had worked up a tremendous thirst by the time we reached the welcome Two Bridges Hotel set amongst expansive lawns, ringed by sheltering trees. The scene was idyllic. People relaxed at tables, or reclined by the sparkling waters of the West Dart River, in the shadow of a rustic packhorse bridge, one of a pair that give the place its name.

In such sybaritic surroundings we almost lost the will to persevere on foot, especially when we observed a young couple, in walking attire, board a passing bus. We dallied in the glorious sunshine, sipping long, cooling drinks.

Forcing ourselves to continue we progressed to a fork in the road, which lay on the fringe of an area badly affected by foot and mouth. Here we took the road to Postbridge, avoiding the infected farm at Dunnabridge.

A hot, strenuous afternoon's walk followed, relieved by a halt at distinctive Powder Mills, where, unfortunately, we could only view the site from a distance. The Powder Mills Pottery Centre and an adjacent row of former worker's cottages guard the entrance to the cluster of buildings and chimneys that huddle silently in a green valley about one quarter of a mile from the road. At the door of the centre a dog sniffed enthusiastically around our legs. The jovial owner remarked that the animal had not had a whiff of a walker for four months. She was referring to the fact that none had paid a visit to her pottery since the introduction of foot and mouth precautions. I replied that the dog could sniff to its heart's content.

Derelict Powder Mills is notable for its former manufacture of black powder, a primitive gunpowder, much in demand in the tin-mining and granite industries, for blasting purposes. The constituents were mixed here as it was considered safest to perform the process near to the point of use. Incorporating mills, charge magazine houses and the finishing house now lie crumbling and forlorn. Between 1844 until nearly 1900, when dynamite was invented, these buildings, where the blending processes and the final mixing took place, were a hive of activity. The finishing house had a tar-paper roof, in case of explosion and the ever present risk of detonation gave rise to a local tale that the area around Powder Mills is haunted by a pair of ghostly 'hairy hands.' They are supposedly those of a worker and on dark nights they grab the steering wheel of passing cars and the handlebars of motorcycles, causing them to swerve and crash. The worker, the tale relates, was an Italian immigrant with a very swarthy complexion and dark, hairy hands. One day he received some startling news from home -

a relative had died and left him a considerable sum of money. Elated, the man decided to return home to collect his new-found wealth. On the day of his departure he returned to the site, dressed in his best attire, to bid farewell to his workmates. Unfortunately, in his excitement he forgot a cardinal rule. All employees wore felt boots to eliminate the chance of sparks from the stone floors and he entered the premises wearing hobnailed ones, with disastrous results. In the resultant explosion he was blown to smithereens and the only parts of him that were recovered were his hairy hands.

Before leaving the pottery a mystery was solved by its owner. Near her premises stood a device resembling a snub-nosed cannon. She explained that it was a proving mortar used to test the potency of the gunpowder. A sample of the mixture was inserted and a cannonball fired from it. The distance travelled by the ball gave an indication of the mixture's strength.

For the last mile and a half of our journey to Postbridge we were able to forego the road and walk through the vast confines of Bellever Woods, one of three extensive forests of Sitka spruce that pattern the locality. Buried within their broad acres are numerous prehistoric sites, which have been carefully preserved, in contrast to earlier years when many were indiscriminately destroyed by over-planting. Sequestered among carpets of spruce are the remains of cairns, stone circles, tumuli and hut circles that can be reached by means of a network of forest walks.

We arrived at Postbridge hot and tired, to be greeted by the sight of a glistening postal van parked outside the Post Office, which seemed apt. After purchasing much-needed drinks we inspected the two bridges, for which the village is famous. They stand side by side, spanning the East Dart River, each a compliment to the skill of their builders. The ancient clapper-bridge, replaced by its neighbour that carries the road, is constructed of unworked granite slabs, worn smooth by centuries of use. It dates from the Middle Ages and would certainly have served one of the early routes across Dartmoor, used by monks and travellers and later by packhorse men.

A frustrating trek of nearly two miles ensued. Our accommodation lay on the very outskirts of the village, at the end of a long winding lane. A spacious, rambling property that was showing signs of wear and tear, it was reminiscent of the guesthouse at St Agnes. It had evidently been a fine building and its location, in enviable surroundings, could not be bettered. Our host, a rather abrupt woman, furnished us with tea and cake on the front patio, from which we enjoyed a superb view to distant Bellever Forest. Roy had the temerity to refuse a second helping of homemade cake. Our host was most put out and demanded to know if he didn't like her speciality, lovingly made from a local recipe.

This was our first inkling of her oddity. Despite her maturity it was evident from her dress and demeanor that she was out to attract men's attention. She gave Roy a shock when she appeared unannounced in his bedroom later that evening on some strange, unsettling pretext. He had an even greater disturbance during the night when he was awakened by a tapping on the bedroom window. When he opened the curtains and looked outside, there was no sign of anyone.

DAY TEN : POSTBRIDGE - CHAGFORD

At breakfast the following morning our host appeared in a very revealing dress and flitted around the other guests, who she appeared to know well, with unctuous familiarity. Her friendliness disappeared swiftly when I announced that after a spate of nine full English breakfasts, I could not face another. She icily announced that they were another of her specialities and it was a cardinal sin to refuse. It was difficult to tell if she was joking, but I stuck to my guns and asked for scrambled eggs on toast.

The scrambled eggs were eventually forthcoming and were unceremoniously dumped before me with an accompanying glare. One of the other guests laughed at this performance, or rather, cackled, in keeping with the creepy establishment. I imagined the elderly woman in question being quite at home, in the opening scene of *Macbeth,* leaning over a cauldron. Her gaunt features were supplanted with a huge hooked nose and her laughter resembled the clucking of a hen. She was as voluble as her mild-mannered companion, a retiring, diminutive person, was reticent.

Roy and I were glad to get away from the unsettling house and eagerly trod the rambling lane, which led us back to the road. It was yet another sunny morning and an interesting day's march lay ahead.

As the crow flies, it is a mere eight miles from Postbridge to Chagford, but our plan was to add several more by leaving the road to join the Two Moors Way as it climbs to Hamel Down Ridge. This long-distance footpath stretches for just over 100 miles, from Ivybridge, on the southern edge of Dartmoor to Lynmouth, on the north coast of Devon. It promised escape from road-walking and extensive views of the surrounding countryside.

Quiet country roads took us past the forest of Soussons Down, where we found a well-maintained cairn circle standing on its fringe. After several miles of tarmac we were able to climb a steep path to open moorland, where we joined the Two Moors Way for what proved to be an invigorating high-level traverse. The rutted track led us to the summit of the ridge at Hameldown Beacon. Here we rested by a small cairn topped by an ancient marker stone and enjoyed the company of a young German couple enjoying a circular walk from nearby Widecombe in the Moor, once one of the most peaceful and picturesque villages of Dartmoor. During the summer it is crowded and noisy, especially on the second Tuesday in September, the day of the famous Widecombe Fair, which was originally a dignified and serious hard-bargaining, hard-drinking matter of selling cattle, sheep and ponies. Since the Rev. Sabine Baring-Gould unearthed an obscure eighteenth-century folk song and made it part of English folklore, the fair has become widely popular and very commercialised.

Bidding farewell to the friendly couple, we progressed along the elevated ridge amongst ancient burial sites, marked by stones identifying various barrows. These Bronze Age barrows are the only known examples of this type of burial on Dartmoor, where the ashes of the dead were placed underground and covered with stone slabs. Some of the identifying stones bear the letters 'DS,' denoting the Duke of Somerset who had interests in the area.

The view from the trig point on Hameldown Tor was panoramic. Wave after wave of hills faded into a distant haze, the ones closer to hand darkened by a covering of heather and whortleberries.

Broad stones, smoothed by centuries of wear, littered the ancient trackway as it began a steep decent to one of the most inspiring archeological sites in the West Country. Nestling in the valley beneath I could discern the remains of the Bronze Age village at

Grimspound, the most famous of the pound settlements. Its massive walled enclosure, covering four acres and used to contain domestic animals, has been reduced to a circle of loosely piled stones, but on closer inspection, the remnants of twenty-four hut circles within the enclosure can be identified. Some of these ancient dwellings have sections of wall remaining, with door-lintels and jambs in place.

Outside the enclosure a young woman was crouching, holding a measuring device to the ground. She explained that she was a post-graduate student, studying for a PhD, and she was measuring the erosion around the sight for a thesis she was preparing. A companion recorded the measurements whilst the woman's dog watched them intently.

Beyond Grimspound the Two Moors Way descends to the Postbridge to Moretonhampstead road and as it does so it is overlooked by the prominence of Headland Warren, on whose slopes rabbits were once bred in buries or warrens. It was an age old occupation stretching back to the Middle Ages when the warreners used nets and gins to catch the rabbits and sold them for their meat and skins.

At the foot of Headland Warren stands the ancient Warren House Inn, a reminder of the area's earlier dependence on rabbits and tin-mining. The roadside hostelry was once a lonely and romantic place, much patronised by early travellers and the tin miners who worked the mines in the nearby valley of the East Webburn River. Its sign displays the curious three rabbit device associated with the Tinners, which portrays three rabbits arranged in a circle with their ears touching. Each rabbit appears to have two ears, yet there is a total of only three ears between them.

The medieval Bennett's Cross stands at the point where the Two Moors way meets the road. This ancient edifice was probably a track marker but it could have denoted a parish, warren or tin boundary. Its most striking feature is a carved pliant figure that resembles a dancing girl.

Here, we were obliged to leave the Way, for the footpaths to the north of the road were within the restricted area of Dartmoor. Consequently, Roy and I marched along the road for a mile, passing further hut circles that litter the grassy inclines of Chagford Common, home to another ancient burial site incorporating a double stone row.

The opportunity arose to escape the main road and join a series of pleasant country lanes that run, between a series of rounded hills, towards the historic town of Chagford. After squeezing between the buttresses of Meldon Hill and Nattadon Common, we reached its outskirts. We were tickled by an array of gnomes in a garden that we passed. Was there amusement and pity in their staring eyes?

As we neared the town centre the road narrowed, barely allowing passage for the cars that crawled between the extensive rows of mature stone and colour-washed facades that lend character to the old stannary town. Chagford, along with its neighbours, Tavistock and Lydford was a tin centre where the ingots were brought for assaying, weighing and stamping. During those times the Tinners formed the equivalent of our modern trade unions and they became so powerful that they began to make their own laws. The right was upheld to invade private property, even to the extent of pulling down buildings that stood on real or imaginary seams of tin. It was declared that no person owning property worth more than ten pounds could dig for tin except on his own freehold. Appeal was useless against the judgement of the stannary courts and victims found guilty were thrown into the dungeons of Lydford Castle.

Chagford nestles in a charming region of the Teign Valley, surrounded by old farmhouses, typical of the countryside in their grey sturdiness. An aged granite bridge crouches over the river and an ancient church occupies pride of place in the main street. The stout granite tower of the church rises majestically above its surroundings, a reminder that worship has been conducted on the site since before the Norman Conquest. Inside stands the original oak rood loft that was erected in 1555 and on the south wall there is an appealing verse commemorating a local girl Mary Whiddon. This unfortunate bride was shot as she left the church after her wedding in 1641. Tradition has it that any girl being married from Whiddon House - now the 'Three Crowns' - will meet the ghost of Mary Whiddon.

In the churchyard I noticed an interesting gravestone, erected in memory of James Perrot, the famous Dartmoor guide who set up the first letterbox at Cranmere Pool. Apparently the pool was formerly much drier than it is now and at one time acquired a mystique that made it a compulsive goal for many who venture into the wilds of Dartmoor. James Perrot was the instigator, in 1854, of the modern pastime of letterboxing, which involves enthusiasts walking over Dartmoor and using predetermined clues and navigational skills to locate boxes placed on the moor by others. The boxes normally contain a visitor's book and a rubber stamp. On finding the box, hunters use the stamp to record the find in their own books or on a series of cards, and then mark the visitor's book in the box with their own personal stamps. The activity has increased in popularity and many adventurers scour the moor for boxes and leave proof that they have located desolate and lifeless spots, such as Cranmere Pool. I could barely believe such a pastime until I checked a map of the area and found Cranmere Pool letterbox clearly indicated. I'll wager John Hillaby never found it!

Chagford is ideal for thirsty travellers. Four hostelries, the oldest of which is the charmingly thatched, seventeenth-century Three Crowns, cluster in close proximity to the pleasant market-square and give it an olde worlde feel. The square's centre-piece is the Victorian Market House, a distinctive hexagonal building topped by an unusual tower. Into this pleasing structure squeeze a number of tiny shops. It is easy to imagine these surroundings in a quieter age when their serenity was disturbed only by the sound of horses' hooves.

Our accommodation for the night was a sixteenth-century, oak-beamed cottage. A delightful residence spoiled by the fact that we were obliged to share a twin-bedded room, large enough for one person. Prettily furnished in country cottons it would have been ideal but for the cramped conditions. We had no complaints regarding the cosy sitting room, its friendly oak beams supplemented by an aged ingle-nook fireplace constructed from large slabs of granite. The timbered walls were pitted with age and, I noticed, ravaged by woodworm.

DAY ELEVEN : CHAGFORD - EXETER

The lady owner offered no complaint when I declined a full English breakfast the following morning. We discovered that she was an accountant by profession and this was borne out when she charged the price of two single rooms for the cramped twin that we had occupied. However, Roy and I were too cowardly to complain and departed sadder and poorer.

This proved to be both a rewarding and frustrating day. After an initial rebuttal when trying to take a local field path we spent much of it following the tranquil upper reaches of the River Teign as it flows between steep and often precipitous wooded slopes.

Road-walking was forsaken when we joined a track that wound through comforting grassland to the river. Gazing down at us from a granite promontory was Castle Drogo. This imposing building, perched more than 900 feet above the River Teign, was completed in 1930 and is the last castle to be built in the country. It was designed for the India tea baron Julius Drewe by Sir Edwin Lutyens and combines the grandeur of a medieval castle with the comfort of the twentieth century. The great country house and its array of gardens are open to the public.

Thus began a riverside journey that stretched for almost eight miles through sheltered woodland, its peace only disturbed by the occasional passing walker and the explosive 'chack' of the woodpecker.

Sunshine filtered through the leafy confines of Whiddon Wood, the first of many that coat the valley. It dappled the layer of moss and stones that overlaid the generous riverside track we were following. The name 'Whiddon' struck a chord. Evidently, the wood was named after Sir John Whiddon, whose town residence was Whiddon House, in Chagford, during the Renaissance. He was no doubt, ancestor to the Mary Whiddon of ghostly legend.

It was late morning when the trees relented to reveal charming Fingle Bridge. A convenient halt, the Anglers Rest, stood nearby. Tables and chairs were arranged on a terrace by the inn, providing an ideal view over the swift-flowing river, once the haunt of salmon. Our push for Exeter was forgotten as we basked in sunshine and watched an angler lazily casting his line into the jingling waters in the search for trout. We could only guess what the man would have given to catch a twenty-six-pound salmon like the one on display in the inn.

A bold chaffinch had no hesitation in perching on our table and eating scraps of food that Roy provided. Eventually, it flew onto the parapet of the sturdy three-arched bridge, its stonework mellowed by the passing centuries, and called to friends watching warily from the surrounding foliage. Evidently, the opportunity of a free meal was not sufficient to lure them from the trees, for none appeared.

By the time we reached Clifford Bridge, in the early afternoon, woodland walking was beginning to pall and I was longing for green fields and rolling hills. A pleasing meal at the nearby inn soon dispelled such craving and I was ready for the final stage of our arboreal journey alongside the River Teign to Steps Bridge, where the valley sheds its tree-cover and the Teign skirts the attractive village of Dunsford. As though tired of forging east the river suddenly veers to the south, heading for its meeting with the Tavey and, eventually, the sea at Teignmouth.

In the open countryside beyond Steps Bridge we joined a narrow road leading to Reedy, where we joined another twisting country road, its high hedges the scourge of motorists, which took us to the busy B3193. To our delight we came upon a sign indicating Exeter, the downside being we had seven miles remaining. A decision was required. Should we take the road that meandered significantly along a roundabout route, or the more direct series of country lanes and woodland paths? Uncertain as to access in the area we decided that the main road was the lesser of two evils and began what proved a hot, tiring and frustrating walk to our destination. The scarcity of pavements and grass verges meant exposure to thundering traffic. Several times my heart missed a beat as we rounded sharp bends, expecting to be swept off our feet with victory almost within our grasp.

Roy was particularly keen to complete the walk and maintained a punishing pace that left me labouring in his wake. He had to halt occasionally to allow me to catch up. We were ruing our decision to keep to the road long before reaching Exeter but once committed we were forced to persevere.

Tired, sweaty and sore-footed, we arrived in the pleasant village of Ide, sequestered in a quiet valley on the outskirts of Exeter. Celebrations were premature, for the final push through the city suburbs was still to be accomplished and, as any walker will appreciate, such a task can be onerous as it involves battling with heavy traffic or a confusing maze of back streets.

At last, with great satisfaction, we wandered through the city centre, admiring its rich variety of buildings. Exeter has an extensive history and came to prominence during Roman times when it was regarded as a frontier town at the western limit of their occupation. Excavations, aided by air raids during the Second World War, have revealed that Roman Exeter was a city of nearly a hundred acres enclosed by a stout wall, parts of which are still visible. During its lively past the Danes took the city twice and William the Conqueror laid siege to it for eighteen days before he triumphed.

It felt a privilege to walk the streets of a city that has survived strife and hardship to reign peacefully as the gateway to the appealing West Country. In Fore Street, where venerable and modern architecture mingle, we came across ancient Tucker's Hall, built for the Guild of Weavers, Fullers and Shearmen in 1471, when Exeter was an important cloth manufacturing and trading centre. Sadly, German bombs destroyed much of the city in 1942 but the Guildhall shopping centre, incorporating much of the Civic Hall of 1838, now stands at its heart. We halted in the shadow of the Cathedral of St Peter. Its massive, yet decorative twin Norman transept towers soared skywards. The largest array of fourteenth-century sculpture in England graces the west front, one of the finest features of this majestic place of worship, set amidst verdant lawns hemmed with trees.

Strolling past an adjacent row of delightful Georgian houses, we discovered a much older medieval dwelling with a massive carved door and vivid trails of wisteria gracing its medley of red sandstone and black and white timbered walls. There seemed something of Bloomsbury about this Georgian haven, which is no coincidence. The Duke of Bedford owned large areas of land in Exeter and London and both sites were developed to a similar design.

The historic significance of the city is portrayed by the remains of Rougemont Castle that we found nestling within Rougemont Gardens. Built by the Normans, soon after they took the city, its only traces are a crumbling gateway, stretches of wall and a tower but their setting is ample compensation. Rougemont Gardens and the neighbouring, more formal Northernhay Gardens, laid out in 1612, are graced with splendid lawns and flowerbeds and have provided ample opportunity for peaceful contemplation and relaxation over the centuries. In fact, it was the ideal environment for Roy and myself to reflect on our accomplishment as we sat in the early evening sunshine.

CHAPTER TWO

Exeter to Chepstow

DAY TWELVE : EXETER - BICKLEIGH

The initial test of my journey from south Devon to the start of
Offa's Dyke Path was to find my way out of Exeter and join the Exe
Valley Way, a forty-five mile trail that begins on Exmoor and travels
to the mouth of the Exe. I intended to follow the Way to the village
of Bickleigh, my destination for the night, and onwards to Tiverton
on the following day. An undemanding walk seemed in prospect
that morning, for the total mileage was little more than twelve and
the route appeared straightforward. The only drawback, I reckoned,
would be inclement weather, which mercifully never materialised.
On such an expectant morning why consider contours, those
perverse indicators of height that have a habit of working against
you? The valley of the Exe, I discovered, has its fair share of these
monsters, which, depending on their mood, can ruin your day or
make life easy. Far from keeping to the valley floor, the Exe Valley
Way wanders uphill and down dale like a wayward child,

occasionally rejoining the river to find a convenient crossing point. Thanks to its intrigue my intended twelve-mile stroll was to last all day, but time was plentiful.

Nearly an hour elapsed whilst I threaded through the city suburbs to reach the village of Cowley lying at the junction of the River Exe and the River Yeo, which begins its life near Yeoford. As it passes Crediton the Yeo flows beneath Yeoton Bridge at the tiny settlement of Salmonhutch, probably a reference to the wealth of salmon found within its waters.

I joined the Exe Valley Way at Cowley, which led me, by footpath and country lane, to Brampford Speke. This agreeable village, consisting mainly of cob and thatch, snuggles by the Exe in pastoral surroundings. I wondered if the inhabitants of this sleepy place were disturbed by the transient legions of Exe Valley Way walkers that tramped through it. No doubt the inn and local store were glad of the passing trade.

Crossing a bridge over the Exe I followed the meandering river for three miles through lush water meadows. I ambled along riverside paths bathed in sunshine with a light breeze fanning my face. Festoons of yellow buttercup and pink willow-herb coated the basking meadows. Birds chirped overhead, butterflies fluttered merrily and grasshoppers flitted in the grass. All seemed right with the world.

The hamlet of Nether Exe slumbered in the warmth, as did a fisherman beside the river when I approached Thorverton. Awakened by my footsteps he remarked that he might as well enjoy a nap, for the fish weren't biting.

I joined a road that entered Thorverton. It crossed a dismantled and overgrown railway, which set me wondering about the line's original purpose. The map indicated a section linking Brampford Speke and the oddly-named settlement of Up Exe that stands roughly one mile north-east of Thorverton.

The attractive village of Thorverton lies at the foot of the Raddon Hills and has an engaging air. From the seat on its tiny, colourful green the view is one of quiet charm. A stream drifts lazily beside the green and passes the butcher's shop, which has the date 1763 over its projecting, pillared porch. Nearby stands another eighteenth-century building, the Dolphin Inn that gives precedence to the ancient fifteenth-century church, which boasts an intriguing

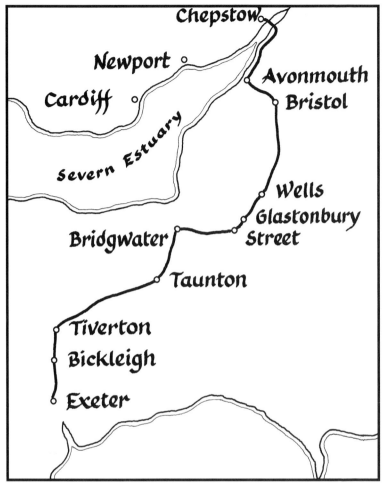

Exeter to Chepstow

carving, incorporating three figures joined in one, in the roof of its porch.

It was a wrench to leave my sun-drenched resting-place amidst sweet-scented roses and rejoin the Exe Valley Way. For the remainder of its journey to Bickleigh the Way follows a series of bucking country roads. They wander high above the valley before plunging down to the river at Lee Cross. It was hot work battling with contours in the afternoon sun but I had the compensation of sweeping views over the green sward of the Exe Valley.

The absorbing Bickleigh Castle stands on a hill above the village and as I passed I paused to examine what resembles a moated manor house rather than a castle. It has a chequered history and contains a fascinating mixture of Norman, medieval and seventeenth-century architecture. After the Conquest the manor passed into the hands of the de Bickleigh family who built the small Norman chapel, which still remains, complete with thatched roof, within the castle's confines. Despite its mixture of buildings Bickleigh Castle is impressive. Delicately crafted wrought-iron gates give access to a well preserved and much altered fifteenth-century gatehouse, originally built by the Courtenays, Earls of Devon. A shapely archway in the gatehouse permits a glimpse of the ancient chapel. During the Civil War a large part of the castle was destroyed by Cromwell's forces and the owners at that time, the Carews, had to rebuild in a more domestic style. The result is the wing of mature stone and thatch, which forms the north side of the inner courtyard. Its impressive façade is topped with a tiny and unusual thatched clock tower. Entrance to the castle is by means of a delightful rustic bridge, which spans a moat, festooned with lilies and rushes, creating a water garden setting.

A short downhill walk brought me to Bickleigh's pride and joy, a sturdy, handsome bridge spanning the wide, tree-fringed River Exe, which flows gracefully beneath weather-beaten arches of sixteenth-century vintage. The view upriver, of thatched cottages and riverside gardens, has made it a beauty spot much favoured by summer visitors. This splendid scene is widely known through its depiction on calendars and promotional literature.

In the bridge's shadow stands old Bickleigh Mill, a working watermill with an adjacent café. It was a pleasure to sit in the afternoon sunshine at an outdoor table and enjoy some refreshment in a stimulating riverside setting, seemingly popular with fishermen. The Fisherman's Cot restaurant stands beside the bridge and the time-honoured Trout Inn can be found nearby.

The village of Bickleigh is situated away from the main road and it contains a wealth of thatched buildings, a graceful Regency vicarage and a secluded medieval church. A notorious member of the Carew family is buried in an unmarked grave within the churchyard. Bampfield Moore Carew, the son of a seventeenth-century vicar of the parish, was romanticised as a king of the gypsies. It is true that he ran away from school, joined a gypsy band

and was eventually elected their chief, but the rest of his life was less glamorous. He became known as 'the noted Devonshire Stroller and Dog stealer' and was convicted of vagrancy. Although sentenced to transportation to America he managed to avoid such a fate and his long-suffering relatives persuaded him to lead a less itinerant life when he won a prize in a lottery. As a result of their pleadings he returned to Bickleigh to lead a quieter existence.

I was intrigued by the Railway Centre situated near the bridge, on what appeared to be the site of a former station. The section of disused railway that I had encountered near Thorverton sprang to mind, which, I reckoned, could be a stretch of the line that formerly ran from Bickleigh to Exeter. There was a length of track remaining at the Centre, which could have been part of this railway but I could find no reference to its existence. What I did find was a variety of model engines and carriages on display that formed a great attraction for young visitors.

DAY THIRTEEN : BICKLEIGH - SAMPFORD PEVERELL

A good night's sleep and a satisfying breakfast provided good preparation for a day of riverside and canal towpath walking. I left my accommodation, a pleasant cottage set amongst spacious and attractive gardens, full of expectation. Planning to spend the morning following the Exe Valley Way, to Tiverton, I noticed from the map that it conveniently kept to the valley bottom.

The major part of the morning's walk was a disappointment. I blundered through endless, dense woodland on a series of frustrating paths. Squelching through swathes of mud I nearly came to grief several times and cursed the mire underfoot. The hidden life of the woods was inescapable. Creaks, sighs and rustles dogged my footsteps, breaking the silence of the seemingly empty forest.

My struggle ended when I emerged from the trees near a Sewage Works, which seemed to typify the journey up to that point. Free of restrictive vegetation I joined a riverside track that permitted rewarding views across the valley. The village of Ashley and the straggling suburbs of Tiverton soon appeared on the opposite bank.

My route into town passed beneath the steeply rising riverbank whose slopes still bear traces of the town houses and riverside gardens of the merchants and manufacturers of wool and lace that made Tiverton famous. A good introduction, I decided, my appetite whetted.

It was a false alarm. There was nothing striking about the array of shops lining the busy streets, their facades regular and undistinguished. Much of the market town was destroyed by fire in 1731 and consequently, most of its buildings are of a later vintage. However, on closer inspection I found there was more on offer. Blundell's School, for instance, a delightful building dating from 1604, when it was larger than Harrow. In the sixteenth century Tiverton became the most prosperous of the Devon wool towns and rich merchants sent their sons to the school after its inception. During the Civil War the building was commandeered by Fairfax after his successful attack on the town.

The general did considerable damage to the castle, whose remains can still be found near the church, with the crumbling pink sandstone ruins of the square south-west tower abutting the churchyard. The gatehouse, a circular tower and part of the wall of the Norman castle, begun in 1106, have been incorporated in an impressive Tudor and Georgian residence.

St George's Church is one of the finest Georgian buildings of its type in the country. When construction began in 1714 it was planned as a chapel for persecuted Dissenters but by the time it was completed conditions had changed and it was consecrated as a church. One of John Wesley's brothers, Samuel, who was headmaster of Blundell's School, is buried in the churchyard.

The River Loman joins the Exe at Tiverton and on its banks stands the school attended by R D Blackmore, the author of *Lorna Doone*. It has been converted into flats, but his name can still be seen carved in its walls. The triangular lawn still exists where John Ridd and Robin Snell had their fictional fight in the acclaimed novel.

Tiverton signified my departure from the Exe Valley. I headed for the terminal basin of the Grand Western Canal, which I planned to follow, and eventually found the terminus, situated in pleasant surroundings, on the outskirts of town. The waterway is only eleven miles long but was originally intended to be part of a system, planned in the eighteenth century, to link the English and Bristol channels. A long barge spanned the end of the canal and served as a floating restaurant. Nearby, passengers were waiting to board another barge and as I stood admiring the handsome vessel the bargee arrived, leading a well-groomed shire horse, its leather straps enhanced with brightly-polished brasses. What a nice touch of nostalgia it presented, in an age where barges are no longer propelled by horsepower. I felt a great urge to leap aboard and give my feet a rest.

I strode along the canal towpath, through peaceful surroundings, on an enjoyable six-mile journey to Sampford Peverell. Assorted shades of green surrounded the waterway that was only disturbed by the occasional unhurried pleasure craft. Lush vegetation overhung the placid water that intermittently sported reed beds and arrays of becoming lilies. Mature cottages peeped over hedges flanking the canal, their rustic roofs adding character to the verdant surroundings. Ducks, white-crested coots and the occasional swan completed a halcyon scene.

Despite my laid back mood, I was making good progress and the castellated tower of Halberton Church soon appeared in the distance. Not wishing to waste energy, I decided to cut out a significant loop in the canal and take the more direct route, by road, into the village.

The hideous rattle of pneumatic drills greeted me as I entered Halberton. Roadworks stretched along much of its main street, causing traffic holdups and frustration to motorists and pedestrians. An otherwise inviting village was ruined by noise and congestion. I ignored an enticing leafy lane leading to the impressive medieval church and hurried past another eye-catching building, the Priory, its dazzling white frontage topped by a lofty stone chimney, the colour of moist sand.

'Blinding nuisance!' exclaimed a passer-by, shouting to make himself heard above the din. I stopped and nodded in reply.

Eyeing my rucksack he inquired, 'Where 'ave you come from?'
'Exeter.'
'Where be you going?'
'Chepstow.'
'Chepstow!' The man retorted. 'That be a mighty long way.'
'Only six days' walking,' I replied.
'You must be pretty fond o' marching round the countryside.'
Stuck for a response I feebly answered, 'Yes.'

'Lord bless your feet!' the man retorted as he went on his way.

Beating a hasty retreat from the clamour I rejoined the canal towpath for the remaining two miles to Sampford Peverell that passed without incident. I received a cheery wave from families aboard a couple of passing barges. They were the first I had seen since leaving Tiverton and of the horse-drawn one there was no sign

As a diversion I made frequent references to the map, hunting for items of interest. I noticed a rash of unusual names in the vicinity. What had caused people to name their properties 'Noble Hindrance,' 'Higher Shutehanger' and 'Battens Farm,' I wondered? It wasn't difficult, however, to guess the origin of 'Muddifords Farm'.

My destination was a farm, lying a short distance from the canal, beyond Sampford Peverell. Anxious for a bath and a meal I followed the waterway through the village, paying it little heed as I kept watch for the footpath leading to the farm. Traffic thundered above me, on the bridge carrying the A361 road, as I found the sign I had been seeking.

A short time later I introduced myself at the old farmhouse. The substantial stone walls and stone-flagged floor of the kitchen created a rustic setting as I chatted over a cup of tea with the amiable couple. I found the rest of the building just as appealing and I was intrigued by the gnarled wooden inner doors until I discovered several of their shrivelled planks had parted allowing a clear view through them. When I used the bathroom I trusted that no one was peering through the unsettling slits in the door.

My hosts suggested I ate at the village inn, which had a good reputation for its food and I found it was worth the three-quarter-mile walk into the village. A friendly atmosphere permeated the place, encouraged by its low, oak beams and glittering brasses. A splendid meal was followed by conversations with several villagers who seemed eager to chat with a stranger. The men, I observed, spoke slowly and deliberately, the women more quickly. In this part of Devon the parlance is colourful and the voice warm with a pronounced burr. Older residents I met claimed that the dialect hasn't altered in over three hundred years. I found the people polite and matter-of-fact, not ones to suffer fools gladly, or to throw their money around. This view was reinforced by a crusty old fellow who walked into the bar later that evening. He asked the price of cigarettes, drinks and several brands of bottled brew before settling for a half of mild. Payment was extracted slowly, coin by coin from his purse and he made the drink last for nearly an hour. When the old man left, the barman smiled knowingly and told me he was a regular patron whose performance was always the same. 'Got more money than he knows what to do with,' the barman added.

DAY FOURTEEN : SAMPFORD PEVERELL - TAUNTON

Dark clouds threatened as I left the farm and returned along the footpath to the canal. I shrugged my shoulders, conceding that the weather had been kind up to that point, apart from my journey in search of Men-an-tol. It soon began to rain. I donned waterproofs and plodded along the canal towpath for several miles in near silence, for there was no traffic on the waterway and very few people around. The bleakness was broken only by the occasional angler huddled over a massive carbon-fibre rod, oblivious to all around him. Not my cup of tea, I thought, especially in such conditions. I was pleasantly surprised when one of them bade me a cheerful, 'Good morning.'

At this stage of its journey the Grand Western Canal runs, arrow-straight, through a country park and, I noticed from the map, within half a mile of the M5 motorway. I thought how much easier it would be to forsake foot-slogging and hitch a lift to Bristol.

Banishing such whimpish notions I trod the towpath to the termination of the waterway, beyond Whipcott. Divested of my trusted companion and guide I took to the road for a mile before locating some convenient field paths. I enjoyed a little celebration as I crossed the county border into Somerset near Greenham Weir, which straddles the broadly meandering River Tone.

The rain began to ease as I tramped through the hamlet of Holywell Lake, named after the holy well that stands on its outskirts, and it had stopped by the time I reached the outlying streets of Wellington. The town's claim to fame is that its name was chosen at random by the victor of Waterloo as his title. He seems to have known little about the place and only visited it once. However, his choice made the townspeople very happy and they demonstrated their pride by constructing a 175-foot column in his honour. Another war-like connection concerns a local factory, which received the largest order ever placed in the country for cloth, in 1915. It was for a million and a half yards of khaki.

In the drying conditions it was with lighter heart I entered a wood and followed a track that eventually meets the Taunton to Exeter Railway just outside tiny Poole. Taunton lay only six miles distant. As I had covered the major part of the day's walk I decided to rest, have a bite to eat and take it easy.

A convenient series of riverside paths provided a scenic afternoon walk to Bradford on Tone, which, like the town of Taunton, nestles in the Vale of Taunton Deane whose name has a rich, succulent ring, evoking images of sun-filled orchards, lush meadows and sleepy villages. The River Tone and I kept fairly close company for the remainder of the day's journey to Taunton. On my arrival I was immediately impressed by the county town of Somerset that retains the sense of a market town and agricultural centre. Sheltered by hills and unsullied by industry, Taunton exudes an air of quiet authority, appropriate for the county seat. It was a pleasure to wander its attractive streets that maintain an intense historical presence. Amongst its highlights is the imposing Georgian Market Hall, and the view of the tower of St Mary's Church as you look down Hammet Street is something to be savoured. Ancient, timbered Tudor House, its rich decoration dating from 1578, stands amongst the shapely lines of its neighbours in Fore Street. Nearly as old are the multi-chimneyed almshouses in East Street, built by Robert Gray in 1635. He was a Merchant Tailor and the coat of arms of his Livery Company can be seen above one of the doors.

At the end of High Street stand the ornate wrought-iron gates of Vivary Park that in earlier times contained the fishponds of the Priory. Since 1894 it has been one of Taunton's cherished spaces. Beyond the park a series of Georgian and Regency dwellings can be seen, immaculate in painted stucco. The Crescent also boasts a fine sweep of Georgian properties, built by Sir Benjamin Hammet and probably modelled on one of its London counterparts. It not merely the buildings that catch your eye. Hanging baskets add dashes of colour to a town centre free of litter and grime and a double, bright red pillar-box adds an unusual touch.

Pride of place must go to the castle, now converted into a

museum, which captures the essence of the town's long history. For twelve centuries Taunton has dominated western Somerset, since the building of an earthwork castle by King Ine who succeeded Caedwalla in 688. Of this castle, by the River Tone, virtually nothing remains, but at the centre of the present range of buildings on Castle Green stand the ruins of the later Norman Castle, once occupied by the bishops of Winchester. Chaucer's son, Thomas, was Constable here and the castle stood stoutly for many centuries, certainly until after the Civil War, for at that time the castle held out against 10,000 Royalists.

It was in the castle that Judge Jeffreys held one of his purges in 1685, after the Battle of Sedgemoor. With the king's encouragement, here and at Winchester he condemned over 300 men to the gallows and had hundreds more transported to the West Indies. The trials, or 'bloody assizes,' as they became known, were often a travesty of justice.

Near the entrance to the museum stands a large stone with a sword embedded in it. The weapon provided my first taste of Arthurian legend, for it is supposedly 'Excalibur.' I was to discover more about King Arthur and Guinevere a little later.

An area where Taunton's identity is keenly felt is that around the churches of St Mary and St James. Here are quiet streets, one with the interesting name of Whirligig Lane, and the former Octagon Chapel opened by John Wesley in 1778. Here too is the home of Somerset cricket, the County Ground, with the towers of the two churches presiding over it. Cricket lovers of advanced years may remember the exploits of JC White, probably the finest player to grace the ground. In his first county match he took ten Gloucestershire wickets for fifty runs and, in 1929, his third season as captain, he took over a hundred wickets and scored more than a thousand runs. Younger supporters will have memories of a more recent county captain, Brian Close, the Yorkshire exile, whose dedication and tenacity transformed Somerset from a mediocre team into one that played attractive cricket and drew in the crowds. He took under his wing a promising batsman from Antigua, Viv Richards and a young all-rounder, Ian Botham. We know what became of them!

DAY FIFTEEN : TAUNTON - BRIDGWATER

Today was to be another episode of canal-side walking. Was I becoming idle and content to follow threads of water? The Bridgwater and Taunton Canal offered the most straightforward route to Bridgwater, with the added bonus of no map-reading required. There were few convenient footpaths and I wished to steer clear of the main road and the M5 motorway that also link the two towns.

The canal led me from the town-centre before threading through outlying Maidenbrook and Bathpool. The urban landscape then relented and I walked through open countryside to Creech St Michael. Conditions underfoot were naturally good and I maintained a fair pace. Apart from the waterway's insistence on wandering hither and thither, thereby adding extra mileage, the journey was trouble-free. I admired cheery canal-side gardens, waved to passing barges and passed the time of day with the occasional angler, anything to add variety to what was becoming a well-established pattern.

Traffic was more plentiful than that on the Grand Western Canal and I was able to watch barge crews wrestle with lock gates and swing bridges. I was becoming familiar with the clever breed, known as 'Gongoozlers,' who observe these labours with amusement and disdain. They usually lean nonchalantly on the handrail of the bridge that spans the lock and always know how to do things better than the poor strugglers beneath. Seldom shy of dispensing advice, they have probably never operated lock gates in their lives.

In order to take a break from the towpath I took a short detour into North Newton, a homely village, unfortunately sited close to the motorway. What did the residents of this peaceful village think, I wondered, when they learnt that a six-lane highway was to scythe through the countryside on their very doorstep? I could imagine them setting up an action group, calling themselves 'Newtonians against Road Pollution,' and sending a deputation to London to chain themselves to the railings of Buckingham Palace. Having no convenient woods available for building tree-houses the poor protestors were powerless to hinder the progress of rapacious bulldozers. It was easy to visualise them prostrating themselves before the murderous machines, being squashed into the Somerset mud and emerging like creatures from the swamp. Thinking of swamps; did they consider sending for 'Swampy' and his colleagues to dig tunnels and render the ground too dangerous for laying a motorway?

In any event, protest would have been futile, for nothing must be allowed to prevent the motorist from saving an hour of his precious time in reaching the honeypots of Devon and Cornwall. Therefore, the good people of North Newton and their neighbours in North Petherton are condemned to live with the ceaseless noise of traffic thundering along the great highway.

As if to further destroy the peacefulness of the village, the West Country Way, a cycle route that forms part of the National Cycle Network, passes through it. The inn and the village store will, no doubt, welcome the trade it brings but the remaining villagers are unlikely to be enamoured by hordes of cyclists threatening to mow them down.

I felt that I should tiptoe from North Newton, so as not to disturb its harassed inhabitants and I trod lightly as I rejoined the canal. It was my turn to duel with cyclists, who seem to have forgotten that a bell is a useful device. There is nothing more disconcerting than being suddenly overtaken by a speeding cycle, or abrupt shouts of, 'Oi!' and the screech of brakes when a rider realises that he is about to propel you into the canal. The West Country Way follows the towpath of the Bridgwater and Taunton Canal for four miles and I kept eyes and ears keenly pricked for marauding cyclists.

Two miles beyond North Newton, at Fordgate, the River Parrett Trail adds to the fun and joins the towpath for a journey into Bridgwater. I was quite happy with this state of affairs, for fellow walkers rarely threaten to pitch you into the water.

I was intrigued by the trail and that evening I did some map research to discover the route of its journey along the River Parrett that stretches for thirty-five miles. The trail traces a rambling course that frequently strays from the river. It starts by the mouth of Stockland Reach, where the Parrett meets the ocean, on a prominent headland culminating at Stert Point. Across the estuary lies Burnham-on-Sea, which heralds seven miles of glorious sand. There is little sand surrounding the headland, for it is an area of marsh, frequented by a large bird population, and the site of a Nature Reserve.

The trail begins where the road runs out at the hamlet of Steart and follows the Parrett southwards until it cuts out a substantial loop in the river and continues south to Bridgwater. From there it follows the canal, as I mentioned, until it rejoins the river near Fordgate. Trail and river travel hand in hand through Langport and onwards to Thorney, where the trail wanders off along a series of tracks to the wonderfully named Kingsbury Episcopi. Pining for the Parrett, the trail rejoins it for two miles until it goes walkabout again and passes through the settlements of South Petherton, Merriott and South Perrott, situated near the source of the river.

My arrival in Bridgwater marked an important point in the walk, for I had arranged to meet my friend Roy, who was to accompany me to Chepstow. I was greatly looking forward to our rendezvous and to having a companion once more. We duly met and went in search of our night's accommodation, where we came across our host, busy in the garden. The man had a strange manner and a queer look to his eyes. Roy and I found him creepy and nicknamed him 'Fred West,' after the notorious serial killer.

We were glad to esape a little later and explore the town. It proved to be undistinguished, but containing some redeeming features. The former bustling port and industrial centre has a rundown air, although the once thriving docks are worth a look. Quayside buildings give the area a Dutch feel. Close-knit facades overlook the river, their varied gables rising and falling atop a range of tall and narrow properties. Most are constructed of brick, for Bridgwater was a centre for the brick and tile industry. Dereliction has begun to creep into the cluster of black roofs, crisp quoins and white window frames.

Castle Street runs from West Quay, flanked by Georgian brick terraces, to King Square, the site of the castle. It was here that the Duke of Monmouth, illegitimate son of Charles II and Lucy Walters, was crowned in 1685 by the mayor and proclaimed from the castle walls as king. There he stood, gazing towards Sedgemoor, where his rebellion ended in defeat during the last battle held on English soil.

The hub of modern day Bridgwater is the statue of Admiral Robert Blake, which stands flamboyantly in front of the porticoed

Market Hall. Few men have achieved renown as leaders on land as well as on sea, yet this former merchant and Member of Parliament for Bridgwater deservedly accomplished this. He rose to fame as a Parliamentarian general in the early days of the Civil War and captured Taunton before successfully withstanding a subsequent siege. Whilst defending the town against attack, Blake reputedly declared, 'I would eat my boots before I would surrender!'

Following the Civil War he became an admiral in the Cromwellian Navy, taking part in the Dutch and Spanish wars. His crowning glory was the defeat of the Spanish fleet at the battle of Santa Cruz, but Blake died at sea an hour before his victorious fleet entered Plymouth Sound. His body lay in state at Greenwich before a state funeral at Westminster. After the Restoration, Charles II had the hero's body exhumed and thrown into a pit, but Blake is still honoured at Bridgwater. His lasting memorial stands not far from the house, now a museum, in which he was born,

Bridgwater possesses several mock Tudor buildings and we entered one of the finest, the Tudor Hotel, in search of a meal. Unfortunately the food did not match the impressive exterior. Our struggle with the overcooked fare was relieved by a radio commentary, floating through the restaurant, featuring England versus Germany in the European Cup.

DAY SIXTEEN : BRIDGWATER - STREET

Our journey on this particular day could be described as a waste of effort. We travelled east for its entirety, which meant that, at the end of it, we were no nearer to our ultimate destination, Chepstow. There were two reasons for this state of affairs. Firstly, a more direct route would have required the negotiation of a maze of rivers, drains and dykes that criss-cross Sedgemoor, Somerset's fenland. Secondly, I had a yen to visit Street, England's largest village, and its neighbour Glastonbury, the cradle of Christianity in this country.

My proposed route followed an intermittent series of footpaths and country roads along a stretch of dry land, bordered to the north and south by an intricate pattern of waterways. I explained to Roy that one of the reasons for choosing it was to keep our feet dry!

As we left Bridgwater a challenging network of back streets had to be wrestled with before we located a path leading to a footbridge over the M5 motorway. Perched on the bridge we watched the traffic thundering beneath us, hell-bent on reaching its objective in the minimum time.

The roar of traffic began to fade as we progressed, by footpath and track, to Chedzoy, one of several settlements ending in 'zoy', which surround the battle-site of Sedgemoor. Together with Middlezoy, Penzoy and Westonzoyland, the village has a 'buzzy' and evocative West Country ring to its name. When Roy and I joined the narrow road into Chedzoy we met the West Country Way that I knew from bitter experience. I explained the problem I had experienced with cyclists on the canal towpath and joked that we had more room to get out of their way on a road. A few cyclists did pass us, but we were thankfully soon out of danger, for after a further mile and a half the Way departed. By this time we had passed through the hamlet of Parchey. Its name was apt, for we had already worked up a thirst that sunny morning. The gardens of Chedzoy and Parchey were revelling in the warm sunshine, their foliage resplendent and many of their blooms spilling over walls to grace the roadsides.

As we left Parchey we crossed one of the main channels that sever Sedgemoor, King Sedgemoor Drain, a band of water, sometimes blue and sparkling, sometimes grey and choppy like a miniature sea. On clear evenings the Drain is often aflame with a golden sunset, stretching the eye along its gilded surface to the very extremity of the surrounding flatlands.

Sedgemoor lies in the Somerset Levels, a plain of church towers, of history, of manor and mariner. Everything hereabouts has the hand of abbot, soldier, engineer and farmer. The land proclaims that it is the bed of history, from Alfred to Monmouth, a place of wide fields and interlaced ditches alive with water-violets, bog myrtle and pondweed, roads that dip and rear, orchards and lonely farms.

Sedgemoor has had its drainage problems but conversely it has provided a prime habitat for withies and teazles. The tough, flexible strands of willow, known as withies, have for centuries been used for canework and for binding bundles. Also, the prickly heads of teazles were valued for dressing cloth.

Roy followed in my footsteps as I led the way to quiet Sutton

Mallet and trod the path that passes beneath Pitt Hill, en route for Moorlinch. Hungry and thirsty we sought the village store where we were welcomed by a genial woman who seemed pleased of the opportunity to chat to strangers. From her remarks it was clear that the store was the focal point of the secluded village and nothing that happened within it escaped her notice.

As we left the store, armed with food and cooling drinks, a tractor pulled up beside us. 'Be you from down under?' inquired the weather-beaten driver. Roy and I laughed. 'No,' we replied. 'We're from Yorkshire.'

It was the farmer's turn to laugh. 'I'm afraid I don't see many folks as I live on my own with my dog, Buster.' He indicated a three-legged dog perched on the tractor.

'Goes everywhere with me, he does,' added the farmer, who clearly led a lonely existence.

'Why not join us?' Roy joked.

'Where be you going?'

'Chepstow,' I replied.

'My lord!' the farmer gasped. 'I think I'll stay 'ere, if you don't mind.'

We left the fellow scratching his head in disbelief. He had probably never been farther than Bridgwater, or Glastonbury.

A series of convenient field paths took us past Greinton and on to Pedwell that stands at the foot of Pedwell Hill and Priest Hill, whose tree-lined slopes dominate the surrounding plain. Our route skirted the hills and as we walked in their shadow I tried to imagine the wide-ranging view from their tops.

Street lay a few miles away and we quickened our pace as we joined a road that leads to Marshall's Elm, which lies on the southern outskirts of the village. Once there we imagined our day's walk to be virtually over but we were premature. The guesthouse where we were staying proved frustratingly elusive and we had to ask for directions on several occasions. Even the locals seemed unsure of its whereabouts.

Street, as I mentioned, is the largest village in the country and it certainly seemed so as we spent the next half-hour searching for our objective. By this time Roy and I had had enough and went in a nearby pub for a meal. As I approached the bar I was greeted by a local wag. 'Going walking?' he asked cheerily, as though my boots, rucksack and walking gear were not proof enough.

This chap doesn't miss much, I thought. 'Well spotted,' I replied, knowing full well what was coming next.

'Where are you going?'

'Chepstow.'

'Bloody hell!'

To rub it in, I added, 'I've come from Land's End.'

The man looked at me as though I had just descended a shaft of light. 'Christ Almighty!'

'It's not far.'

'Too bloody far for me, mate,' he declared patting his sizeable stomach.

'It would do you good,' I responded.

The man laughed. 'Kill me more like.' He smiled at his companion, who was also propping up the bar, before giving me a searching look. 'You must be mad.'

'You want to try it sometime,' I suggested.

'Not likely,' he replied, 'I've better things to do.' He glanced at Roy who had commandeered a vacant table. 'He's as daft as you are. What are the pair of you doing galavanting around the country at your age?'

'Getting some exercise,' I quipped. '

'Silly bugger,' the chap replied and returned to his drink.

'What was all that about?' Roy asked when I had ordered our food and joined him at the table. He had a good laugh when I explained.

When we had had our fill a woman from an adjoining table came over to us. She must have heard us bemoaning the search for our accommodation and offered to take us there in her car. We jumped at the chance and were soon relaxing at the amenable guest-house.

I found a book on the area and learnt that Street took its name from an ancient causeway, which ran north to Glastonbury. I also discovered that it is the home of the shoe industry founded by Clarks, the local family that inherited the tanning craft, in 1825. From there it was a short step to fleecy slippers and it became a cottage industry until 1858. When the business expanded the honest dealing Quaker family began to provide schools, a library and, above all, decent homes for their factory-hands. Thus developed Somerset's 'Bournville,' or 'Saltaire,' and today Street is home to Clark's village, a large factory-shop complex. It is also home to the famous Millfield School that developed from a house that WS Clark built for himself and called 'Millfield.' In 1935 it became a school, inspired by principles of excellence and individual development. It currently houses an Olympic standard swimming pool, which can be hired at a cost of £3,000 per day, half the price of others of a similar grade.

DAY SEVENTEEN : STREET – WELLS

Roy and I were about to venture into the Somerset of legend and mystery. From Street it is but a mile to revered Glastonbury and the traveller moves back many centuries as that short journey is made. He enters the mists and meloncholy of Avalon that appeals to the primeval streak in man. Beyond Glastonbury rises its Tor, an island amidst a mystic land where Arthur of Camelot reigned and pilgrims journeyed to the seat of Christianity. In early times the Tor formed an island, in a watery wilderness, which attracted settlers. During the Middle Ages it became a place of pilgrimage, for as legend claims, Joseph of Arimathea came here with the Holy Grail.

Hereabouts, as at Sedgemoor, the battle has always been for dry land. In medieval times the great land-owning abbeys tried to change the landscape but still the floods came. It was not until fifty years ago that significant progress was made, athough this brought another dilemma. The inefficiency of the old rivers, Axe, Brue and Parrett, had encouraged a rich variety of wildlife. It is only now, when the water levels have been lowered and the land made more productive for agriculture, that the cost to plant, insect and bird population is appreciated. This problem aside, the area retains its broad vistas of field and sky, its secret lanes and sentinel towers that make it so distinctive.

We were required to cross the channelled River Brue during our approach to Glastonbury, whereupon we climbed a hill that provided a fine view of the town. The twin towers of its two churches presided over an expanse of buildings littering a landscape free of industrial sprawl. The tree-studded slopes of Edmund Hill formed a green backdrop to the neat array of red roofs and white walls slumbering beneath. Glastonbury looked decidedly neat and tidy.

Our eyes were drawn to Glastonbury Tor soaring from a flat land interspersed with willow and ditch, where every mound and farm is emphasised. What a pity so little remains of the lake villages that surrounded Glastonbury. Excavations were begun in the nineteenth century, which presented a clear picture of their design. They consisted of circular huts, almost floating on the marshy surface, supported by piles driven down to the peat. With constant use the huts began to sink and the solution was to lay fresh floors on top of the old ones, sometimes as many as ten.

A mixture of ancient and dignified buildings lined the streets as we neared the slender Gothic War Memorial in the centre of town. White-paint and timber added lustre to the rows of immaculate façades, engendering an old-world charm. The medieval George Inn, with its rich mouldings and fine mullioned windows, appeared a most inviting hostelry. It was built in the fifteenth century for the accommodation of pilgrims, for whom no room could be found in the abbey. The 'George's' little brother, 'The Abbot's Tribunal,' looked very homely, but in the past, when the abbey was all-powerful, or when the king's judges were on the circuit, there must have been many a ruthless sentence passed in its chamber.

You are made perfectly aware of the 'Avalon' connection in Glastonbury. The name is bestowed on numerous premises, a reminder of the Arthurian folklore that enriches the area with a dense web of unproven tradition. Glastonbury, it is reputed, is the Isle of Avalon – rising from the Dark Age marshes – where King Arthur is buried.

To find out more, we toured the remains of the abbey set amongst well-manicured grounds that were once the site of a Celtic monastery, established in 500 AD. A notice indicated the spot where Arthur and Guinevere are supposedly buried. Nothing remains of a tomb, which might add authenticity to the claim.

Shattered remnants of the abbey are scattered around the green sward and there is actually one building still intact, the Abbot's Kitchen, which is probably the finest of its kind in Europe. It was most likely saved from demolition because of its secular purpose. The building would have been used by the last abbot, Richard Whiting, who was eighty years old at the time of the Dissolution in

1539, when the abbey was destroyed. His great age did not save him from a sticky end, for he was executed on Glastonbury Tor, his head stuck on the abbey gate, and his body quartered and sent around the county.

The most eye-catching of the abbey remains are the twin twelfth-century transept arch supports, 175 feet high, framing the great ruined nave, open to the sky. What a tragedy it seems that such a worthy edifice should be desecrated so soon after its completion in 1524. To add insult to injury, stone was plundered from the abbey for many years afterwards.

So engrossed was I in this historic place, I almost forgot that the bulk of our day's walk still remained. There was also the intriguing Glastonbury Tor to be visited. We hurried out of town and began the 520-foot climb to the top of the great conical mound. It was a hard one and, sweating with the heat and our exertions, we neared the summit of the steep-sided Tor and saw a vast panorama unroll beneath us. The green canvas of the Somerset Levels stretched into the distant haze as we reached the tower, all that remains of the late thirteenth-century St Michael's Church, perched on top of the Tor.

The view from our superb lookout evoked a strong sense of history and legend, for this was the land that pilgrims trod and King Arthur and his knights reputedly roamed. Unfortunately our musing was short-lived, for we had to return to reality and head for the village of North Wooton, where we planned to join the Monarch's Way. Five miles of determined walking brought us to this little-known long-distance footpath that covers nearly 500 miles and closely follows the route taken by Charles II during his retreat after the Battle of Worcester in 1651. His flight followed a crushing defeat by Cromwell and, at the age of twenty-one, he became a fugitive forced to flee for his life.

In some confusion, the royal party initially headed north with the intention of crossing the River Severn into Wales and obtaining a ship to the continent. The river was heavily guarded, however, and the plan had to be aborted.

After a day spent in the legendary oak tree at Boscobel a new plan was developed. A royalist supporter, one Colonel Lane, had a sister, Jane, who was in possession of a permit to travel to Abbots Leigh, near Bristol and it was arranged for Charles, disguised as a servant, to accompany her and try to obtain passage on a ship to

France. For five exciting weeks, hotly pursued by the Parliamentary forces, he travelled south through the Cotswolds and the Mendips to the south coast. Finally he progressed along the South Downs to Shoreham, near Brighton, where he made his escape to France. Loyally supported by his followers, many at great risk to their own lives, he was given shelter in places both great and humble, some of which exist today.

We followed the Monarch's Way northwards towards Wells. In parts it was adequately signed but in others difficult to detect. I am unsure of the conditions when Charles trod the route but sections of it appear to retain the succeeding 350 years' growth of vegetation. I was pleased to learn, however, that a Monarch's Way Association is to be formed, or indeed, may already have been by the time this book is published. Its purpose is to consolidate the walk. I wish them good fortune.

North Wooton, we discovered, is a quiet, secluded village, set away from the main roads. At the time of the Domesday Book it belonged to Glastonbury Abbey and for much of its history has been known for wine production. Even today it possesses its own vineyard.

As it leaves the village, the Way climbs steep-sided Worminster Down, a flat-topped hill from where we enjoyed a fine view of the Somerset Levels. The hard work of the day was over, for a gradual descent from this prominence brought us to the outskirts of Wells. The cathedral is a dominant landmark as you near England's smallest city, which takes its name from the wells that rise in the grounds of the Bishop's Palace. Water from the wells feeds the moat that surrounds the palace and also flows through the gutters of High Street.

Glastonbury is a treat, but Wells is a gem. It boasts the oldest medieval street in Europe - completed in 1348 - and houses many decorative buildings. In fact it is impossible to walk round the city without coming across unbelievably attractive premises. Here a medieval doorway set among windows of all centuries, there an elegant Georgian facade or a many-gabled hotel.

The market square is a sight to behold, presided over by the gateways of Penniless Porch and the Bishop's Eye, flying the eye-catching episcopal flag. Behind loom the towers of the first completely Gothic cathedral in the country, built during the twelfth and thirteenth centuries. Georgian bay windows overlook the commemorative slab marking Mary Bignal Rand's world record long jump, whose dimensions are etched in the pavement.

Pass through Penniless Porch, dating from 1450 and once frequented by beggars, and you come face to face with the magnificent west front of the cathedral, overlooking Cathedral Green. This most decorative façade, elaborated with many statues and a representation of the Last Judgement, ranks amongst the finest in Europe.

Resting in the grounds of the thirteenth-century Bishop's Palace we gazed across the tranquil, tree-fringed moat to its ancient precincts, still occupied by the Bishop of Bath and Wells.

Our accommodation lay some way from the city-centre and, as we crossed Cathedral Green we passed the Cathedral School, from whose windows floated melodic strains. A concert was in progress, continuing the great musical tradition of Wells. We were surprised to hear the tempo change to jazz, an indication that the school caters for all musical tastes.

Our host that evening was a jovial character who kept a highly presentable establishment. We discovered he was a cricket enthusiast, like us, and a friendly rivalry developed between the counties of Somerset and Yorkshire. A regular visitor to matches at Taunton, he declared that his county team would thrash ours when they next met. I am pleased to relate that since his boast Yorkshire have won the county championship!

DAY EIGHTEEN : WELLS - CHEW STOKE

Stout legs were required for the initial stage of our day's walk, which involved climbing the testing Mendip Hills. Our first objective was the village of Wookey Hole, whose claim to fame is the famous Wookey Hole cave complex, which is situated in a beautiful wooded valley. The caves, over a million years old and first inhabited in the Iron Age, are surrounded by legend and superstition. One tale, concerning the infamous Witch of Wookey, may well be based on fact, for in 1912 excavations revealed a female skeleton together with a dagger and a round stone rather like a crystal ball.

With a long day in prospect and a stiff climb facing us we decided to forsake the caves. A scorching sun showed no mercy as we struggled up the steep escarpment, frequently pausing to recover our breath and mop sweating brows. At last the top of the limestone plateau was attained and we were treated to a wonderful retrospective view of the Vale of Avalon and the distant hump of Glastonbury Tor, protruding from the flat landscape like a giant carbuncle. We enjoyed a brief respite on our grassy perch and drank copious amounts of liquid.

Progress became easier as we followed field paths to an area of heathland, called Priddy Mineries, a Nature Reserve covering 123 acres. The site and the neighbouring land were worked for lead over a lengthy period, which may stretch back to Roman times. Earlier workings were obliterated by those of the Victorian era, which give rise to the pores, spoil heaps, buddle pits and condensation flues found today. Due to lead contamination of the vegetation, no stock graze the area, which is also an ancient burial site, littered with prehistoric circles, tumuli and barrows. The finest means of interpreting the true character of the Mendips is to stand atop Priddy Nine Barrows and survey the history that surrounds you.

The Reserve is a Site of Special Scientific Interest and its spoil heaps are home to spring sandwort and sea campion. Marsh and spotted orchids flourish in the damper patches and there are areas dominated by purple moor grass. Dank pools abound, which are inhabited by small reptiles and a variety of water bugs, an attraction for naturalists and fishermen.

Unfortunately, Priddy Mineries is threaded with a confusing network of paths and this caused us to lose our way. The temperature had soared and we were in no mood for frustrating diversions. Eventually, hot and flustered, we reached a car park where a kind motorist offered us drinks. Extremely grateful, we gulped down the welcome liquid. In fact we became so thirsty later on we were compelled to knock on the door of a house and ask for a drink of water. The helpful occupant willingly supplied us with cooling soft drinks and gave us pitying looks.

A period of woodland walking beckoned as we entered Stockhill Plantation, its thick coat of conifers giving relief from the searing sunshine. We needed to remain alert, for route-finding was complicated, courtesy of the maze of tracks that permeate the forest. Just prior to emerging from its confines we crossed the line of a former Roman road that merges with the modern B3135.

At Pitt Farm, on the fringe of East Harptree Woods, we began our descent from the Mendips, along a delightful series of lanes, to the village of Compton Martin. Originally a Bronze Age, and then a Roman settlement it nestles in Chew Valley astride the River Yeo, which flows into Blagdon Lake. The valley forms a huge water store, for it also houses sizeable Chew Valley Lake, nearly three miles in length.

The mid-afternoon sun was unrelenting and, despite the generous drinks we had received, the thirst was upon us again. To our joy we spied the 'Ring o' Bells' pub and hurried past tall hedges, resplendent with hawthorn blossom, to dive inside. Re-emerging with drinks in hand we savoured the delights of sun-drenched Compton Martin. White walls, many adorned with garlands of roses, glistened in the blistering sunshine. Ducks waddled from the nearby pond and the sturdy church tower kept watch over a scene of rural tranquility.

It was an effort to get tired limbs moving once more but our aches eased as we steered a course between the two lakes until we reached the hamlet of Breach Hill. Here we were rewarded by an extensive view over the placid expanse of Chew Valley Lake, which is, in reality, a reservoir.

A further mile and a half of field paths brought us to Walnut Tree Farm where we bade a temporary farewell to the Monarch's Way and joined a path that veered towards Chew Stoke. The fine tower of the village church, crowned with stone balustrades and slender turrets, rose majestically above a cluster of trees and guided our footsteps over the final lap of our day's journey. Horses grazed in meadows on the fringe of the village as we spied the red roofs of mature cottages that formed a welcome sight after one of the hottest and gruelling days I have experienced.

I was immediately attracted to the quiet charm of Chew Stoke, which, along with its neighbour, Chew Magna, huddles at the northern end of Chew Valley Lake. A feeder stream of the River Chew glides, almost apologetically, through its peaceful centre and passes between ivy-covered walls to a timeless rustic bridge. Here it widens and tumbles over a tiny waterfall overlooked by a pattern of neat dwellings fit to grace any English country scene.

We peered over stone walls at lush gardens patterned with yew, chestnut and ash. Lupins lined paths winding to mellow-stone dwellings that invoke names such as 'Rose Cottage' and 'Shady Nook.' Chew Stoke is a reminder of a gentler age.

Our accommodation was just as inviting and proved very agreeable. Here we met an elderly couple who regularly visited the area and had nothing but praise for it. The other guest was a young London taxi driver who enlivened breakfast with tales of ferrying passengers around the capital. Roy asked how long it had taken him to familiarise himself with its maze of thoroughfares, to which he replied, 'I just picked things up as I went along.' I told him that my eldest son lived in London and knew of many short cuts through its back streets. This, I explained was very convenient until he was obliged to get back onto main roads clogged with traffic.

DAY NINETEEN : CHEW STOKE - CHEPSTOW

Our plan for the final day was to follow the Monarch's Way to Abbott's Leigh, on the outskirts of Bristol, where we hoped to pick up the Avon Walkway and follow it to Avonmouth. Here the route looked hazy, along a series of roads, until the Severn Way could be joined, leading to the old Severn Bridge, near Aust. It is all of twenty-four miles from Chew Stoke to this river crossing and a further four to the centre of Chepstow. Accordingly, I had not booked overnight accommodation, preferring to leave things open-ended.

Once again, the weather was on our side. The sun was busy burning off a slight haze and it appeared we were in for another scorching day. Apart from the section through Avonmouth, the route seemed straightforward, but how many times has that assumption been proved wrong?

Bidding a fond farewell to Chew Stoke we retraced our steps to the Monarch's Way, en route for Winford, a pleasant, sleepy village, nestling in a hollow amidst acres of grassland, patterned with mature trees and luxuriant hedgerows. Elder, hazel and maple encroached on the village, partially obscuring its handsome church. Our progress towards Barrow Common was impeded by a series of overgrown and muddy stretches of path. At Castle Farm, near

Dundry, we walked into a quagmire created by the daily milking routine. With boots squelching and legs plastered with mud we ploughed onwards trusting that the warm sun would dry them out and allow us to scrape off some of the mess. A field of maize proved our next obstacle, forcing us to follow the field edge and search for a gap in the hedge that revealed a footbridge. I dared not imagine how long the day's walk would take if conditions remained as hostile.

During our descent to Barrow Common we glimpsed a chain of three reservoirs and the beginnings of Bristol's urban sprawl. Beyond the hamlet more mud appeared as we left an earthen embankment, a remnant of the ancient Wansdyke. This is believed to date from the Dark Ages, possibly the sixth century. The area on the other side of the embankment is named on the map as 'The Wild Country!'

More squelching followed until the mire relented and we reached a cutting through which the A370 road runs. A little further on we crossed a bridge over a railway line, which, together with the road, occupies the major transport corridor linking Bristol and Weston-Super-Mare. At this point we entered Long Ashton, an ancient village with three pre-Roman hill encampments in the vicinity. The Romans themselves built a large settlement and villa at nearby Gatcombe. In more recent times WG Grace's father, probably the village's most notable inhabitant, was born here

Two miles of pleasant walking along leafy country lanes brought us to Abbott's Leigh and permitted our first view of the Bristol Channel and the Welsh hills beyond. Abbott's Leigh is another old settlement, for there is evidence that a Celtic community existed well before the Romans came. It was also an important halt during Charles II's flight. The large house in which the king sheltered was the home of George Norton, to whom the king's identity was not revealed, for he was posing as a servant to Jane Lane. However, the family butler had served in the Royalist army and recognised the king. Consequently Norton was taken into Charles's confidence and charged with finding a ship in Bristol bound for the continent. Unfortunately, the prospect of a ship sailing to that destination proved doubtful and it was decided to head for the south coast and a secure base from which to obtain passage.

After the king's escape to Europe and the subsequent

Restoration, many people who had helped him were rewarded. Strangely, there is no record of such granted to George Norton. However, in the church there is a monument to Sir George Norton (1622-1677) and reference to the historic royal visitation.

We followed another section of the Monarch's Way into extensive Leigh Woods that line the west bank of the River Avon for over two miles. The area is a National Nature Reserve, threaded by forest walks and is home to a variety of birds and fauna. Descending the steep Nightingale Valley we emerged at the riverside, close to the Clifton Suspension Bridge. This commanding landmark hangs, like a giant cobweb, between the abrupt sides of the Avon Gorge, 245 feet above the river. The unique structure is a tribute to the skill of Isambard Kingdom Brunel who also designed Bristol Temple Mead Station and the *SS Great Britain*, the largest ship of its era, which lies in dry dock at Bristol. The ship was launched by Prince Albert in 1843 and marked the beginning of a new concept in ocean travel. Over 320 feet long, it was the largest ship in the world and the first to be fitted with an iron hull and driven by a screw propeller.

At this point we joined the Avon Walkway, which can be followed into the heart of the great seafaring city of Bristol that derived much of its wealth from slave trading. Despite the dangers, Charles II insisted on a diversion into the city, curious to see if the defences had changed since he was last there. Today, little remains of the castle, which was demolished in 1656, five years after the king's clandestine inspection, but an excavated section of its south wall is visible in Castle Park.

Fourteen miles of our day's journey still remained so we headed north, away from the city, along the riverside trail. The wide, even track ensured that we made good time, despite a sizeable loop in the river and we were soon approaching Avonmouth Bridge that carries the M5 motorway. Here we lost much of the time gained, for access to the conspicuous concrete structure was by a circuitous path and the bridge stretches for a mile on its gigantic stilts. Road-works were in progress and traffic was crawling, a frequent occurrence, from all accounts. The walkway was unfortunately partially obstructed by men and equipment engaged on repairs. However, we managed to squeeze past such obstacles without straying into the extensive line of crawling traffic.

A lengthy descent from the bridge was followed by the tortuous negotiation of Avonmouth's suburbs. Unable to find any footpaths in the vicinity an uncomfortable period was spent walking along the busy A 403 road with traffic hurtling past.

Avonmouth is a flourishing port and the original village is surrounded by docklands and large industrial estates. Fuel depots litter the riverside area, known as the Oil Basin and storage tanks, cold stores and grain silos sprout at every turn. Aerial ducts, conveying materials and ores to the factories and smelting works, criss-cross the bleak, urban landscape, making our desire to be rid of the industrial squalor more intense.

At last we were able to escape the main highway and join a path running parallel to it but this proved a mixed blessing. To say it was overgrown was an understatement, for we battled with head-high brambles and nettles. In desperation, we were forced to return to the road until we neared Severn Beach where an attractive promenade and defensive wall has been constructed, known as the Binn Wall. Walking would have been pleasant along the concrete walkway, permitting good views across the river, had it not been for our sore feet. The long day and the heat were taking their toll and progress became slower until we took an enforced rest on a seat at a riverside viewpoint. Whilst quenching our thirst, we surveyed the imposing concrete mass of the new Severn Bridge that was almost within our grasp. It arched over the wide estuary, supported on gigantic columns, almost fading into infinity, such is its great span. Opened in 1996 it replaced our objective, the older version, as the gateway to South Wales and it now carries the M4 motorway. The first Severn Bridge has been relegated to transporting the M48 motorway across the river but it has retained its visitor centre.

The new bridge looked even more impressive at close quarters and, far from being straight, a distinct curve could be detected. The bases for the concrete supports resemble massive houses with four chimneys atop that bear the weight of the huge bridge. A sizeable metal cradle is suspended beneath the bridge, running on rails for the complete span. It carries a scissor lift, used for maintenance. Roy and I agreed we would not relish using the cradle beneath the apex of the bridge.

Three miles remained to the village of Aust that lies in the shadow of the old Severn Bridge. Although walking was easier, having joined the Severn Way, the concrete underfoot further inflamed our feet and slowed our progress until the hump of the old Severn Bridge, its twin, fabricated metal supports thrusting skywards, dominated the skyline.

Our proposed crossing of the Severn by this bridge would hopefully be simpler than that of John Hillaby. He was told by a tramp, who fell in with him as he walked from Bristol, that he could pass amongst the construction gangs onto the brand new bridge of the unfinished England-to-Wales motorway - the M4 as it was to become. He approached the bridge plagued by an almighty din. Bristol aircraft engines were under test at nearby Filton, pile-drivers and pneumatic drills pounded the final section of the super-highway, but worse was to come. At the point where the road began to run over the estuary, suspended on ferro-concrete stilts, he noticed a gap of several hundred feet. Cursing his luck, he walked to Aust Ferry and missed the ferryboat by minutes. He had to wait two frustrating hours for the next one.

Beyond oddly-named Cake Pill Gout we were able to take a series of field paths, which ran to the outskirts of Aust. These were kinder to our abused feet, which were sorely in need of a rest. As we entered the compact hamlet of Aust, a welcome pub appeared and it was agreed that a halt and a rejuvanating meal were in order. We hurried into the hostelry extremely glad of the respite.

After the meal I booked accommodation in Chepstow by telephone, explaining our situation and that we would be late in arriving. This lifted a load from our shoulders and meant that we could take our time over the remainder of our day's journey.

Suitably fortified we climbed from the village and joined the foot and cycle path of the old Severn Bridge. The river crossing, as it did at Avonmouth, took longer than anticipated. By the time we had crossed the Severn and left the bridge, two miles had elapsed. A further mile of road-walking beckoned before we could take the path onto Sedbury Cliffs and reach the stone that marks the southern extremity of Offa's Dyke Path.

Fatigue crept upon us once more as we trod the road that hugged the riverside. Undaunted, we persevered until we reached our goal and touched the stone that signified the end of our journey from Exeter. Weary, but happy, we rested on the grass by the stone that is inscribed in both Welsh and English, as are the markings on the majority of the signs along the long-distance footpath.

We could have gladly slept overnight by the stone, but Chepstow beckoned, with its promise of a comfortable bed. In the glow of late evening we trudged the remaining distance into the ancient town, stopping frequently to gather our strength and rest our feet.

When we reached our accommodation our hosts remarked that we looked shattered, which was an accurate description. We were truly exhausted. Their mouths dropped open when we explained that we had walked from Chew Stoke that day. They were unsurprised that we proposed to go straight to bed after a hot bath.

The exertions of the day melted away as I sank into my welcome bed and in the brief moments before falling asleep I reflected on the highs and lows of the absorbing eight-day journey from Exeter.

CHAPTER THREE
Offa's Dyke Path

DAY TWENTY : CHEPSTOW - MONMOUTH

I walked onto windswept Sedbury Cliffs, eager to experience Offa's
Dyke Path that basically follows the great earthwork, built by Offa,
King of Mercia in 757, the first year of his reign. As the sixth
century dissolved into the seventh, the Anglo Saxons renewed their
inexorable expansion, driving the Welsh to the foothills of the central
mountains. By the eighth century, Mercia was one of the most
powerful kingdoms in Britain and Offa constructed the great earth
mound as a demarcation, probably intended to keep the warlike
Celtic Welsh at bay. Wales had for the first time acquired an eastern
frontier, not far removed from the present national boundary.

Compared to Hadrian's Wall, Offa's Dyke can hardly be
regarded as a serious line of defence. It was not intended to be
permanently manned, neither was it a continuous structure, but its
creation was a monumental achievement, considering the lack of
today's earth-moving equipment. There were many breaks along its

length, in thickly wooded river valleys for instance, where its construction would have been very difficult and pointless, for the forests acted as a natural barrier. A deep ditch was dug on the Welsh side. Above this, an earth mound rose up to twenty feet high. The overall structure, ditch and earthwork, was over seventy feet wide in places.

The 1245-year-old barrier has vanished along much of its route but where it does survive -usually in high remote places - it conveys a profound sense of the past. The untravelled uplands around Knighton are such an area.

Offa's Dyke Path runs from Sedbury Cliffs to Prestatyn, a distance of 168 miles and was created in 1971. The opening ceremony was held at Knighton, midway along the route, in the Offa's Dyke Riverside Park, where Sir John Hunt, later to become Lord Hunt, performed the unveiling of the commemorative stone.

On towering Sedbury Cliffs, overlooking the mudflats of the wide Severn Estuary, I began my assault on the Path that would involve eleven days of arduous, but stimulating, walking through attractive and undulating border country.

Departing from the marker stone I headed towards Chepstow along field paths that provided an amenable introduction to the walk. I strode through meadows adorned with swathes of buttercup and cowslip, radiant in the morning sunshine. Cattle, chewing contentedly, followed my progress with large languid eyes and the 'chit-chat' of birds floated from the hedgerows. Dry, ruckled mud underfoot signified a lack of rain for several days.

Pastoral contentment was soon halted when I entered a housing estate on the outskirts of Sedbury. The pleasant path was transformed into a narrow, overgrown channel sandwiched between high fences. Nettles and brambles attacked my legs until I reached an estate road. Obliged to weave through the estate, I passed along Mercian Way and Offa's Close, before skirting a sewage farm and reaching the cliffs lining the River Wye.

The tidal river was at its lowest and an array of boats languished on its muddy banks like beached whales. Across the river stands an engineering works that was formerly used for shipbuilding and the rusting remains of a launching ramp are partially embedded in the riverbank beneath. Metal supports for the old Severn Bridge were fabricated at this site and transported down the river for erection.

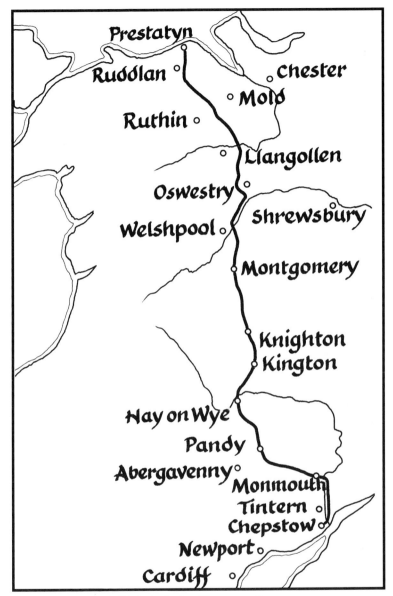

Offa's Dyke Path - Chepstow to Prestatyn

The confluence of the Wye and the Severn, roughly one and a half miles to the south, is plagued by treacherous, swirling currents and the barges carrying the stanchions would have had to negotiate these.

It was necessary to follow the wide sweep of the river before entering Chepstow, but my reward was the sight of John Rennie's iron road bridge, painted a pristine white and its lattice-work frame resting on sturdy stone ramparts. From this gently arching structure I obtained a magnificent view of the Norman castle, seated on limestone cliffs, high above the river. It remains partially intact, dominating the town with its tremendous presence.

Although playing a key role in the Norman control of the turbulent Welsh, the fortress came into its own during the Civil War when it was associated with Henry Marten, a leading Parliamentarian. He signed Charles I's death warrant and suffered for this 'treacherous' act when Charles II was restored to the throne. The tower, in the castle, where he was held prisoner for twenty years is still known as Marten's Tower.

The significant loop of the River Wye acts as a natural moat for the castle and also aided the sealing off of the town, from the end of the thirteenth century onwards, in conjunction with the building of the Port Wall. This structure, still intact for the greater part of its length, enclosed the medieval borough on the west and the south, and the river sealed off the remainder.

Near the river, in the old streets of the town, one can visualise Chepstow as it was 200 years ago - a hive of activity with craft of all sizes, plying the Wye and the Bristol Channel. Like most ports it would have been a bad, mad place, its dozens of alehouses crammed with sailors and harlots. It is said that the tide has been known to rise to over forty feet here, depositing brackish water into the local ale.

The Chepstow of today is gentler. It typifies medieval towns that grew alongside military strongholds and evolved through the centuries into busy market centres. Its church, castle, tangled street pattern and surviving fortified gateway give it a timeless and absorbing air.

Evidence of the town's strong links with the Dukes of Beaufort is demonstrated by Beaufort Square and, overlooking one of the narrow streets that branches from it, the Beaufort Hotel. In the square stands a rather incongruous German gun, which serves as a memorial to Able Seaman Williams of Chepstow, who won the Victoria Cross at Gallipoli.

Bidding goodbye to the 'Gateway to South Wales,' as the town is frequently described, I followed a lane leading past the mellow ruins of Tutshill Tower that was probably a sixteenth-century coastguard beacon.

Thus began a journey to Monmouth following the notable Wye Valley. It was to be a day of meadows, leafy lanes, narrow roads, tree-lined paths, a good measure of forest glades and tangles of badger-haunted woodland. I switched from road, to track, to field, to wooded path, and a period of resolute stile-climbing brought me to Wintour's Leap, a 200-foot precipice that dives into the grey waters of the Wye where it winds between tree-carpeted banks at Lancaut. It is named after the supposed feat of Sir John Wintour who, pursued by Parliamentary soldiers, escaped by leaping, on horseback, from the cliff into the river. It stretches the bounds of credulity to imagine such an action would not result in certain death for horse and rider.

Another exciting vantage point over the Wye was reached at the Devil's Pulpit, a rocky outcrop providing a magnificent view of the remains of Tintern Abbey, 600 feet below. On this rocky knob, as legend has it, the devil stood and raged at the monks in their handsome abbey and pelted them with rocks.

Tintern Abbey stands in a perfect riverside setting, framed by attractive wooded slopes. The Cistercian site inspired William Wordsworth to pen one of his finest poems, *Lines*, and one can understand the inspiration behind this illustration of his firm belief that God is to be found in nature.

Hereabouts Offa's Dyke reveals itself and I followed its overgrown profile until it descends to the Brockweir Valley and emerges from the woods much diminished. The quiet village of Brockweir heralded a transfer to riverside walking and, as I left its confines I passed a Bentley, of 1929 vintage, that displayed infinitely more character than the modern Ford Fiesta parked alongside.

I was enjoying the sight of the river gurgling over patterns of beetling rocks when a walker, wearing a floppy sun hat quickly overtook me. I discovered he was from Manchester and a man of few words, except those he used to brag about his prowess. He was marked down as a 'mile cruncher,' eager to tell you how far he had walked, but vague about what he had seen. I began to explain about my traverse of the Path, but he swiftly departed as though my activities were of no interest.

As I watched him forge ahead we were herded towards the river's edge by a rope fence. The path deteriorated and I passed a terse notice declaring, 'No boating, no bathing, no picnics.' I reckoned it ought to include 'no breathing!' Visitors were obviously unwelcome and conditions were deliberately made uncomfortable. However, a family across the river appeared to ignore the instructions. Mum was preparing sandwiches whilst dad and their son played football. Less happy was a straggling party of schoolchildren that filed past me, loaded down with bottles of orange squash and billowing anoraks. Some were limping, others hung their heads and the odd scuffle was taking place. Instead of being glad of a day out in such surroundings, most of them seemed to resent their teachers dragging them through the Wye Valley.

I stopped for respite in the shadow of Bigsweir Bridge, a not unattractive metal span, across which trudged three women shouldering rucksacks as large as themselves. I can never see the fun in carrying everything but the kitchen sink, but these walkers evidently needed a mountain of equipment that could only serve to slow their progress and make them sweat buckets. They struggled past me ignoring my proffered greeting, eyes staring straight ahead as though focused on something of importance down-river. I had to subdue a smile when, a few minutes later, they passed once more, heading up-river, without a smile or a 'hello.' Their antics smacked of *The Grand Old Duke of York*.

Between Bigsweir Bridge and Redbrook the Path climbs to a superb viewpoint near Highbury Farm. The tree-lined river could be seen snaking through the narrow, steep-sided valley and the forthcoming section of my route was revealed. The rippling Vale of Monmouth and the profile of the Black Mountains beyond stretched into the afternoon haze. Redbrook, a former industrial village, hunched by the riverside, amidst a profusion of trees, and my attention was drawn to the adjacent eye-catching iron railway bridge straddling the waterway on massive stilts. The settlement derives its name from the brook that flows from the hills above, whose water was valuable to the busy iron-producing industry that sprang up during the industrial revolution. When large supplies of coal were discovered further west in South Wales, the village lost its ironworks.

In the late afternoon, with roughly two miles remaining to Monmouth, I reached the National Trust owned Kymin, the site of a Naval Temple and Round House, standing on the crest of a hill overlooking the town and its surrounding vale. The 'Temple' is a large stone column topped by a statue of Britannia. It was erected as a memorial to the eighteenth-century British admirals and their significant naval victories. In 1802, Lord Nelson, Emma and Sir William Hamilton visited the site.

The culmination of a hot and testing day's walk was a steep descent into Monmouth, the former county town, with its promise of rest and recuperation. Monmouth is an attractive town, steeped in history. An important centre since Roman times, it was a popular stopping place on the fashionable Wye Valley Tour. Its hub is Agincourt Square, named after its most famous son, Henry V, who was born in Monmouth Castle in 1387. His statue is set into the decorative façade of Shire Hall and it gazes down on the bronze figure of Charles Rolls, co-founder of Rolls-Royce, who was the first man to fly across the Channel from England to France and back without landing. Tragically, that same year, 1910, he was killed in a flying accident.

Near the square stands Agincourt House, a venerable, half-timbered building, typical of the pleasant old houses and inns, which grace the town. Lord Nelson stayed in one of the hostelries when he was awarded the Freedom of the Borough in 1802. The Nelson Museum contains an unrivalled collection of relics left to the town in the will of Lady Llangattock, the mother of Charles Rolls. Amongst the Nelson memorabilia are his sword and models of the ships on which he served.

DAY TWENTY-ONE : MONMOUTH - PANDY

The route out of Monmouth is conveniently along its main thoroughfare, the wide Monnow Street, which leads to the River Monnow and an outstanding bridge. This delightful red sandstone structure was built in 1262 and is a most attractive reminder of Monmouth's vivid history. It still supports the tall tower that was formerly the gatehouse for the town. Through the centuries the tower has also been used as a watchtower and small prison.

The Path leaves the outskirts of Monmouth along Watery Lane, an ominous name. The weather was, however, once again set fair and towards lunchtime the heat was such that I was desperately seeking shade.

It was to be a day spent traversing the rolling hills of the Vale of Monmouth. The terrain was very pleasant but offered more of a challenge than I anticipated. Those seemingly innocuous hills made me pour with sweat.

Around lunchtime I arrived at a delightful little church, sporting an unusual wooden tower, at Llanfihangel-ystern-llewern. Try pronouncing that name after a few drinks! Reputedly, the church is founded on the spot where Ynr, King of Gwent escaped onto dry land from a bog into which he had stumbled.

The church porch looked inviting as it offered welcome shade - the church itself was unfortunately locked. As I sat mopping my brow and eating a sandwich a party of Dutch walkers joined me. It transpired they were walking part of Offa's Dyke Path, which they had learnt about through their local Tourist Information Centre. Apparently, our long-distance footpaths are well publicised in Holland, a fact that I can substantiate, for I have met several walkers from that country.

I fell in with their party and we covered the next few miles together, beginning our communal journey through meadows, flecked with radiant yellow, and a blue sky above. Several kissing gates had to be negotiated, those annoying contraptions designed to snare rucksacks and squeeze the breath from your lungs. We soon reached Llantilio Croesenny and its church in a commanding position atop a hill. This sturdy edifice, possessing a tall slender spire is lord of all it surveys. From the churchyard there are distant views of the Skirrid-fawr, the 'Holy Mountain,' an oddly shaped prominence with a protruding small lump. Its top forms a saddle in which the Ark is believed to have rested. In the hazy sunshine the faint profile of Sugar Loaf Hill could also be detected, greatly resembling that of Pendle Hill, a familiar landmark in Lancashire.

These outliers of the Black Mountains heralded the next phase of my journey along the Path, but first I had to reach the village of Pandy, nestling at their feet.

As the red-hot afternoon wore on our party reached another reminder of border strife, one of three castles that stand in close proximity. It was to defend Monmouth that the 'Three Castles,' as they are known, were built - Skenfrith and Gromont, on the Upper Monnow, and White Castle, whose gates we were at, on the hills above, guarding an important road over the pass to Abergavenny. Formerly under the Lordship of Hubert de Burgh and Edmund of Lancaster, the three are impressively maintained and admission to Skenfrith and Grosmont is free.

My Dutch friends held a quick debate to decide if they should visit the former stronghold that got its name from the original white colouring of its walls. I peered through the entrance gates and saw an answer to my prayers - a cold water tap! So hot was I that my flask and water bottle had been drained, both failing to quench my raging thirst. The tap convinced me that it was worth the admission fee to enter the castle grounds and I hurriedly did so, closely followed by the team from Holland. I made a beeline for the tap and drank lustily before replenishing my flask and bottle. As I toured the castle's remains I took frequent gulps of sweet, ice-cold water.

The ruins of the Norman fortress were formidable, the majority of the ramparts being clearly identifiable. Its solid towers and curtain walls, more or less intact, were protected by a defensive moat although the drawbridge and portcullis had perished. At points where the walls had crumbled their vast thickness could be discerned, which must have provided sound protection against arrow, musket and cannon.

My Dutch friends lingered at the castle. They had discovered the tap and were drinking eagerly from it. I pushed on, ungratefully cursing the cruel sun that refused to let up. My pace gradually slowed as I plodded uphill and down-dale for the remaining miles, my rucksack seeming to grow heavier by the minute. It was early evening before I arrived in Pandy, weary and slightly footsore. My accommodation for the night, an ancient farmhouse, lay an agonising two miles from the village. My heart sank until I recalled that the farmer's wife had offered transport from Pandy. I made a hurried phone call and was delighted when her car drew up about ten minutes later.

The old farmhouse, Oldfield Court Farm, lies in the very shadow of the Black Mountains, whose southern, grassy slopes rise sharply behind the building. Part was in ruins and I discovered that this was the original structure, built in the thirteenth century.

Around eight feet of wall remained, pitted with numerous doorways and windows that had been modified over the centuries.

When I entered the intact section I was struck by its coolness. Its interior appeared impervious to the current spell of boiling-hot weather and I understood why when I was told that the stone walls were eighteen inches thick.

A good meal was provided and I spent the evening chatting to the farmer and his wife who outlined the history of the farm and its original occupants. As the name implies, they were the Oldfield family whose most notable member was Sir John Oldfield who was born in 1360. His Grandfather was a Member of Parliament during the reign of Richard II. Sir John distinguished himself as a soldier and statesman, being granted the title of Lord Cobham. However, his honesty and forthrightness were his undoing, for he sent correspondence to Parliament criticising the leaders of the established church and praising the clergy. His remarks caused great animosity and a warrant was issued for his arrest. When a party of soldiers arrived at the farm he slipped out of a small rear window and escaped into the hills. He was soon captured, but managed to escape once more. His freedom was short-lived, for he was eventually recaptured and escorted to London where he was imprisoned in the Tower. He was tried, found guilty of treason and hanged in 1417.

DAY TWENTY-TWO : PANDY - HAY ON WYE

The farmhouse proved a most convenient halt, for it lies virtually on the Path, which I soon rejoined, as it climbs the steep slope of Hatterrall Hill. It was hot work, for the sun was already beating down from a clear-blue sky. This was pleasing in one way, for I was beginning what is probably the most exposed section of the Path, along the elevated Hatterrall Ridge.

As I struggled up the testing incline Skirrid beckoned beyond an emerald landscape, a vast patchwork laced together by dark green hedgerows. The occasional fawn of a hay meadow intruded into the verdant panorama and lines of gigantic black bin liners patterned several newly mown cornfields. A squadron of crows hovered above me like vultures licking their lips over easy pickings. They must have been bitterly disappointed when I reached the ridge and they flew away in disgust

The terrain became harsher as I began to traverse Hatterrall Ridge, towering 2,300 feet above sea level and stretching for ten miles along the eastern fringe of the Black Mountains. There is no habitation on its heights, necessitating a long decent for anyone requiring food or accommodation. The views, however, give adequate compensation and I was fortunate to experience them in perfect weather. A shiver ran down my spine as I imagined the bleak highway shrouded in mist with no landmarks to guide a lone walker. I looked tentatively over my shoulder. There is a sense of dark Celtic mystery in the air hereabouts and no shortage of local myths and legends to create such an aura. It is said a castle once stood at Craig Pwll-du owned by a chatelain with a fondness for ravishing local womenfolk. I should be safe then! After taking his pleasure he reputedly hurled them into a dark pool in the river below. It is also a convenient habitat for ruffians and brigands, like Tebris who reputedly recruited captains that levied tolls on travellers. I patted my wallet to ensure it was safely stowed.

The wide, well-trodden track was easy to follow and, pulling myself together, I reckoned it would provide a lifeline to wimps like me, even in bad weather. I could imagine the ancient green route being used by early travellers like the Celts and later by hardy monks and packhorse men who must have endured the harshest conditions. Here was I with food and drink in my rucksack and stout boots on my feet, in blazing sunshine, dwelling on all kinds of imaginary pitfalls. Compared to those early wayfarers I was in clover.

I savoured a feast of panoramic views. Behind me lay the intricate land of villages and castles bounded by the Wye Gorge and the southern face of the Black Mountains. To the east the land dropped sharply towards the Herefordshire Plain and to the west huddled the sequestered Honddu Valley.

Some hardy sheep ignored me as I passed, content to rummage amongst the thick entanglement of heather and blueberry, oblivious to the wind that swept across the exposed heath. According to local shepherds, sheep are very partial to blueberry and, as it begins to sprout in springtime, flocks are driven onto the hills in the knowledge that they will be content in the wild environment and unlikely to stray down into the valleys. The shepherds kick off the sprouting heads of the bracken, which eventually withers and makes space for more amenable fodder.

Inquisitive birds provided me with some entertainment. A watchful pair of curlews circled above, their warning calls drifting menacingly on the bracing morning air. Prying red shanks and plovers, after a cursory inspection, quickly retreated and the occasional buzzard wheeled on the brisk currents. I was beginning to enjoy my high-level jaunt. Stretches of drying peat felt springy beneath my feet, giving relief from the hard surface of the baked track and the clear conditions meant I could relish the Welsh Border country at its finest.

The village of Llanthony nestled deep in the Honddu Valley amongst a spread of lush meadows topped by shadowy carpets of coniferous forests. The steep 'rhiws' above were carpeted with bracken and pebble-dashed with vivid-white hawthorn blossom. In this romantic setting, within the Brecon Beacons National Park, stand the remains of the twelfth-century Priory, which began life as an Augustinian monastery. Although roofless, the priory displays fine traces of Norman and Early English architecture. Transitional work can be clearly discerned from the remnants of the west front, transepts and portions of the nave and choir. The chapter house, prior's lodge and south-west tower are partially incorporated in a hotel.

In 1807, the poet Walter Savage Landor purchased the Llanthony estate but ambitious plans for a school, 10,000 cedars of Lebanon, and merino sheep soon put him at loggerheads with his tenants and the local authority. He eventually went bankrupt and was forced to assign the estate to trustees.

Beyond Llanthony the valley steepens and the crags close in creating a secluded sanctuary where, long after the border feuds, escapees from the more frenetic town and city life came in search of peace.

Suddenly I was not alone, for I came across a group of wild ponies busily cropping the stunted grass. Amongst them was an incongruous donkey, probably a fugitive from Blackpool beach in search of a more tranquil existence. Hatterrall Ridge forms one of the breeding grounds for Welsh ponies whose concave profiles and delicate muzzles are said to be a legacy of Arab blood brought in by Roman pack horse.

People were thin on the ground and I passed only two couples during my traverse. Walkers are normally friendly and talkative, but these were unaccountably reticent. In fact they stared unblinkingly at me and all but turned up their noses. I was tempted to touch the forelock and would have welcomed some conversation.

A rustic sign by the Path points towards the head of the Honddu Valley and the hamlet of Capel-y-ffin, where, I assumed, walkers can seek sanctuary during inclement weather. It has been such a place since the time of the Reverend Joseph Leycester, an Anglian clergyman who took the name Father Ignatius. He claimed to have seen a vision of the Virgin Mary in one of the fields and he founded a monastery in 1870. Soon after his death and burial in the church in 1908, the buildings fell into ruin and in later years it became a retreat for the Roman Catholic community.

The trig point near Hay Bluff signifies the highest point of Offa's Dyke Path at 2,306 feet and as I reached this objective I noticed a hang-glider circling a little way ahead. This puzzled me until, a little farther on, the ground suddenly fell away beneath my feet. I was on the renowned Bluff, where the Black Mountains come to an abrupt halt and the Vale of Hay rolls out beneath you like a giant carpet. A steep track plunged down to a road and a car park, where vehicles, resembling tiny models, shimmered in vivid sunshine.

This unexpected panorama was breathtaking and I stood transfixed as I gazed towards my objective, Hay-on-Wye. As I descended to the road I passed a man and his wife labouring up the track. It transpired they were touring the area by car and wished to take in the view from the Bluff. They were glad of the respite, for they had not realised the severity of the climb when they left the comfort of their car. 'We're from Manchester,' the man informed me, 'and we're glad of a break from its urban sprawl'.

Hay-on-Wye lay four and a half miles away and I spent a confusing two hours negotiating a series of paths that led me a merry dance before I entered the compact border town. For book lovers, the place is either paradise or a vision of hell. In an array of bookshops, ranging from the cosy to the enormous, glossy hardbacks rub shoulders with the battered works of long-forgotten novelists and Harry Potter consorts with frayed Ian Flemings.

As far back as the seventeenth century Hay was a book centre and even undesirables imprisoned in the stocks were permitted to read, though it is doubtful if many could. The current popularity of Hay as a book town began in the 1960's when Richard Booth set up a book and antiques shop and soon found that the old books did by far the best trade. Buoyed by his success he began to purchase other properties and soon the former Plaza cinema was stocked with books, along with the redundant fire station, the workhouse, a chapel and even the castle, a decrepit building he procured for £6,500. He employed a local carpenter to fashion a replica of the original stocks, complete with book rest, and these were sited outside the castle. Above them he placed a sign proclaiming 'Erected in 1690,' and outlining Hay's history as a book town. It caught the attention of tourists who began to photograph this supposed antiquity and it became a significant attraction.

Booth's ethos was straightforward. Hay was facing economic isolation as local shoppers were lured away to large supermarkets in nearby towns and its only salvation was to specialise. Books, he believed, are an international market and Hay was handily placed to supply the needs of large metropolitan areas such as Bristol, Birmingham and Manchester. He knew his scheme was working when other booksellers began to seek premises in the town and even Oxfam opened a secondhand bookshop. Bus tours included the town in their itinerary and in 1989 the first Hay-on-Wye Festival of Literature was held. Hay had become firmly established as a book town and the tourists continued to pour in. Its Festival has become nationally and internationally renowned.

However, things did not end happily for the instigator. Booth's book keeping did not match his entrepeneurial skills and the 1980's brought a host of problems. The castle was nearly destroyed by fire and Booth was forced to consolidate by shedding many of his properties.

Despite gaining the title of 'biggest secondhand bookshop in the world,' the border town has managed to retain its rural character and boasts some fine half-timbered buildings. One of its more unusual features is an open-air 'Honesty Bookshop' situated in the shadow of the castle. Here one can browse around an array of bookshelves containing countless secondhand books of every type, entirely unguarded and open to the elements. Their only protection is canvas screens that can be pulled over the fronts of the shelves, at night, or in inclement weather. An honesty box is provided should you wish to make a purchase and a battered, hand-painted sign declares, 'Paperbacks 30p, Hardbacks 50p.'

On Castle Street an old bookshop with bed and breakfast accommodation above caught my eye. It is named 'Rest for the Tyred,' which is certain to strike a chord with weary walkers. An intriguing sign hangs from its façade offering 'Rest for the Tired,' and 'Books for the Inspired.'

DAY TWENTY-THREE : HAY-ON-WYE - KINGTON

The following morning saw me rejoin the River Wye in bright sunshine. I passed the sketchy remains of a great Roman camp before visiting tiny Bettws Clyro church, set in a field with fine views across the river. Francis Kilvert led worship here as curate of Clyro more than a century ago and his stimulating diary has become renowned as an evocation of the surrounding countryside and its people. The curate was a keen observer of life and had a passion for gossip, the bizarre and, an eyebrow-raising liking for scantily dressed young girls! It is lucky for him that he lived in more tolerant times, for his vivid description of stroking the soft curls of a little girl who pressed her face to him and kissed him again and again would have caused an uproar today. However, such behaviour probably stemmed from his passion and sensitivity. He certainly displayed a strong affinity with the simple people and children of his parish.

Cows studied me intently as I walked through inviting meadows and I turned for a last look at the retreating Black Mountains that shimmered in the morning sunlight. As I trod a narrow lane a car squeezed past. Its occupants, a man and his wife, wore matching sun hats, causing me to dub them 'Bill and Ben.'

I teamed up with another lone walker as we ventured into the valley that enfolds the village of Newchurch. Chalky farmhouses sparkled under a clear azure sky and sheep contentedly cropped the green meadows amidst cordons of brilliant-white hawthorn. It was lunchtime as we reached the village church where we decided to rest and cool our fevered brows. As we ate I studied a notice posted on the gate of the churchyard. It read, 'Annual Race Day Service. All welcome - The liveliest church music on the Borders!' I had no idea of the race referred to, perhaps it involved pulling a bedstead, or carrying a heavy load round the village. Whatever it was I gave the notice-maker full marks for effort.

A little later we passed through a farmyard where we found a very welcome cold water tap together with some drinking mugs that the kindly farmer had supplied for Path walkers. Above the tap was a little rhyme, guaranteed to raise a smile. It read as follows:

> If you are walking Offa's Dyke
> And this should catch your eye
> If your pack is feeling heavy
> And your throat is feeling dry
> There's water flowing in this tap
> It's cool, its fresh, it's free
> It may not be as strong as wine
> But neither is the fee!
> You may imbibe the elixir
> Avoiding spill or waste
> And having thus refreshed yourself
> Be on your way with haste.

During that hot afternoon I crossed numerous valleys and trudged over testing hills with David, my companion. The Dyke began to come into its own on our roller-coaster journey, for as we approached Gladestry, the remains of its hump and ditch became clearly visible. At times we walked on a broad track atop the Dyke itself that could often be seen snaking into the far distance.

The sleepy hamlet of Gladestry, coated in glorious sunshine, positively beamed and the narrow road threading through it remained stubbornly silent as we crossed and steeled ourselves for yet another climb. This particular one led us onto the green road, once used by drovers, that traverses elevated Hergest Ridge. A racecourse was formerly sited on the grassy level top of the ridge but it is now home to wild ponies and sheep. They wander at will across the fine open grazing land and drink at a large pool set in its midst. The newly shorn sheep, sporting brightly painted numbers on their backs, wore bemused expressions as though wondering why their warm coats had been purloined.

We looked to the north, over irregular hills of ancient rock, to the secluded Vale of Radnor that encompasses Old Radnor and its striking church, before approaching the weird irregular triangle of the Whet Stone boulder. Energetic birds frolicked in the warm air and a skylark sang its heart out as we identified the remnants of the ancient race-track surrounding the stone. The origin of the Whet Stone is uncertain but there is a strange legend associated with it that purports at cock crow it rolls down to a brook to drink and then climbs back to its original position. Some people believe it was a plague stone, like that at Zennor, where the inhabitants of disease-struck villages came to leave their goods. Its most likely use was as a way mark, particularly to aid drovers in ill weather, for it is sited where the Path prepares for its descent to the compact market town of Kington.

The innkeepers of the town, when they got wind of the drovers' approach - who usually travelled in large groups for safety - would hurriedly place tempting signs outside their premises advertising 'pleasant pasture, good beer and comfortable shelter.' In the meantime their wives would take up the carpets in the bedrooms and throw the curtains on top of the four-poster beds for safekeeping.

Kington possesses a web of narrow streets that lie between the River Arrow and the church, situated on high ground at the opposite end of the High Street. This main thoroughfare was surprisingly deserted as we wandered between buildings that have suffered the blight of Victorian restoration and rebuilding. The town is, however, home to the 400 year-old Talbot Hotel and some tasteful Georgian houses.

In comparison with other border towns, Kington appears to have taken little part in great events. The most startling incident in its existence occurred in 1862, when a fire in a building where blasting powder was stored woke sleepers for miles around. Thankfully, no one was hurt and services of thanksgiving were held in surrounding churches for this miraculous deliverance.

Kington is noted for its association with the Hergest Court, which was a centre of Welsh culture throughout the fifteenth century. It was here that the *White Book of Hergest* and the *Red Book of Hergest*, with their tales of Welsh legends and folklore, were preserved. The former was destroyed by fire in 1808 but the latter was more fortunate and is currently held in the Bodleian Library at Oxford.

Approximately a mile from the town lie the extensive Hergest Court Gardens, containing one of the best displays of trees and shrubs in Britain and noted for its rhododendrons and azaleas.

By coincidence, David and I were staying in the same cottage that night, an ancient and cramped abode. We had no complaints regarding its friendly ambiance but we had a headache before the evening was out. This was caused by the tiny guest lounge being sited under the sloping roof of the building and our inability to move around without banging our heads on the low beams.

DAY TWENTY-FOUR : KINGTON - KNIGHTON

As I left the cottage the following morning, after saying farewell to David who was walking to Ludlow that day, I discovered there was life in Kington after all. Numerous people were abroad and the shops in the main street were doing brisk business.

On my way out of town I crossed the Black Brook that flows past a delightful row of whitewashed cottages. Their facades had no window ledges so, instead of window boxes a clever display of flowers had been created by planting them in holes cut in a strip of concrete bordering the fronts of the cottages.

A stiff climb followed, amidst bracken and gorse, onto Bradnor Hill where a sign warned me to beware of flying golf balls, as a fairway of the surrounding course, one of highest in country at 1,284 feet, lay straight ahead. I kept a keen eye out for such missiles as I crossed the head of Bower Dingle and ventured onto Rushock Hill. Here the Dyke becomes prominent once again and an Offa's Dyke Path sign indicates the well-worn path on top of the remains of the earth mound.

I followed the Dyke uphill and down dale as it traces the southern sector of the boundary between the ancient Welsh principality of Powys and the Mercian kingdoms. I passed three yews, believed to be planted for three Garbett sisters, of Knill Court, in the eighteenth century. They are known as the 'Three Shepherds' and are regarded as a landmark of great antiquity. The trees reminded me of the three Scots pines planted in open country by farmers wishing to indicate to drovers that they were able to provide food, shelter and grazing. Although many of the drovers knew the countryside like the back of their hand they frequently used the pines as way marks.

The Dyke sweeps round the steep, gorse-studded slopes of Herrock Hill and I had a clear view of the Vale of Radnor stretching before me. As I descended, the Dyke could be plainly detected, striking north from the foot of the conifer-planted Burfa Hill Fort towards strange-sounding Evenjobb.

Near Old Burfa Farmhouse a massive section of the Dyke remains, one of the most prominent stretches in the whole of its length. The ancient fifteenth-century building has undergone considerable renovation and extension in recent times but still retains much of its original character. A plaque, relating to Offa's Dyke can be seen on its wall.

A little farther along I crossed a road near the border between Radnorshire and Powys. I was amused to see that the white lines running along the centre of the road stopped abruptly when it entered Powys. This administrative county, created in 1974, must be strapped for cash!

Hereabouts, the old ridgeway from Radnor Forest to Presteigne was blocked and deflected through a narrow opening intended as a frontier control point for authorised traffic between Offa's realm and Wales.

The area was also the scene of a bloody battle in 1402 between the Welsh national hero Owen Glendower and the English forces under Sir Edmund Mortimer. On this occasion Glendower was victorious and Henry IV subsequently invaded Wales to put down the rebellion. The 'Prince of Wales,' as Glendower had proclaimed himself, proved a formidable opponent but he was finally defeated in 1406. Twice offered a pardon by Henry V, he declined on both occasions. Forced to become an outlaw, Glendower died ignominiously in a hiding place that was never discovered.

On the crest of Hawthorn Hill, near Knighton, I met my Waterloo. My undoing was sitting on the crumbling steps of a monument, erected in memory of Richard Green Price, a local MP and landowner who was responsible for bringing the railways to Radnorshire. Taking a mid-afternoon break, I foolishly wedged my back against the foot of the slender memorial and aggravated my deep-rooted injury, partially displacing a disc. When I tried to rise the pain was searing. Cursing my bad luck I hobbled the remaining few miles to a converted farmhouse where I planned to stay the night. The place had been very tastefully renovated and would have proved extremely comfortable had I not suffered so badly from the pain in my back. I spent a disturbed night, barely managing to shuffle down for breakfast on the following morning.

A little later I set out to walk to Montgomery but the pain became so severe when I reached Knighton I was forced to abandon my journey and return home. I was devastated. It was the only time that I have been unable to complete a long-distance walk and all my aspirations and planning for that venture had come to naught.

DAY TWENTY-FIVE : KNIGHTON - MONTGOMERY

Eventually my disappointment receded and, determined to achieve my goal I began to plan another attempt. Returning to Knighton some time later with my friend Derek, who had agreed to accompany me to Prestatyn, I trusted he would not have to carry me if my back let me down again!

Having been preoccupied with my problems when I first saw the town, which lies on the abrupt Welsh bank of the River Teme, I took the opportunity to give it a good appraisal. It has the relaxed air of a friendly market town and mature buildings line its steep, narrow streets. The focal point is the tasteful clock tower, erected by Thomas Moore in the nineteenth century, which dominates the town-centre.

Knighton is fortunate to retain its railway station, which survived the Beeching axe of the 1960's. It is sited just over the English border, in Shropshire and stands at the end of the line, so to speak. It has convenient links with Shrewsbury, Ludlow and the south-west.

The town is at the heart of Offa's Dyke Path, for it was here that the idea of a long-distance route along the Welsh border was conceived. In 1970, the Knighton Amenity Society, in co-operation with the Offa's Dyke Association set about recovering an overgrown stretch of Dyke and riverside, which was threatened by factory extensions. Despite official apathy and opposition they transformed it into the Offa's Dyke Riverside Park and purchased the adjoining old school, later sold to the YHA and converted into a Youth Hostel and Offa's Dyke Association headquarters. The building is also a Heritage and Information Centre, in addition to being the nerve-centre of the association, providing detailed information, including an accommodation guide, concerning the Path,

In 1971, as I mentioned previously, a commemorative stone was unveiled in the park by Sir John Hunt, leader of the first successful assault on Mount Everest in 1953. Over 2,000 people gathered for the unveiling of the commemorative plaques on the three-ton monolith, erected by local volunteers. A lost cause of the 1950's had thus become a recognised national amenity of the 1970's. Following the unveiling, Sir John, as he was at that time, then led an inaugural walk over Panpunton Hill, above Weir cottage where he was living when he was chosen to lead the Everest expedition.

Our first task on leaving Knighton was to climb Panpunton Hill. On its flat grassy top we rested on a memorial seat and surveyed the swathe of Radnorshire countryside beneath us. The Teme wound lazily through a wooded valley and the railway swept up to the viaduct below Knucklas Castle Hill.

A plaque on the simple wooden seat denotes its dedication to Frank Noble, one of the instigators of the Offa's Dyke Path. Nearby stands a small memorial cairn inscribed to Roy Walters another of the tenacious workers committed to the realisation of a dream. Both men were founders of the Offa's Dyke Association.

At the triangulation station on Cwm-sanaham Hill we gazed over another valley, abounding with legends of Arthur and Guinevere, also of Dafyd Ddu and the Devil at Llanfairwaterdine. I was immediately reminded of Avalon and reckoned, like Robin Hood, King Arthur pops up everywhere.

The Dyke continued its roller-coaster ride over the Radnorshire countryside, wriggling up and down valley-sides and crossing rolling uplands like a giant snake. At Springhill Farm we came to a road that follows the line of the ancient ridgeway, along which flint implements from the English chalk lands were traded in pre-historic times. There is a fine collection of flint arrowheads and other tools in the old village hall at nearby Clun, a quiet place that retains the grim ruins of a Norman castle.

Clun Forest, which we were traversing, is as much desolate open land as it is trees and what forests there are have been planted, in recent times, by the Forestry Commission. Once again the Dyke was clearly visible and provided excellent guidance. Apart from a modern barn, adjacent to the Path, there was scarcely another building to be seen. It is reputed that the Saxon, Wild Edric, hunting in these parts, seized his fairy wife, who supposedly accompanied him when he made peace with William the Conqueror. People say that his wild hunt still haunts these hills.

As Derek and I descended to Lower Spode great blotches of resplendent hawthorn blossom surrounded us. Inquisitive sparrows hopped from branch to branch, assessing the heavy-booted walkers disturbing their rural idyll. We wiped the sweat from heated brows. Yes, the sun was shining once more, keeping up the remarkable sequence of my first attempt at the Path.

At Lower Spode we spied another delightful rustic farmhouse, its facade retaining some remarkable timber work. Behind the house stands a distinctive and carefully preserved cruck-built barn.

Our switchback ride ended when we descended to the Plain of Montgomery. As we did so we were treated to fine views north to Long Mountain and the Vale of Severn. By this time Derek and I were parched and desperately seeking a watering hole. Unfortunately, on discovering the Blue Bell Inn at Brompton crossroads we were mortified to find it closed.

Hot and gagging we made for a farmhouse, about a mile from Montgomery, where I had booked accommodation. Our disappointment at finding no refreshment on that scorching afternoon was quickly dispelled by the hospitality we received at the farm. A splendid meal was provided and the room we shared was superb. I had found the place, courtesy of the Offa's Dyke Association's accommodation booklet, which served me well.

The Path skirts Montgomery, which is a pity, for it is a pleasant and traditional mid-Wales border town, whose pride and joy is its castle ruins pitched upon a high crag on its outskirts. Erected by Henry III in 1223 the castle was established to quell the uprising led by Llewelyn the Great, a forerunner of Owen Glendower. Despite the town being sacked six times, on the last occasion by Glendower, the castle was never captured by force of arms during the Welsh rebellions. Its site, a long, narrow and rocky ridge is ideal for defence, accessible only from the south. The ridge is occupied by the remains of four rectangular wards, two of which were probably never completed. In 1644, at the height of the Civil War, the first Lord Herbert of Cherbury tamely surrendered the fortress to Parliament. It was demolished in 1649 because the second Lord Herbert was an ardent Royalist.

Montgomery, although small, is attractively Georgian in character and stands on a hill near the ruined castle. Buildings of mellow red brick vie for attention with those of the half-timbered variety and the town hall, with its prominent clock tower, presides over the tiny and homely market-square. As the former county town, it housed the court and a jail. This former house of correction, still with cells beneath, is currently owned by a couple who provide bed and breakfast accommodation.

The church, mainly thirteenth-century, but with a tower rebuilt in 1816, houses the fine Renaissance tombs of Sir Richard Herbert, father of Lord Herbert, and Sir Edmund Mortimer, grandson of Owen Glendower. In the churchyard lies John Newton Davies, hanged for murder in 1821. He protested his innocence to the last and prophesied no grass would grow on his grave in proof of the injustice of his death. Some writers have testified that after a long period grass did eventually grow there. Others have found a strange bare patch in the form of a rough cross, but who is to say that this was not created by some lover of tradition?

DAY TWENTY-SIX : MONTGOMERY - LLANYMYNECH

On yet another bright morning Derek and I crossed the road leading to Chirbury, the village three miles from Montgomery, from which Lord Herbert took his title, although not the spelling. We followed tracks and paths through the fertile valley, amidst waving banks of ripening cereal crops and lush hedgerows. The Dyke began to run out as we approached the marshy 'Devil's Hole' and we turned across meadows to Salt Bridge where we found a remarkably straight road, not Roman, but probably eighteenth-century turnpike, which points directly to Montgomery Castle. It crosses the little Camlad, the only river to rise in England and flow into Wales.

We rejoined the Dyke and followed it past Nantcriba Crag with its ruins of a long-destroyed castle belonging to the Corbets of Cause. As we trudged the steep Long Mountain road we wondered why Offa did not run his dyke straight to the river, thus saving four miles of awkward digging, or keep to a lower contour, which would have provided a more reasonable line. There are two possible reasons. First, the Princes of Powys had probably staked their claim to the nearby Leighton meadows and second, it acted as a fall-back line for Mercians who might be driven back from the river by Welsh attackers. This was of no comfort to us as we laboured to the top of Long Mountain.

Here lie the remaining ramparts of Beacon Ring, an Iron-age fort and earthwork, which commanded the surrounding circuit of hills and valleys and the wide Shropshire plains to the north-east. It is an atmospheric place and the presence of early man and the ancient travellers who passed this way can be sensed. Our old friend King Arthur crops up again and Henry Tudor journeyed through the area on his way to Bosworth and the throne of England. The shadowy Elystan, founder of the last 'royal tribe' of Wales was killed here and buried at the tiny half-timbered church at Trelystan, on the south-east slope of Long Mountain.

From our lofty resting-place we could see Welshpool spreading its tentacles across the green carpet beneath. A handsome market town of tall buildings and a wide main street, it is home to the narrow-gauge Welshpool and Llanfair Light Railway, which runs for eight miles along a scenic route through the hills to Llanfair Caereinion.

Like Montgomery it has its castle, sited one mile from the town. Powys Castle, or 'Red Castle,' as it is sometimes called because of its mellow red walls, is still intact and is currently owned by the National Trust. It is open to the public and its treasures include many mementos of Clive of India. The Clive connection came about during the tenure of the Herberts, when one of that family married the second Lord Clive.

Although reconstructed in the seventeenth century, the fortress retains its basic early fourteenth-century characteristics. It was here the Princes of Powys reigned, who were the only princes of Wales to survive the fateful year of 1284. Spurred on by hatred of their Welsh rivals, they had more often than not been allies of the English, wielding their power as English barons rather than as Welsh princes. It is due to their skill as scheming negotiators that the castle remained intact and was never seized by a Marcher lord.

Rivalling the exotic grandeur of the castle itself are the gardens, a series of four grand terraces of Italianate design. Created between 1688 and 1722, they are horticulturally and historically important, for they are the only formal gardens of this date to survive in their original form.

The Path descends from Beacon Ring through a plantation and down to Stone House where we joined a road that led us past a newly created and aptly-named Offa's Dyke Business Park. From here it was a short walk to the flood banks of the youthful River Severn that has recently set out on its semi-circular course to the Bristol Channel. I found the short section of river we encountered particularly attractive on that sunny afternoon. It wound through verdant pastures and tree-fringed banks beneath the backdrop of a steep, but shapely range of hills called the Breiddens.

Faint traces of the Dyke accompanied us across the flood-level fields where we joined the former jungle-bordered bog that is the Montgomery branch of the Shropshire Union Canal. Recent remedial work had been carried out and nine miles of towpath reopened. Glad of a change of terrain we happily began a stretch of canalside walking that was made particularly pleasing by the vivid colour and variety of the bordering shrubs and plants, allowed to mature during the years of the canal's demise. There was very little traffic in evidence on the waterway, apart from families of ducks.

Cooled by tall, overhanging hedgerows we found the going easy until we reached an uncleared section of towpath. Our tempers frayed as we ploughed through entanglements of brambles and irrepressible weeds. After a spell of struggling with ensnaring undergrowth we met a walker coming in the opposite direction, who made us feel guilty for cursing the conditions. The poor man's legs were nearly torn to shreds. Beneath his short shorts scratches and blotches covered his abused limbs and he winced with each step taken. We discovered that he had persevered for several miles in this agonising state and we watched sympathetically as he hobbled away.

Determined not to suffer the same fate we abandoned the canal and made for the nearest road where we found a convenient hostelry, at Four Crosses, near Llanymynech, and hurried inside to quench our raging thirst. It was very quiet, the only customer being a weather-beaten farmer. He asked what we were about and laughed when we told him about our tribulations on the canal towpath. 'I've been coming in this pub for over thirty years,' the man indicated, 'and I remember when the old back rooms of the pubs in Llanymynech, on the English side of the Dyke, were a godsend for thirsty Sunday drinkers crossing the border from 'dry' Wales.'

Much refreshed after a couple of drinks we completed the final mile and a half of our day's journey to Llanymynech without incident and were soon settled in our accommodation, another commendable stopping place recommended by the Offa's Dyke accommodation guide. Here we learned of a possible alternative, unfortunately discounted by officialdom, to the stretch of overgrown canal we had encountered. Apparently, the old Cambrian railway formerly ran to Llanymynech and its bed could have provided a good walking track had the powers-that-be not pulled out the bridges and wired the subsequent gaps. What a boon it would have been to our friend with shredded legs!

'Llanymynech' means 'Enclosure of the Miners,' denoting the former mining of silver, zinc, lead and copper on local Llanymynech Hill. I was chastised for pronouncing the name of the village as it is spelt. 'No, bach!' I was told. 'It is 'Llanymanach!'

DAY TWENTY-SEVEN: LLANYMYNECH - BRONYGARTH

The morning began with a climb from a deep lane to an old quarry set amongst the limestone cliffs of Jones' Rough. The pleasant path wound between banks of vibrant-yellow buttercups and course grasses as we progressed onto the slopes of Llanymynech Hill. Evidence of the mineral mines, used as far back as Roman times, can still be seen in the form of disused shafts leading to the narrow galleries of the 'Ogof' Cavern. The Earls of Shrewsbury built an early castle here and, up to 1213, it figured prominently in Welsh border warfare and in royal silver-mining projects.

After the hard work of scaling the heights we were obliged to follow the Path down the steep face of the hill and across to Port-y-waen. The views were extensive as we continued along the top of Blodwell Rocks and followed the Dyke along Lynclys Hill. On one side the Shropshire Plain rolled out like a giant carpet and on the other intricate valleys snaked up into the Berwyns.

A spell of road-walking intervened before we began the climb up

Moelydd Hill, another fine viewpoint. Here we met a fellow walker who was attempting to reach John O'Groats, having set out from Land's End three weeks previously. His chances of reaching his final destination seemed slim for he had injured his knee, which was strapped up and causing him to limp badly. Derek and I stopped to take in the view as the poor fellow hobbled away, wilting under the weight of a massive rucksack. We never met him again and I often wonder how he fared.

The cool confines of Llanforda Wood provided welcome shade before another climb loomed, onto the flat summit of the hill that formerly housed Old Oswestry Racecourse. The site of the course is marked by a stone edifice incorporating a saddle and twin horses' heads. Derek mounted the edifice and grasped imaginary reins as he posed for a cryptic photograph.

Remnants of stone buildings, probably the grandstand of its day, could be clearly seen and the line of the track still remained. Why were ancient racecourses sited on hilltops well away from the towns, I wondered, for did not the old Kington Racecourse occupy a similar position? The reason, I reckoned, is that gambling was frowned upon.

The Path prefers to remain aloof from Oswestry and bypasses it before continuing towards the Dee. However, the town is worth a detour as it is one of the oldest on the Welsh border. It was once the headquarters of the Cambrian Railway and of a network of delightful branch lines, which have sadly disappeared.

Set between the pastoral plain of Shropshire to the east, and the Berwyns to the west, it was continually a centre of warfare in its earlier years. It was sacked and burned by King John, Llewelyn the Great and Owen Glendower, before being accidentally incinerated three times in the 1540's, which gave little encouragement for rebuilding. The town is said to have derived its name from Oswald's Tree, a cross on which the Christian king of Northumbria, St Oswald, was hung when defeated by Penda, the pagan king of Mercia. It contains some fine ancient buildings, including a timbered house dating from 1604. There are several old inns, of seventeenth-century vintage and one of them, the Fox, had a gable that extended across the full width of the pavement. It was reduced in 1870, owing, it is said, to a guest from the Wynnstay Arms colliding with it and spoiling his new top hat!

Sir Henry Walford Davies, who succeeded Sir Edward Elgar as Master of the King's Musick, was born in Oswestry in 1869 and he is best known for composing the *RAF March* and the hymn tune, *O Little Town of Bethlehem.*

Another native of Oswestry was Wilfred Owen, one of the gifted young poets killed in the First World War. His *Strange Meeting* is one of the most memorable poems of its time.

The last good walking stretch along the Dyke itself runs for eight miles beyond Oswestry's Old Racecourse to the Dee. Eventually it sweeps towards the mouth of the Vale of Llangollen as it crosses the lower slopes of Selatyn Hill. At this point Derek and I were nearing the end of a strenuous day's walk and tiredness was setting in.

We were extremely glad to reach the village of Bronygarth, where we were due to stay at the 'Old School,' which sounded an interesting halt. Eventually we came upon the old building, nestling on the side of the Ceiriog Valley and surrounded by a delightful garden. We received an enthusiastic welcome and were invited to rest our weary limbs and take tea on the lawn.

The toil of the hot afternoon drifted away as we reclined on the sun-baked lawn that thirstily absorbed water from a steadily rotating sprinkler. Likewise, we absorbed several cups of tea whilst admiring the bold features of Chirk Castle, rising majestically above a dense cordon of trees across the valley. It perches like a picture-book fortress on a bold hill above the hollow where Henry II's expedition was ambushed in 1164 and it now resembles a large stately home rather than a medieval castle. It was formerly a late baronial stronghold on lands taken from the Welsh princes of Northern Powys after the final conquest of Wales in 1282. The home of the Myddletons since 1595, it had to be largely rebuilt following the sieges of the Civil War, when its inhabitants fought for the Parliamentarians.

The castle is normally open to the public between Easter and the end of September and, like Powys Castle, it contains many treasures. The story is told of a guest at the castle, in recent times, coming down to breakfast and finding his host sitting in a full suit of armour and reading a newspaper.

The entrance gates to the attractive castle gardens are magnificent. Superbly crafted, in 1721, their intricate wrought-ironwork is a delight to the eye. They are the work of the Davies brothers and I was to pass another fine example of their craftsmanship and finesse on my journey from Offa's Dyke to the Pennine Way.

Suitably cleaned and refreshed, Derek and I were whisked by car to a local hostelry where we enjoyed a substantial meal and made an evening of it by watching a World Cup soccer match on television.

DAY TWENTY-EIGHT : BRONYGARTH - LLANDEGLA

Sunshine, yet again! Hardly able to believe our luck with the weather we descended the Ceiriog Valley and crossed the river, having reluctantly decided to give Chirk Castle and the impressive Chirk Aqueduct a miss, due to lack of time.

Angling up the far valley side, by Crogen Wladys, we followed the path across a ridge and along lanes and quiet roads, a little to the west of the surviving stretches of Dyke, until we rejoined the Shropshire Union Canal.

We strode along the uncluttered towpath alongside Telford's waterway, one of his great engineering projects. Several boats passed us as we skirted Froncysyllte and approached Telford's masterpiece of industrial archaeology, the mighty Pont-Cysyllte Aqueduct that spans the River Dee. Its innovative design, of 1805, incorporates a cast-iron trough, over a thousand feet in length, the first time metal was used to a major degree in bridge building. A pleasure boat passed along along the narrow thread of water, barely wide enough for a single craft, as we edged along the accompanying walkway 120 feet above the energetic river. We had the comfort of a metal barrier fence alongside us but on the opposite side of the aqueduct there was no such protection and the passengers on the far side of the boat overlooked an alarming drop. Fortunately, none of them tried to abandon ship during the crossing!

Beyond the aqueduct we entered a dramatic limestone area by climbing through plantations onto the metalled 'Panorama Walk,' a fine piece of scenic road-building, which provides a stunning high-level traverse above the Vale of Llangollen. The terrain is reminiscent of the Yorkshire Dales, our home area. It was a thrill to walk amongst shapely limestone bluffs set high above the verdant valley beneath.

We found a convenient seat near the narrow road as it passes beneath the towering escarpment of Creigiau-Eglwyseg and as we rested we could make out the ruins of Castell Dinas Bran. This tiny fortress, once an Iron-Age hillfort, and later a stone castle, perches on a lofty limestone hill in a superb defensive position. I jested that I was glad not to be an attacker struggling up its steep slopes, only to have boiling oil, or arrows, rain down on me.

There were two slight drawbacks to our elevated idyll. We had left Llangollen in our wake and we could not see Valle Crucis Abbey sequestered in the valley. Our apologies to both but the Path pays homage to neither. I had visited the popular town many years before, with my young family, and marvelled at the dramatic Horseshoe Falls, one of its main attractions. Many changes have taken place over the intervening years, but some things solidly remain, such as the annual International Music Eisteddfod, first held there in 1947 to help heal the wounds of a world ravaged by war. The July event still attracts over 100,000 visitors who flock to enjoy performances by choirs, folk-singers and dancers.

The impressive remains of Valle Crucis Abbey occupy a fine site on the bank of the Eglwyseg River near its confluence with the Dee. The Cistercian abbey was founded in 1201 by Madog ap Gruffyd, a prince of Powys who had no scruples about siding alternately with his own people and the English. A serious fire later in the same century led to major alterations and the tower collapsed in 1400. The abbey was dissolved in 1535 and its quite extensive ruins include two walls of its church that point dramatically skywards.

A little farther along our panoramic traverse we came to a sign indicating that we were approaching 'World's End.' This caused great consternation. Were we about to drop off the end of the world? It made us doubt the clever chap who said it was round. We need not have worried, however, for the road deteriorated to a track and led us into a limestone amphitheatre strikingly similar to Malham Cove, one of the wonders of the Yorkshire Dales. We felt we were on familiar ground until the wide track shrank to a narrow path that contours the steep sides of the bare limestone crags of Eglwyseg Mountain. Could this be the end of the world we wondered? If we strayed from the path and careered down the menacing slopes beneath us, it could easily be the case.

Emerging unscathed from the crags we ascended the old drove track beneath the buttress of Craig Arthur before crossing the wooded World's End Valley, with its abandoned mining tunnels. A spell of moorland walking brought us to Llandegla Forest, a large area of woodland penetrated by forest trails. As we crossed the exposed moorland we kept an eye out for gamekeepers who are known to watch for unauthorised disturbers of the indigenous grouse.

Hafod Bilston Youth Hostel nestles at the spot where the Path emerges from the dense Llandegla Forest, a welcome sight for hostellers. Here we fell in step with another Offa's Dyke walker who, we discovered, hailed from Exeter and earned a living buying property and converting it into flats for students. Derek has family in the city and knew many of the areas the man mentioned.

We parted company in Llandegla, where Derek and I planned to stay the night. Our companion still had a fair distance to cover, having set out late that morning from Llangollen. As we said our goodbyes he added that he might cross paths with Derek when he next visited Exeter.

Miraculously, the sun disappeared, the skies darkened and wretched drizzle set in. We donned waterproofs as we scoured the village for our accommodation. When we found the house, a dreary-looking place, it took a long time before a woman finally answered the door. It transpired that she had been in the back yard feeding her chickens. Our mood fitted the dismal weather when we were shown our room, for it did not live up to expectations. We were glad to escape later and hurry to a local hostelry for a meal and some company.

Like the village, it was quiet, apart from a few regulars and some passing trade - motorists returning from Bala to Chester. The landlord, who indicated that walkers were always welcome, seemed happy to chat, as he was hardly overwhelmed with work.

'Have you seen the holy well?' he inquired.

We shook our heads.

'It was once known for curing epilepsy,' he said proudly.

There was apparently little else of note in the village for the conversation turned to the Clwydian Hills. We told him they were our next objective.

'You're right on their doorstep and you'll enjoy walking them,' he said, 'Provided the weather's kind.'

'The fine spell seems to have ended,' I replied, looking at the rain-spattered windows.

'Never fear,' said the landlord jovially. 'It could clear by tomorrow.'

DAY TWENTY-NINE : LLANDEGLA - BODFARI

His optimism was well founded, for the rain had dispersed during the night and the sun reappeared as we hurried from the village. For the first mile or so we followed the meandering River Alyn, which flows north towards Mold. In its gathering grounds several tumbling streams drain the crevasses of Llantysilio Mountain, a great buttress that overlooks the scenic Horseshoe Pass.

At Pertichwareu the Path briefly joins the B5431 and, near an old quarry lay-by on this road a series of small caves burrow into a low limestone ridge. When these were excavated in the late nineteenth century they were found to contain an intricate arrangement of prehistoric burials.

We soon left the road and its companion, the River Alyn, to begin a gradual climb onto the shapely Clwydian Hills, their summits ranged in line like a giant roller-coaster. The landlord was correct, they looked extremely inviting. Gentle grassy slopes angled up to dark heather-strewn tops that stretched as far as the eye could see. This barrier of hummocky, rounded hills guarding the Vale of Clwyd is designated an Area of Outstanding Natural Beauty.

In perfect visibility we strode along a pleasant track above a dense blanket of woodland. Fluffy, white cirrus floated languidly in the azure sky and the sun was smiling upon us once more. A perfect morning for walking

The gradient sharpened as we scaled Moel y Plas flanked by heath and bracken. It was the first in a series of 'Moels' (meaning 'bare hill') that we would conquer that day. In fact, I remarked to Derek later in the day that whoever devised the path seemed determined not to miss out a single one!

Moel Llanfair and Moel Gyw came next on that bright, stimulating morning and I suffered a twinge of conscience about bemoaning the rare wet period of the previous afternoon. I had read in a guide book that the Welsh border is to some extent sheltered by the higher mountain ranges to the west and there is consequently better chance of reasonable weather than in most parts of western Britain. I should have remembered this fact before whining about a small blip in the exceptional conditions.

At lunchtime we approached a cluster of sparkling-white buildings and the foremost among them, the Gyrn Motel, looked very inviting. We resisted the temptation to call in for a drink and, as we passed, two elderly walkers tottered from it. We discovered that the men had a very relaxed attitude to walking. That morning they had strolled four miles and homed in on the motel for an extended lunch, accompanied by four or five whiskies. Consequently, they were feeling very mellow and were steeling themselves for the demanding return journey. Derek and I smiled as they wandered merrily away.

A little later we lunched, on sandwiches and fruit, in the shade of a snow-white hawthorn tree. The sun was really getting into gear by this time and we were glad of the respite. Whilst we rested, a group of walkers, who turned out to be RAF recruits on a training march, passed by. They headed in our intended direction and we decided to follow them.

It was not long before their party halted and we caught up with them. It transpired that they were covering a section of the Path and that one of the recruits was suffering badly with blisters and was falling behind his colleagues. It was decided that one of the instructors would accompany him so as not to hold up the main party.

We watched them march swiftly away, their boots scuffing the rough surface of the track that ascends Moel Eithinen and wondered if they would maintain their punishing pace. Not for long, as it turned out, for when we climbed to the summit of Foel Fenlli, there they lay in varying stages of exhaustion.

They looked at us approvingly. 'You're not bad for two old-timers,' one of the recruits quipped.

'More haste, less speed,' Derek replied. The reference to our maturity fired us up and made us determined to show these young whippersnappers what we could do. In order to get a head start we hurried on, passing the remains of the impressive hill-fort that surrounds the summit of Foel Fenlli. Its ramparts are larger in places than any section of Offa's Dyke and they enclose a former settlement area of more than twenty acres. According to legend, Benlli, a Dark-Age tyrant who occupied the fort was destroyed by fire called down from heaven by St Germanus as retribution for the slaying of a Christian convert who arrived late for his work from the plain below.

We barely had time to admire the inspiring views to the west as we hastened down the grassy slopes of Foel Fenlli towards a cattle grid. Set amidst the wide, open landscape lay the fortress town of Ruthin, its early history centering on its castle. Since the eleventh century the curfew has rung out each night over its delightful jumble of black and white timbered buildings. Beyond the town and its surrounding patchwork vale, we could decipher the hazy outline of the distant mountains of Snowdonia.

When we reached the cattle-grid, at Bwlch Penbarras, the RAF lads galloped past once more, but we had the last laugh. During the afternoon we pushed on resolutely and caught up with the party whenever they stopped to recover. A classic example of the tortoise and the hare!

At this point we entered the Moel Famau Country Park that encircles the hill of that name. There were numerous cars in the adjacent car park, indicating the area's popularity. We toiled up a wide track on a gradual ascent to the blackened summit of Moel Famau. There was no mistaking the elevated crest, for the remnants of the Jubilee Tower perched upon it are visible from a considerable distance. Built to commemorate the jubilee of George III, only its restored base remains. However, it does provide an excellent vantage point, for it is perched on the highest hill of the Clwydian range.

As you stand amidst the remains of the tower, tidied up by volunteers in European Conservation Year, 1970, much of North Wales is visible. On top of each section of wall is an etched diagram of the features on display in that particular direction. The most interesting view was to the north, for we could see the northern extremity of the Clwydian Hills descending to the coastal plain and eventually, the sea. Journey's end was in sight!

'Don't get too excited,' warned Derek, 'there's nearly a day's walk still ahead.'

I didn't care, for I knew the hardest part of our walk was behind us and we would soon be feeling the sand of Prestatyn beach in our boots.

My relief, however, was a little premature for several remaining hills had to be conquered. The Path took us resolutely over a further three summits before relenting and skirting the crest of Moel y Parc, the final hill of the main Clwydian range. Here we were able to wave goodbye to the still visible Jubilee Tower and the line of hills that provide some of the finest walking on Offa's Dyke Path.

Trackways led us down below Fron-haul and field paths took over for the final descent to Grove Hall. The rich-green vale beneath shimmered in blazing sunshine as we approached Bodfari, our destination for the night and the last stopping place before Prestatyn.

Several stepped Flintshire stiles were encountered as we crossed the meadows that run down to the River Wheeler, a popular trout and salmon stream, which skirts Bodfari and has made it a haunt of anglers. The elegant thirteenth-century tower of the church beckoned as we drew ever closer to the sun-drenched hamlet with its promise of hospitality and a well-earned rest.

The village lies at the foot of Foel Gaer, surrounded by verdant woods, and contains the ancient St Defier's Well. According to local folklore, children were immersed in the well, up to their necks, to prevent their crying at night. A somewhat drastic remedy! Another local custom, in the seventeenth century, was the offering of a cockerel for a boy and a pullet for a girl, after nine visits to the well.

We reached our accommodation tired and ringing with sweat, so we were delighted to be offered refreshing drinks by our hosts who were soaking up the sun in the garden. The couple were happy to talk and wished to know about our journey and what we thought to the Welsh border.

It was a wrench to eventually shower and change for a trip to the local hostelry, which has the date of 1640 over its doorway. Conveniently, the inn lay a mere couple of hundred yards away and served good food in an affable atmosphere. The lilting tones of the locals mingled with the brogue of a group from over the Cheshire border. A good-humoured argument was in progress about the merits of their respective dialects.

'Look you,' said one voice, 'I'll at least give you credit for speaking better than those heathens in the Black Country, with their loose vowels.'

'Thanks,' one of the Cheshire contingent responded. 'Your lot are not so bad, apart from your singing.'

'Jealousy, it is bach,' said a red-haired local, who began a raucous rendition of *We'll Keep a Welcome in the Hillsides*. The man's singing was so terrible that even his friends begged him to shut up and everyone dissolved into laughter.

Whilst listening with amusement to the banter Derek and I speculated on our finishing time on the following day. A mere eleven miles remained and, if things went well we could reach Prestatyn by the early afternoon. In our impatience we determined to make an early start and reach the sea without delay.

DAY THIRTY : BODFARI - PRESTATYN

Our first task that morning was to traverse the minor outposts of the Clwydian Hills. When we had scaled the steep lanes leading to Moel y Gaer, we were treated to extensive views over the coastal plain to distant horizons. The vistas ranged from the industrial installations surrounding the Dee Estuary and the rash of small farms covering the Vale of Clwyd.

As we skirted the summit of Moel y Gaer we noticed the remains of a small hill-fort, another garrison of the early Celts. Heading for the next prominence, Cefn Du, we came upon the tiny settlement of Sodom, nestling between the two hills, which set us wondering if Gomorra was thereabouts.

Other evidence of the early inhabition of this upland area is the numerous ancient burial cairns and tumuli that litter the Clwydian Hills. We passed beneath a tumulus and an aged stone cross as we began to decend the west slope of Moel Maenefa, the most northerly of the Clwydian outliers, which are bounded to the north by the A55. It was gratifying to walk into the valley and reach this major arterial road, which runs from Chester to St Asaph that lies three miles to the west. It formed another landmark in our conquest of Offa's Dyke Path and prompted recollections of journeys in my youth along the coast road, the A548, before this convenient highway was constructed. It seemed to take hours, when travelling with my family for holidays at Llanfairfechan and Penmaenmawr, along that bottleneck of a road as we passed through every town and village on the North Wales coast.

Rhuallt snuggles in a pronounced curve of the A55 and, at one time, a Roman road passed through on its way to St Asaph, which was probably the site of the Roman station of Varae. St Asaph boasts a cathedral, the smallest of the ancient ones of Britain, which perches on a hill-top. Its fine proportions and well-chosen site give it a certain grandeur.

A thought should be spared for Sir Henry Morton Stanley who was educated in St Asaph workhouse. He eventually rose to become the world-famous journalist who uttered the immortal line, 'Dr Livingstone, I presume?'

The Path climbs out of Rhuallt by a circuitous route due to opposition by forestry interests. It skirts the woods above Bodlonfa before traversing country roads over Mynydd y Cwm and crossing fields to Marian Ffrith, an unusually named small hill.

The Dyke ends hereabouts, on Gop Hill, two miles north-east of Dyserth, in a form that suggests it was never completed. Tradition has it that Offa died at nearby Rhuddlan in 795 and his Dyke was left unfinished at its northern end, probably because his guiding hand was withdrawn. It is said that marking-out trenches were in place right to the sea that lies a mere five miles to the north.

Above us, on Moel Hiraddug summit stands another once proud hill-fort overlooking a scene of desolation caused by unsightly quarries that provided employment in former times for the people of Dyserth.

The older parts of this large village occupy the lower slopes of Moel Hiraddug and they lead down to the unusual attraction of a waterfall in its centre. The water flows from St Asaph's Well in the neighbouring parish of Cwm and spills forty feet down the face of a limestone rock before flowing through the main street of the village. Dr Johnson is said to have 'trudged unwillingly' to see it in 1774 and was 'not sorry to find it dry.'

Offa's Dyke Path veers away from the site of Dyserth Castle, built by Henry III and demolished by Llewellyn the Last, and makes for the old cliffs of Tan-yr-allt before climbing between brambles and gorse to the crest of 'King Charles' Bowling Green.' Here, we enjoyed a bird's eye view of Prestatyn and it seemed that with one mighty leap we could reach journey's end. The straggling resort ended abruptly at the blue band of sea that stretched to the horizon. What a welcome sight!

Burning with anticipation Derek and I hurried down a series of pronounced zig-zags in the road that descends to the town. The most northerly signpost on the Path pointed in the direction of the main street and we strode amongst crowds of holiday-makers towards the beach.

It is hard to imagine that before the spread of nineteenth-century hotels and houses, modern flats, vast caravan parks that merge into those of Rhyl and all the paraphernalia of a modern seaside resort, Prestatyn was merely a cluster of fishermen's dwellings and a hotel. Like its neighbour it provides light relief for the regions of Lancashire, Cheshire and the West Midlands, an outlet where they can relax and enjoy the bracing air, fish and chips and candy-floss.

The few hundred yards to the beach along the bustling pavement seemed interminable. Threading through the throng milling around the gift shops and cafés it took us all our time to avoid collision in our haste to reach our goal, the newly built Offa's Dyke Centre beckoning from the promenade. The building of an extensive concrete rampart that stretches for several miles to Rhyl and Colwyn Bay is good for combating erosion but has done little to enhance the seafront. Until we had touched the marker stone beside the Centre this was of little concern in our eagerness to be photographed at the moment of triumph. When the end of our challenge was suitably recorded we surveyed the seemingly endless concrete barrier, its steps almost dipping its toes in the Irish Sea. The tide was at its highest and the golden sands, what we could see of them, were virtually non-existent. People were using the concrete steps as convenient seats whilst others frolicked on the tiny sections of exposed beach.

Our gaze turned to the gorse-covered cliffs, from which we had recently descended. It was a reminder of longed for quiet hills, the great boundary earthwork of a forgotten kingdom and Offa's Dyke Path, which I had successfully traced, with Derek's help, from the Bristol Channel.

CHAPTER FOUR
The Cestrian Link

DAY THIRTY-ONE : PRESTATYN - MOLD

Walkers, beware of the Cestrian Link! To traverse this unofficial long-distance footpath can seriously damage your resolve! If, despite this warning, you are determined to conquer it you are advised to take a machete.

I refer particularly to its route through North Wales, where I sank knee-deep in slime, fought vicious vegetation, received shocks from unauthorised electric fences and was forced to leave the path and take to roads on many occasions.

The Cestrian Link is named after Cestrians - natives of Chester, the ancient city that the path skirts. It is well-devised and has a guide to the route - from Prestatyn to the southern end of the Pennine Way at Edale. The guide I took with me was comprehensive, and conscientiously researched, but unfortunately out of date, as I discovered when I came across sections that were overgrown, fenced-off, had disappeared, or been diverted.

It stretches for 112 miles but I covered considerably more due to enforced diversions. Without these it would have proved very enjoyable, for it is an attractive and varied walk that contains much of interest. It passes through the appealing countryside of Clwyd (Flintshire), Cheshire and Derbyshire and includes a mixture of footpath, road and canal-side walking. I began the journey on my own but was joined once again, for the final three days, by my walking companion, Roy.

I left the Offa's Dyke Centre in Prestatyn and retraced my steps through the town before tackling the stiff climb up the hill that I had hurriedly descended in my haste to complete Offa's Dyke Path. When I reached the crest I turned for a final look at Prestatyn and the surrounding coast. As it had been on the previous occasion the area was bathed in sunshine and I could see the gnarled fingers of Little Orme and Great Orme thrusting into the ocean. I waved farewell to Prestatyn and descended grassy slopes in the direction of the village of Llanasa.

Way-markers were conspicuous by their absence and the paths were difficult to follow. Frustrated, I headed for a country road that I knew would lead me to my destination. The sun-baked tarmac made my feet hot but I was at least following a reliable route.

Delightfully peaceful, Llanasa basked under a cloudless sky as I approached. The sun-dappled village pond provided a pleasing introduction to the village and a striking avenue of vibrant roadside flowers led me to its tiny centre. I sat in a walled enclosure and drank in my congenial surroundings. The whitewashed walls of the Red Lion Inn shimmered, cottage gardens glowed with assorted hues and a rustic church added the perfect dignified touch. This ancient place of worship embodies an unusual pointed tower and appealing stained glass windows. At the Reformation, Basingwerk Abbey, near Holywell, was dismantled and many of its features and relics re-housed in the locality. The stained glass, of 1500 vintage, came to Llanasa and the timber roof of the choir went to St Mary-on-the-Hill at Chester.

It was with regret that I left this rural idyll and I managed to follow field paths to the small hamlet of Trelogan that nestles on the slopes above the Dee Estuary. Its claim to fame concerns the accomplished Welsh actor and dramatist Emlyn Williams, who attended the village school.

A mile beyond Trelogen I came to a junction of several roads and noticed an ancient stone cross standing in an adjacent field. Ornately carved and incorporating a Celtic wheel at its head this eleven-foot high edifice is the tallest of its type in Britain. It is known as 'The Stone of Lamentations' and it dates from the tenth century.

As I trod the field-paths that lead to Lloc I passed an elderly walker, giving him a cheery greeting as I did so. The man did not stop until he was several yards beyond me and I was surprised to hear his utterance, 'You miserable sod. Can't you speak?'

I turned round in amazement and went up to him. 'I spoke to you,' I responded.

'You what?' inquired the man as he put his hand to his ear. His expression changed from one of anger to sheepishness. 'I'm sorry,' he said. 'I forgot to switch on my hearing aid!'

We had a good laugh before continuing on our respective ways.

My route nearly coincided with Offa's Dyke as I entered Pen-y-parc Wood, on the outskirts of Lloc. The remnants of the earthwork intrude into the wood but I never found them because I was busy wrestling with the numerous tracks within it. I was intent on reaching a field-path at the exit from the wood that leads to the A55, which I was due to re-cross. Little did I realise the battle that was about to take place.

I found the elusive path and, at its termination I climbed a stile giving access to the road. Unfortunately I had not anticipated the jungle of nettles and briars that barred the way to its steep embankment.

I fought my way through the entanglement and reached the roadside burning with nettle-stings and my legs covered in scratches. The next part of the game involved 'dodge the traffic' that roared along the road, hell-bent on Llandudno, or Bangor. When the busy dual carriageway was finally negotiated I was met with another overgrown embankment, which enforced a detour of several hundred yards before I could clamber down it and reach the beckoning stile.

Nursing my wounds I ploughed on along paths and country lanes to Babbell (pronounced 'Babbeth') where I passed the ancient Black Lion Inn, which dates from 1259 and was used by drovers for many centuries. An adjacent road-sign pointed in the direction of

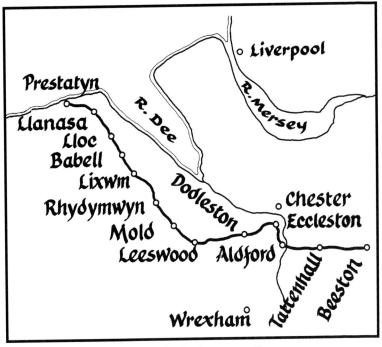

The Cestrian Link - Prestatyn to Beeston

Caerwys (pronounced 'Carewith'), which has been a notable town since early times, judging by the numerous prehistoric sites within its parish. It lies in an attractive region of small hills and woods, beneath the eastern slopes of the Clwydian Hills and amongst its varied occupants were the Romans who established a station there. The Welsh princes had a Courthouse in Caerwys, and the Great Sessions were held there until the middle of the seventeenth century, when the courts were removed to Flint.

Caerwys was the only Welsh borough in Flintshire created by Edward I and the pattern of the town then laid out is still to be seen in its long, wide streets, but it is best known for its long association with the eisteddfod. The first of these was enacted there in 1100 under the Prince of Gwynedd and there are written records of eisteddfodau held in 1523 and 1568. The commission granted by Elizabeth I for the 1568 eisteddfod is still in existence and also the little silver harp awarded to the best harpist.

This eisteddfod was re-enacted on the four-hundredth

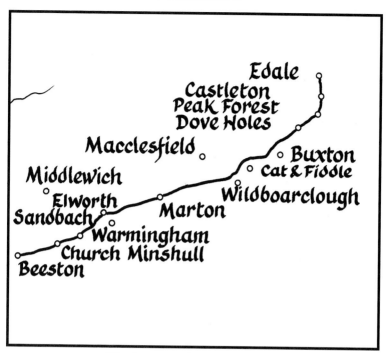

The Cestrian Link - Beeston to Edale

anniversary in 1968 when the proceedings were opened by H.R.H. Princess Margaret. On the final day, the Gorsedd of bards, in their robes, together with the people of Caerwys in Tudor costume, made a colourful procession through the main street.

From Babbell I kept to country lanes until I reached Lixwm, a quiet place that lines the B5121 road linking Holywell and Nannerch. It has its share of venerable cottages and also an inviting inn, the Crown Hotel. No one could call Lixwm a one-horse village. As I walked through its environs they were everywhere. Most of the local farms have stables and many horses could be found cropping the grass in the surrounding fields. The weather had deteriorated and I walked in rain for most of the afternoon. This put a damper on the former industrial landscape that surrounds Rhes-y-cae and Moel-y-crio. They lie on a limestone plateau that bears the scars of quarrying and lead-mining, the latter having been carried out since Roman times. Its grassy slopes now provide grazing for a large population of sheep

My next port of call was Rhosesmoor. The elevated hamlet provides extensive views across the fertile valley to those great humps, the Clwydian Hills. They hunched beneath a thick blanket of stratus and I could imagine Offfa's Dyke Path walkers toiling along their tracks in bleaker conditions than I had experienced.

I stopped for a well-earned rest on the tiny village green. Having made good time so far over what was to be a long day's march of twenty-one miles I needed to conserve my strength for the final push. The map indicated I had approximately four miles to cover to the farm where I intended to stay the night, which lies to the west of Mold.

A convenient path left the village outskirts and descended a steep hillside into the valley of the River Alyn, which had changed course since we parted company near Llandegla and was now flowing south-east. I could not escape the Clwydian Hills. They towered above the tree-cloaked, undulating vale that separated us, reluctant to be left behind.

As I approached a gap in a tall hedgerow, the sprawling village of Rhydymwyn suddenly appeared beneath me, a most welcome sight, for it would be level walking from now on. The village itself is sandwiched between the A542 road, which links Denbigh and Mold, and the river. It possesses a very attractive church and the remnants of an abandoned railway that formerly ran from Chester to Mold and onwards to the foot of the Clwydian Hills beyond Nannerch.

The chief feature of the area is The Leet, a highly popular four-mile riverside Nature Trail along the Alyn, amongst fine limestone cliffs and woods. An inconspicuous plaque at its entrance denotes that Charles Kingsley frequently walked there and that Mendelssohn composed *The Rivulet* in 1829, a recollection of the River Alyn, whilst staying in the locality.

I crossed a bridge over the defunct railway, which, unfortunately is not on the recommended route and has not been dedicated as a right of way. What a sad sight the rusting equipment and fragments of rail presented, all that remains of a once thriving railway. Its bed, I reckoned, would make an ideal approach to Mold. Even better, if it was restored to its former self, what a fine tourist attraction it would make.

The long day's mileage was beginning to take its toll. My legs ached and I slowed considerably as I crossed the bridge over the River Alyn and joined a quiet road leading to Maes Garman Farm. When I finally reached the lane leading to the farm I wondered what lay in store. I need not have worried, for I was confronted by a magnificently renovated building as I rounded a bend in the lane. The lady of the house gave me a polite welcome and showed me to my room in the annex, a spacious restored barn. The facilities were first-class and the only drawback was the recall of painful memories of my stay at a similar establishment, near Knighton.

During the evening I gleaned much about my accommodation and its surroundings, courtesy of my hosts. The seventeenth-century farm is now solely used for housing guests, following extensive restoration. Renovation work was carried out over a hectic and challenging period of twelve months and at one stage the couple temporarily moved out to allow the work to proceed more quickly. It had all been worthwhile, I was told, for the results, as I could confirm, spoke for themselves.

They explained that the farm derived its name from the 'Field of Germanus,' a field by the adjacent Gwernafield road that is traditionally the site of the 'Alleluia Victory' of 430. This was achieved when the native Christians under Germanus, Bishop of Auxerre, who had been sent to Britain to combat the Pelagian heresy, decisively defeated the heathen Picts and Scots. Terror-stricken by the simultaneous shout of 'Alleluia!' by the Christians, the pagans fled without striking a blow. The site is marked by an obelisk, erected in 1736, which stands near the road.

That night I slept soundly, thanks to the comfortable bed and the fresh Clwyd air. My long day's journey ensured that nothing disturbed my dreams.

DAY THIRTY-TWO : MOLD - CHESTER

To Mold's credit, it looked attractive, even on a damp and dismal Monday morning. The rain had persisted through the night and refused to relent. It was restoring the balance somewhat for my days of glorious sunshine. I walked into the ancient market town full of anticipation and I was not disappointed. A pleasant mixture of Georgian, half-timbered and whitewashed buildings line its spacious High Street, which descends almost imperceptibly from Bailey Hill, the site of the Norman castle, around which the town originally grew. The hill is now a public park but over the centuries it was a place of fierce battles and much bloodshed. So much so that when the castle was captured by Llewellyn the Great in 1199, it was recorded that the 'Alyn ran red with blood.' It was a victory that marked the beginning of Llewellyn's rise to power and after his death it changed hands several times before the Edwardian Conquest. The Parliamentarian forces occupied the castle during the Civil War, but little now remains of it.

The adjacent parish church, dedicated to St Mary, is the finest in the diocese of St Asaph. There can be little doubt that Margaret Beaufort, Countess of Richmond and Derby, had a hand in its fifteenth-century rebuilding. The Earls of Derby held the barony of Mold from 1442 until the execution of one of their number, James Stanley, in 1651. The castellated knave and eighteenth-century tower are studded with impressive round-arched windows. One of these commemorates Richard Wilson, the landscape painter who died near Mold and is buried in the churchyard. When the Disestablishment Bill was going through Parliament, the south porch was restored and one of its pinnacles was re-carved with a diminutive, but unmistakable likeness of Lloyd George.

I strolled through what is now the county town of Clwyd and into the surrounding countryside that lay damp and dreary in the unremitting rain. It is amazing how wet weather transforms even the most scenic landscapes and I had little to cheer me as I followed country roads towards Leeswood until I arrived at the magnificent gates of Leeswood Hall. These are known as the White Gates and their counterpart, the smaller Black Gates guard another entrance to the hall. Dubbed 'Heaven's Gate' and 'Hell's Gate' respectively they are a further example of the craftsmanship of the Davies brothers' work who, you will recall, fashioned those of Chirk Castle. The White Gates represent over 100 feet of magnificent wrought-ironwork and form a fitting tribute to the famous brothers who were pupils of Tijou.

Leeswood Hall is an early fifteenth-century crenellated house, to the south side of which stands a Queen Anne mansion. The latter was built by Sir George Wynne, a reckless spendthrift and flamboyant eighteenth-century aristocrat. It was he who paid for the artistic education of his young kinsman, the artist Richard Wilson. Jacobite relics preserved in the house include locks of the Old Pretender's and Bonnie Prince Charlie's hair, tickets for Jacobite meetings, and portraits of the Stuarts. A gruesome event took place at the Hall in 1470 when a Welsh chieftain hanged the Mayor of Chester and burned alive 400 citizens who tried to take him.

The sight of Leeswood Hall proved an interesting prelude to a frustrating attempt to reach the hamlet of Pontblyddyn. I found my path blocked by fenced-off woods and an annoying stream that took ages to cross. To cap it all I received a shock from an unmarked electric fence that barred my way. Consequently I was not in the best of temper when I finally stormed through Pontblyddyn, well behind schedule and determined to report such a blatant obstruction of the footpath.

The afternoon was not trouble-free, for I encountered more problems in locating paths before eventually reaching the sanctuary of Higher Kinnerton. The appearance of appealing red-brick buildings, which, I discovered, characterise the surrounding eastern fringe of Wales and the Cheshire Plain, improved my temper as I passed through the tasteful village.

As I traversed obscured paths and pleasant country lanes, the tranquility of my surroundings had a calming influence. I was assailed by the scent of honeysuckle, dog rose and cow parsley and I admired the long-stemmed rose-bay willow herb and convolvulus that enlivened the roadside verges. I found this corner of Welsh border country an area of marked contrasts. I had left behind the more remote and thinly populated moors and mountains with their small, grey-stoned villages, typical of traditional Wales. The landscape was gentler, pleasantly rural and, as I was about to discover, threaded with busy roads.

The region is also a cultural amalgam. It consists of traditional Welsh rural hill communities and, in complete contrast, the industrial and urban incursions into the flatlands around the Dee Estuary and Wrexham, which have introduced an anglicised culture. A typical example is the English labourers, mainly from Staffordshire, Lancashire and Cornwall who came to work in the clay pits and coal mines, particularly around Buckley, about three miles from Mold. Buckley clay has been used for making earthenware since the Roman occupation of Chester. The manufacture of bricks, from fire and acid resistant Buckley clay, commenced in 1737 and became a major industry. This vivid-red clay is responsible for the unique colouring of the buildings of Higher Kinnerton and countless settlements.

Welsh was the prevailing language around Buckley until the invasion by English labourers, which resulted in a singular form of dialect, used only by the people of that district for over 200 years. So potent are cross-border influences that speakers in parts of Clwyd, to this day, can sound as if they come from Liverpool.

The next village I encountered, Dodleston, has evidence of substantial earlier fortification. There are the remains of a Motte and Bailey, several moats and Mill Mound, which was possibly an ancient defensive site, or burial mound. It was no coincidence that on my approach to the village I had crossed the frequently fought over border with England.

Beyond Dodleston I reached an attractive mere and stopped to rest. My surroundings would have been idyllic if it were not for the roar of distant traffic on the busy A483 road that links Chester and Wrexham. A little later I was forced to walk the overgrown grass verge of this busy highway due to the lack of a decent footpath and spent an uncomfortable twenty minutes being bombarded by traffic noise and stared at by the occupants of vehicles that flashed past me.

At last I was able to escape the uproar and join a quiet road leading to Eccleston that lies uncomfortably close to the A55 road, around two miles to the south of Chester. I had chosen this particular route rather than travelling directly to Aldford, my next destination on the Cestrian Link, because I wished to explore the Roman city and had booked accommodation there. From the map I also discovered a convenient footpath linking Eccleston with Chester.

I was pleased I had made this choice when I arrived in Eccleston, for I found it to be a little gem. Red-brick buildings, to which I was becoming accustomed, dominated the village and I stopped to admire the shapely and unusual features of Eccleston Hall that basked in welcome sunshine. In the centre of the settlement stands a tiny, but unique shelter with a high, tiered roof and a weather vane perched on its top. This quaint structure, set amidst a wealth of alluring, mature trees that encircle the hub of the village, proved one of the highlights of the day.

Eccleston and its neighbour, Aldford, stand on the former

Roman highway of Watling Street and the footpath I followed to Chester runs parallel to its modern counterpart, an arrow-straight minor road. The majority of my two-mile journey was through woodland, which restricted views of the locality. The path suited my purpose, however, for I was anxious to reach the city as quickly as possible and have minimal interference from traffic.

I headed directly for the guesthouse where I was to stay, eager for a bath and a meal, reckoning there would be sufficient time on the following morning for exploring the city. My accommodation was typical of many such establishments in popular locations. It could be described as a 'wheel 'em in, feed 'em the bare essentials and wheel 'em out again,' sort of place. I was tired after my day's walk, extended by the morning's mishaps so I was content to refresh myself, 'stoke the boiler' and get a good night's rest.

DAY THIRTY-THREE : CHESTER - BEESTON BROOK

I spent two absorbing hours that morning taking in the sights of the fine city of Chester. There is a true sense of history about the place, from the remains of its ancient walls and Roman amphitheatre, to its dignified mixture of medieval and Victorian architecture. Its two-mile circuit of Roman and medieval walls, black and white timbered buildings, galleried streets, flights of uneven steps and double-tiered shops, combine to provide a unique atmosphere.

The morning was still young but crowds of visitors were beginning to throng its streets and cluster around the ancient cross that marks the city centre. It is a curious mixture of styles, for after its destruction by Parliamentarians in 1646 it was reconstructed using some of the original fragments.

Another popular attraction is decorative Eastgate Clock that was gifted to the city in 1897 by Edward Evans Lloyd, a freeman of the borough. It is poised high above street level and causes all eyes to admire its intricate ironwork.

As I surveyed the remains of the Roman amphitheatre, the largest of its kind in Britain, I was aware that those empire builders chose their site well when they built their stronghold on the River Dee. Sea-going vessels had good access and were able to moor virtually under its walls. The pronounced bend of the river protected the southern and western flanks of the settlement and its encircling wall provided extra protection.

When the Romans left Britain, Chester fell into decay and obscurity for several centuries until, under Norman rule, it became a virtually independent state governed by a succession of earls. Their control ended when the last of them had no male heir, and the king, rather than let the city fall into female hands, took it over and conferred the earldom on his son. Ever since that time Chester has been the property of the eldest son of the reigning monarch.

Chester flourished most profitably as a port between the twelfth and fourteenth centuries, until the river began to silt up and was no longer navigable to ships of any size. Trade subsequently declined and was diverted to the village of Liverpool.

During Tudor and Stuart times the remarkable street frontages of today were built and even earlier, probably in the thirteenth century, the unique Rows appeared. The latter are the arcades and galleries forming continuous passages along the first floors of the houses and shops, some of which contain preserved medieval crypts.

I realised that I should have allocated a full day of my itinerary in order to do justice to the city, steeped as it is in history and tradition. However, my accommodation for the remainder of my walk was pre-booked and I had a planned rendezvous with Roy at Elworth on the following day.

Beeston Brook beckoned and I retraced my steps to Eccleston where I continued along the line of the Roman road to pass impressive Eaton Hall. This mansion, home to the Grosvenor family since Norman times, was built in 1972 and replaced the former vast hall, damaged during the Second World War. The family's fortunes improved in 1676 when Thomas Grosvenor married a wealthy merchant's daughter, whose father owned Ebury, in London. She was only eleven years old at the time and she eventually inherited the land that became London's West End, giving the names to Grosvenor Square, Eaton Square and Eccleston Square. One of her descendants became Duke of Westminster in 1874 and he embarked on a resurgence of building on the Grosvenor estates, which covered much of Chester and the banks of the Dee. The family had close associations with Chester and the Grosvenor Gardens were donated to the city by one of its members. Another connection is the Grosvenor Museum that devotes considerable space to Roman antiquities and the extensive history of Chester.

I continued south along the bank of the Dee, a riverside walk that has been popular since Victorian times. I caught a glimpse of a kingfisher and watched moorhens strutting on the muddy riverbanks. Hoping that I might see a heron swooping low over the water, on a hunting expedition, I kept a sharp lookout. Unfortunately none appeared.

The Cestrian Link was rejoined at Aldford, named after the 'Old Ford,' where the Roman road forded the River Dee. A delightful red sandstone bridge spans the river, a fitting introduction to the charming village with its assortment of mellow-red buildings and decorated facades. Its many attractions include a splendid church and numerous buildings with twisted chimneys and windows with diamond-shaped panes, typical of Westminster estate houses.

At Aldford I changed direction and headed east towards the old settlement of Tattenhall, a pleasing mixture of old and new. Modern houses lining the main street vied for attention with black and white Tudor properties, one of which bears the date, 1601.

The day was warm and sunny and a fair proportion of road-walking had made my feet sore. Anxious to take the most direct route I threw caution to the wind and ventured across a half-mile stretch of pathless countryside that lay between two farms. I nearly suffered for my misdeed, for as I skirted a market garden, two gardeners spotted me and headed in my direction. Terrified that they were about to apprehend me for trespassing, I hurriedly sought a place to hide. A tall yew hedge bordering the gardens seemed a good bet and I squeezed myself into a narrow crevasse in its thick foliage, not daring to move.

Expecting to be caught at any moment I cowered for several minutes, hardly daring to breathe. Tentatively, I peeped from my hiding place and caught a glimpse of the retreating gardeners. They collected their tools and wandered from view, much to my relief. When I thought the coast was clear I emerged from my lair and went hot-foot across a neighbouring field.

Unfortunately, retribution was at hand, for a few minutes later my way was barred by an electric fence. Rather than trying to step over the obstruction, a tricky prospect, I rolled underneath it, which would have been fine had it not been for a dangling strand of electrified wire that gave me an unpleasant shock. Convinced that this was divine justice I vowed not to trespass again.

I found a legitimate path that skirts the next farm and had my boots filled with oozing mud for my pains. Once clear of this annoyance I crossed grassy meadows and enjoyed my first view of the densely wooded Peckforton Hills bathed in sunshine. I would have liked to explore the Sandstone Trail that traverses them and visit the Table Rock at their northern extremity, but it was late afternoon and hunger got the better of me. I hurried on unable to see Peckforton Castle sequestered amongst the blanket of trees obscuring the hills. Apparently it is a folly with no defensive significance and was built in the mid-nineteenth century as a residence for a local landowner.

As I rounded the northern fringe of the Peckforton Hills I caught sight of distant Beeston Castle, its remains protruding from tree-cover on the summit of a prominent crag. This fortification occupies a superb defensive site, perched on a block of sandstone with a sheer rock face soaring up to its walls. Unlike its neighbour it has a lengthy pedigree stretching back to the thirteenth century and was largely destroyed by Parliamentarians at the end of the Civil War. It is now an impressive ruin, maintained by English Heritage, with a museum housed within its nineteenth-century turreted entrance. It possesses a well, 370 feet deep, which must have rendered it virtually 'siege-proof.' History relates that Richard II hid treasure worth 20,000 marks here, consisting of coins, gold and jewels.

Anxious to complete my day's stint I tramped along a narrow lane towards Beeston, its verges bursting with colour. Stately hollyhocks and foxgloves lined my route into the sleepy hamlet and the hot sun was taking its toll.

A mere mile remained to my night's halt at Beeston Brook, on the outskirts of Tiverton and I covered this with as much speed as I could muster. I trod the final quarter-mile alongside the A49 trunk road that slices through the small settlement, searching for my accommodation. I found it standing by the side of this busy thoroughfare and I hoped that traffic noise would not disturb my night's sleep. I need not have worried, for after a good meal in a nearby inn the day's exertions ensured that I spent an undisturbed night.

DAY THIRTY-FOUR : BEESTON BROOK - ELWORTH

Much of the day's journey was spent on the towpath of the Shropshire Union Canal, which conveniently passed within a hundred yards of my stopping place.

The morning dawned fine and sunny once more and I joined the canal happy in the knowledge that my route that morning should be straightforward and trouble-free. Initially it would run south-east, away from my destination, but the convenience of following the waterway was too good to miss.

Traffic was brisk on the canal as I strolled along the ample towpath and waved to several passing boats, my feet thankful for the release from tarmac. The obviously popular waterway forms a strategic part of the canal networks of north-west and central England. It is linked to the Manchester Ship Canal, the Cheshire Ring and, to the south, the system that encircles Birmingham. Like many canals it gradually declined in the face of stiff competition from the new railway companies after the boom period of the late eighteenth and early nineteenth centuries. Large-scale commercial carrying had ceased by the time of the Second World War and today leisure traffic is its mainstay.

As I covered the five-mile section to the canal's junction with its Middlewich branch I noted the variety of names given to the passing fleet of boats, several of which indicated their owner's sense of humour, such as 'Canality J'aime,' which I took to be a corruption of 'Calamity Jane.' The unflattering 'Flat Bottomed Lady' caught my eye and I'll wager its possessor is a bachelor!

The Shropshire Union, known to the locals as the 'shroppy,' and the Trent and Mersey were both vital to the development of Middlewich, which more than any other town in Cheshire deserves the title of 'Canal Town.'

Around lunchtime I called in a canal-side shop to purchase some food and drink. The friendly woman behind the counter seemed most impressed when I told her I was walking to Edale.

'How exciting!' she exclaimed. 'I wish I was coming with you.'

What would your husband say to that, I wondered?

As she had sold out of sandwiches the woman suggested cake as an alternative. I was so hungry I would have eaten anything and readily agreed. She unwrapped a slab of Dundee cake and helpfully cut it into slices, adding that she would not see me going hungry. When I left the shop she wished me luck with my 'great adventure,' as she described it.

I found a convenient seat on the grassy towpath and enjoyed the cake, followed by biscuits and fruit, to keep me going through the afternoon. The sun was beating down and I drank copious amounts of liquid. It was so hot that a little later I passed a herd of cows drinking eagerly from the canal.

At Barbridge I joined the Middlewich branch and found it even more crowded. At one of the locks a queue of boats awaited passage through it and at a popular mooring site there was hardly room for boats to pass the double row of moored craft.

I spent a worrying ten minutes trying to pass a pair of swans jealously guarding their brood of young cygnets that reclined on the towpath. Their intimidating hisses forced a party of walkers coming in the opposite direction to beat a hasty retreat. I tried the soothing approach as I began to edge round the angry swans whose beaks came too close for comfort. I'm unsure if my quiet, placating words had any effect but after what seemed an age I finally passed them and heaved a sigh of relief.

As I approached Church Minshull I discovered from a fisherman hunched over his rod that the towpath had only recently been cleared. I had disturbing visions of the treacherous growth on the flanks of the Montgomery Canal.

Church Minshull proved disappointing. My view of the place was probably coloured by the digging up of its main street and the fact that I was nearly bowled over by a young idiot driving his car very fast along a lane leading from the village. This particular thoroughfare was unexpectedly busy with traffic and I realised it was being used as a 'rat-run' by motorists wishing to avoid the congestion caused by the roadworks.

To be fair to Church Minshull, if conditions had been different I may have been more charitable, for its unusual red-brick church was quite striking and it possessed a number of attractive timbered houses. Its most tranquil setting is seen from the bridge over the languid River Weaver. Flanked by luxuriant trees, amongst which a mixture of tasteful modern and mature properties are camouflaged, this inviting portion of the river makes an ideal subject for a landscape artist.

My next objective, Warmingham, is a quiet hamlet astride the River Wheelock. I negotiated a series of field-paths and crossed the course of a Roman road as I headed for it. Consulting the map it appeared that the line of this highway, King Street, runs from Middlewich, about three miles to the north, and heads for Nantwich, but disappears without trace whilst skirting Crewe. It forms part of the great legacy of the Romans that was designed to carry not only troops but also goods and, equally important, information. Their road system had three main arms that radiated from London, one of which led to Chester and onwards to Carlisle.

The tower of Warmingham church rose from a cordon of trees as I followed the well-signed footpaths towards the village. Unfortunately my entrance coincided with a heavy shower and it put a damper on the place. I donned waterproofs and quickly left, hoping to reach Elworth before I received a soaking.

A mile and a half of soggy paths brought me to the outskirts of my destination and as I joined a road that led through an attractive residential area, the rain stopped, the sun returned and I was presented with a vivid rainbow. Elworth was glad to see me I reckoned as I crossed the hump-backed bridge that spans the Trent and Mersey Canal. The entrance to Foden's Motor Works lay a little farther along the road. Famous for its diesel engines and its brass band, the company was the brain-child of E.R. Foden, who's initials, 'ERF' are a common sight on the front of trucks.

I was hoping to find Roy waiting at the guesthouse where I was due to stay. Unfortunately he was delayed and turned up during dinner. We had much to talk about and he was anxious to know how my walk was progressing. I'm sure I must have bored him with my tale of access problems and unexpected electric shocks. He asked how far we were walking the next day. 'I hope you're leading me in gently,' he added.

'Of course,' I replied, 'we're only doing fifteen miles.'

What I didn't say was that the mileage would probably expand considerably if it followed the pattern of other difficult route-finding days.

DAY THIRTY-FIVE : ELWORTH - OAKGROVE

I felt happy as we set out next morning. I had a long-standing companion to talk with and whinge to when things did not go according to plan. The day began in promising fashion as we crossed level countryside to the tiny hamlet of Bradwall Green. I felt sorry for its inhabitants, for on the outskirts of the village the peaceful surroundings were shattered by traffic tearing along the M6 motorway.

We hurriedly crossed a bridge over the disconcerting highway and returned to quiet paths making for the less frenetic Brereton Green. Just beyond this village, at the end of a narrow road, lies the Church of St Oswald, in its own quiet graveyard. It fared badly during the Civil War when the puritanical Roundheads removed the fourteenth-century font and stripped much of its fine furnishings.

Adjacent to the church stands the entrance to Brereton Hall, former home of the prominent Cheshire family, the Breretons. This manor house, now used as a school, has an attractive brick frontage and two solid towers linked by a bridge-like structure. The Brereton family crest, a boar's head, is depicted on the sign of the local Boar's Head Inn, an ancient ivy-clad and timbered hostelry built in 1617.

A quiet lane leads to Brereton Heath Park, a pleasant area of woodland and heath, which once belonged to the Brereton family and was later used for pure sand and silica quarrying. The quarry closed in 1973 and the park is currently managed by Congleton Borough Council. As we skirted a peaceful lake situated within the park, the tranquility of this natural habitat for birds was insensitively disturbed by a woman throwing a stick into the water for her dog to retrieve. However, our annoyance subsided somewhat when we learnt that the lake is used for water sports during the summer.

We lingered in the pleasant surroundings before crossing the River Dane near Swettenham Hall and heading along country lanes towards Marton. The massive radio telescope at Jodrell Bank Observatory stood out clearly on the skyline and we could also see the town of Congleton nestling in a valley to the south. One of the inns of the town, the Bear's Head, is a reminder that Congleton was the last town in England to abolish bear-baiting. It is still nicknamed 'Bear Town.' Another of its ancient inns, the White Lion, is said to have been used as an office by John Bradshaw. He was High Steward of Congleton and president of the court that sentenced Charles I to be beheaded in 1649.

Derbyshire seemed close at hand, despite the county border being a day's walk away. For some reason for I mistakenly associate Congleton with that county, despite its reputation as the second most notable town of Cheshire's silk industry, after Macclesfield.

'No need to get my hopes up yet,' I told Roy. 'We're still a long way from Derbyshire.'

At Marton we joined the A34 road and, to our delight we found a welcome roadside café and dived inside. It was an effort to leave after eating lunch, as it often is when you take a break from a strenuous walk. However, we soon got back into our stride as we followed road and track to Gawsworth. This tiny settlement, encircling a series of delightful ponds, was a revelation. An impressive fifteenth-century church, two ancient rectories and two historic halls vie for prominence in a leafy setting reminiscent of feudal times. We walked between hedges of beech and yew, past gardens bedecked with mature trees, which enhance the watery idyll. Beyond the largest of the serene ponds, in splendid isolation, stood Gawsworth Hall, a half-timbered manor house reflected in the mirror-calm waters. The present hall, constructed in 1480, underwent extensive re-modelling in 1701, which does not detract from its innate beauty. It is privately owned and lived in, although open to the public daily between the end of March and mid-October. An open-air theatre operates during the summer, which specialises in the plays of William Shakespeare.

> Shall I compare thee to a summer's day?
> Thou art more lovely and more temperate:
> Rough winds do shake the darling buds of May,
> And summer's lease hath all too short a date:

These are the opening lines of a sonnet that Shakespeare wrote to 'The Dark Lady,' but who was she?' She is supposedly none other than Mary Fitton, the headstrong member of the Fitton family, former owners of Gawsworth Hall. This feisty girl, who is said to have turned the head of the bard, was appointed Maid of Honour to Elizabeth I in 1596. It is not beyond the bounds of possibility that Shakespeare called at Gawsworth on his way north to Rufford and was beguiled by this beautiful young lady.

Mary's court life did not last long, for she reputedly misbehaved and by 1602 she was pregnant, probably by the Earl of Pembroke. The Queen was intolerant of such misdemeanors and they were both dispatched to the Tower. Elizabeth died the following year and Mary was eventually allowed to return to Gawsworth.

A serious event in the long history of the hall occurred in 1712, when one of the most famous duels ever enacted took place. Lord Mohun and the Duke of Hamilton fought over the Gawsworth estate and both died of their wounds. Their deaths caused great distress to the reigning monarch of the time, Queen Anne.

Music still resounds around Gawsworth Hall, filtering through its fabric from the chapel, the first of which was built in the fourteenth century. In times gone by it was not just religious music that filled the hall as the lion headed fiddle in the dining room amply proves. The instrument belonged to the Gawsworth Jester, Samuel Johnson, better known as 'Maggoty.' This eccentric gentleman is buried in Maggoty Johnson's Wood and he was perhaps the last professional jester in England. However, he was nobody's fool and wrote plays under the pseudonym of Lord Flame. One of his creations ran for two months at London's Haymarket Theatre.

A pair of majestic swans swam towards us, eager for titbits, and rooks called from their nests high in the trees as we took a final look at the hall and the shimmering reflections in the pond before beginning the final stretch of our day's journey. By this time the straps of Roy's rucksack were beginning to chafe his shoulders and my feet were protesting. We spent an uncomfortable three quarters of an hour covering the remaining two miles to Oakgrove, a hamlet straddling the A523 road that links Macclesfield and Leek.

When we asked the location of the farm where we were due to spend the night a man told us gleefully, 'It's quite a way out of the village.'

'How far?' asked Roy, tentatively.

'You take the track up yon hill,' our guide replied, pointing to a steep path climbing the far valley side, 'and follow it for about a mile. That'll bring you to the farm.'

The disappointment must have shown on our faces.

'Do you reckon you can make it? You look all in?'

'Of course we will,' I replied with more enthusiasm than I felt.

'Then you'd best be off,' said the man who turned on his heel without another word.

'I think he enjoyed that,' Roy commented.

'You're probably right. Let's get to it.'

The mile along the tortuous meandering track seemed endless. I was limping and Roy grimaced with pain as the shoulder straps of his rucksack bit deeper into his shoulders.

'Pad your shoulders with your spare socks,' I suggested.

'I'm okay,' Roy insisted. 'It can't be much farther.'

At last we rounded a bend in the track and came upon the farmhouse nestling in a picturesque setting amongst shapely hills. The view was inspiring as we sat outside the farmhouse drinking tea and chatting to the farmer's wife.

'We can't give you a meal,' she said, 'but you can get a nice one at the inn in the village.'

Roy and I looked at each other in dismay. A return trip along the punishing track seemed the only option. Not wishing to reveal our aches and pains we said nothing.

A short time later, having showered and changed, we began the mile-long journey back to Oakgrove. Roy's shoulders were sore but much better for discarding the rucksack that someone had lent him. My feet were marginally better for wearing trainers, but I was still limping.

We mulled over the day's events as we plodded towards the village. Eventually we reached the roadside inn and thankfully took the weight off our feet. The meal was splendid and we were feeling quite mellow until it was time to leave and make the tiresome return journey to the farm. Had someone extended the track since we left the farm? It seemed twice its original length and it was dusk before our objective finally came into view. The most welcome sight of the day, we reckoned. Fresh air and exercise worked their magic a little later, for we fell sound asleep and did not stir until the following morning.

DAY THIRTY-SIX : OAKGROVE - BUXTON

The weather had deteriorated overnight and a clinging mist hung over the surrounding hills. The forecast did not predict much improvement. It seemed we were in for a much cooler day, with restricted views. This was a pity for we had left the Cheshire Plain behind and would be heading into the hills that straddle the border with Derbyshire. These form part of the southern fringe of the Pennines, whose very name conjured up visions of Edale and the start of the Pennine Way.

Bidding goodbye to our companionable host we set off along a winding track that penetrated the bleak, sodden hills. Initially the cart-track meandered east, before annoyingly turning south and away from our desired route. As there seemed no alternative we were forced to follow the writhing thoroughfare that seemed reluctant to head for our next target, Croker Hill. We could see the tall mast, just visible in the mist, on its summit, long before we reached it. When we finally scaled the gorse-studded hill we had travelled twice as far as the crow flies.

Some miles to the east we could see the dark humps of the Pennines, cowering beneath a leaden sky. 'Derbyshire ahoy!' I said to Roy, who seemed less than enthusiastic. Despite padding his shoulders they were still very painful and he was cursing his unfamiliar rucksack. My feet felt much better but gradually worsened as the day wore on.

We continued our weaving route through the green and sombre landscape to the foot of the Pennines, land of the mountain pansy, lady's mantle and wild rose. We began a gradual ascent in steady rain and the clouds began to press down on us as we climbed. We were entering wild, wet country where bird-watchers are in their element. Skylarks, meadow pipits and curlews inhabit the high wasteland and you may even catch sight of breeding merlin.

To the north lies Macclesfield Forest a fine walking area much favoured by naturalists. A chain of reservoirs lies within its confines, which are not densely packed with trees. It was formerly a popular hunting-ground of the Bromley-Davenport family who lived at Capesthorne Hall situated roughly six miles north of Congleton, off the A34 road. The family origins hark back to Norman times and part of its crest shows the head of a felon, indicating that poachers could expect little mercy. The hall is reputedly haunted, and in 1958 William Bromley-Davenport was awakened by what he described as a severed hand scratching at his bedroom window.

Roy and I descended from the hill-country into the hamlet of Wildboarclough, embedded deep in a tree-lined valley. Here we found an inn that served good food and spent a pleasant hour inside fortifying ourselves for the climb out of the cleft through which channels lively Clough Brook.

At the rear of Clough House we joined a track that climbs steadily between rounded green hills before branching off along a soggy and eroded path through comfortless peatland. The uncompromising wind was in its element as we squelched over exposed moorland towards the Buxton to Macclesfield road. From a distance we could see traffic snaking over the bleak watershed of the Pennines under a glowering sky.

As we neared the road we spied one of the highest inns in the country, the Cat and Fiddle, an oasis amidst a pitiless, barren landscape. It resides in Cheshire by a cat's whisker and virtually straddles the county border. I could well imagine it being a place of refuge during the heavy snows of years gone by, which now seem less commonplace. At 1,690 feet it is the second highest hostelry in England, giving precedence to the Tan Hill Inn, which lies on the Pennine Way high above Swaledale.

We crossed the main road near the inn and took a minor road to Derbyshire Bridge at the head of the scenic Goyt Valley. It was hard to believe that the quiet and secluded upper valley once supported a thriving farming community and factories making paint and explosives. The latter disappeared beneath Fernilee and Errwood Reservoirs, constructed in 1938 and 1968 respectively, to provide water for Stockport.

Buxton lay a tantalising two and a half miles away but to remain faithful to our route we descended the valley to the head of the Errwood Reservoir, before taking a path leading to Edgemoor and Buxton. An unfenced road snakes down to the reservoir but we left it as soon as possible to take a path that contours the side of Goyt's Moss and provides more amenable walking. We met several fellow walkers, confirming that the area is extremely popular with our ilk.

Deep cloughs cut through the shales that descend to the Goyt and thin bands of low-grade coal have been mined hereabouts during the nineteenth century. It was mainly burnt with limestone to produce quicklime for treating the land.

Speckle-faced Dale O' Goyt sheep eyed us suspiciously as we

passed. The breed originated here and has become commonly known as the Derbyshire Gritstone.

Across the valley, shrouded in woodland stand the ruins of Errwood Hall, now a sad scene of crumbling stone. In its heyday during the early 1800's it presented an entirely different picture. At that time the Grimshawe family occupied the hall, which was a vibrant place. They lived a bizarre, almost frenzied life of luxury in the impressive Italianate building. The Grimshawes were fond of travelling on their ocean-going yacht and many of the trees and bushes on the estate were brought back from foreign lands, rhododendron bushes frequently serving as ballast for the yacht. Sadly the last of the Grimshawe family died in 1930 and was buried alongside her relatives in the small burial ground above the hall. It is said she was hastened to her death by worry after hearing the news that Stockport Council was to build a reservoir in the Goyt Valley.

Above the head of Errwood reservoir we joined a path leading out of the valley and towards Edgemoor. When the valley crest was reached a superb view of Buxton, nestling in the fertile plain beneath, unfolded. What a contrast it presented to the windswept moorland beneath our feet, a rain-washed landscape, aptly named Wild Moor, inhabited by bad-tempered grouse that cackled indignantly when disturbed.

There was a time when Buxtonians who commuted outside the town could guarantee a few extra days off work during the winter months, with the excuse that they were snowbound. Many would climb onto these moors into a magical snow-sculptured world, the moorland roads impassable and the town muffled and silent under its white blanket.

From thereon it was downhill all the way. We descended, as fast as our injuries would allow, alongside the tumbling Wildmoorstone Brook to Beet Wood and Edgemoor, before taking the convenient Bishop's Lane into Buxton.

Famed for its waters, architecture, international festival and surroundings, Buxton is Derbyshire's highest town and England's second highest after Alston, in Cumbria. The fresh and exhilarating air brought the Victorians in large numbers when it was fashionable to visit spa towns for rejuvenation.

Among the town's prestigious visitors, Mary Queen of Scots was probably the most enthusiastic. Whilst imprisoned by Elizabeth I and in the custody of the Earl of Shrewsbury she often came to the spa for the good of her health. Closely guarded, her every movement was watched, confirming suspicions that Elizabeth felt Mary could easily escape over the open moors and threaten her position on the throne.

Sadly the opulence of John Carr's Crescent of 1786, built to emulate the Royal Crescent at Bath, is no longer apparent but thankfully other buildings still display traces of their former glory. Most prominent among them are the Devonshire Royal Hospital with its great dome, possibly the largest unsupported one in Europe, and the Opera House of 1903, which each year plays host to the town's international festival.

The town stands just within The Peak National Park, designated in 1951, and the first of its kind in Britain. Wedged between Manchester, Sheffield and Derby, it is effectively the lungs of central England and is easily reached by the fifteen million people who live within an hour's drive of its boundary. Buxton represents one of the Park's very popular venues and serves as a good base for touring it.

After settling into our accommodation it was a must for us to explore the town. We strolled its absorbing streets before searching for a suitable place to eat. We chose a Chinese restaurant as Roy is partial to Chinese cuisine. We ate our fill, which is not difficult with Chinese food and returned, feeling bloated, to our respective rooms to recover. Little did I know that I would be made to pay for my greed the next day.

DAY THIRTY-SEVEN : BUXTON - EDALE

The final day of my trek to the foot of the Pennine Way had arrived. I felt well and truly in Derbyshire, and couldn't wait to complete the last lap of the journey to Edale, which seemed a mere stone's throw away. My exhilaration was slightly premature for we still had a testing day's walk ahead.

Unfortunately, weather-wise, Derbyshire had been less than welcoming and it was about to get worse. Much of the day was spent in waterproofs, which cast a shadow over the normally appealing limestone terrain of the Peak District.

At the outset conditions were reasonable as we began our return to the track on Wild Moor that we had left the previous afternoon. Rounded masses of white cloud predominated and it thankfully remained dry. We laboured up Bishop's Lane and above Edgemoor we discovered a tunnel in the hillside that had gone unnoticed during our descent. According to the map it provided access for a disused railway that runs through the Goyt Valley. The railway probably served the coalmines in the valley and also the great limestone quarries to the south-east of Buxton.

We retraced our steps in the company of the lively Widmoorstone Brook onto the wild tops and met the railway once more where it crosses Goyt's Lane. The next hour and a half was spent closely studying the map as we negotiated a complicated, twisting route across hill and dale until the secluded village of Combs appeared, snuggling amidst a rolling patchwork of meadows and cereal crops.

My map-reading was not helped by a worsening stomach ache, a legacy of the Chinese meal that had obviously not agreed with me. We made a good pair. Roy's shoulders were troubling him again and I had a slight limp, brought on by three miles of road walking to Dove Holes. It was, despite our difficulties an enjoyable scenic route through a green landscape predominated by gentle, rounded hills. The fields and higher pastureland were threaded with dry-stone walls, some of which were erected after the passing of the Enclosures Acts between 1780 and 1830. I admired the solidity of a roadside wall, built upon one or two foundation courses with a rubble filling and occasional 'through' stones to give strength, a tribute to the craftsmen that fashioned it. Their work, however, is continual, for repairs are often needed to sections damaged by ewes at lambing time, as they try to escape the rest of the flock. They jump onto the top and kick backward with their hind legs as they leap off, dislodging capstones. The damage is normally made more severe by other sheep following in their wake.

The countryside around Dove Holes is scarred with limestone quarries and coated with conifer plantations, and the village of today seems unremarkable. It was formerly an important settlement and the site of the 'Bull Ring,' a Neolithic henge that may also have served as a market and trading centre. Adjacent to the henge lies a tumulus, one of the many Neolithic tombs and barrows that litter the Peak District. Thomas Bateman, the famous nineteenth-century archaeologist excavated hundreds of such burial sites

Lunchtime was approaching as we entered Dove Holes and Roy made for the village store in a search for food and drink. Thanks to the pain in my stomach I was not feeling hungry but I managed to force down a ham roll. To add to my woe it began to rain.

We beat a hasty retreat from the village, made difficult by a lime-works obstructing our climb into the hills. The rain came with a vengeance and we were soon drenched and miserable. As we skirted the Bee Low lime quarries the path became indistinct and I had to forget my troubles and concentrate hard on route-finding. Fortunately, it also took my mind off the increasing urgency to reach a toilet.

After two rain-sodden miles we walked through the hamlet of Peak Forest seeking a public convenience, which was highly optimistic. It was a fruitless exercise and the village pub seemed the only alternative. We dashed in and I made a beeline for the toilet, much to the amusement of the landlord. When I returned to the bar he said, 'I hear you have the yellow peril.'

'That's the last Chinese I'm having,' I replied, forcing a smile.

We removed our sodden and dripping waterproofs and put them to dry on a nearby radiator. A great help that was, for they soon got wet again when we left the pub.

'Nasty day for walking,' said a man seated at the next table.

'It is,' replied Roy, 'a good day for ducks.'

The man laughed. 'You'd best stay in here for the afternoon.'

We explained that we were making for Edale.

'Then you've about five miles to walk,' our acquaintance declared.

'It doesn't sound far,' I responded, my excitement mounting now that we were nearing journey's end.

'Do you live in the village?' Roy inquired.

'Have done all my life.'

'It seems a strange name, 'Peak Forest.' I don't see many trees around.'

'There were some in times gone by,' the man replied. 'It stands in what was the centre of the Royal Forest of the Peak, used by Norman kings as their hunting ground. That's how it got its name.'

'Ah,' said Roy.

The man continued. 'It wasn't heavily wooded but mainly open country where wolves and wild boar roamed. It stayed like that for 500 years until it lost its status as a hunting forest.'

'It seems a nice area,' Roy ventured, 'despite our seeing it at its worst.'

The man smiled. 'There's nowhere like it. I wouldn't move from here for a million pounds.'

Roy laughed. 'Not even if you won the lottery?'

'We'll have to move shortly,' I indicated, 'if we're going to make Edale before evening.'

'Aye, you will,' the man replied. 'Have a look at the nearby church as you leave, it was quite famous at one time when our village was known as 'the Gretna Green of the Peak.' Marriage licences were given with no questions asked, provided you gave a small fee to the incumbent. It was built as a private chapel, you see, and was outside church jurisdiction. There were lots of runaway marriages conducted in it.'

We chatted a little longer with the cordial villager, reluctant to stir ourselves, until Roy said, 'Time's moving on, we'd best be on our way.'

'Yes,' I said, turning to the man. 'Thanks for your company.'

'Goodbye, and good luck,' he replied, 'you'll need it in this weather.'

We left the inn, glanced at the distinctive church and walked out of the village in steady rain. A good hour of traversing convenient paths brought us within sight of the dark bulk of Mam Tor that overlooks the Vale of Edale.

'We're nearly home and dry,' I said to Roy.

'Less of the dry,' he quipped, 'I'm soaking wet.'

Through the gloom I could see the exposed eastern face of the tor, known as the 'shivering mountain,' due to its instability. The precipice, its striped rock formation clearly visible, was produced by a great landslip, caused by the alternating layers of soft, impervious shale and porous, harder grits sliding over each other when wet. This has had serious consequences for the road at the foot of the hill. Originally constructed for horse transport, it had to be rebuilt in 1945 only to slip again in 1977. It has remained closed to traffic since that time.

The hill is significant, not least because it towers above the Hope Valley and forms the western end of the pronounced ridge to Lose

Hill that effectively separates the White Peak to the south and the Dark Peak to the north.

Despite our eagerness to reach Edale we decided that we should climb the highest hill of the Peak and see the remains of the Iron Age hill-fort on its 1,695-foot summit. As we clambered onto its undulating ridge we disappeared into cloud which prevented any views over the coveted Vale of Edale. Part of the fort's original sixteen acres have disappeared through landslips but a pronounced ditch was still discernible. Our curiosity satisfied, we did not linger on the summit, preferring to quickly touch the trig point before a hurried descent.

As we crossed the saddle below Mam Tor we caught up with a group of schoolgirls on a weekend hike. Many of them were struggling, demoralised by persistent rain, blisters and heavy packs. Roy and I felt sorry for the poor girls, dragged onwards by their teachers. We chatted to one or two of the pupils who, we found, were definitely not enjoying their weekend.

Eventually we left the party to their suffering and hastened, as fast as our feet and Roy's sore shoulders would allow, into the saturated Vale of Edale. My stomach was much improved - it's amazing what nearing a goal can do - and we made good time along a wide track through Harden Clough, which brought us to the outskirts of Edale itself. A mere few hundred yards remained to our objective, the Old Nag's Head Inn, the recognised starting point of the Pennine Way. Tired, but elated we dived in for a celebratory drink and a swapping of a few tales with some fellow walkers.

'Well, we did it!' I said triumphantly to Roy, as we stood outside the inn a little later. We turned towards the sombre view that has intimidated many a walker - the bleak moorland edge of Kinder Scout. 'That was my initiation to the Pennine Way,' I told him.

CHAPTER FIVE

The Pennine Way

DAY THIRTY-EIGHT : EDALE - CROWDEN

The night before tackling the 270-mile walk to Kirk Yetholm on the Scottish Border was spent at Edale Youth Hostel. At that time I was happy to use such accommodation rather than craving the comforts of Bed and Breakfast. It was here that I met Ben, a retired schoolteacher from Harrogate, which is not far from my home in Baildon. He was also attempting the whole of the Pennine Way and by coincidence had chosen the same accommodation as myself. We struck up an immediate friendship and decided to join forces. I looked forward to having a companion to share the next two and a half weeks. Ben, I discovered was in his early sixties and had taken up walking rather late in life like myself.

We spent a comfortable night in the hostel, but I was awake early the next morning and lay wondering what fate had in store for us. At breakfast I chose the high-protein option of baked beans on toast. What I actually got was an orange mound floating on an ebony raft. The beans were glutinous and the toast was burnt to a cinder. I struggled with this culinary disaster, urged on by the thought that the beans would give me added momentum during my struggle up Grindsbrook Clough. It was one way of making flatulence work for you!

(I should emphasise here that the section I am about to describe is not included in subsequent route revisions.)

Fortified by this explosive mixture I headed up Grindsbrook Clough, accompanied by Ben, and we reached brooding Kinder Plateau, without undue difficulty. The sight before us was daunting. Low cloud enveloped us and over the few yards of visibility available, all we could make out was a sea of glutinous brown peat disappearing into nothingness.

We stood teetering on the brink until, grasping the bull by the horns, we took our first step into the morass with much trepidation. The best way of describing the conditions underfoot would be mounds of clinging peat surrounded by water. The strain of extricating peat-laden boots and legs from the quagmire was tremendous. There was not a soul in sight and we were enveloped in an eerie silence that you could almost reach out and touch. The fellow walkers that we had met climbing Grindsbrook Clough, or standing apprehensively looking at the peat hags from the edge of the plateau, had disappeared. They had probably taken one look at the terrain and gone home!

I fought the temptation to shout for my mum as Ben and I ploughed, on a compass bearing, towards the Kinder River. After what seemed an age our objective appeared out of the mist and we were soon following this lifeline to Kinder Downfall. Here we found groups of walkers sitting around, chatting, or simply enjoying the view over the waterfall. Where had all these people been when we were desperate for company? Presumably taking the easier route around the plateau's edge!

With lighter hearts Ben and I descended from the grim plateau and soon reached the Snake Road, which we crossed and headed for Bleaklow, a place as notorious as Kinder Scout, if not worse. The view of more peat hags as far as the eye could see did not offer any comfort, especially as the higher reaches of the hill were obscured by cloud.

After floundering through this quagmire for a time we hit on a

The Pennine Way - Edale to Kirk Yetholm

better scheme, for we had noticed several streams that drained the summit. Although it increased the distance by weaving in and out of the hags, we followed a convenient streambed, which was reasonably solid and made walking much easier.

After a period of steady climbing through these meandering channels a group of stones could be seen through the gloom. These weirdly shaped boulders were the Wain Stones and although not signifying the summit, gave reassurance that we were near to it.

It was lucky that the mist was down because the view from these stones to the barely discernible Bleaklow Head is not one to be enjoyed. It is akin to being in mid-ocean, with the waves substituted by mounds of peat.

We tentatively squelched our way across this sea of peat to attain the highest point of Bleaklow, our legs nicely soaked and stained by the morass. Once there we had to find the route down to the Longdendale Valley. If the weather had been kinder, we could have taken a bearing towards Holme Moss television mast, which stands roughly five miles to the north. We headed in that direction and, much to our relief, eventually found the valley of Wildboar Grain that we knew from the map runs into Torside Clough, which in turn would take us down to the reservoirs near Crowden Youth Hostel, our stopping place for the night.

As we descended Torside Clough we came out of the low cloud and got our first view of the valley and its reservoirs. The path became exceedingly steep and rocky as we dropped down towards Reaps Farm. Unfortunately, this was the cause of Ben's demise. So intent was he on taking in the impressive view over Longdendale that he did not watch where he was putting his feet. Whilst extolling the virtues of the wonderful panorama Ben missed his footing and pitched forward to the ground, putting out his hand to lessen the impact. In so doing he dislocated his little finger. Without more ado he grabbed the injured digit and, remarkably, pulled it back into position. I was quite unprepared for what happened next. Not having learnt his lesson, he fell in exactly the same way a few moments later, this time letting out a loud yell. I turned to look at his now grotesquely shaped finger with a nasty gash at its base. He was obviously in considerable pain but I was no expert in replacing dislocated digits. Rooting inside my rucksack I found my first aid kit and bound the injured finger to the others. I had no idea if this was the accepted practice but it was all that I could think of at the time and hoped it would at least ease Ben's pain and prevent further damage.

We made our way gingerly down to Reaps Farm and once on to solid ground we made better progress across the end of Torside Reservoir and along the far side of the valley to the Crowden Youth Hostel. After checking in, I explained Ben's predicament and asked if there was a hospital in the area. We were told that the nearest was at Ashton-under-Lyne on the outskirts of Manchester. I rang for a taxi to ferry Ben to the hospital and duly saw him off, with a promise to arrange that there would be some hot food available on his return.

The evening meal was a rather subdued affair for me as I was concerned about Ben. There was one bright spot, however. I overheard an elderly gentleman telling everyone within earshot that he was seventy-four years old and delighted to be walking the Pennine Way. He was accompanied by a mere stripling of sixty-six in his attempt and he began to tell anyone who cared to listen how superbly fit he was. It became obvious, however, that he was not too clever at route-finding. He revealed that he and his companion had completely lost their way on Kinder Plateau and never made it to the Downfall. Instead, they had blundered from the plateau not knowing where they were and had made an unscheduled overnight stop at a convenient pub. They had managed to reach Crowden on their second day, already a day behind schedule. I wondered what problems might lie in wait for them, and I was eventually to find out as I encountered them in the most unexpected places. They were to prove a wily pair and I conferred on them the nickname of the 'Brothers in Law.'

Shortly after supper, Ben returned with his hand heavily bandaged and a splint on his injured finger. He had received a tetanus jab where it hurts most and been sent on his way with the sobering thought that they considered him mad to be attempting such a venture. The warden did Ben proud and provided a hot meal for him. Then later, suitably fed and watered, Ben telephoned his wife to give her the sorrowful news, and assured her that it would not distract him from his task. She probably tried to persuade him to go home, but you know how stubborn men are.

DAY THIRTY- NINE : CROWDEN - DELPH

Next morning we were amongst the last to leave the hostel and noted that the 'Brothers in Law' had got away much earlier. Ben's hand wasn't giving too much pain from its injury.

It is quite a stiff climb onto Lladdow Rocks but the view from there down the valley and over Longdendale is very impressive. On a fine day the flat top of Kinder Scout can be seen on the southern horizon. There was low cloud on this occasion and it had begun to rain but we could see below us into the valley where Crowden Great Brook flows from the flanks of Black Hill. Lo and behold, the 'Brothers in Law' could be seen making uncertain progress along it - despite the fact that it was not the official route. They were going slowly and we saw no more of them that day.

We began the descent from the rocks on pretty rough going and Ben carefully watched where his feet were landing. He had obviously learnt his lesson!

Once in the valley the ground became quite boggy. We crossed Crowden Great Brook high up and made our waterlogged way onto the lower slopes of Black Hill. Eventually, the climb stiffened and it was quite a pull up to the flat top. The conditions underfoot deteriorated the higher we went and when we reached the summit plateau an unappetising sight met our eyes. Wainwright said with great emphasis that it is not a place to be enjoyed. How right he was. In the middle of a seemingly impregnable quagmire stood the triangulation point, known as the 'Soldier's Lump.' I could not help but admire the skill and tenacity of the Royal Ordnance Corps who erected the column in such a spot. How had they managed to stop it from sinking into the oozing peat I wondered?

It took us a good twenty minutes of bog-hopping to reach the marooned Ordnance column. You may have reached the conclusion that all the high ground on the Pennine Way consists only of oozing peat. Never fear it does improve.

Ben had not complained at all of his injury. He had covered the affected hand with a plastic bag whilst crossing the boggier sections, which prevented his bandages from being dirtied by the ever-present peat.

As we sat at the base of the column on the only bit of solid ground available, the sun broke through the clouds. With our spirits lifted, we made short work of our lunchtime sandwiches provided by the Youth Hostel. We had met quite a few walkers during our climb but none of them apparently wanted to leave the path and fight their way to where we were sitting. It is surprising how a shared challenge or adversity fosters companionship. Although barely halfway through our second day together, Ben and I knew a great deal about each other and were firm friends. As we sat chatting and enjoying the warmth of the sun, I felt glad once again that he was with me. We were actually perched on the county boundary, which passes over the summit and were about to cross from Derbyshire into my adopted county of West Yorkshire. The clouds for once had moved away and the landmark of the television mast on Holme Moss was clearly visible about a mile away. Now that we did not need it for a compass bearing, there it was staring us in the face. Isn't life perverse, I thought.

I suggested to Ben that for the next part of our journey we take the route that passes the Wessenden Reservoirs. The most immediate challenge was to get off the summit of Black Hill in the right direction. Luckily, a pile of stones stood virtually on our compass bearing, so we struck out for this. After another period of squelching, weaving and hopping we got clear of the peat and were able to follow piles of stones marking a dry channel that took us down towards Dean Clough. We found the boundary ditch which runs down to the road without difficulty and, before we knew it, we were clear of Black Hill and had the firmness of tarmacadam under our boots on the A635 Holmfirth-Greenfield road.

Once across the road we could see the broad, dry track running towards the distant reservoirs and made good progress down to them. The scenery was impressive around the reservoirs with several small waterfalls cascading from the surrounding moorland. All too soon the pleasant walking came to an end. A sign told us to leave the track and strike out across the moorland. With reluctance we dropped into the valley below the track, crossed a rippling stream and made the steep climb onto the moor itself. As we passed Swellands Reservoir the conditions underfoot were reasonable, with young summer bracken and heather much in evidence.

Our destination was the Oldham to Huddersfield road, the A62. There are many reservoirs in this area that serve Huddersfield and Manchester's needs. As we reached the road we passed the fifth of these, Redbrook Reservoir, which appeared to be very popular with yachting enthusiasts. We joined the main road at the head of Standedge Cutting where it runs between steep embankments up to the watershed between Yorkshire and Lancashire. Below the road run three tunnels. When these were constructed in the nineteenth century, they provided a vital link between the industrial areas of east Lancashire and West Yorkshire. One of them, the Marsden

Tunnel has recently been re-opened to canal traffic as part of the refurbishment of the Huddersfield Narrow Canal.

A detour of roughly two miles along the road to Delph brought us to our designated stopping place for the night, Globe Farm Bunkhouse. This is in a good position, sheltering beneath Standedge Edge and having extensive views over Greenfield and Oldham. We were made very welcome and the food was excellent. After supper Ben and I walked to a nearby pub with two chaps also staying in the bunkhouse. They too were walking the Pennine Way and we spent a pleasant couple of hours swapping stories. I was later to team up with one of them, John, for part of the walk.

DAY FORTY : DELPH - MANKINHOLES

The sleeping quarters at the bunkhouse were somewhat cramped. Ben spent an uncomfortable night tossing and turning with pain from his injured finger. By morning it had swollen badly and turned rather an ugly colour. The weather, in contrast, was cool but clear to start with and got pleasantly warmer as the day progressed.

Our route up until lunchtime took us along the gritstone edge of Standedge, over the M62 motorway and across another gritstone bastion, Blackstone Edge. The M62 was crossed by means of a narrow footbridge strung across the gorge at Windy Hill on the crest of Saddleworth Moor. The spot is well named, for the wind, which had been strong all morning, tore through the channel, buffeting the footbridge, causing it to swing appreciably from side to side. Crossing it was not for the faint hearted and my knuckles were white with gripping onto the handrails. The sight of heavy traffic roaring beneath us did not provide any comfort.

Staggering from the bridge we began the long pull up to Blackstone Edge where, on the weathered crags with massive gritstone blocks tumbled at their feet, is Robin Hood's Bed. When we reached the top, since the weather was still on our side, we stopped for a while to admire the view of Rochdale and Manchester below us. Leaving the Edge we crossed a Roman road, which has one of the best preserved sections in the country. Its stones have stayed in remarkable condition for nearly two thousand years. The Pennine Way crosses the ancient highway near a solitary standing stone, known as the Aiggin Stone, which toppled over some years ago but has thankfully been re-erected.

The walking is easy from this point to the main A58 road linking Halifax with Rochdale. Skirting round an old quarry, the road comes into full view, with the welcoming sight of the White House pub, a convenient watering-hole. Ben and I approached it at lunchtime and spent a pleasant half-hour outside with a well-earned pint to accompany our sandwiches. We struck up a conversation during our meal with a friendly couple who were walking a few miles of the Way before returning to their car. They said they envied us attempting the whole distance but when we jokingly offered to change places with them they hastily declined.

We joined a good flat track that passed three reservoirs before rejoining the rough moorland, which was now becoming pretty familiar. Good views over Bacup and Todmorden opened up on our left as we approached the stone sentinel of Stoodley Pike. A short distance from the Pike we crossed a stone-flagged path that was an old trackway running from Crag Vale in the Calder Valley to Mankinholes, which nestled below us. This path now forms part of the Calderdale Way, a fifty-mile circular walk around the Calder Valley.

Our route from here should have taken us down to the Youth Hostel in Mankinholes, but fate took a hand. To be precise, Ben's hand. The swelling around his affected finger was increasing by the hour and it was turning all colours of the rainbow. He obviously needed immediate treatment so, checking the map, we decided we had to head for either Todmorden or nearby Hebden Bridge to find a hospital or health centre. Although Ben must have been in considerable pain all day, he had not complained once and I felt the least I could do was to help him get some treatment. Despite his predicament, he insisted that we should first pay our respects to the monument of Stoodley Pike.

Accordingly we gave the 125-foot high obelisk a close inspection. It was built to commemorate the peace following the Battle of Waterloo and it stands by the Pennine Way on a hill overlooking the Calder Valley. As conditions were clear, we could see for many miles in all directions and were loath to leave our lofty vantage point.

We made our way into the steep-sided Calder Valley where the lines of communication - namely canal, railway, river and road - squeeze through a narrow gap. The footpath intersected the A646 road between Todmorden and Hebden Bridge. Not knowing the area, we asked about medical facilities at a nearby filling station. The owner couldn't have been more helpful: he rang the health centre in Hebden Bridge and booked an appointment for Ben. He also arranged for us to be taken there by car, thus saving us a walk of two miles, and told us the times of buses back and where to alight. I have never forgotten his generosity and whenever I drive along that road, which I have done many times since, I salute his thoughtfulness.

Ben and I were met in the reception of the health centre by a smiling nurse who cheerily exclaimed, 'Welcome to the Pennine Way Blister Unit!' Apparently they were used to frequent visits from walkers whose feet had rebelled after three days' abuse. Ben explained that blisters were not his problem and held out his injured hand. The nurse grimaced and whisked him away for examination.

A short time later he was back with a face as long as a fiddle. A quick look at his finger by the medics had been enough. He had been told to go straight home and report to his local hospital. This, of course, was the kiss of death to his Pennine Way aspirations and meant that I would lose a companion and new-found friend.

The next task was to get Ben home. He rang his wife and gave her prior warning of his unscheduled return. I then accompanied him to the local bus station, but didn't feel that any comforting words would lift his spirits. Accordingly, I had to be content with suggesting that we keep in touch and promised to inform him of my progress. I saw him safely on the bus and waved a disconsolate farewell as I watched it pull away.

My immediate problem was to get to the Mankinholes Youth Hostel in time for my evening meal. I caught a bus back along the main road towards Todmorden, from whence I had a brisk walk to Mankinholes. I reached the hostel in time for supper and explained to the warden the reason for Ben's non-attendance. Unfortunately he would not let me eat Ben's share, which was a shame since I was ravenously hungry.

Although I missed Ben's friendly chat during supper, I was otherwise entertained - by that canny pair, the 'Brothers in Law'.

Once again I was surprised that they had found their way here, as they were not doing very well when last seen approaching Black Hill. They had some hairy adventures to recount like being half submerged during their crossing of Black Moss, which we had fortunately avoided. To illustrate their predicament, the older of the two brandished a broken walking stick that he had snapped whilst trying to heave himself from the peat. Despite their misfortunes, they still seemed in high spirits and were determined to carry on.

I also met some young walkers who were doing the Way much more quickly than I could. One couple had walked the twenty-five miles from Crowden that day, thereby condensing two of my stages into one. Another pair, who were walking in the opposite direction, had come from Kirk Yetholm in just twelve days, including a rest day. One of them was paying a high price, for although he was wearing trainers, his feet were an ugly mess.

DAY FORTY-ONE : MANKINHOLES - HAWORTH

My abiding memory of the hostel at Mankinholes is of the warden oversleeping the following morning. He was awakened by impatient walkers hammering on his bedroom door demanding breakfast.

As I set out on my first day alone, the rain, which had been falling since dawn, conveniently stopped. I found a path on the edge of the moor that returned me to the main route at Stoodley Pike. Then I took the same journey into the Calder Valley that I had taken the previous afternoon. Wishing to thank the kind proprietor at the filling station I made a short detour along the A646 road to tell him how Ben had fared, but unfortunately I had to leave a message as he was not there. I returned to the Pennine Way path disappointed that I had not been able to thank him for his kindness.

I tackled the steep climb out of the valley with the comforting feeling that things were about to improve. Much of the route was along paved paths that ran between stone walls, a feature of the area. My lack of a companion did not last long. Before I reached the top of the valley I came across John, a young walker from Sheffield whom Ben and I had met at Globe Farm a couple of days previously. I explained how I had lost my earlier companion and when we discovered we were staying at the same locations until Malham we joined forces.

The next section of the route, over Pry Hill and onwards to Colden Water was quite complicated and we had to follow the map closely to avoid straying from the path. During much of that section the towers of Heptonstall's two churches kept a watchful eye on our progress. They lay about one and a half miles to the east and the squat tower of the old church (circa 1260) stands proudly beside its taller Victorian counterpart.

We reached another deep valley with rich woodland carpeting much of its floor. Through the attractive setting flows the lively Colden Water, which we crossed by a fine old stone footbridge. At this point we were crossing the Calderdale Way once more.

Another climb followed towards the hamlet of Colden and in a short time we reached Long High Top where were on open moorland again. The going was reasonable as we followed one of the many paths, used in times gone by as packhorse routes and salt ways, that cross Heptonstall Moor. Ancient crosses also mark routes used by the monks of Whalley Abbey.

As it leaves the moor, the Way passes the Pack Horse Inn that still stands on the Hebden Bridge to Colne road. From here it is a long and gradual climb onto Haworth Moor and as we made the steady pull out of the valley we passed the three Walshaw Dean Reservoirs that are interlinked and controlled by Halifax Corporation.

The reservoir lodge was undergoing renovation and we called out a greeting to a man lying precariously on the roof up a ladder. He paused in his work to respond that he thought we were right barmy to be wandering the countryside with huge packs on our back. We told him that we stood less chance of breaking our backs than he did if he happened to fall from his ladder. With a broad grin and a rude gesture he sent us on our way.

As we left the reservoirs behind the familiar battle with boggy peat was resumed during our steady ascent to the watershed that overlooks Stanbury and Haworth Moors. John was making good progress in the conditions with his long legs that were a good deal younger than mine. I was struggling to keep pace with him and was glad of the occasional respite when we stopped to take in the view over the wide expanse of moorland behind us.

The weather was quite humid that afternoon and John and I were wringing with sweat as we reached Withins Height. Unfortunately the now overcast conditions hid the fine views we should have had down to Haworth and over Stanbury Moor. What we could see was the nearby ruin of Top Withens. Deciding that this would make a good spot for a late lunch stop, we hurried down to it. A persistent wind, one that reeked of consumption, whistled around the moor and we were glad to get some shelter from it. As we took our well-earned break we were all but molested by ravenous, sandwich-partial sheep.

I tried to picture Emily Brontë struggling up here from Haworth in her long skirts and high-laced boots. I could imagine her sitting in solitary silence, a thick shawl clasped around her shoulders and her teeth chattering. She would probably be doodling with her quill pen as she dreamed of some hunky male taking her into his arms in a passionate embrace. Longing for her hero to ride past on his white horse, she may have gazed at the farmhouse where we now sat and imagined herself and the object of her desires living in it. Thus was sown the seed of Heathcliffe and *Wuthering Heights.* In case any Brontë lovers take umbrage, this is purely my personal version of the creation of her most famous novel!

When John and I and the sheep were replete, it was time to leave the Way and make what turned out to be a four-mile detour to the Youth Hostel situated between Haworth and Oakworth. We took the path that dropped steeply to the Brontë Falls, another tourist attraction. Unfortunately this turned out to be little more than a trickle, but perhaps we caught it on a bad day - although I would have thought there'd been quite enough rain for it to put on a better show. A broad, level track took us to the outskirts of Haworth and within easy reach of its main tourist attraction, Brontë Parsonage. This is well worth a visit as it is now a museum with many of the rooms laid out exactly as they were when the Brontës lived there, depicting life in those austere times. Across the churchyard, bulging with gravestones, stands the Parish Church where the Rev Brontë was the rector for many years. The cobbled main street of the village is flanked by shops and cafés and is thronged with tourists throughout the year. Haworth certainly is indebted to the Brontës as the shops are packed with souvenirs of the family and almost all the articles seem to have acquired a Brontë connection. There had even been a bakery at the bottom of the main street that used to make Brontë biscuits.

John was fascinated by the village and its literary connections, but as I lived only a few miles away I knew it quite well already. When planning the walk, the thought had crossed my mind that I might go home for that night. However, honour prevailed and I had decided not to cheat by sneaking off.

Leaving the village, we made our way along the road from Haworth to Oakworth, and after about a mile we reached the hostel, which stands well back from the road. It is a very handsome former mill-owner's house, with an imposing stone exterior. Inside is a beautiful oak-panelled staircase and hallway, overlooked by some fine stained glass windows.

As there were not many staying that evening we had a free choice of meal, as opposed to the set menu, which was very enjoyable. After supper, John and I struck up a conversation with three Australians who were walking in the area. We discovered that the Brontës' fame had reached the other side of the world.

DAY FORTY-TWO : HAWORTH - EARBY

The following day the sky was overcast at breakfast but cleared later and we enjoyed sunshine, blue skies and a temperature in the seventies. Quite a change from what we had been experiencing.

We walked back to the point where we had left the path at Top Withens the evening before. From there it was easy walking down to Ponden Reservoir that lies beside the Haworth to Colne road. The last section of the descent is very steep with good views of the reservoir and valley below. Near the reservoir stands Ponden Hall, which is another reminder of the Brontës as this was supposedly the Thrushcross Grange of *Wuthering Heights*. It looked well preserved with an interesting stone frontage but we were anxious to keep going so did not stop to look around.

The next obstacle was Ickornshaw Moor, which stood between us and the village of Cowling. It is an arduous stretch of countryside with paths that are conspicuous by their absence. We made reasonable progress across the peat, which was fairly dry for a change. The sunshine encouraged John to don his shorts and wide-brimmed sun hat. He was unfortunately brought down to earth when he got a bootful of water by not watching where he was treading. At least he didn't pay the same price as Ben for his carelessness.

There is not much interest on the moor itself, apart from several signs imploring you to sample Cowling's accommodation, tea shop and village store, but as it stands high up, there are decent views from its flat top. On a good day you can make out Pinhaw Beacon to the north and behind it in the far distance some peaks of the Yorkshire Dales. It was comforting to know that we would soon be amongst them, out of the peaty terrain and into the lovely limestone country around Malham. As we dropped down to Cowling, the broad outline of Earl Crag dominated the skyline to the east. Superimposed on this gritstone edge were the twin monuments of Wainman's Pinnacle and Lund's Tower.

At the point where the Way joins the A6068, the Keighley to Colne road, Cowling bombarded the walker with arrows painted on everything in sight including a fence, the pavement and kerbstones. The village seemed keen to ensure that Pennine Way walkers take the correct route. On the other hand they may have had the devious intention of luring them away from the centre of Cowling, which somewhat negates the signs on Ickornshaw Moor. Whichever purpose they serve, they lead to a series of field paths that skirt the village, ending at the road to Lothersdale.

By a remarkable coincidence, the direction signs disappeared abruptly and we were left to use the map to follow the route to Lothersdale across farmland and along lanes. The signs had obviously served their purpose of relieving the walker of his cash or ushering him away from the village. Cowling obviously had no further use for us, or was glad to be rid of us. To be fair, I must point out that this situation is much improved, as a good system of direction signs now leads the way to Lothersdale.

It was pleasant, firm walking over meadows decked with buttercups. Lothersdale is a lovely village and, tucked away between attractive hills, does not reveal itself until the unsuspecting walker is almost upon it. As we approached, the first intimation of the village was the appearance of a tall, well-preserved mill chimney rising from the valley like a solitary finger. As we descended the steep hillside, the mill came into view in its most attractive setting.

The mill wheel has since been rebuilt and part of the mill itself is still in use, as are the adjacent mill-worker's stone cottages with their neat gardens and colourful window boxes. We had already travelled a fair distance that day and had worked up a thirst, so we tried to get a drink in the village, but annoyingly the Post Office-cum-village shop was closed. To add insult to injury the inviting pub was also shut. John was so thirsty he asked at one of the houses for a drink of water, but was told it was unfit to drink.

It was with annoyance that we dragged ourselves away from Lothersdale, still perspiring and gasping for a drink. We were to sweat even more as there followed a long pull up to Pinhaw Beacon. The going was good as we climbed from the valley across fields dotted with sheltering copses and threaded by gurgling streams. After a while we reached the higher moorland approach to the Beacon. We crossed this on a wide track that kept us away from the worst of the peat.

As we stood on Pinhaw Beacon we were rewarded with superb views in every direction. The beloved Yorkshire Dales were coming ever closer although a slight haze prevented us from seeing much further than Penyghent to the north. We were able to see landmarks ranging from Pendle Hill in Lancashire, the Bowland Fells to the west and the fells around Wharfedale and Ribblesdale. The limestone hills above Malham could also be seen dominated by Fountain's Fell. Pinhaw was a place to rest, take stock and drink in the wide-ranging countryside that Yorkshire and Lancashire have to offer.

Having toiled our way up there, it was a wrench to leave that fine viewpoint but we were only a few miles from journey's end for that day. This was at Earby, hidden in the valley that runs from Skipton to Colne. So we came down from Pinhaw and skirted Elslack Moor, the last stretch of moorland before joining the pastureland that heralds the start of limestone country. We unfortunately had to make a detour here, which proved to be decidedly muddy, from the main path down to the industrialisation of Earby.

Our stay that night was at a Youth Hostel, which comprised two converted terraced cottages. It turned out that John had arranged for his wife Anne to join him for the evening, to relieve the daily monotony of foot-slogging. She was there to greet us on our arrival, and after John and I had showered and changed we all went out for a meal, I having accepted their kind invitation with alacrity. Anne drove us to a nearby inn with a good restaurant and we enjoyed a first-class dinner, which was most welcome after the strain of the last five days. I fear that we must have bored Anne rigid with tales of our journey but she had the good grace to appear interested.

DAY FORTY-THREE : EARBY - MALHAM

The weather on the following morning was ideal - blue sky, bright sunshine and a light breeze. The sun streamed through the windows of Earby hostel as I tucked into a large plateful of bacon, eggs, sausages and fried bread. Then, during our climb back to the Pennine Way path, I suffered pains in my chest, which I put down to indigestion, heartburn or an impending heart attack. I agree with Mike Harding's comments in his *Walking the Dales* that if you are going to expire, it might as well be in style, whilst walking the hills, rather than growing old and infirm and having to be looked after like a baby. I pressed on, thinking that if I was stricken, at least it would be whilst doing what I enjoyed. You will have gathered by now that it was merely indigestion and that I am a confirmed hypochondriac.

Regain the path I did and headed with John towards Thornton in Craven, which lay one and a half miles away in the valley ahead. We were onto grass now and were descending a fairly steep slope when I nearly came to grief. My feet slid on the rather slippery surface and my rucksack took me off balance, depositing me flat on my back in the middle of the field. A flock of sheep grazing nearby had been watching our progress idly, apparently unconcerned but as I lay spreadeagled on the ground they suddenly broke into lusty bleating, which could only be interpreted as laughter. Sheep are not as dumb as they are made out to be.

John, laughing too, pulled me to my feet and checked that I was sound in wind and limb. Only my pride was dented.

Thornton is a pleasant village but unfortunately spoiled by traffic that thunders through it on the main A56 road. We didn't linger, therefore, but found the path out of the village for the Leeds and Liverpool Canal, which it then follows for a mile or so. There were many boats moored on the canal, people sunbathing, or angling and contented families of ducks.

We left the busy stretch of canal for more field paths that took us to Gargrave on the A65 road running from Skipton to Settle. We ate our sandwiches by the attractive stone bridge over the River Aire. In springtime there is a profusion of daffodils and blossoms of every hue here. Gargrave is a place to savour, for all too often one rushes through it on the drive to the more spectacular Lake District. The Dalesman Café stands on the main road where the Way crosses it and is a well-loved haunt of cyclists and walkers.

In front of us lay a lovely seven-mile walk to Malham, and this began at the foot of Eshton Moor. Once over the crest of the moor we took in the splendid view along the valley of the infant River Aire. Walking carefully to ensure no slip-ups on my part as we descended the grassy slopes of Eel Ark Hill, the river was soon reached. John and I then enjoyed a delightful riverside walk that took us past the hamlet of Airton with its shapely stone bridge and onwards to Hanlith. Here we passed the impressive Hanlith Hall, which displays some intriguing stone carvings on its frontage. We were not far from our objective of Malham at this point and we were rewarded during the final section of the day's walk with the dramatic view of Malham Cove. Its sheer face dominates the skyline beyond the village of Malham, one of the most visited villages in Britain.

Malham stands in a beautiful limestone setting, but sadly suffers the scourge of tourism. The lovely Malham Beck flows peacefully through its centre and as we joined this watercourse we realised we were at a critical point of the walk. Was it not common knowledge among the aficionados that if you reach Malham the odds that you will complete the whole walk will have swung in your favour? So here we were, one-third of the Pennine Way completed, with a good chance of reaching Kirk Yetholm. To celebrate our achievement, we spent the latter part of the evening in the Buck Inn. However, there was another reason for our visit to this popular watering hole. John and I were to part company as he was staying for two nights in Malham. Looking forward to his first visit to the area, he had planned to explore the surrounding countryside on the following day. So, it was with some sadness that we drank to each other's success at the end of our last meeting together.

Prior to this, as we sat down for our evening meal at the Malham Youth Hostel, suitably scrubbed, we found that there were only two other walkers for company. These turned out to be a married couple, Ian and Sheila, who were walking part of the Way. John and I were to soon discover that Ian, although of slim build, could eat like a horse. The first course of our meal that evening was soup, which was in plentiful supply. When we had all consumed at least four helpings, the warden deposited a large pan on the table telling us to eat up or it would go to waste. It was still half full of soup and everyone laughingly agreed that this was too much of a good thing. Everyone except Ian that is, who said he would happily finish the remaining contents. To our amazement, not only did he polish off every last drop, he even scraped out the pan and the dregs from the ladle! He appeared to have no problem eating the rest of the meal.

After supper, Ian produced his party piece, in the form of a tea bag. He claimed to hold the world record for the number of cups of tea obtainable from one bag - sixteen! As I kept company with Ian and Sheila for much of the remainder of the walk, I was able to witness his remarkable prowess. However, I'm glad that I never had to sample the tea that he produced after the third cup.

That evening I rang Ben to see how his injury was progressing. His arm was in a sling, he told me, but the swelling in his hand was going down. When I told him how much I was enjoying the walk, especially now I was in limestone country and the weather was good, he said that he was longing to join me.

DAY FORTY-FOUR : MALHAM - HORTON IN RIBB'DALE

I left Malham, after saying goodbye to John, as I had entered it, along the Malham Beck for a short distance. After a brief road walk I joined the well-trodden field path leading to Malham Cove. Thousands of visitors to Malham each year walk this route to gaze at the great limestone buttress and the nearby strip 'lynchets', or medieval cultivation terraces, on the surrounding slopes. The cove, created by a great upthrust of limestone, is one of the most photographed sights in Yorkshire.

On top of it sits a fine limestone pavement, which is a mecca for geologists and students who come from far afield to study the features and development of the landscape. A series of stone steps leads up the side of the cove - quite a test of endurance for the unfit walker. The effort is well rewarded with the view that opens up to the south. On the rugged, sheer face, climbers of varying skills can be seen clinging like limpets.

Once across the pavement I made a slight detour into the Dry Valley, which squeezes between the weathered limestone formations that overshadow it. This valley is a dramatic representation of sculptured limestone and formerly had a stream running through it, which plunged over the cove. To leave the valley, I had to clamber up a steep rock-strewn barrier to reach the grassy moorland beyond.

The morning was again warm and sunny and there was a slight breeze. As I walked along the springy turf to Malham Tarn I decided I could not wish for more pleasant walking conditions. There was a slight haze hanging over the tarn, but this added to the atmosphere. The Pennine Way is certainly not all about slogging through peat.

Malham Tarn is set in superb surroundings and lies on a bed of hard Silurian slate, which is how it comes to exist amongst an area of limestone. On its northern bank stands a grand house that formerly belonged to the Victorian industrialist Walter Morrison. He was fond of entertaining and amongst his guests were Charles Darwin, John Ruskin and Charles Kingsley. Tarn House is now owned by the National Trust and is used by the Field Studies Council as a training centre.

My contented mood was punctured as I began the climb past Tennant Gill Farm onto the slopes of Fountains Fell. To be accurate, the ascent of the fell is a long drag, with the peat reappearing as an added obstacle. As I neared the top, who should I come upon but my new-found friends Ian and Sheila. We made our way together to the flattish summit and investigated a hole, which was poorly fenced. I dropped a stone down it to test the depth and estimated it to be around fifty feet. Coal mining was prevalent here centuries ago and the hole may have been one of the numerous shafts that were sunk.

The view from the summit was superb in the fine weather that we were enjoying. Across Silverdale could be seen the extensive hump of Penyghent, its outline resembling the 'Sleeping Lion', as it is nicknamed. This was to be my next port of call. Ian and Sheila were having an extended stay for some refreshment, so I left them to relax and take in their beautiful surroundings. As I descended the rough, stony path into the sheltered valley, I came across two fellow walkers also enjoying their lunch. They were walking the Pennine Way as far as Hawes and were doing it in easy stages. It had taken them a fortnight since leaving Edale, but they were savouring the experience. I was introduced to the jungle telegraph that operates along the Way, walkers swopping items of interest as they pass. These fellows had heard about Ben and his accident and they asked if I had news of him.

There is rather a boggy descent across fields at the base of Fountains Fell before the road is reached. A spell of firm roadside walking along grass verges took me to the track to Dale Head Farm past some limestone outcrops that appeared to be popular with picnickers. A sign indicated that I must leave the road and join the well-trodden path up to Penyghent. The ascent from the road is steady at first, and the shape of the fell changes rapidly from this angle as you make a curved approach to it. The gritstone cliff that forms the southern edge of the summit reveals its variety of buttresses and crevices. I worked up quite a sweat as the climbing became stiffer and as I paused too get my breath back, I was able to savour an already commanding view of Fountains Fell back across the valley. Although the going was hard, I paced myself and climbed steadily before negotiating the steep clamber up the rocky gritstone section.

As the slope to the summit was reached, I was pleased to see that the bogs were drying nicely in the sunshine. When I finally reached the trig point a panorama spread beneath me. Through a shimmering heat haze I was able to make out a number of landmarks ranging from Pendle Hill in the south, to Great Shunner Fell, my next objective to the north. Whernside, Ingleborough and Baugh Fell stood out from the rippling landscape that surrounded me. As I stood drinking in the inspiring vista, two young ladies brought me down to earth by asking if I would take their photograph. They were camping in Horton in Ribblesdale for a few days and wanted to prove to their friends that they had climbed Penyghent.

Progress down the western flank was relatively smooth although I watched the rocky ground carefully at the start of the descent. I had no wish to get down to Horton in record time by missing my footing. As the ground levels out the Way follows one of the numerous green lanes in the area, Horton Scar Lane, as it makes for Horton.

I found my night's resting place, a cottage in the village, without difficulty. To my delight it stood right on the Way, opposite the welcoming Crown Hotel. After a glorious soak in a steaming hot bath, I had a good meal in the hotel, which brought on a satisfying feeling of contentment and also extreme tiredness. I retired early to my bed and was luxuriating in its enveloping softness when I was jerked from semi-consciousness by the sound of voices in the corridor. It sounded like late arrivals being shown to their room, but I was too tired to take much notice of their conversation and fell sound asleep.

DAY FORTY-FIVE : HORTON - HAWES

After a restful night I dressed and went down to breakfast the following morning to be met with two familiar faces. Who should be sat at the table but the 'Brothers in Law.' They had been the late arrivals the previous evening. I was intrigued to hear how they had managed to get this far, after their earlier disasters: apparently, they had stayed for the previous two nights at Lothersdale and Gargrave respectively. This explained their lateness in getting to Horton for they would have walked twenty-two miles from Gargrave. This seemed a pretty tall order, considering their navigational skills.

They appeared none the worse for their ordeal thus far and were going to make an early start for Hawes that morning. After chatting for a bit about the day's walk, they left me finishing a leisurely breakfast. Starting off a little later than usual, the first part of my journey was along another green lane, this one called Harber Scar Lane, one of a network of tracks used centuries ago by the monks of Jervaulx Abbey who bred horses in Horton.

I was now walking through an area containing numerous potholes, with several situated near the path. I paused to gaze down Sell Gill Hole, but even looking down one gives me a feeling of unease, and actually descending one is unthinkable as far as I am concerned. For people who like potholes there are plenty to choose from hereabouts: the largest and most distinctive being Hull Pot. This particular hole can be more conveniently examined following the descent from Penyghent on the previous day's walk, as it lies a short distance from the point where the Way joins Horton Scar Lane.

After an hour's walking I came upon the 'Brothers in Law' sitting at the side of the track at its junction with the one that descends from Penyghent and heads for the road leading to Ribblehead. They were pondering over their map, obviously uncertain where to go next. One of them pointed along the path in the direction of the Ribblehead road and suggested that they should follow that route. Knowing the area fairly well, I pointed them in the right direction and on the map finger-traced the route to their destination at Hawes. I offered to walk with them, but they declined, saying that they would take their time and should have no further problems.

Satisfied that they could not go wrong on the straightforward route, I carried on and was soon climbing the winding path up to Cam End where the Roman road from Ingleton to Bainbridge is joined. At the approach to the climb, in Ling Gill, a fine packhorse bridge is crossed, recalling the times when this was a well-trodden route. The Roman road, or Cam High Road as it is known is now a muddy, deeply rutted track. Its extensive erosion is a sorry sight, aided and abetted by the presence of motor cycles, which have gouged the deep ruts that make walking almost impossible.

Putting aside my anger at the loutish treatment of the ground underfoot I pressed on and soon reached the point where the Pennine Way runs in a channel between the lower slopes of Dodd Fell and the Snaizeholme Valley. Here I met a walker who told me of the time he had found three feet of snow blocking the channel in early April. He was forced to walk along the higher slopes of the fell to avoid the snow and had noticed several dead sheep embedded in it. That was a sobering reminder of the harsh conditions that can affect a hill farmer in the Yorkshire Dales.

My progress had been good and, as I only had the descent into Hawes remaining, I stopped for a late lunchtime snack. The sunshine that had accompanied me for so long deserted me. Menacing black clouds loomed overhead and a chill wind was blowing. This was not the time to stop and admire the view, I decided as the cloud began to envelop me. My stay was brief, therefore, and I was soon on my way down to Hawes to escape the worst of the elements.

As I entered the pleasant market town at the head of Wensleydale, which I had become familiar with through my walks around the Yorkshire Dales, I was in for a surprise. No sooner had I reached the market place than who should I see a short distance away? You have surely guessed right - there as large as life were the 'Brothers in Law' walking along the road. I was puzzled as to how they could have overtaken me. First, they were not fast walkers, taking into account their age and lack of map reading ability; second, I had made good time and was sure that they had not passed me. There was only one other possible explanation. They must have taken the path to the Ribblehead road and got a lift into Hawes. It now became clear how they had managed to keep up with me so far. They were obviously not above a little bending of the rules. Deciding to keep my peace, I did not wish to embarrass them into explanations for their remarkable progress since I felt that their secret would be exposed sooner or later.

I strolled around Hawes market and shops, which cater for a variety of tastes, ranging from walking, reading and souvenir hunting to rope making. This ancient craft is still carried on here, as is cheese making, for this is the home of Wensleydale cheese. Some time ago the Hawes Creamery where the cheese is made had been taken over by a large dairy company and plans were in hand to close it and move production elsewhere. This caused a public outcry but spurred people into action and fortunately local business people purchased it and retained this proud heritage, re-naming it the Wensleydale Creamery. Traditional methods are now being used and customers are not only enjoying an improvement in quality, but also an opportunity to see cheese making in action in its modern visitor centre.

The town stands amongst some of the finest Dales scenery, not least being the limestone features of Abbotside Common, which was formerly owned by Jervaulx Abbey. Many of the surrounding fields are traversed by stone-flagged paths, laid to provide a walkway for quarrymen. Not for their convenience, but to prevent their boots from wearing away the grass.

At the appropriate time I made my way to the Youth Hostel,

whose facilities were good. As I was enjoying a tasty meal I struck up a conversation two ladies who were also walking the Way. They appeared to be enjoying themselves and our paths continued to cross until we reached Bellingham.

After supper I spent a relaxing couple of hours watching television. So much for the rigours of the Pennine Way!

DAY FORTY-SIX : HAWES - KELD

The following morning I headed for the bridge that spans the River Ure on the outskirts of Hawes. As I leaned over its parapet, the river looked resplendent as it rushed beneath me, hurrying on its journey to Bainbridge, Leyburn and beyond.

It was now my turn to take one of those stone-flagged paths across the fields to Hardraw whose claim to fame is the highest waterfall above ground in England. It is just below one hundred feet high and tumbles into a secluded limestone amphitheatre whose acoustics render it suitable for brass band concerts. The only access to the waterfall is through the Green Dragon Inn and there cannot be many pubs with such an impressive attraction in their back garden. What a treat for its customers!

As you leave the hamlet of Hardraw the gradient increases where the lower slopes of Great Shunner Fell are encountered. Although it is a long drag to the top of this barrier that divides the head of Wensleydale from that of Swaledale, the climb is not too onerous. During my steady progress to the summit I met a young walker who had spent the previous night in the porch of a church. As the vicar arrived to open the church that morning, he almost fell over the sleeping walker. When they had both recovered from their surprise, the vicar told the man he would have been more than happy to put him up at the vicarage. A very kind thought - but somewhat too late. The young man told me that he was wandering around the Dales for a short holiday with no pre-planned route. He was travelling wherever his fancy took him.

Other walkers I met included a man and two women who were walking together from Kirk Yetholm south to Gargrave. I learned that one of the ladies was seventy-two years old but she seemed fit and sprightly. No sooner had I said goodbye to them than I came across three Dutchmen who had also walked from Kirk Yetholm. As they had approached me at a good pace, I christened them the 'Flying Dutchmen'. This seemed a good day for walkers doing the Pennine Way in the reverse direction.

Leaving the boggy summit, which, at 2,340 feet was the highest point of the Way so far, I hoped to get below cloud and enjoy the view down the upper reaches of Swaledale - one of the finest in the Yorkshire Dales. This is enhanced by the stone-built villages of Thwaite and Muker that nestle in the verdant valley, flanked by meadows bursting with wild flowers in springtime.

On entering Thwaite I was met by several signs shepherding walkers in single file through the adjacent fields. At one stage, I was forced to walk between two lengths of twine, which defined the footpath, but I do appreciate that these conditions may have been brought about by damage to property and crops. It is probably a case of a few irresponsible walkers spoiling things for the majority.

However, I did have a look around this tiny village that was named by the Vikings who settled in the area, its name being the Norse word for a clearing. This hardy race inhabited the upper reaches of the valleys and the higher ground, as they were basically hill farmers.

Just as Haworth owes much to the Brontës, Thwaite is indebted to the Kearton brothers who were two of its favourite sons. Richard and Cherry Kearton became famous naturalists and early wild life photographers, and their achievement is marked in various ways in the village including the Kearton Guest House, a very nice establishment.

As I was not pressed for time that afternoon I made a short detour to Muker, an attractive village lying at the foot of Kisdon Hill. The tea shop, village store and literary institute give it a pleasant air. It is very popular with visitors and is jammed with cars during the summer months. Who did I see emerging from the pub but the 'Brothers in Law' who were still making remarkable progress. I did not wish to approach them as their secret would be revealed, but I did enjoy a good chuckle to myself.

I made my way back onto the Pennine Way and started up the steep climb to Kisdon Farm that stands high up on the impressive hill of the same name. I found the subsequent walk above the Swale Gorge one of the most enjoyable sections of the Pennine Way.

Words cannot adequately convey the beauty of the area but suffice to say that the views from this high-level path are magnificent. The infant River Swale cuts through surrounding hills that, in autumn, are ablaze with colour. Walking was rough along the flank of Kisdon Hill but I was compensated by the view across the valley to the deep cleft of Swinner Gill and the distant hump of Rogans Seat. The path forming the low-level route of Wainwright's Coast to Coast path could also be discerned hugging the opposite bank of the river.

As the approach to Keld is made, the ruins of Crackpot Hall come into view in the valley and the alternative high-level Coast to Coast path can be seen snaking up Swinner Gill onto the high moorland beyond. This path traverses the higher reaches of the former lead-mining area, crossing the desolate expanses of mine spoilage at Merry Field and Old Gang, before rejoining the river route at Reeth.

The Swale Gorge is evidently a popular walking area, borne out by the numerous people that I met during my traverse of it. Several family groups and other walkers passed me and a number of them commented on the beauty of the surroundings.

When the bridge over the River Swale is reached, on the approach to Keld, a superb view of East Gill Force is obtained, where the peaty-brown water surges alongside the Way to plunge into the main body of the river. Close by, the Pennine Way and Coast to Coast path merge for a mere hundred yards. This is the only part of both walks where they march together - a true crossroads.

Keld is a throwback to earlier times. Seemingly untouched by the passing years, its scattered stone buildings recall a peaceful, bygone age. There are two chapels in the village but no public house. This was closed around forty-five years ago. Known as the Cathole Inn, it was puchased by a local farmer, Jim Alderson, and converted to a house. Anyone wanting a drink will have to stay at East Stonesdale Farm, which has a residential licence and is a popular stopping place on the Pennine Way and Coast to Coast routes.

My destination was the Youth Hostel, which was formerly a shooting lodge. I found it to be a comfortable, well-run hostel, with good food. To my delight Sheila and Ian, who I had not seen since leaving them on top of Fountains Fell, re-appeared. They had stayed in Horton and Hawes as I had done but at different lodgings and had wandered around indulging in a little sightseeing. During supper Ian scraped the soup pan once more and produced innumerable cups of tea from his single tea bag. He promised he did not carry the same tea bag from hostel to hostel!

Later that evening we walked along the river, which looked resplendent in the mellow sunshine. It was a pleasant feeling to be surrounded by such beauty on the Pennine Way.

DAY FORTY-SEVEN : KELD - BALDERSDALE

The following morning it was time to say farewell to Swaledale and head for the highest public house in England at Tan Hill. Sunshine and a slight breeze accompanied me as I climbed from the valley, frequently turning to take in the retrospective view of Swaledale, which expanded with every step that I took. After crossing Lad Gill, ravaged moorland engulfed me that was formerly bustling with activity. Like Fountains Fell, cheap coal was mined here by workmen who, struggling for survival, didn't apparently have the time or the inclination to fill in the redundant shafts.

A little further on an old mine track is joined which leads directly to the Tan Hill Inn, but before entering I crossed from the familiar county of Yorkshire into the unknown reaches of Co. Durham. The old inn formerly quenched the parched throats of coalminers, packhorsemen and sheep drovers - and now Pennine Way walkers. It is a friendly place where travellers have met for centuries and nowadays is just the spot to enjoy a relaxing drink with fellow walkers whilst steeling yourself for the forthcoming dubious privilege of squelching your way across Sleightholme Moor.

All too soon I had to leave the lovely old stone fireplace, blackened by smoke from countless welcoming fires. Once outside, the fresh air invaded my nostrils and I blinked in the bright sunlight. I gazed over the foreboding stretch of bleak, featureless moorland that stood between me and the A66 road, which cuts through a strategic channel in the Pennines - the Stainmore Gap.

Fortunately the spell of good weather that I had recently enjoyed had started to dry out some of the more treacherous bogs and my passage was therefore made easier. I crossed the moor with a feeling of relief for myself, and pity for those less fortunate souls destined to make the crossing in foul weather. Even so, I was accompanied for part of this stretch by a group of walkers who continually complained about the hard going.

At Trough Heads Farm a tantalising route decision was necessary. The main path heads for God's Bridge, which is a natural limestone rock bridge over the River Greta, before crossing the A66 road at Pasture End. I plumped for the delights of Bowes by taking the alternative path or the 'Bowes Loop' as it is known. This makes a wide detour to the east but it is well worth the effort if time permits. Accordingly, I set off for East Mellwaters, forsaking God's Bridge, which a walker in the Tan Hill Inn had told me was a beautiful spot

I was not disappointed by Bowes' historic remains, but found the place itself fairly undistinguished. The castle, or more accurately the remains of its Norman keep, stand proudly in isolation amongst fields that were formerly the site of a Roman fort. All but a few ramparts of the fort are long gone but the strategic importance of Bowes did not diminish when the Romans left. As I stood on that historic site and thought about the Roman legions marching through Stainmore Gap, so must have done the Normans who, realising how crucial it was to guard this important route through the Pennines, built their castle or watchtower here.

When I had had my fill of Bowes' history, I walked through the centre of the village and bumped into none other than the 'Brothers in Law' who seemed to be dogging my footsteps. They were conveniently staying here whereas I had several miles of open country to negotiate before my overnight stay at Baldersdale Youth Hostel. I struggled to keep a straight face whilst listening to the account of the hardships of their journey to date.

I bade my two friends farewell as time was pressing and set off on what turned out to be a difficult section of the walk. On the outskirts of the village I passed a building, which was, supposedly, the 'Dotheboys Hall' depicted in *Nicholas Nickleby*. The hardest task was negotiating the route, for the path was indistinct in places and I was overcome with a nagging feeling that I would not find the hostel before dark. Much of this section was over rough terrain, which made the going tough.

After a further mile of toil I reached Goldsborough, a distinctive hill that thrusts itself above the undulating countryside and stands sentinel over Blackton Reservoir. With a sigh of relief, I eventually succeeded in reaching the narrow road running into Baldersdale. A thankfully short journey then brought me within sight of the hostel, a converted farmhouse, which stands at the head of Blackton Reservoir.

Baldersdale is counted as the halfway point of the Pennine Way. I now had a cause for a double celebration, for I had found the hostel before nightfall and had covered half of my journey.

Another piece of good fortune presented itself, for who should I see as I entered the hostel but Ian and Sheila. As the place was self-catering only, we set to work with a will, having purchased provisions from the hostel shop. My supper menu consisted of soup, meat pie and beans - yes, beans again! - rounded off by two Eccles cakes. This was hardly sparkling fare but I did have great entertainment watching Sheila and Ian struggling to create a mouth-watering meal from the most basic ingredients.

Having no soup pan to scrape out, Ian made up for it after supper by seemingly drinking gallons of tea from the now obligatory tea bag. As we relaxed after our meal they described their day's journey from Keld, having chosen the main route from Sleightholme over God's Bridge. They were full of praise for the bridge and waxed lyrical about the numerous wild flowers in that area.

A capable and friendly young warden ran the hostel and during a chat with him I learnt that Hannah Hauxwell lived at Low Birk Hat, a neighbouring farm, and that he had been able to assist her during the hard winter months. Many people will be familiar with the television programme *Too Long a Winter* of some years ago in which she was immortalised by Barry Cockcroft. The depiction of her harsh and lonely life at the farm made her a national celebrity. Hannah has since moved six miles down the valley to enjoy village life in an attractive cottage. When asked how life at the cottage compared to that at Low Birk Hat, Hannah replied, 'better in some respects, worse in others.' She likes the modern conveniences of her present home, such as running water and washing facilities, but misses the open spaces and the 'sands of the Mississippi,' her name for the shore of Blackton Reservoir where she used to wash her clothes. Despite the rigours of washing garments and household linen in its chill waters, she found the setting theraputic, as she does all those that surround water.

DAY FORTY-EIGHT : BALDERSDALE - LANGDON BECK

When I set out from the hostel the next morning, to make my way to Middleton in Teesdale and my destination at Langdon Beck, I was looking forward to visiting the farm at Low Birk Hat that lay a short distance away. The warden had told me that Hannah loved to chat with walkers as they tramped past. Unfortunately, she was not around when I went through but, lingering by the farm I tried to picture it in the depths of winter, with the wind howling over Cotherstone Moor. Tearing myself from the scene, I turned my sights northwards and passed through a field at the front of the farm that is now known as 'Hannah's Meadow.'

My journey to Middleton was one of anticipation, for I was looking forward to my first view of the River Tees, which several friends had told me was such a lively and attractive river. The going at the outset was not hard and I was able to enjoy a fairly relaxed pace, unlike the previous evening. There were several interesting features as I progressed through the Lune Valley and onwards to Crossthwaite Common. The view from Grassholme Bridge across the waters of Grassholme Reservoir is one to be savoured as the Lune valley at this point is in its most attractive mode. The rolling green carpet of the reservoir's grassy banks and surrounding fields is scattered with the darker hues of copses and a lattice-work of steel-grey stone walls. In the far distance, beyond Middleton, the high, austere moorland provides a subtle contrast to the lushness of the valley.

Shortly after leaving the bridge I crossed the Middleton to Brough road. Here I met two fellow Pennine Way walkers who strode up behind me in determined fashion. They were considerably weighted down with their expansive rucksacks but this had not prevented them from making very good time from Bowes, where they had made an early start that morning. Now well into their day's walk they could afford to relax and take a well-earned rest, for their destination was Newbiggin, which is only about three miles past Middleton. I discovered that they liked to get away early in the morning and accomplish most of their day's journey by lunchtime. On this particular day they were planning to take a leisurely look around Middleton before strolling along the banks of the River Tees in the afternoon. Their approach differed significantly from mine as I prefer to keep up a fairly even pace and when I intimated this they laughingly said it would not do for all walkers to be the same.

Wishing them luck as I left them I climbed through the pastures flanking Crossthwaite Common, following my map closely, as they are bounded by an intricate pattern of stone walls. Eventually the route became clearer and the landmark of Kirkarrion appeared. This is a distinctive tree plantation that stands proudly on top of a hill, which was the site of a large tumulus, or burial ground.

I was now entering Teesdale, a delightful area. Middleton came in sight, spread before me, in an inviting setting. The forthcoming seven-mile walk along the River Tees to Langdon Beck ranks with the Swale Gorge as the most outstanding sections of the Pennine Way. That was a treat to be savoured since I stopped for a while in Middleton to explore its agreeable streets. The weather, which had been dull with a light drizzle up to then, suddenly cleared and the sun came out. It was as though the little town seemed determined to be seen at its best. Glinting in the sunshine was a monumental fountain, which trumpets Middleton's history as a lead-mining centre; in fact, the place owes much of its growth and present appearance to the London Lead Company, which was very active in the area.

Looking forward to an enjoyable afternoon's walk, I ate my sandwiches perched on the steps of the ornate fountain that stands beside the attractive tree-lined main street. It is dedicated to a gentleman called Bainbridge, an employee of the London Lead Company.

My lunch completed, I crossed the sturdy stone bridge over the teeming River Tees as I retraced my steps to the Pennine Way path that would take me upstream. The rushing waters beneath my feet were already hurrying towards Barnard Castle, paying no heed to Middleton, as they passed by the town. Their vibrancy eventually decreases as the river matures and threads its way through the sprawling industrialisation of the Vale of Teeside.

The path that hugs the southern bank of the river proved a fine vantage point from which to see its magnificence as it surges over and through some impressive rock formations. Millions of years ago a sheet of dolerite intruded into the strata over a wide area of Upper Teesdale and formed what is known as the Whin Sill; this hard rock is responsible for the three dramatic waterfalls of Low Force, High Force and Cauldron Snout. All three are passed by the Way and the cascades provide splendid spectacles. The path also skirts lush meadows, containing a profusion of wild flowers. I am no connoisseur but there must have been at least thirty species of blooms on display.

As I reached High Force there was a superb view overlooking the falls. The prospect from this bank is free; to view them from the opposite bank one has to pay for the privilege of using the path that runs down from the High Force Hotel. Either way, it is an impressive spectacle. A foaming torrent of water, seventy feet high, crashes over the crest with a roar that invades the ear drums.

It was a wrench to pull myself away and walk on up the river for about one and a half miles. At this point I bade a temporary farewell to the Tees as I headed for my night's rest at Langdon Beck Youth Hostel. The beck from which the fairly remote hostel takes its name is followed for a further half-mile until the Alston Road is reached and it is but a short walk from there.

A formidable lady warden ran the hostel, assisted by her quiet and retiring husband. Susequently, the evening meal was a rather amusing affair. We did not not queue to be served nor have our food brought to the table. We were served through a hatch in the kitchen wall and the husband, whom we never saw apart from fleeting glimpses, would open the hatch prior to each course, place the food on the shelf and then slam down the hatch behind it. This act became part of folklore between Pennine Way walkers and was referred to in several visitors' books at succeeding hostels. There were references to the 'Dragon of the Langdon Beck Youth Hostel', and 'Mr Invisible,' her better half; I wondered how many hatches he got through in a season. I personally found no fault with the way the hostel was run and I had a good laugh at the slamming hatch, which threatened to chop off the fingers of anyone who was over anxious to snatch their food.

After supper that evening I enjoyed swapping tales with fellow hostellers who included a variety of walkers and cyclists. I was particularly intrigued to meet a nun whose interest was acid peat bogs, rather an unusual hobby for one of that calling. She was spending her holiday studying the geology of Upper Teesdale. Walkers doing the Pennine Way in the opposite direction told me that they had not enjoyed the Cheviot section but things had improved since then. They were very impressed with Upper Teesdale, particularly Cauldron Snout, which I would see the following morning.

DAY FORTY-NINE : LANGDON BECK - DUFTON

The following morning dawned sunny and warm, with a cooling breeze to keep perspiration down to a reasonable level. Walking amidst beautiful surroundings on such a bright morning was a pleasure. Although not as dramatic as the section from Middleton to Langdon Beck, Cauldron Snout excepted, the upper reaches of the Tees were still a sight to behold. The river rippled between ever-narrowing rocky clefts, its waters a deep, shiny blue under the sun's rays. How different from the bog-hopping of Kinder and Bleaklow, which now seemed a world away.

The lone building passed that morning was Widdybank Farm, which offered refreshment and camping facilities. Its unusual name is derived from a 'widdy,' or slate pencil, for a small layer of Skiddaw slates had been mined in the area; there is also a ruined pencil mill nearby.

At this point I was overtaken by five young Pennine Way walkers dwarfed by their heavy packs and striding purposefully with heads lowered. A brief conversation revealed that they were aiming to complete the walk in fourteen days and that up to then things were going according to plan. It seemed a bit like a forced march to me but I kept my thoughts to myself and wished them well as they hurriedly strode ahead.

Accommodation is virtually non-existent between this farm and Dufton, twelve miles away across wild country. Many walkers hole up here in bad weather before the long trek to High Cup overlooking Dufton. On this part of the route, walkers actually head in a westerly direction, which is not desirable for laggards like myself who want to progress northwards and get to journey's end as soon as possible.

After leaving Widdybank Farm the river twists and turns and walking becomes difficult on its rocky bank. Negotiating the wide loop under Falcon Clints is helped by the presence of duck-boards, which relieved the strain on my ankles. Beyond the loop a roaring sound could be heard, shattering the peacefulness of the surroundings. As I turned the corner, 150 feet of foaming water confronted me. I had reached the impressive Cauldron Snout that cascades from Cow Green Reservoir. Negotiating the steep scramble up the side of the torrent, I dared not dwell on the possibility of slipping on the wet rocks and falling into the foaming mass.

From the top of the climb it is only a short walk to the reservoir that caused a swarm of protests from naturalists prior to the commencement of its construction in the late 1960's. Amongst its opponents was Wainwright who was disturbed by the prospect of submerging many acres of attractive countryside. Probably the worst effect of this ravage of nature by man was the destruction of countless rare Alpine plants, although some were moved to higher ground to escape the flooding. In lighter vein, I did notice from my map that the county boundary dividing Co. Durham and Cumbria, created in 1974, runs through the centre of the reservoir. I wondered if the residents of each county could only have water from their half!

The view over the reservoir stretched for many miles and on the skyline could be seen the adjacent humps of Great Dun Fell, Little Dun Fell and Cross Fell. The latter at nearly 3,000 feet is the highest point on the Pennine Way. I gazed at those ramparts dominating the horizon with expectancy, tinged with apprehension.

At this point I caught up with a group of walkers travelling part of the Pennine Way. I discovered that they lived under the shadow of Kinder Scout at Hayfield; at least they didn't have far to travel to the start of this 270-mile challenge. We joined forces for the walk to Dufton, which I was grateful for. I had heard it was a lonely moorland stretch to High Cup and companions were just what I needed.

We passed two farms at Birkdale and progressed over the bleak moors until we found the Maize Beck, which would be our guide for part of the journey. After a further mile the path began to improve and there were beautiful wild flowers in abundance. Our progress quickened but it was not long before we were halted in our tracks. The ground suddenly dropped away beneath our feet without warning. We had arrived at the geological phenomenon of High Cup. A vast basin lay before us through which we could look down upon the lovely Eden Valley, with the Lake District hills forming a fine backdrop. The horseshoe-shaped cleft is lined with vertical columns of the now familiar Whin Sill, which has resisted erosion.

This was an ideal spot to eat our lunchtime sandwiches, so we picked a comfortable vantage point on our lofty perch. Having time to study the rugged outlines of the great basin, the myriad fantastic rock formations were a source of wonderment. My eyes were drawn to a stone wall, which soared up the opposite face of High Cup, its highest section appearing almost vertical. I felt great admiration for the builders of that drystone wall because it must have been a feat of endurance to get the stone to its higher reaches and then construct a wall that had obviously stood the test of time.

After skirting the northern edge of the escarpment, we began the three-mile descent to the village of Dufton. On the way we came across Ian and Sheila who had been ahead of us but were just getting ready to start again after a rest stop. Catching up on our respective happenings since leaving Baldersdale, we jauntily descended into the village. The welcome sight of Dufton's village green was soon upon us, surrounded by a fine array of cottages. The hostel was sandwiched amongst them and we lay on the grass nearby waiting for it to open.

I have stayed in many hostels but Dufton wins the prize for supplying first rate food. The helpings were so large I found it difficult to get up from the table when the meal was over. After the gigantic supper a group of us strolled out of Dufton to check the beginning of the route to Great Dun Fell for the next morning. As we did so clouds began to swirl over the fells. That, I was informed, signified the famous 'Helm Wind' that blows down from Cross Fell. It was this wind, my informant unsettlingly rubbed in, that may have given Cross Fell its original name of Fiends' Fell.

Among the hostellers staying was a group of children in the charge of two teachers who kept them under strict control. The school party was walking to Garrigill the following day like myself.

I took the opportunity to talk to one of the teachers who I came to know as Mac McGregor. He was an experienced walker and told me about some of the forthcoming sections of the Pennine Way, particularly the last stretch over the Cheviots. I revealed that I was due to complete that part of the journey in two stages and stay at an isolated farm known as Uswayford. Mac kindly gave me directions to it, such as needing to turn right at the fourth cairn past Windy Gyle before a trek through a forest. I asked him about the Cheviot itself but he did not advise a detour from the path to climb it - 'dull, uninteresting and very boggy.'

I overheard Mac telling his charges that one of the lessons walking teaches you is patience. I have never forgotten that piece of astute advice and agree wholeheartedly that impatience should be avoided, particularly when faced with a challenging climb. It is rare to be able to see the summit of a fell throughout a climb up to it. Most summits are deceptively hard to reach, especially in bad weather. Many times I have thought I am just below the summit when another slope looms up in front - and then another, and quite possibly another. When this happens, you just have to grit your teeth and press on until you achieve your goal. A good tutor of children was Mac McGregor.

DAY FIFTY : DUFTON - GARRIGILL

The scene was idyllic next morning as I walked along the road that separates the two parts of the village green. I was flanked by trees on either side, their ample foliage virtually forming a triumphal archway. The sun shone brightly on the impressive red sandstone of the village pump as I raised my eyes above a backdrop of white-walled cottages to the beckoning distant hills. How tempting it was to delay my plans and remain in the enticing surroundings for a further day. Could it be that my enthusiasm for the village was a ploy to avoid tackling one of the most testing sections of the walk? I could see other walkers heading towards the lane leading out of the village and forced myself to follow them. My delay meant that I was probably the last to leave, despite a hard seventeen-mile journey ahead of me. The realisation of this caused me to step out at a good pace.

Dufton Pike basked in the sunshine as I began to skirt its broad base and a little later I crossed the Great Rundale Beck to begin the ascent of Knock Fell. My feeling of contentment was quickly evaporating with the effort of climbing but even more disturbing was the sight of thick mist beginning to roll down from the heights. It was not long before I was completely enveloped and had to resort to taking a compass bearing for Knock Old Man, a cairn not far from the summit.

Curiously there was not a soul around. I was now paying for my dilatory start by being behind all the other walkers. An eerie silence had descended and there was nothing for it but to press on alone hoping that my bearing was accurate. Longing for some company I stuck to my task up the rapidly increasing gradient. My breathing became laboured as I forged ever upwards and after what seemed an eternity a cairn loomed out of the mist. A quick look at the map indicated a line of cairns on the approach to Knock Old Man. Reckoning this was a false alarm I carried on past more cairns until I reached a grander one, which proved to be my destination. Who should be sheltering beside it but my old friends Ian and Sheila. We had left Dufton separately since they were not staying at the hostel and I was both relieved and elated as I joined them for a cup of tea. The pleasant interlude ended when Sheila suggested that I went on alone as they were in no hurry and didn't want to hold me back. Too macho to admit that I could do with their company I smiled bravely and left them to their second cup of tea. Ian's tea bag was certainly going to get plenty of use that day.

Alone once more in the mist I tackled the steep, but thankfully short climb over the summit of Knock Fell and eventually found the road leading to the radar station on Great Dun Fell. This was originally a track to the surrounding mines, which had been surfaced to provide access to the tall masts and attendant equipment on top of the fell.

As I approached the station I was surprised to find a new encircling boundary fence under construction. It was eight feet high and was obviously there to keep walkers like myself from passing through. The map showed the path leading through the various buildings but it was evident that a detour round the fence was necessary. Unfortunately I became disorientated in the thick fog and found myself plodding round the large circular fence at least twice. I couldn't find the path leading from it and twice ended up at the spot where I had joined it. By this time I was more than a little concerned. Fearful that I could carry on circling the fence all day I took a hopeful compass bearing and left the fence. In the swirling mist I blundered out over the fellside. It was my lucky day, for who should I bump into but Ian and Sheila, who had also lost the path and taken a bearing towards Little Dun Fell. We teamed up and after about twenty minutes of struggling over featureless fellside we met up with the elusive path.

Determined not to lose it we stuck to the path like limpets. Progress onto Cross Fell was steady and we were soon straining our eyes for the numerous summit cairns we knew surrounded the trig point. As the ground levelled out a minor miracle occurred. We walked out of the mist into bright sunshine. The features of the summit plateau stood out clearly before us and, hardly able to believe our luck, we made our way easily to the trig point, at 2,930 feet. We enjoyed a celebratory lunch in the large stone shelter and out came Ian's tea bag for a toast to our achievement. Unfortunately the mist was still below us, blotting out any surrounding views but we were just grateful to find the summit clear.

I was pleased to discover that Ian and Sheila were staying at the same place in Garrigill that evening. We decided to complete the day's journey together. This also provided an opportunity to see how his tea bag would stand up to the strain of a hard day's use.

Before starting our descent we met up with the school party from the Dufton hostel once more. They all made it safely to the top although one or two were limping slightly. We let them go first and followed their route past a row of cairns. They looked to be going in the wrong direction but the masters were good guides and we soon joined the track that took us down to the cairned path that was formerly the old corpse road from Kirkland to Garrigill. The most demanding part of our day's walk was over and we were able to relax with the prospect of only an easy seven-mile descent to come.

There were signs everywhere that lead had been mined extensively in the surrounding area. Spoil heaps, mine shafts, tunnels and ruined buildings were commonplace. One of the buildings was in a reasonable condition and contained fireplaces. This, I discovered, is Greg's Hut, which is used as an emergency shelter by anyone caught in bad weather, or behind schedule.

The mist had disappeared and the journey down to Garrigill along a good track was completed without difficulty. In the improved weather conditions it was possible to see down to the valley of the River South Tyne, our next destination. During our descent we caught up with the back-markers of the school party and I walked with Mac for the last couple of miles to where their minibus was waiting. Being the kind man he obviously was, he had dropped behind their main group to accompany a girl who was hobbling painfully. She would never have made it without his continual encouragement.

Garrigill straddles the River South Tyne but lies a little off the beaten track, probably starting life as a lead-mining settlement. Like Dufton it has a pleasant village green and I was looking forward to my night's stay at the nearby Post Office.

We were made very welcome that evening, the meal lived up to expectations and pleasant company was enjoyed, Ian keeping us entertained with a string of humorous stories. Everyone staying there that night was either doing stretches of the Pennine Way, or the whole thing so we had much in common. As if we had not walked enough that day, we went for a stroll round the village after supper.

DAY FIFTY-ONE : GARRIGILL - ALSTON

The following morning I did not hurry breakfast, which was worth savouring. Gone was the apprehension of the previous morning when I had Cross Fell in front of me; I only had a short walk to Alston that day. Navigation would be simple as the four-mile journey basically follows the river. I made a leisurely start around ten o'clock as I was treating the short journey as a rest day. The hardest task would be to make it last all day and I began to wonder if I had adopted the correct strategy.

Just outside the village I joined a riverside path for an amble alongside the River South Tyne. What the day's walking lacked in quantity, it made up for in quality; it proved to be a decidedly attractive area. Looking at the river in its natural and unfettered state made me conscious of the dramatic change that would eventually befall it. Following its meeting with the River North

Tyne near Hexham it would form the majestic River Tyne that had for so long been the life's blood of the North-East, serving now defunct shipyards at Jarrow and Wallsend. For the time being the infant river was content to ripple towards Alston, its bed and banks strewn with boulders and overlooked by trees of differing hues. The surrounding meadows were speckled with wild blooms and I took the opportunity to stop and study some of them; so often one takes them for granted as one marches past.

As I passed the gateway of a field a farmer emerged from it on his tractor and alongside bounded a large Alsation, barking menacingly. I gave the farmer a cheery, 'Good morning,' whilst keeping a wary eye on his fierce-looking dog. He shouted a terse command at which the animal stopped barking, but approached me with a low growl. Stopping his machine the farmer demanded to know if I was one of the Pennine Way crowd. When I confirmed that I was he replied, 'I thought so. We get a lot of your sort through here and most of you shouldn't be let loose.' The dog was now circling round my legs. 'Staggering about with damn great packs on your backs looking absolutely knackered,' was his next retort. 'Some of you couldn't find your way out of a paper bag, God knows how you expect to walk that Pennine Way!' Before I could reply to this insult the redoubtable farmer, now in full flow, continued: 'walkers come knocking on my door at all hours asking to camp in my field. I can't understand why they can't make proper arrangements instead of wanderin' around like nomads.' When I tried to explain, whilst struggling to remain calm as the animal snarled and nudged at my ankles, that some walkers prefer the flexibility of staying wherever it is convenient, I was met with a snort. 'Can't they do a bit of proper plannin'; where would I be if I didn't plan my work? You should hear some of the horror stories they tell me about wanderin' around like lost sheep.' Mercifully, he stopped to shout at the dog. Seizing my opportunity to escape I made a speedy withdrawal with a quick wave of farewell. Thankfully his dog did not chase me as his owner sat nonplussed on his tractor. Scurrying away, I breathed a sigh of relief at escaping with my ears and legs intact.

My leisurely stroll to Alston that had been so rudely interrupted seemed to be over all too quickly and I was soon at the Youth Hostel. It was now only lunchtime and the hostel itself would not open for several hours but the washing and drying room was conveniently open. I took the chance to do some necessary laundry and then ate my sandwiches. Trusting that my drying clothes would still be there when I returned, I went for a walk around the market town. I have always found hostellers honest people, except for an isolated experience at Bellingham, which I will come to later, and my clothes were untouched upon my return.

There was plenty of time available for an amble around Alston's cobbled streets and for gazing in its shop windows. The place has a relaxed, unspoiled appearance and the shops are handy for self-catering walkers, enabling them to replenish shrinking stocks of food. It claims to be the highest market town in England, but unfortunately there was no market that day, the lovely stone market cross standing in splendid isolation in the market square

As I surveyed the pleasant town centre I was joined by an elderly man who sat down beside me to pass the time of day. He turned out to be a local inhabitant who had lived in the town all his life. Having noticed me studying the market cross he inquired if I would like to know more about it. The original was erected in 1746 he explained, and the present structure was a grade two listed building. Unfortunately, due to wear and tear, and more recently to battering from passing lorries, it had required re-building three times. He indicated a line of stone pillars by the cross and laughingly told me that they were protecting the building from the ravages of passing traffic.

As we parted I thanked him for the information and his farewell remark brought a huge smile to my face. Apparently he had met a pair of elderly walkers in the square the previous day, who had proudly told him that they were walking the Pennine Way. When I asked if one of them had happened to mention that he was seventy-four years old, the man nodded, confirming my suspicion that he was referring to the one and only 'Brothers in Law.' I explained about their adventures and the remarkable progress they had made to forge ahead of me.

The afternoon turned to evening and I was eager for the morrow and to be on my way again. After supper in the hostel I overheard voices with a familiar accent coming from the self-catering kitchen. I went to investigate and found three ladies from Mansfield, the town of my birth, preparing a meal. More accurately, two were cooking and the third, who was suffering terribly from blisters, sat watching her companions. It transpired that they were walking the Pennine Way to raise money for their local hospice. They had never walked any great distance before and, as far as I could make out had not done any preparatory training. Consequently they were plagued by sore feet. Things had got so bad that they had come by taxi from Dufton as the worst sufferer was unable to walk, hoping that a day's rest would enable them to carry on and finish the walk. They must have achieved their aim, for on my next trip to Mansfield I was delighted to see them featured in a lengthy article in the local paper. I felt pleased that they had raised a good sum for charity because they were keen not to let their sponsors down.

It was these ladies who first told me about a fellow walker nicknamed 'Road Runner.' Before my walk was finished his name was on many Pennine Way walkers' lips relaying stories of his great speed and stamina. Apparently this young man had been a great help to these ladies during their trip from Langdon Beck to Dufton. They happened to mention to him at Langdon Beck Youth Hostel that they were apprehensive about finding their way across the moorland. Although he was due a rest day, he offered to accompany them for part of the way. In the event, he guided them the whole distance to High Cup and then returned to the hostel to make the official journey to Dufton the following day. Anyone that helpful was in my view worth meeting. I was to make his aquaintance later, but not for some time.

DAY FIFTY-TWO : ALSTON - GREENHEAD

The first part of the day's route hugged the picturesque valley of the River South Tyne, which had now become a welcome companion. Fortuitously I met Ian and Sheila who had enjoyed the luxury of bed and breakfast accommodation the previous evening. I had only just set out across Alston Bridge and we stayed together for the journey to Greenhead where they were also staying at the Youth Hostel. Discussion centred around our fitness and unimpeded progress. We agreed that we were lucky to have no serious problems with fatigue or blisters. After early rain the skies cleared and we optimistically decided that the weather would be kind to us for the rest of the day.

Maintaining a lively pace we were soon crossing the A689 Alston to Brampton road that threads through the valley, keeping close company with the disused railway that formerly linked Alston to Haltwhistle. We were to re-cross the road several more times that day. A study of the map revealed the Alston stands at an important road junction; no fewer than five roads radiate from it, hence its use as a staging post in former times.

We were looking forward to linking up with the Maiden Way, an ancient marching road heading for Carvoran that stands alongside Hadrian's Wall. However, it was difficult to find as its line was indistinct. According to the map we were to meet up with it several times during our approach to the site of Whitley Castle, a Roman fort, where the soldiers would have rested their tired limbs before their final push to Hadrian's Wall

Ian and Sheila were singing the praises of the river scenery, particularly when we made our way through the attractive meadows beyond the tiny hamlet of Kirkhaugh. They were bemoaning the fact that Bellingham, their finishing point, was looming ever closer but were determined to enjoy the remainder of their journey.

The easy walking brought us rapidly towards Slaggyford, which nestles by the river. This we decided would be a good place to eat our sandwiches and admire the meandering, yet still lively river. Upon reaching the hamlet we relaxed on the riverbank and while we ate we speculated on who Slaggy was, and when he had forded the river. I later discovered the name is derived from the river clattering over its stony bed.

The afternoon section of the walk began well enough as we veered away from the river and onto the rounded contours of Glendue Fell and Hartleyburn Common. It was here that we rejoined the Maiden way, now more clearly discernable as it cut straight through the heathland. We followed the ancient highway for two and a half miles to our farewell intersection with the A689 road.

From this point onwards our surroundings deteriorated and became decidedly uninteresting until the approach to Greenhead. With a mere quarter of the Pennine Way remaining I was not about to let such minor irritations upset me, so, gritting our teeth we struck out over the rather tedious stretch of countryside that would take us to the A69 Brampton to Greenhead road. The path, indistinct and difficult to follow, initially led us through fields before depositing us on trackless moorland. Only the landmark of the trig point on top of Wain Rigg, at a modest height of 900 feet, served to relieve the monotony. However, we we received a little light relief by chatting to a group of Pennine Way walkers that we came upon as they rested. They were still hoping to accomplish the whole distance despite two of their party dropping out at an early stage. Overcome with the pain of ripe blisters on the third day, one of the girls in the group had decided that she could go no further. Her boyfriend, not wishing to leave her, had also dropped out. Their depleted party had remained intact thus far but its members expressed varying reactions to the demands of walking every day for more than two weeks. The more experienced walkers among them were quite enjoying themselves but some of the others, who had come along for company, were not as impressed. We were treated to the full spectrum of their feelings concerning the various sections of the walk. Keen to press on we bade them goodbye and wished them well. I wonder if they ever made it to Kirk Yetholm?

The three of us had by now grown tired of the hummocky grass that had dogged our footsteps for so many miles during our crossing of the foothills at the northern end of the Pennines.

During our approach to the A69 road my eagerness to reach Greenhead was mounting with every step. I was greatly anticipating my first view of Hadrian's Wall, about which I had heard so much, but never seen.

We were striding out as we crossed the road heading for the Roman road known as Stanegate, which signifies the beginning of 'Wall Country.' So intent were we in reaching our objective that I nearly missed the fact that the 200-mile point was rapidly approaching. Hurrying through the hollow depression that forms part of Stanegate we fairly leapt over the stile at the end of it to be confronted by the Vallum, a large ditch, which formerly defended the south side of the Roman Wall. The beckoning 200-mile landmark lay a little way along the path running parallel with the Vallum near its intersection with the B6318 road. We hurried to the spot and stopped to recover our breath, taking the opportunity to survey our surroundings. Annoyingly there were no remaining traces of the Roman Wall at this point and we had to wait until the following day for our first glimpse of it. A consolation was the sight of Thirlwall Castle, now sadly a ruin, standing above the path. This fourteenth-century pele tower stands on a green hill overlooking the footbridge spanning a burn heading for Walltown Quarry.

A detour was now necessary to the Greenhead hostel - a converted church - which lies a quarter of a mile off the path. It was a long quarter-mile for tired legs. Unfortunately, I was feeling somewhat below par by the time we reached the hostel. This was due to a head cold, which had very suddenly developed. I had no idea how I managed to acquire it. There had been no early warning signs; it had just sneaked up on me. Not being able to concentrate on the good chat, which always seemed to follow supper, I went to bed early.

DAY FIFTY-THREE : GREENHEAD - ONCE BREWED

I awoke the next morning feeling much better for the good night's rest, and raring to get going. This I attributed to the tablets that Ian had given me the night before. He was a man prepared for any eventuality.

At breakfast I met a young chap who was walking the entire length of Hadrian's Wall, seventy-three miles from Bowness-on-Solway to Wallsend-on-Tyne. He was being sponsored, the money going to Cancer Research. Waving his toast and marmalade around in the air, he explained the construction of the Wall, which is approximately fifteen feet high and eight feet thick, with a six-foot parapet. Seventeen forts are spaced evenly along its length and at every Roman mile is a small fortification known as a milecastle.

Ian and Sheila were to accompany me once more as they were also having a leisurely day's walk in order to explore the Wall. Our common destination was the hostel at Once Brewed. We were licking our lips in anticipation of a journey through history along the boundary of the great Roman Empire. Our day was to be extremely gratifying, but also surprising, because the actual appearance of the Wall was very different from what I had imagined.

We were to find it in various stages of disrepair along the seven-mile stretch that we covered. Its line follows an escarpment that appears man-made, but is actually a series of crags that necessitate alternate climbing and descent.

The day started bright and sunny; perfect for views along the Wall and of the striking Northumberland scenery. We walked for one and a half miles before we received our much anticipated first sight of the Roman Wall. Eagerly we marched alongside the Roman Ditch that marks the original line of the Wall, quickly skirted Walltown Quarry, where the Wall has unfortunately been destroyed by quarrying, to finally feast our eyes on the first section of the impressive stone rampart. Although sadly a shadow of its former self at this point, its massive bulk undulates over the escarpment, reaching around half of its original height in places.

A little farther on, part of the Wall was being renovated by a group of enthusiasts. The work was being done painstakingly and progress appeared to be very slow. There were many miles to be done stretching in front of them - a daunting task. They certainly earned my admiration for their tireless efforts.

Alongside the Wall a military road ran, replacing the Stanegate and acting as an artery for supplies to the fortifications. I didn't envy the Roman's their task of manning the Wall or transporting provisions in the depths of winter. We were lucky, for we were enjoying pleasantly warm and dry weather.

Ian suggested that I join them on their trip to the Roman Fort at Housesteads and I readily agreed. Although it involved a detour of two and a half miles and a retracing of that distance, the day's mileage would not be onerous. It also meant that I could remain with Ian and Sheila who had only one more day left.

We carried on our intriguing journey in the footsteps of the Roman's, even walking on top of the Wall where its dimensions and solidity allowed. Our undulating and demanding progress was accompanied by remarkable views from the crags that tower above the surrounding countryside. Some have intriguing names, such as Windshields, Peel and Hotbank and all carry their burden of the man-made stone rampart. The highlight was a view over the shimmering blue waters of Crag Lough from Highshield Crag. Ringed with trees and a backdrop of rolling Northumberland hills, it forms a memorable setting.

Our visit to Housesteads proved very worthwhile. The ancient five-acre site, shaped like a playing card, formerly included streets, barracks for the legionaires, granaries and a commander's house. It now displays, in addition to its ruins, more modern attractions, such as a visitor centre, museum, picnic site and other amenities. The museum houses an original plan of the fort and many artefacts portraying the military and civilian roles that it played in those times.

Retracing our steps along the Wall to Once Brewed we surveyed the Wark Forest in the distance, which we would encounter the next day. Before checking in at the hostel we visited the adjacent Tourist Information Centre, from where I purchased some excellent literature about the Wall and its other attendant forts. I asked in the Centre about the unusual names of Once Brewed and its chum down the road, Twice Brewed, and was told that originally there had been an inn and a bothy in the surrounding hamlet. The inn stood in West Twice Brewed and the bothy a quarter of a mile away in East Twice Brewed. Ale supplied by the inn was fermented twice to give added strength, hence the name; the bothy was supplied for walkers who could obtain refreshment there. This bothy was replaced by the Youth Hostel, which was opened by a lady from a local Methodist family. At the opening ceremony she expressed a wish that nothing stronger than tea would be consumed in the hostel and that it would be brewed only once, thus giving rise to the name of 'Once Brewed.' I was confident that Ian would ensure the brewing of large amounts of tea during our stay, but was less convinced that it would qualify as a single brew.

The hostel was seemingly run on a tight budget. Food was in short supply; portions were measured and small and did nothing to satisfy Ian's rapacious appetite. When he had the temerity to ask for more bread with his soup, he was told that there was none available. Amazingly, we were restricted to one cup of tea with our supper, but Ian came to rescue, as I knew he would. We were later able to supplement our liquid intake by a visit to the inn at Twice Brewed to sample the strong ale.

DAY FIFTY-FOUR : ONCE BREWED - BELLINGHAM

Next morning I managed to get another half-slice of toast at breakfast to supplement the one I had been rationed to. A group of friends whom I had met along the Way, including Ian and Sheila, assembled for a photo-call after breakfast. We were now entering the last stages of our walk and wished to have some record of our respective companions; something to bore our relatives and friends back home.

The day's walk was to the market town of Bellingham (pronounced 'Bellinjam') and it would be my last opportunity to accompany Ian and Sheila as their journey ended there. Apparently the hostel in which we were to stay that evening was, according to Ian, rather cramped. He had been telling me frequently that on his previous stay there he had slept in a broom cupboard as space was so limited. Never being absolutely sure wether his stories were true, I wondered what I was letting myself in for. I would leave Ian and Sheila with some regret as they were a great couple and good company. Ian had kept my spirits up with his mealtime antics and his humorous tales. I will always remember their companionship, which was particularly welcome during our foggy climb to Cross Fell.

I set off with them to join Hadrian's Wall for the last time before leaving it a few miles farther on to head north. Once again we were treated to sunshine and a slight breeze, perfect walking weather. The familiar pattern of alternating climb and descent was recommenced as we passed Crag Lough and Hotbank Crags once more. The appeal of those superb views had not diminished. At Rapishaw Gap, within sight of the picturesque Cuddy's Crags, we said a reluctant goodbye to the Wall.

Undistinguished moorland now stretched before us. Views of Broomlee and Greenlee Loughs added some variety before we found ourselves enveloped by the brooding pine trees of Wark Forest. As Northumberland has many such forests, I was to spend a great deal of time walking through them during the next couple of days. The first experience of traversing forest tracks in warm sunshine was a pleasant one, but, after the umpteenth mile of this, I began to long for the fells and open spaces. I was even prepared to settle for a return to the peat and a little bog hopping.

Eventually, we emerged from the Wark Forest but this tempered by the lack of a distinct path through the open countryside. However, things soon improved and we came upon the delightful Warks Burn, a pleasant stream, which is a tributary of the North Tyne. It lies in an attractive, wooded glade, which made a wonderful change from Sitka Spruce for hour after hour.

The following section proved a complicated one until a road was reached. Concentration was required to follow an indistinct route through pastureland. After a spell of road walking we headed over more fields until the landmark of the unfortunately named Shitlington Crags came into view. We stopped at a nearby farm, which displayed a sign with a welcoming message that tea and refreshments were available. The lady appeared glad of some company and we enjoyed a leisurely half-hour chatting on the lawn of the farmhouse and admiring her garden furniture, which consisted of a commode and a curious assortment of old tables and chairs. The tea was very satisfying and it was hard to terminate this relaxing interlude in the sunshine.

The remaining distance to Bellingham proved trouble-free. It stands in pleasant countryside and the approach is particularly impressive as we dropped down to the River North Tyne, which skirts the town centre. A sturdy stone bridge over the river was undergoing reconstruction, but there was room to pass over it and make our way into the little town. I was eager to see the hostel that Ian had told me so much about, but as it lay on the opposite side of town, that pleasure was to come later.

Before making our way to the hostel there was a little time to inspect the Norman church. This was sturdily built to repel attacks and has narrow windows in its thick walls. Bellingham's history is interlinked with the border disputes and Scottish raids that were prevelent centuries ago. The church was seriously damaged by fire during two particularly punitive raids by marauding Scots.

The hostel, when I finally saw it, was a revelation. It had the appearance of a simple wooden hut that had been banished to the outskirts of the settlement. A party of youngsters was staying, as were some fellow walkers from abroad. These included an American who was hoping to complete the Pennine Way in fourteen days. Then he planned to attempt it again and halve that time. Rather him than me, I thought, but he had the advantage of Marine training.

Space was at a premium in the communal area that also served as a dining room but we just managed to squeeze in. The adjacent dormatories were thankfully larger than the broom cupboard that Ian swore he had slept in on his previous visit and I jokingly asked him if it had been enlarged.

After supper Ian had a captive audience for what was his farewell performance with the single tea bag. They could hardly escape his swan-song as there was nowhere else to retire to, except to bed. Ian's humour was infectious and everyone enjoyed the cosy and friendly atmosphere, and many tales of walking exploits were exchanged.

As I mentioned earlier, this hostel was the only one where any of my belongings went missing. We noticed that items such as soft drinks, tea bags and small personal articles had a habit of disappearing. Ian, Sheila and I went to a local hostelry later that evening for a little celebration and when we returned I was annoyed to find my map and its case had disappeared. Kind man that he was, Ian gave me his map case and the missing map, insisting that he had no further use for them.

DAY FIFTY-FIVE : BELLINGHAM - BYRNESS

At breakfast the following morning I made some porridge for Ian as a parting gesture. He said it was the best he had eaten on the Pennine Way - a fine compliment, for he took his porridge very seriously. The warden had been conspicuous by her absence during breakfast. She did not live at the hostel, for reasons of space and her house was quite a distance away. We had to suffer the indignity of walking there to reclaim our membership cards before we could start our day's walk.

I bade a very sad farewell to Ian and Sheila, for they had been ideal companions. We had liked to walk at much the same pace and had enjoyed talking when we felt like it, but were also content to swing along in silence at other times.

As they disappeared from sight my attention reverted to the job in hand and I made my way to Hareshaw Linn along the attractive Hareshaw Burn, a recommended detour. I was not disappointed, for following a pleasant walk up the wooded valley, a lovely waterfall greeted me. I drank in the view in the morning sunshine before retracing my steps, as one is recommended to do, to regain the main route.

I took my time over the four miles of congenial countryside walking to reach the Bellingham to Otterburn road that takes a different route out of the village. Disused quarries and shooting butts were much in evidence. Part of the track follows an old wagon-way that served the quarry and colliery situated near to the road. The colliery had been in use for over two hundred years until its demise around forty years ago. Many raw materials had been hewn from this area including ironstone, limestone and coal. One of the quarries still has traces of an accompanying lime-kiln.

The journey between this road and the next one linking Byrness to Troughend was awkward to negotiate, as no clear path was visible. However, I found the countryside to be an agreeable mixture of forest and hill. I crossed three summits, namely those of Lough Shaw, Deer Play and Lord's Shaw, all of which are of moderate height but they do have the advantage of affording the first views of the Cheviots, the final barrier of the walk. I tried to contain the excitement that I could feel welling up inside.

The next landmark, approximately a mile past the road, was the monument on Padon Hill. Although not directly on the route, I had only to make a short detour to the summit, and though the hill was of no great height I was perspiring freely in the heat of a warm, early summer afternoon. The stone monument appeared to be a solid construction, roughly the shape of a salt or pepper pot. It was erected in memory of the Scottish Covenantor Alexander Padon who held religious gatherings at this remote spot to escape persecution. A convenient fence runs along this section of the path, which must be a great help in bad weather. I realised that my mind was being inextricably drawn to the Cheviots still in front of me. Perhaps their notorious bogs would have dried out a bit after the extensive spell of good weather. Following a period of respite during the descent of Padon Hill, I worked up a fine lather whilst climbing the final hill before Byrness, Brownrigg Head. My climb was made more enjoyable by the fact that the surrounding boggy landscape was favourably drying out under the hot sun.

Following a mile of descent from Brownrigg Head it was time once again for some more forest walking. The next three miles were through Redesdale Forest, which encloses the hamlet of Blakehopesburnhaugh and the village of Byrness. The former has the longest name of any settlement on the Pennine Way and is a test of pronunciation, particularly if one has had a few drinks!

It was cooler in the forest but I found the endless rows of pines intensely boring and I was glad to emerge from the claustrophobic place. I then followed the River Rede for a couple of miles to reach Byrness, which is little more than a collection of forestry cottages arranged in neat rows. Two of the cottages are converted into the Youth Hostel.

The roadside café and store was the first place I headed for at the end of the hot, tiring day's walk. Sweat was pouring from me and I had a raging thirst, the drinks that I had with me having been consumed due to the heat. It was too early for the hostel to open so I made for this convenient watering hole. When I tell you that I drank a litre bottle of mineral water virtually straight down, you will know how thirsty I was. A few minutes later I paid the penalty for bolting that large amount of fizzy liquid. Eruptions began to tune up in my stomach and took a long time to abate.

As I checked into the hostel I saw a notice on the wall proclaiming, 'Baths can be taken by prior appointment with the lady warden.' I felt tempted to ask her if I could take advantage of the offer, but restrained myself. The lady was much more helpful than the warden at Bellingham hostel. At supper I met another two fellow Pennine Way travellers. One had unfortunately damaged a leg muscle, which had delayed their progress by four days. They had heard about Ben and his finger (what an age ago that seemed), and had met the 'Road Runner.' He had told them of his assistance to the three ladies from Mansfield. The Pennine Way grapevine is truly remarkable.

Amongst further acquaintances made at the hostel was a Scotsman who was walking the Way from north to south. Apparently he had covered the twenty-nine miles over the Cheviots in nine hours, which seemed a remarkably good time to me. He confirmed my hope that conditions underfoot were as good as could be expected, reporting that the peat had dried out considerably. The character that topped them all was Canadian and something of a masochist, for in his rucksack he carried a fifteen-pound rock, in addition to all the normal gear. Obviously he wanted to do the Pennine Way the hard way. When I asked him what on earth possessed him to carry a darned great rock, he replied, 'Well, its something to do.' If the Cheviots had not been drying out so rapidly I could have visualised him sinking into a peat grough up to his neck with all that weight.

Later that evening I accompanied my new-found friends to the local hotel for a couple of hours relaxation and to forget about the formidable task awaiting me the next day.

DAY FIFTY-SIX : BYRNESS - USWAYFORD

I awoke early to find another hot, sunny day in prospect. On the one hand this was a welcome sight as the drying of the bogs would continue and visibility would be good. The downside would be losing another few gallons of sweat. As I set out my thoughts were mixed. Here I was on the last lap of my journey with high hopes of finishing, but the prospect of twenty-nine miles of tough country with virtually no habitation was a sobering one. There was, however, the comforting fact that I was to break the crossing at the remote farm of Uswayford, high among the Cheviot Hills. That was assuming I could find it and, as I set off, I tried to recall 'Mac' the schoolmaster's precise directions to it.

The initial climb out of Byrness turned out to be confusing, as I got lost in a forest. I missed the official path that appeared to be nothing more than a narrow gap between pines that were shrouded in eerie darkness and extremely uninviting. Consequently I spent quite a time plodding along forest tracks, which looked identical. Finally I got back onto the proper route, picking up the path as it emerged from the forest. This diversion did nothing to bolster my spirits, for if I couldn't find my way at this early stage, what hope was there on the exposed hills?

Pulling myself together, I said goodbye to the forest at last, glad that those infernal trees were behind me. A short climb up the remainder of the steep path took me to the summit of Byrness Hill. Anxious not to lose more time, I stayed on the summit only long enough to look back, with considerable satisfaction, over the last of the forest to the valley of the Rede spread out below.

As often happens, the anticipation of an event is more awesome than the event itself. So it proved with the Cheviots, although I did have the benefit of good weather and reasonably dry conditions. I found it hard work, but enjoyable, and the Border fence between England and Scotland provided a lifeline for much of the way. In misty conditions, I could imagine clinging to that fence like a limpet. The scenery was impressive with myriad rounded hills stretching in all directions. Peat groughs abounded and some were many feet deep. I thanked God for the reasonable solidity of the ground. As I was emerging from a particularly deep chasm of peat I was staggered to see a chap hurtling towards me on an all-terrain vehicle. He paused just long enough for me to ask what he was doing riding such a beast up there. He replied that he was a shepherd looking for his sheep. Apparently he had overslept that morning, jumped on his machine and was trying to make up lost time. After wishing him well in his search for his sheep I watched him ride his bucking bronco into the distance.

I turned north and set off at a brisk pace to find the Border fence, which was to be my companion, on and off, for the rest of the day. There was no one about apart from the ubiquitous sheep and I amused myself with quirky thoughts about the oddly-named hills that I passed. Houx Hill - did it really exist or was it just a hoax? Raven's Knowe - what did the ravens know that I didn't? Ogre Hill - no giants in attendance, but its name rhymed with toga, which was appropriate as I was about to pass some ancient Roman camps not far beyond. Just before the Chew Green settlement the path crossed the border into Scotland for the first time. This was another milestone achieved.

At Chew Green, however, I passed back into England and joined Dere Street, a high level section of Roman road. It was used to control the south of Scotland for more than a hundred years during the Roman occupation. Dere Street continued as a main route between England and Scotland until the Middle Ages, so the road built by Agricola remained vitally important to trade for many centuries after the departure of the Romans.

Brownhart Law and Black Halls were the next two hills to be passed and once again my sense of humour began to run amok. Brownhart Law triggered thoughts of the 'Brothers in Law.' Where were they? Had they succumbed to the Cheviot peat or were they still maintaining their remarkable progress? Then came Lamb Hill - an apt name considering the local sheep population. This was followed by Beefstand Hill and Mozie Law - reminiscent of the Wild West - 'mosey down to the old corral.' Plea Knowe and Foul Step came next (who dreamt up such names?) - a request that I watched where I was putting my feet?'

As I approached Windy Gyle I met several walkers, some doing the Pennine Way and others out for a circular walk. I was glad of the company up there on the 2,034-foot summit, which was reached after a stiff climb.

I concentrated on Mac's instructions for leaving the path as I vacated the top of Windy Gyle. As one would have expected, they were very accurate and I found the farm at Uswayford without difficulty. It lies in a lovely spot surrounded by shapely hills and lush pastureland.

Unfortunately the welcome on my arrival was less than courteous and I was abruptly asked if I had booked accommodation. I told the farmer's wife that a booking had been made for me and she visibly softened. I gathered that her attitude was caused by inconsiderate walkers. Apparently some made a booking and never appeared; if the weather was fine they just carried straight on to Kirk Yetholm. The opposite often happened when walkers would appear at her door without a prior booking and expect to be accommodated. It transpired that four other walkers were expected that evening and she was concerned that they would not turn up. This probably explained the fact that I was not offered a cup of tea after my hot, tiring day. She spent most of the next two hours looking out of the window, through a pair of binoculars for a sight of my missing fellow guests. When I inquired about the possibility of a bath I was told that there was not enough hot water. The long-lost walkers finally made an appearance just before eight o'clock, which eased the atmosphere a bit.

After supper, which was delayed due to the late arrivals, I found out quite a lot about Uswayford. The farmer told me that they were eighteen miles from the nearest shop and, worse still, twenty-two miles from the nearest pub. There was no power supply and they relied on their own electricity generator at the back of the farmhouse. We were warned not to turn on any lights in the middle of the night, or the noisy generator would automatically start up and wake the household.

There were more than 1,200 sheep and 150 cattle on the farm and a good class of sheepdog was essential. Conseqently there were several border collies in evidence and the farmer was a keen breeder. I was leapt upon by numerous pups whenever I left the house. In fact, my stay was quite pleasant once the initial difficulties were overcome The food was good and wholesome, as you would expect on a farm.

DAY FIFTY-SEVEN : USWAYFORD - KIRK YETHOLM

As I awoke the following morning, the realisation quickly dawned on me that this was to be the last day of my walk. My feelings were mixed. I looked forward to achieving my goal of Kirk Yetholm but I had become accustomed to my daily routine and the challenge that each day brought. Would I find it hard to readjust after nearly three weeks of walking and living out of a rucksack? That I would find out soon enough but the immediate task was to return to the path and cover the remaining sixteen miles to journey's end.

The remarkable weather was true to form for the final test, the sun shining yet again. There was a spring in my step that morning and I was eager to put the remaining miles behind me. I reckoned that the final part of the route should not be too arduous. Once Auchope Cairn was attained, it would be downhill all the way to the end.

Testing peat groughs were soon in evidence and I fairly leapt up and down these obstacles in my haste. I was soon approaching Auchope Cairn and, remembering Mac's description of it, I decided to give the two-mile detour to The Cheviot a miss. It may have been the highest point of the Cheviot Hills, at 2,676 feet, but it didn't look very inspiring and I was in a hurry.

I pressed on to the summit of Auchope Cairn feeling that the hardest work was over. I was wrong. The next hill, known as the Schil, although nearly 400 feet lower than Auchope Cairn, proved to be a stiff climb.

As I decended from the Schil and the ground levelled out I passed a survival hut, not as spacious as Greg's Hut on Cross Fell, but obviously welcome in a storm. Some kind benefactor must have sited it there for Pennine Way walkers in a state of collapse with just a few miles left to go. At the bottom of the slope from the Schil, the path divided. The Low Level Route dropped down into the attractive Halterburn Valley and, as I had been told by Mac, this was the best way if the weather was bad. But good fortune still smiled on me, so I took the High Level Route and strode along

Steer Rigg. My momentum was temporarily slowed by the pull to the top of White Law but from that hill's summit it really was downhill to the edge of the Cheviots.

They say that the longest mile of any walk is the last one and so it was on the Pennine Way. As I dropped down the last hill on the Cheviots I saw cars parked where the path ended in the valley below. I wrongly assumed that this was the finishing point of the Way. There was a sting in the tail, for on consulting the map I discovered that I still had some road walking to do.

Feeling deflated, I was immediately faced with the prospect of another slope to climb, albeit on tarmac. My legs suddenly lost their spring and I found this last unexpected obstacle a real drag. After what seemed an age, the road decended into habitation. I paused a moment to enjoy the marvellous sight of the buildings of Kirk Yetholm, smiling at Wainwright's comment that any village would look wonderful to someone who had walked 270 miles to reach it.

As I covered the last two hundred yards to the village green the Border Hotel beckoned and I had my final duty to perform. Shedding my rucksack with great relief, I hurried into the bar to claim a free drink on Wainwright, as all Pennine Way walkers had the privilege of doing. The lady behind the bar eyed me suspiciously when I made my request. She asked for proof that I had walked the whole Pennine Way, although it was obvious from my weather-beaten appearance and my well-used walking gear, let alone the sweat on my brow, that I had not just driven there in my car. Proof was requested in the form of Wainwright's *Pennine Way Companion*. I happily produced it and was rewarded with my free half-pint of bitter. A full complimentary pint was the original prize but the ravages of inflation had obviously eaten into Wainwright's generous donation. Now convinced of my authenticity, the landlady signed my *Companion* to signify my receipt of a free drink and handed me a book containing the signatures and dates of the Pennine Way completions. I added my own details and casually studied the recent entries. Imagine my surprise when two signatures leapt from the page. They were those of the wily 'Brothers in Law' who had finished *two days ahead* of me! I should have guessed that those two were capable of anything.

Carrying my well-earned drink from the hotel into the glorious sunshine, I sat on the village green to savour my moment of achievement and to send Ben a postcard. Moments later a young walker came tearing down the hill into the village. I have never seen more sweat on a man and, judging by his rapid pace, I reckoned that he must be the 'Road Runner.' He was obviously making a beeline for the Border Hotel and liquid refreshment. Tearing off his rucksack he leapt into the bar to claim his reward from Wainwright. He too must have been thwarted by the laconic landlady who had obviously asked for the same proof that he had completed the 270-mile walk. Within half a minute he hurriedly re-emerged, tore open the pocket flap of his rucksack and returned to the bar, brandishing his *Companion.*

A few moments later he came out with a drink in his hand and a grin on his face, and crossed over to where I was sitting. He was indeed the 'Road Runner' and I was not surprised to learn that he had accomplished the complete twenty-nine-mile journey from Byrness in less than eight hours. He smiled when I told him of his fame amongst fellow Pennine Way walkers and that he had earned admiration from everyone who had come across him. We sat there companionably, drinking the last of our refreshing beer and reflecting on our own achievement. Wainwright sums up the feeling admirably in his *Pennine Way Companion* when he writes, 'The satisfaction you feel is intensely personal, and cannot be shared: the sense of achievement is yours alone simply because you have earned it alone.'

CHAPTER SIX

The Scottish Borders

DAY FIFTY-EIGHT : KIRK YETHOLM - JEDBURGH

It was a nostalgic return to Kirk Yetholm. I gazed over the village green where I had sat with the 'Road Runner' during our moment of triumph. The Border Hotel remained as impassive as ever and I wondered how many excited Pennine Way walkers would leap into its portals that day to claim a free drink, courtesy of Wainwright.

I was there for another purpose; to link the Pennine Way with Scotland's first officially designated long-distance footpath, the West Highland Way that begins at the little town of Milngavie on the outskirts of Glasgow. The itinerary of the journey was of my own making and, being forever the optimist, I visualised myself as the first walker to devise a route connecting these well-established long-distance paths, thus bringing closer the prospect of a recognised cross-country route from Land's End to John O'Groats

I felt some sympathy for Tom Stephenson, the prime mover of the Pennine Way. It took him thirty years to establish rights of way and link up the various paths and here was I hoping to do it in a week. However, I had a head start because much of my route was on designated rights of way. On the other hand there was a considerable amount of road-walking involved, which is not convenient for an official long-distance route. My efforts to keep from walking on roads wherever possible meant following a meandering course and I covered 131 miles compared to the eighty-four miles as the crow flies. My abiding memories of the walk are two exceedingly long days and sore feet from a surfeit of tarmac as I progressed through a land with a frontier character, riddled with violence and strife, more bloody than any other part of Britain, for 1500 years. Monuments to its warlike past remain in the form of hill-forts, brochs, peles, ruined castles, abbeys and tower houses. Recalling the evocative nature of the conflicts are the border ballads, and diverse place names reflect the history of invaders from Celtic to Norman.

As I strode out of Kirk Yetholm I was mindful of the centuries of border strife and trusted that the area had become much less warlike. I didn't relish the prospect of continually looking over my shoulder for hordes of reivers or those still hostile to the 'auld enemy.'

It was grey and damp as I crossed Bowmont Water that separates the twin villages of Kirk Yetholm and Town Yetholm. A clue to their origins are 'The Palace' and 'Gypsy Row' in Kirk Yetholm. The former, a cottage painted a startling pink, was the home of the last queen of the gypsies Esther Fay Blyth, descended from a long line of gypsies that inhabited the twin settlements. In the early days the Yetholms were the home of the notorious gypsy clan, known as the 'Faas' who gave the locality an evil reputation. Hordes of tinkers issued from them each spring and took to the road. Travellers gave the villages a wide berth, for if strangers ventured into them they were likely to be set upon by men wielding sticks and accompanied by fierce dogs.

Town Yetholm was peaceful as I entered and, as it has no connection with the Pennine Way, exhibited less of an atmosphere than its neighbour. It does, however, share Kirk Yetholm's attractive valley setting where the hills recede and the river cuts through a verdant strath. Its broad main street is bedecked with an array of pleasing sycamores and neat cottages.

I left the village along a quiet road that accompanies Bowmont

Water as it ripples merrily beneath a backdrop of bracken-coated hills. The countryside at the foot of the Cheviots has an air of tranquility and quiet charm - quite a contrast to the peaty heights and their streams of Pennine Way walkers. Several sparkling streams tumbled into Bowmont Water, eager to swell its inviting waters, as I progressed along the valley to the hamlet of Clifton. I stood on a delightful old bridge and watched the river dancing beneath me before turning my eyes to a track climbing alongside the Curr Burn into the Cheviot Hills. This is one of the old trackways that became border crossings before the construction of roads. These border traverses often followed drove roads along which cattle were driven to markets in the North of England.

I soon reached the collection of farms at Cliftoncote where I joined a track that climbed sharply before contouring the flank of Hownam Law, which has the remains of an Iron Age fort on its summit. Its extensive walls were originally over ten feet thick and shallow depressions in the ground indicate the presence of former dwellings. It was occupied for over 800 years until the Romans arrived. As I passed beneath this relic a clinging mist descended and peversely the path became indistinct. Where was the wretched thoroughfare when I needed it most? Out came my compass and I began a careful descent into the next valley. I eventually walked out of the mist to see my objective, a cluster of cottages at Hownam Mains that huddle on a shelf above the appealing Kate Water. An old mining track led me down to the tiny settlement of Howgate, which lies beneath ancient cultivation terraces that line the valley side. I turned for a retrospective look at Hownam Law, partially obscured by mist. It is separated from its neighbour Grubbit Law by the amusingly-named Weary Stream that looked anything but weary as it tumbled energetically into Kate Water.

Another steep climb faced me as I left the deep cleft along a good path heading for Whitton. Visibilty was poor but as I approached the compact settlement of Whitton I could make out another row of miners' cottages, a prelude to sighting the ruins of an ancient tower abutting a restored stone barn. I was to come across several of these ancient fortifications attached to farm buildings that must have provided protection during the Border raids. The collection of farms was linked by the muddiest tracks in Christendom. As I squelched through these glorified mudbaths I

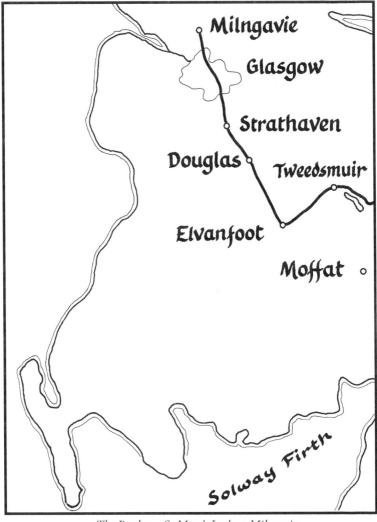

The Borders - St Mary's Loch to Milngavie

fully expected to spy a herd of wallowing hippos.

Dragging several kilos of mud and other unmentionable substances on my submerged boots I struggled with the quagmire for quite a distance making a mental note to suggest that the All-Britain mud-wrestling championships be held at Whitton. Eventually, I began to climb a field path, which extricated me from the vice-like grip of the mire, but returned me into mist. Steady rain spattered my waterproofs as I plodded through several shrouded

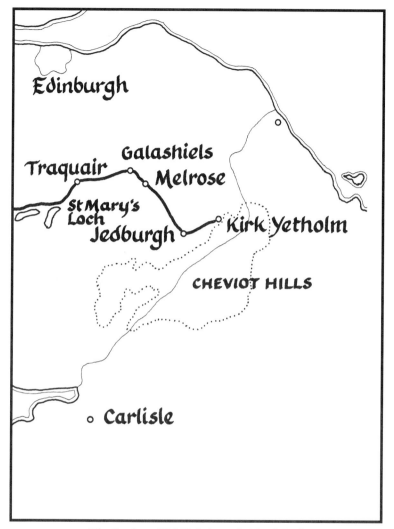

The Borders - Kirk Yetholm to St Mary's Loch

fields until I suddenly stopped, my heart thumping. Dark, eerie shapes suddenly appeared out of the thick mist. I heaved a sigh of relief and cursed myself for my timidity, for it was merely a herd of inquisitive cows. They watched with pity in their eyes as this mud-spattered walker blundered past them heading for God knows where.

A misty traverse of more field paths followed until, as I skirted a brooding wood, the ground began to decline. As I descended past the farm at Marchcleuch I thankfully emerged from the mist to be treated to a somewhat damp, but encouraging view of the valley below. The rain had stopped and the afternoon warmth gave a humid feel to the surroundings. I could see steam rising from the valley road that winds alongside the Cessford Burn and I hurried down to it to stand amidst high hedgerows weighted down with hawthorn blossom that sheltered a profusion of wild flowers. The resplendent verges were a medley of white, blue and pink beneath the steel-grey backdrop of a leaden sky.

At the nearby hamlet of Rennieston I was re-united with the ancient Roman road, Dere Street, which I had encountered high on the Cheviots. Its line was arrow-straight and I was able to follow it for about two miles before forsaking its grassy track in favour of a detour to Jedburgh, my night's stopping place. Before heading for the Border town I paid a quick visit to the adjacent hamlet of Crailinghall where I was rewarded by a view of its mature Old Hall set amidst pristine lawns edged with a variety of handsome trees. An unusual stone pillar by the roadside at the entrance to the village caught my eye, displaying the name 'Crailinghall' and the ornamental heads of a sheep and a cow.

My final task of the day was a two-mile walk along a pleasant country road that brought me to the outskirts of Jedburgh. Long before I reached it I could discern the imposing tower of the ruined abbey that dominates the town. It is one of a cluster of four Border abbeys that have survived from David I's twelfth-century feudalism. Jedburgh is the most imposing, Melrose the most ornate, Dryburgh the most romantic and Kelso the richest of the four.

I hurried into the inviting town, an ancient royal burgh on the Jed Water whose weavers claimed the discovery of tweed, the diagonally ridged fabric produced by passing the weft threads over one and under two or more threads of the warp. The abbey looked even more impressive at close quarters. Its Norman tower rests on the gaunt, roofless shell of the nave and north transept and it is one of the best-preserved abbeys in the Borders despite the hostile attentions of the English. It was sacked and looted several times and after each attack the monks painstakingly restored it. The building remains much as it might have been left after the final sacking during Hertford's so called 'rough wooing' in 1545 when Henry VIII was trying to force Scotland to accept a marriage between his son and the young Mary Queen of Scots. Mary, the Catholic pretender to the throne of England, is indelibly linked to Jedburgh through Mary Queen of Scots' House, which still serves as a museum. In 1566 she lodged there and almost died through illness after a rash and over-energetic ride to see her lover the Earl of Bothwell at Hermitage Castle. Jedburgh also had its castle, the original version being built in the twelfth century, which became the home of the Scottish kings. Unfortunately it was vulnerable to attack by the English and was demolished in 1409. In 1823 a County Prison was built on the site and that in turn was superceded by the present building of 1886, currently a museum containing displays of prison life and a potted history of the town.

DAY FIFTY-NINE : JEDBURGH - MELROSE

After a comfortable night in a rambling old house on the outskirts of Jedburgh, I headed out of town to rejoin my convenient companion Dere Street that continues its unswerving progress towards St Boswells and eventually the Firth of Forth. In Roman times it linked that great estuary with the strategic fort at Eboracum, as York was named during that era.

As I walked along the ancient arterial highway I was conscious of following in the footsteps of the Roman legions as they traversed a hostile countryside. This vital route took them almost to their most northerly outpost, the Antonine Wall. Built by Hadrian's successor this massive turf rampart linked the Firths of Clyde and Forth and marked the northern extremity of the Roman Empire in Britain. My overactive sense of humour got into gear again to relieve the monotony of walking in a dead straight line. I reckoned the Romans felt disinclined to chase the warlike Celts into the inhospitable Highlands so they called it a day and, without planning permission stuck up the great barrier to keep them at bay. It was easy to picture the fierce Picts hammering away at this Roman monstrosity, helped by a marauding band of their mates in those troubled times, the Brigantes. The attackers eventually won the day after a mere forty-four years and the Romans abandoned the Wall.

Such daft thoughts kept me amused until I was obliged to leave Dere Street at the point where it metamorphosed into the modern

A68 road about two miles from St Boswells. However, I couldn't complain, for it had been a good aid for several miles that fine morning and I had made good time up to that point.

My route became much more circuitous as it weaved through St Boswells and its neighbour Newton St Boswells. At St Boswells I had my first meeting, albeit a brief one, with the sparkling River Tweed that I was to encounter on several occasions. The village, I discovered, is named after St Boisil who was the seventh-century prior of Old Melrose Monastery. In July of each year, on St Boisil's Day, gypsies gather from all over the country for the annual horse fair. I wonder how many of them came from the Yetholms?

My lunchtime stop was on the banks of the Tweed just beyond St Boswells, a lovely scene of quiet contentment. Anglers lazily cast their lines into the energetic waters that danced on the stony bed and the verdant riverbanks were alive with buttercup and meadow sweet. Across the river, hiding demurely behind a curtain of ash and elder stood the second of the great Border abbeys, Dryburgh. I could just discern part of its ox-bowed structure piercing the trees and from that glimpse I realised what a fine sight it must have been when intact. It was home to monks of the Premonstratensian Order (a branch of the Augustinians), from Alnwick. Destroyed by the English in 1322 and rebuilt, it became another victim of Hertford's attentions, whereupon it was left to decay. The romantic ruin captivated Sir Walter Scott and it became his burial place along with Field Marshall Earl Haig.

After hungrily demolishing my sandwiches I left my riverside idyll to hurry through Newton St Boswells, eager to catch my first sight of Melrose, my day's destination. A disused railway runs through the town and I tagged on to this convenient walkway as it arcs, in the shadow of the Eildon Hills, towards the attractive market town of Melrose, lying in the heart of Scott Country. Because the surrounding countryside is flat, the three humps of the Eildons stand proud, like ancient watchdogs keeping guard over Melrose and the winding Tweed. These distinctive hills are the remains of groups of volcanoes complete with lava flows and intrusions. On the North Hill stood the ancient fortified town of the Selgovae, requisitioned by the Romans as a signal station and given the name of Trimontium. Its dominant position gave it great strategic significance and not surprisingly this spectacular site

Bleaklow - Wainstones

Kirkby Malham

Penyghent

Upper Teesdale

River Tweed - near Melrose

Galashiels

Church at Douglas

Strathaven

Loch Lomond from Conic Hill

Tyndrum

Buachaille Etive Mor

Fort William from Ben Nevis

Shiel Bridge

Coulin Pass

Kyle of Tongue

John 'O' Groats House Hotel

became a place of legend. The wizard, Michael Scot, is said to have cleaved the three hills from one and the ubiquitous King Arthur and the Knights of the Round Table are reputed to sleep within it, ready to rise again in Scotland's hour of need. A far cry from Avalon!

On that balmy afternoon, heather lazed on Eildon's slopes as cloud-whisps sailed silently above and I felt a strong urge to climb the gentle, tempting hills. However, Melrose beckoned with its prospect of exploration and a night's rest. My lodgings stood in the very shadow of Melrose Abbey, a great seat of worship, founded by monks from Rievaulx in Yorkshire, which played an important role in the making of Scotland. It suffered the same fate as its neighbours and was virtually destroyed in 1385 by the English. The stately ruins upon which I gazed are mainly of fifteenth and sixteenth-century reconstruction that was tragically curtailed through lack of funds. A mesh of scaffolding obscured a section of the impressive red sandstone structure but enough of the ravaged shell remained to give it the timeless air of a proud haven of Christianity. In its grounds stands The Commendator's House, which is now a fine museum containing details and artefacts from the days of Roman occupation.

I was very impressed by my accommodation that evening and knew that I was in for a comfortable night's sleep. However, my first task was to remove the day's grime and find a good restaurant. When that was accomplished, I wandered the streets of the old town as the evening sun cast deepening shadows over its late medieval remains, such as the sixteenth-century mercat cross in Market Square. I was quite taken by the agreeable feel of the place but my eyes were continually drawn to the three bastions of early occupation, the Eildons. The hills were a reminder that in my haste to reach Melrose that afternoon I had completely ignored the site of another Roman connection. This was a camp and important staging post on Dere Street that was established at the time a signal tower was planted on their Eildon fortress. Its site is near the village of Newstead about one mile to the east of Melrose.

Having played school and club rugby in my youth I was interested to discover that Melrose is the birthplace of seven-a-side rugby and the town possesses an impressive ground. Such is the lure of the Melrose 'Sevens' that teams from many countries annually compete for the trophy.

DAY SIXTY : MELROSE - TRAQUAIR

The weather remained favourable the following morning as I headed out of Melrose to rejoin the banks of the Tweed. It had lost none of its sparkle of the previous day; a glorious silver thread winding through rich farmland - squared fields of green, gold and blue. I saw anglers casting into deep pools where salmon lie, perpetuating the Tweed's centuries old fame as a prime source of Scotland's most coveted fish. I stopped to chat with an angler who told me that the salmon-fishing season runs virtually throughout the year, from the beginning of February to the end of November. 'There's a variety of fish in the river, if you can get your hooks into them!' he said laughingly. 'There's trout, another migratory fish, and freshwater varieties, such as grayling, perch, roach and dace. Did you know?' he asked, 'that salmon and trout have a completely different status to freshwater fish under Scottish Law?' I shook my head. 'Aye,' the angler replied, 'there's no public right to fish for salmon and trout; that's vested in the landowner.' These technicalities were a little beyond me and, after a brief natter about the weather I left him to his sport.

I followed the pleasant riverside path as it steered though carpets of lush grass spread with buttercup until it was time to abandon the Tweed at a delightful red-tinted rustic bridge. At this point I joined a long-distance footpath, the Southern Upland Way, which I planned to follow for the best part of the next two days. I didn't know it at the time but this coast to coast route, from Portpatrick, near Stranraer, to Cockburnspath, north of Berwick upon Tweed, was to provide some of the finest walking I have experienced. Things were looking up, for the Way joined the dismantled railway that I had used the previous day during my approach to Melrose. The bed had been levelled and surfaced with tarmac; quite a boon. I marched along the amenable highway for a mile before crossing the Tweed and joining its tributary Gala Water on the outskirts of Galashiels.

At this point I entered the industrialised floor of the Gala Valley, leaving behind the splendid vistas of rolling hills through which the Romans under Agricola pressed their campaigns against the Selgovae in AD 80 as they pushed north to the Lothian Plain and Edinburgh. Galashiels has suffered some undistinguished modern housing development but I was thankfully immune from such spoilage as I followed the river, walking through avenues of vibrant hawthorn blossom. Gala Water was a shimmering blue under the hot sun, but as I approached the town centre its clear waters began to be blighted by debris, such as a forlorn supermarket trolley that rather spoiled the setting.

I crossed Gala Water and approached the hub of the town. As I entered the main street all was grey stone interspersed with a modicum of modern brick. The burgh chambers, topped with a shapely clocktower, occupied a prominent position at the head of the street, a reminder of the town's importance as an industrial centre and a focal point of ancient Roxburgh. Galashiels has long been at the heart of the tweed manufacturing industry and its mills go back to the early days of the industrial revolution. It had the first carding machine and the first woollen mill in Scotland to use water-power for producing weaving yarn. The view down its main street is of a pleasant mixture of stone-built properties, some possesssing tastefully coloured facades, and rows of flamboyant flowerbeds that line a splendid roadside park. I took the opportunity to sit among these iridescent blooms to eat my lunchtime sandwiches, in glorious sunshine.

There is much more to Galashiels than its industrial heritage. It contains another splendid park and many reminders of the past, including its oldest building Old Gala House. There is a bust of Sir Walter Scott, the celebrated poet and novelist who was a great lover of the district and lived at nearby Abbotsford House for twenty years. The Border reivers are recalled by Thomas Clapperton's statue of the Mounted Border Reiver, one of a number who were said to prize the early textiles of Galashiels known as 'Hodden Grey.'

After lunch I visited Old Gala House, eager to discover what lay within the former home of the lairds of Gala, built in 1611. It was a fascinating tour, for its rooms tell the story of the house itself and also of the development of Galashiels and its inhabitants. Most impressive was the Painted Wall Room containing murals on each of its walls depicting the house's long history, the lairds, and life as it was in the early seventeenth century. I developed a crick in my neck when I surveyed the Painted Ceiling Room in the 1611 tower, through admiring the splendid example of a Scottish painted ceiling dating from 1635.

It was an effort to leave Galashiels but I still had a long day's journey to complete. I quickly rejoined the Southern Upland Way as it climbs from the town into enticing hills. The first section of ascent skirted a forest but once this was left behind the splendid countryside rolled out like a relief map beneath my feet. Galashiels looked a world away in the distant valley and the vista of rolling hills before me made my heart sing. I made a gradual climb to Hog Hill through brilliant patches of gorse and outcrops of spruce and pine. It was hot work and I stopped several times to wipe the sweat from my brow but my superb surroundings more than compensated for my discomfort. The higher I climbed the stronger became the welcome breeze as it fingered my hair and soothed my brow.

The Way skirts the summit of Hog Hill before descending to another rendezvous with the Tweed. I followed the path as it contours the higher reaches of Hog Hill before joining a broad track leading down from the farm at Calfshaw. My descent was trouble free and I soon found myself watching the now familiar river bubbling beneath the mighty stone arches of the bridge at Yair. However, it was not time to say goodbye to the Tweed, for I was to follow it virtually to its source and, although it was a wrench to leave the river as it flowed merrily through idyllic surroundings, I knew there would be other opportunities to admire its unrivalled beauty. As I crossed the bridge I noticed a lodge at the entrance to inviting grounds a short distance up river. Luckily it stood on my route and I ventured through its gates hoping that I would not be apprehended. There was no one around and I plucked up courage to intrude a little further. I was rewarded by a glorious display of rhododendron of varying hues lining the driveway. I quickly produced my camera and captured the striking blooms before beating a hasty retreat through the gates.

A stiff ascent awaited me as I left the valley with the sun still beating down. An arduous and frustrating climb through a dense forest followed, awakening memories of the great tracts of vegetation in Northumberland. The foliage did offer good shade until I emerged from it on a broad, steep track that heads for three large cairns on an approaching hilltop. The retrospective view was panoramic and despite having left them far behind the distinctive Eildons were clearly visible in the distant haze, rising like three giant carbuncles on the posterior of Border country. I met three more, albeit much smaller carbuncles at end of my exhausting climb in the form of the Three Brethren - massive cairns marking the meeting-point of three of the old Border counties. It was a magnificent 1,520-foot vantage point, from which to view the vast tract of rolling Border hills that encircled me.

I sat on my enthralling perch for as long as was prudent. It was well into the afternoon and I still had seven miles to cover that day, and there were two higher summits to conquer before I could begin my descent to Traquair. As I left the Three Brethren I joined another track, identified on the map as the Old Drove Road, which climbs from Selkirk and would hopefully lead me over the hills to Traquair. This old routeway took me over a saddle beneath the summit of Broomy Law before beginning the climb to Brown Knowe, at 1,719 feet, the highest of the summits I had to attain. Gritting my teeth I plodded up its testing approach before stopping for a breather on its exposed top. There was a pleasant, cooling wind and the sun's rays were losing some of their ferocity, which augered well for the remainder of my journey.

It was a fairly level walk to the final summit, Hare Law, which is 50 feet lower than Brown Knowe, and I reached it without much effort. The downside was that I had entered Elibank and Traquair Forest, which would shroud most of my descent. This meant an end to my scenic delights but I was able to relax in the knowledge that the hard work of the day was over. I trudged for two miles through the ancient forest that was granted by David I to Melrose Abbey, together with royal lands and the Forest of Selkirk, plus the three granges of Melrose, Eildon and Darnick. These lands provided pasturage for sheep and cattle, wood for building and burning, and rights of fishing in the Tweed.

In the centre of the forest I passed through an extensive clearing, from which rises the great hump of Minch Moor, the highest hill in the area at 1,860 feet. Another spell of forest walking took me beneath Pipers Knowe, which sounds like a song title. Once clear of the claustrophobic trees it was merely a short walk into Traquair. As I approached the village I was treated to a view of Lee Penn, its conical crown thrusting into the early evening sky beyond Innerleithen. The bracken and fir coated slopes of this prominent hill were softened by the mellow glow of the weakening sun.

A decorative red sandstone cross, the local War Memorial, greeted my arrival and a row of neat and compact white-walled cottages beckoned. These, unfortunately were not my night's resting place, for I had a further three quarters of a mile to cover to my accommodation at Traquair Bank, a neighbour of the famous Traquair House, home of the Maxwell Stuarts. Waving farewell to the agreeable hamlet I plodded the remaining distance along the road to reach the inviting old house where I was to stay. I was impressed. It was tall and stately with an attractive stone frontage and large bay windows that overlooked a terrace and spacious grounds.

I was made very welcome and enjoyed a good meal in the company of several other guests who were touring the area by car. After supper we retired to the terrace to chat and admire the superb view of Lee Penn towering above banks of vibrant rhododendron that lined the garden. My companions were excited to hear of my trek and I was questioned for quite a time about my exploits. However, no one volunteered to accompany me for the rest of my journey.

DAY SIXTY-ONE : TRAQUAIR - TWEEDHOPEFOOT

Another sunny day was in prospect as I ate breakfast the next morning. Excitement was building, for my first appointment of the day was a visit to historic Traquair House. Unfortunately time was pressing as I had twenty-four miles to cover and had no desire to finish my day's walk in the dark.

I hurried away after breakfast, but not before thanking my hosts for a most comfortable stay. I back-tracked for a quarter of a mile along the road to the entrance to Traquair House where I viewed the impressive Bear Gates that formerly gave access to the house. I say formerly because they have not been opened since 1745 when Bonnie Prince Charlie rode through them to continue his march south to Derby. The Stuarts, whose descendents are the Maxwell Stuarts, were the incumbents at that time and were stout Jacobite sympathisers. On the prince's departure they swore that the gates would remain closed until a Stuart king sat on the British throne. History relates that this never came to pass and consequently the gates, with magnificent carvings of a bear on top of each of their posts, have remained tight shut. I wondered how rusty the hinges had become?

There was no one manning the lodge at the normal entrance and I ventured along the drive unchallenged. From a discreet distance I studied the house, its façade partially obscured by annoying scaffolding. With a history stretching back almost one thousand years, it has remained unaltered for the last 300, and is said to be the oldest inhabited home in Scotland. It was a pleasure house for the early kings of Scotland, from David I to Alexander III and it only ceased to be a royal residence when the Wars of Independence made it untenable for them. The first Stuart laird fell with his king at Flodden in 1513 and the current laird has worked tirelessly to encourage visitors to the house in order to defray the enormous cost of running the estate.

The imposing four-storey building, embellished with towers and tall chimneys, was indeed a stirring sight. My heart beat a little faster as I thought of the triumphs and tragedies played out within its solid walls. I realised that I was viewing a microcosm of Scottish history.

Tweedhopefoot beckoned so I turned on my heel and strode from the grounds to return to the village and rejoin my faithful companion the Southern Upland Way for our final journey together. I planned to leave the Way at St Mary's Loch that lay a tantalising eight miles away. Full steam ahead was required on this long day's march and I hurried along the B709 road out of Traquair. I caught sight of the delightful tree-lined Quair Water flowing through the meadows, eager to join the Tweed near Innerleithen. A mile from the village I thankfully left the road, crossed the engaging stream and took to the hills once again. I climbed across the flank of Fethan Hill through pleasant pastureland until the path levelled out as it approached Blake Muir. The gorse was resplendent, adding splashes of yellow to the emerald landscape. An inquisitive skylark hovered overhead and the raucous calls of a pair of watchful lapwings floated on the breeze. Despite it being mid-morning the sun was getting into its stride and I knew that another good measure of sweat would be wrung out of me before the day was out. What had I to complain about? The day was young, the sky was a brilliant blue and my surroundings were first-class; what more could a walker ask for?

I stuck to my task as I covered those eight hard miles to St Mary's Loch, determined not to waste precious time. However, I was careful not to overstretch myself at this early stage, making occasional stops, not only to rest but also to take in my invigorating surroundings. When Blake Muir was behind me, level walking on a good track followed, amidst a cordon of shapely hills, until the forest of Brakehope Rig was reached. At this point the long descent to St Mary's Loch began and initially I was cooled by the leafy confines of the forest before emerging to join the lively Craighope Burn that ripples past the farm at Blackhouse. Blue sky and bright sunlight combined to create a serene and appealing setting, two miles from the nearest road. As I passed the farm many pairs of eyes watched me intently. Goats, geese, ducks and hens roamed freely but I had their rapt attention as I srode along the track, my boots leaving a trail of dust. Near the farmhouse stood another ruined tower, its grass-infested stonework crumbling from centuries of neglect. Small trees sprouted from gaps in the red sandstone relic that was formerly the stronghold of the Black Douglases. It seemed a good place to eat my sandwiches so I had a short lunch stop.

I reached the A708 road, which runs along the north shore of St Mary's Loch, just beyond Dryhope, where stands another ruined tower, the birthplace of Mary Scott, the 'Flower of Yarrow.' It was time to leave the Southern Upland Way, which prefers the south shore of the loch as it heads towards the famous Tibbie Shiel's Inn. The old inn is named after Isabella (Tibbie) Shiel who began taking in lodgers after being widowed in 1824. In the visitors' book can be found the signatures of Sir Walter Scott, James Hogg, Robert Louis Stevenson and Thomas Carlyle, poets and writers of great acclaim. It was here that the Southern Upland Way was officially opened in 1984 and a plaque denotes the occasion.

I had enjoyed my two-day traverse of the amenable long-distance path and vowed to explore it further some time in the future but at that moment I was studying my route. Unfortunately there appeared no alternative to a lengthy spell of road-walking past St Mary's Loch, the largest in southern Scotland, and its neighbours Megget Reservoir and Talla Reservoir. My boots scuffed the tarmac as I strode past the shimmering blue waters of St Mary's Loch but there was the compensation of good views across the loch to the wooded hills beyond. I was pleased to leave the main road at Cappercleuch and join a minor road that links St Mary's Loch with Tweedsmuir. It began its twisting, but scenic, journey through the Lowther Hills, intitially following Megget Water that links St Mary's Loch with the extensive Megget Reservoir before passing the Megget Stone and Fans Law.

As I passed the third water-store, Talla Reservoir, my feet began to protest at the miles of road-walking they were forced to endure, but I pressed on at a good pace, eager to make good time to Tweedsmuir. The stream issuing from Talla Reservoir was a delight as it danced playfully through a tree-lined channel towards Tweedsmuir, throwing up frothy white spume as it hurried merrily on its way. For me, the scene portrayed the essence of Scotland: distant hills, afforested slopes and rushing water, overlooked by a radiant azure sky.

It was early evening as I entered the scenic environs of Tweedsmuir set in the lush valley of the Upper Tweed. Many of its buildings, including the attractive red sandstone kirk, hid shyly among clusters of trees and the surroundings included a liberal scattering of fine broad-leaved woods. On closer inspection, the kirk, perched on a hillock, looked resplendent. Its tall spire, burnished in the glow of evening, presides over the graves of several Covenanting martyrs.

Eleven miles of pounding tarmac had done nothing for my feet but I hurried for a reunion with the Tweed, which flowed, more sedately than the infant stream that poured into it, towards Drumelzier. At nearby Broughton the John Buchan Centre is housed in the Free Church where his father was minister. It immortalises the renowned author who became the first Lord Tweedsmuir and eventually, Governor-General of Canada. His memorable novel *The Thirty-Nine Steps* is a favourite of mine.

Several miles still remained to the sheepdog centre at Tweedhopefoot where I had booked accommodation and I hoped a meal would be fortcoming on my arrival, for I had eaten little during the day in my haste. The final part of my journey took me south towards Moffat, with the Tweed a close companion. It was nearly eight o'clock when I arrived at the white-walled cottage with 'Tweedhope Sheep Dogs' emblazoned on its gable-end to be greeted by Viv Bellingham who declared, 'I thought you weren't coming.'

I apologised for my late arrival and asked if a meal was available. It transpired that I was the only guest that evening and Viv swiftly produced a plate of meat and vegetables, which she placed in a microwave. A few minutes later I sat down to a steaming supper whilst Viv told me about herself and the sheep dog centre that she ran with her husband Geoff. They were in the business of rearing and training sheep dogs, which included frequent displays of working Border collies at the centre. The couple are nationally and internationally known in their field, having appeared many times on television and judged at sheep dog trials in a variety of countries. Viv has written several books and she kindly presented me with a signed copy of *Tweedhope Sheep Dogs* despite her comment that I must be mad to undertake such a long walk on my own.

After my welcome supper I was so tired after my gruelling day's walk I went to bed and fell asleep almost as my head touched the pillow.

DAY SIXTY-TWO : TWEEDH'FOOT - CRAWFORDJOHN

I awoke at eight o'clock the following morning having slept like a log. There's nothing like fresh air and streunous exercise for ensuring a good night's sleep. Today would seem like a rest day after the rigours of the previous day. A mere seventeen miles was in prospect!

I said goodbye to Viv and the River Tweed, for two of its tributaries meet at Tweedhopefoot and neither lay directly on my route. I continued my journey south and entered an extensive plantation, which would take me all that morning to traverse. I was obliged to follow the A701 Moffat to Edinburgh road for the first two miles and this boring section was only relieved by a sign at the roadside denoting the source of the Tweed at nearby Tweed's Well. All I could see from the road was an expanse of tussocky grass and there was no sign of the starting point of the river's 100-mile journey to Berwick upon Tweed and the sea. This was a pity for the Tweed and I had been good companions.

At the foot of Bog Hill I left the main road with a sigh of relief to join a track, heading west, which cut a dead-straight channel through the sea of Scots pine and spruce. I was on the line of another Roman road that was heading for the former Roman camp near Little Clyde, close by the M74 motorway. The monotony of my surroundings was occasionally relieved by views of the Lowther Hills and the flat land beneath me. Another break from remorseless forest walking was provided by a chance meeting with a walker who knew the area well. When I mentioned my dislike of such terrain he told me that in earlier times the woodland landscape was much more varied. 'There's a long history of attempts to reverse the loss of woodland and to give it greater appeal,' he indicated. 'There was an experiment conducted in Ettrick Forest in the early 1900's to see if indigenous woodland would grow again if left undisturbed,' the man said. 'It showed that the ancient forest was not a uniform canopy of trees. In early times the valleys were a dense brushwood of hawthorne, birch and sallow, whereas the hills were coated with Scots fir, ash and oak.' It put me in mind of a visit to Mar Lodge in the old Forest of Mar, in Royal Deeside, which is now owned by the National Trust for Scotland who have plans to revert the lands to their former state - Caledonian forest. 'That's a far-reaching investment,' the walker observed when I mentioned this. 'Such a project will take many years to mature.'

I shook hands with the knowledgeable fellow and he wished me well as I returned to my arboreal tramp. As I neared the site of the Roman camp the trees finally relented and I looked down on the great artery linking England with Glasgow and Edinburgh, the M74. It wound like a giant snake over Beattock Summit and through the gorge at Elvanfoot, my next destination. My release from the wooded confines was tempered by the noise of speeding traffic as I contoured the slope alongside the wide highway. It was a relief to finally leave the forest behind, walk under the motorway and into the hamlet of Elvanfoot. The sky was clouding over and I probably did not see the tiny place at its best. It appeared to have little of note.

As I left the village I joined a track that climbs into the hills to the west of the M74 and as I laboured along it I kept the motorway in intermittent sight for the next three miles as it burrowed through the valley below me. For a period it was obscured by Mid Hill but re-appeared as I descended to Glencaple. It was rough, open country but it gave sweet release from forest tracks. Beneath a grey foreboding sky I followed the pleasing Glengonnar Water that cut through a verdant valley.

At Lettershaws I crossed a tiny bridge, constructed of logs topped with ling, and bemoaned the sun's disappearance. The weather did not do justice to this attractive dell tucked between green, rolling hills. As the last lap of my day's journey was about to begin I trusted that the rain would hold off until it was completed. Unfortunately this was not to be and when I joined a narrow road that cut through a short section of yet another forest, down it came. I donned waterproofs glad that I had not been caught in open countryside and strode along the road eager for a night's rest. As I covered the remaining two and a half miles to my destination my feet began to trouble me, a legacy of the eleven-mile pounding of roads on the previous day. I determined to give them a thorough inspection when I reached Crawfordjohn, for I had no desire to abandon my walk now that victory was within striking distance.

I reached the small village in pouring rain and thankfully found my night's accommodation without incedent. I was welcomed by a young couple who seemed used to walkers dripping with rain and making puddles on their doorstep. A hot bath soon refreshed me but the sight of a blister on each foot did nothing for my confidence. I gave them some soothing ointment and applied a pad to each of them in order to relieve the pressure. When I headed for the dining room I was pleased to learn that my wet boots and outer clothing had been put to dry by my thoughtful hosts. After a wholesome meal I felt drowsy and decided a quiet evening was in order. I was the only person staying and I retired to the residents' lounge to scan any available reading material. There was the usual mixture of tourist brochures, assorted magazines and books of diverse interest. I picked up a book about the area hoping to find what was in store on the next day's walk. My first destination was the village of Douglas and it was prominently featured. I was intrigued by its coverage of the Douglas Family, having passed Blackhouse Tower the previous day, with which the Black Douglases had associations. Apparently they were very prominent in Scottish history and their origins can be traced back to the twelfth century. It was in the early fourteenth century, with the emergence of Sir James, the 'Black Douglas' that the family fortune and power base was founded. Sir James was a powerful ally of Robert the Bruce in the Wars of Independence, fighting in the

Battle of Bannockburn and distinguishing himself by recapturing his castle from the English. As Robert the Bruce lay dying he requested that Sir James should carry his heart to a resting-place in Jerusalem. During his journey Sir James became involved in the crusades in Spain and died bravely, with Bruce's heart protected beneath him as he fell, at the hands of the Moors.

After Sir James' death the family became very influential in Scotland through a few well-chosen marriages, and is said to have designs on the throne itself. In the mid-fifteenth century James II set out to crush the powerful Black Douglases who held land and titles throughout Scotland. The fifth earl, who had too much power and influence for James' comfort, was invited to dine with the king. This was his undoing, for it is said that he was done away with over dinner by the king himself. The Douglases must have been quite a family!

As I read, my eyelids began to droop and I fought tiredness for as long as I could before capitulating and going to bed. It had been another absorbing day, packed with interest, which seemed to be the norm on my Borders Walk.

DAY SIXTY-THREE : CRAWFORDJOHN - STRATHAVEN

The weather was much improved when I set out out for Strathaven the following morning. My feet felt better for the night's rest. According to the map the initial section of my day's route appeared devoid of paths or thoroughfares, so when Crawfordjohn was left behind I cut across open country heading directly for Douglas. The walking was fairly strenuous over heathland but it was preferable to a wide detour by road. I traversed several gentle hills and crossed bubbling Braidknowe Burn and Black Burn, which should be in Lancashire! On the summit of Auchensaugh Hill, the highest in the area, at 1,286 feet, I came across the remains of an ancient burial cairn, another remnant of early occupation.

From the summit of Pagie Hill I began a gradual descent to Douglas and soon joined a narrow road that took me into the village. I was looking forward to investigating the home of the Douglases and their family seat, the castle. Douglas stands astride the A70 road that heads towards Edinburgh and is consequently very busy. I hurriedly vacated the modern part of Douglas to escape the traffic and came upon the deserted old village with its church and charming collection of eighteenth-century buildings. The place was like a ghost town and I was able to stroll the streets without interruption and study its distinctive church at length. The remains of its fourteenth-century chancel still stand beneath the imposing and shapely tower that houses the oldest working clock in Scotland, reputedly gifted by Mary Queen of Scots in 1565. Inside the church are carved stones from an earlier version built on the same site, together with effigies and tombs of the Douglases. Two heart-shaped caskets contain the hearts of Archibald, the fifth Earl of Angus, and Sir James, the Black Douglas.

I went in search of the castle only to be thwarted, for the seventeenth-century version was demolished in 1938 due to subsidence. All that remains is a ruined tower that I found in the surrounding parkland. I left the village in a huff along a good track and soon crossed the black waters of Douglas Water that gives a clue to the name 'Black Douglas'. The family name of Douglas is thought to have been derived from the Gaelic word Dubhghlais meaning 'black or dark water.'

My curiosity sated I began the long trek to Stratheven, which was to prove extremely tiresome. As I headed for the village of Coalburn I encountered a dismantled railway, which I thought would make a good walking track. Unfortunately its bridges had been dismantled and I was forced to leave it several times and battle through undergrowth in order to rejoin it. After several bouts of this I abandoned the idea and found a path leading to Coalburn an aptly-named place, for it resembles a typical coal-mining village. I paid it scant attention, for I was still annoyed at my disused railway debacle.

A series of field paths led me to a country road heading towards Porterhall. This marked the beginning of a frustrating and painful nine miles of road-walking across a flat and uninteresting plain to Strathaven. As the miles rolled by the sun beat down, my feet were hot and my blisters were almost unbearable. I became so desperate to relieve my abused feet I was unable to resist a tempting stream running parallel to the road, but through adjacent farmland. I trespassed along a farm track in order to reach the stream and bathe my blisters. As I sat with my feet in the soothing water a farmer drove up in his landrover.

'What do you think you're doing?' he asked angrily.

I guiltily explained my predicament and the irate man calmed down. 'That's alright,' he said affably. 'I've had trouble with thieves coming onto my property and I wondered who you were.' He went on to explain how he and neighbouring farmers had been plagued by gangs trespassing on their land and stealing equipment or anything else they could lay their hands on. I assured him I had nothing like that in mind and he smiled. 'Take all the time you need,' he said. 'I hope you make it to Strathaven.' With a cheery, 'Goodbye,' he jumped into his landrover and left me soaking my feet.

When I rejoined the road I felt much better but the relief was only temporary, for as more monotonous miles were covered the blisters began to complain once more. Thankful that only one day remained of my journey, I hobbled into the pleasant market town of Strathaven in the late afternoon and began an immediate search for my night's stopping place. I was given a welcoming pot of tea on my arrival and my host commiserated with my predicament. 'You'll feel much better after a good soak in a hot bath,' she suggested.

The lady was right, for after a prolonged lie in the bath my feet were less painful. I applied more ointment and fresh pressure pads, which also helped. Unfortunately an evening meal was not supplied at the guesthouse so I was obliged to walk into the town centre to find a restaurant. I virtually tiptoed into town to ease my blisters and it was a relief to sit down and enjoy a good meal. As I ate I had disturbing thoughts about my final day's journey to Milngavie, which would be another twenty-four mile trek. Would my feet last out? Should I call it a day and take a bus into Glasgow? My stubborn streak dismissed the cowardly way out. I was determined to reach my destination even if it meant crawling on my hands and knees.

As there was no time to lose on the following morning I recklessly decided to explore the town that evening. If I trod carefully, I told myself, I should be able to manage a short tour. It began in Common Green, the attractive market-square, which is full of character, as are the tasteful buildings that surround it, several of them half-timbered. I discovered that there is more to Strathaven than meets the eye, for it has a long history. The original medieval village grew up alongside its castle, which was probably built during the eleventh or twelfth century. By 1150 Strathaven was large enough to be granted a special Charter and become a Free

Burgh of Barony with its implication for the development of trade. Weavers from Flanders brought hand-loom weaving to the area and towards the end of the eighteenth century cotton and silk weaving replaced that of linen. On Castle Street I found a monument to James 'Purlie' Wilson, a Scottish radical and weaver who invented the stocking frame on which the purl stitch could be worked. His fame was short-lived for he was executed in Glasgow in 1820 for being at the forefront of an uprising and a subsequent march to Cathkin Braes on the outskirts of the city.

I walked slowly to the castle, which was a disappointment, for it fell into disrepair in the eighteenth century and its crumbling remains are declared unsafe. Only one of the original two towers and part of the outer wall remain. I did learn that it was granted to the Earls of Douglas in 1370 who strengthened the fortification. A legend attached to the castle concerns a lady reputed to have been bricked up into a cavity in one of the walls by an angry husband. Apparently, he was thoughtful enough to include a final meal of bread and water for the poor woman whose bones are said to have been found when part of the wall fell down.

In order to rest my feet I sat for a time in the engaging John Hastie Park. It was cool and pleasant, a little different from the hot afternoon. In one corner of the park stands a museum that houses many relics from the time of the Covenanters. The town saw intensive activity in this regard and today the well-established Covenanters' Trail passes through it.

I sat in quiet contentment until a chill wind began to blow across the park, whereupon I hobbled back to my lodgings wondering what the following day would bring.

DAY SIXTY-FOUR : STRATHAVEN - MILNGAVIE

Footpaths were once again conspicuous by their absence as I began my journey on another bright morning. There was no alternative to following minor roads to East Kilbride, a 'new town' of the 1950's situated on the southern outskirts of Glasgow. My feet felt better, but tender, and I had no idea how they would stand up to another bout of road-walking. I kept to any available roadside verges to lessen the impact on my blisters and maintained a fairly slow pace.

I didn't care if I arrived in Milngavie after dark, so determined was I to triumph.

As I plodded towards East Kilbride, bathed in sunshine, the surroundings looked quite pleasant. Mile after mile of lush farmland lined the road and I knew that I would soon have to forsake the bracing countryside to enter the brick and concrete environs of Glasgow. On the outskirts of East Kilbride I crossed the attractive Calder Water where it begins a winding course through a scenic wooded valley. Prefering not to enter the town the river skirts its eastern fringe and hurries to join the Clyde.

A dramatic change of landscape occurred as I entered East Kilbride. Green fields were exchanged for concrete blocks and wide streets. Traffic careered around nearby Murray roundabout as I gazed across the wide thoroughfare of Queensway towards the regular lines of The Plaza and The Olympia, set in the heart of town and housing expansive shopping malls. The Local Authority's proud boast is that you can walk from one end of the Olympia Centre to the other end of The Plaza, a distance of over three-quarters of a mile, all under one roof and completely protected from the weather. East Kilbride was not always like this. As recently as 1947 it was a charming rural village huddling around the eighteenth-century Parish Church. Its character was doomed to be changed forever in May of that year when the East Kilbride Development Corporation was established to oversee the creation of Scotland's first new town with the village as its nucleus. Over the succeeding years the population grew from 2,400 to 82,000 with the building of new houses, shops, factories, offices, churches and schools.

I wandered through the town centre and found the quiet haven of Cloverhill Park where I walked between lawns edged with white-blossomed hawthorn and elder. It seemed a good place for a lunch stop and as I munched my sandwiches I could see the stately tower of the Parish Church rising from the old village. I felt that I must pay my respects to the original East Kilbride, so, when my lunch was completed I walked between its warm stone buildings that exhibit a quiet charm amidst the bustling town that surrounds them. I was particularly drawn to the seventeenth-century coaching inn, the Montgomerie Arms. Outside the hostelry stands a stone platform known as the 'loupin' on stane,' which gave an easy leg up into the saddle for travellers on horseback.

As I headed north out of town I had one further call to make; to view Mains Castle, which fortuitously stood almost on my route. It is the oldest surviving building in East Kilbride, built by Roger de Valoins and dating from the sixteenth century. It gradually fell into disrepair but has thankfully been refurbished and is now an unusual and arresting private residence.

Once clear of the town I headed by road and path through the open land that separates East Kilbride from the urban sprawl of Glasgow. It was quite a pleasant walk and I passed the tiny settlement of Rogerton with a reservoir nestling nearby. Before I entered Glasgow's suburbs I reached Cathkin Braes, the nemesis of James 'Purlie' Wilson. Apparently when the poor fellow was executed he was hung and then beheaded before a crowd of 20,000 who shouted 'Murderers!' at his executioners. His body was thrown into a pauper's grave but during the night his daughter retrieved the corpse and had it interred in Strathaven.

I began a nightmare journey through the suburb of Rutherglen along a series of confusing roads and backstreets. My pace slowed due to the increasing discomfort from my ripe blisters and I was forced to rest periodically to ease them. Two and a half miles of purgatory brought me to the River Clyde at Dalmarnock. As I crossed the bridge over the evocative river I consulted the map to check the remaining distance to the city-centre. It indicated three miles. Would my blisters and I make it, I wondered? There was only one thing to be done. I removed my boots and put on trainers hoping their padded soles would lessen the pain.

Whilst changing my footwear my eyes were drawn to the writhing River Clyde, which has been the life-blood of Glasgow for centuries. At this point on its journey it is wayward, as if trying to escape the shackles of its urban surroundings, but after twisting for a further mile it widens and untangles itself. Eventually it shrugs off the city confines and opens its arms, as it passes Craigendoran and Port Glasgow, to become the majestic Firth of Clyde. It is thanks to this sheltered estuary that Glasgow became one of the prominent ports of Britain in the early eighteenth century when the Act of Union lifted the embargo on trade between Scotland and America. A handful of Glasgow businessmen seized this opportunity to join forces and charter a ship, which returned from Virginia loaded with rum and tobacco. This was sold at a good profit and by 1735 trade between Glasgow and America was thoroughly established and great fortunes were about to be made.

Reluctant to further abuse my feet, I left the river, conscious of the vast changes it must have witnessed over the years. The glory days are all but gone when its banks were lined with thriving shipbuilding yards and docks, but it still flows unperturbed on its well-worn path, much quieter and cleaner than it was in those industrious times. What a pleasure it would be if it reverted to its old self, for up to the middle of the eighteenth century it was a salmon river.

My trainers made a marginal improvement to my progress, and after a slow crawl, with frequent stops, I arrived in the heart of Glasgow well over an hour later. My ordeal was far from over, for I still had to reach Milngavie, which by my reckoning lay eight miles away. Eight miles! The very thought of it made me wince. Why not catch a bus and save youself grief? No one will ever know. The persuasive voice in my head was talking sense. But I would know and I couldn't cheat.

Feeling it would be foolish to plough on in my present condition, I decided to rest and have a meal before attempting the final lap of my journey. I rang the bed and breakfast residence where I was due to stay in Milngavie to let them know that I would be arriving late in the evening. When that was done I felt easier in my mind and went in search of food.

I wandered through stone and concrete lined city streets that were pulsatingly alive. How frenetic was the activity compared to the peaceful and serene countryside that I had relished on my walk through the Borders. Tempting, plate-glassed high-street stores and densely packed shops, brimming with bargain offers, were a magnet for the lively crowds surging along the pavements. Traffic streamed continually through their midst and the noise was incessant. However, to do justice to the great city it does offer far more than shops and crowded thoroughfares. It is justly proud of its art galleries, museums and its music in addition to the fine examples of historical architecture that have survived the City Fathers' attempts at 'improvement.' Foremost of these, the imposing cathedral, nowadays sits in incongruous surroundings with a backdrop of uninspiring modern buildings. The Cathedral Kirk, begun early in the thirteenth century, is the oldest surviving property in Glasgow and its central spire, the most ambitious of its kind in medieval Scottish architecture, rises to a height of 220 feet above the crossing. A prominent reminder of Glasgow's illustrious past, it remains an edifice of rare Gothic distinction.

Anxious to escape the seething mass of humanity I found a quiet back-street restaurant and recharged my batteries for the final onslaught. I planned to take a circuitous route to Milngavie, which added extra miles but avoided the urbanisation that has turned the town into a city suburb. The most direct route, going north, appeared to follow the A879 and A807 roads and I discounted these busy thoroughfares. For the first section of the journey I was obliged to follow minor roads until I was able to join the Forth and Clyde Canal at Lambhill. Pounding tarmac did little for my blisters and I was reduced to periodic halts to rest my feet. The luxury of towpath walking was enjoyed for a mile and a half as I headed for Wilderness Plantation and the Antonine Wall. It was pleasing to be in open country once more and an added bonus was passing the serene Possil Loch that borders the canal.

When I reached the plantation I was quite a distance to the east of Milngavie but I had the benefit of pastoral surroundings and the prospect of seeing the site of a Roman Fortlet when I crossed the line of the Antonine Wall. This I came across as I emerged from Wilderness Plantation and my thoughts returned to my first contact with the great Roman barrier near Newton St Boswells. How long ago that seemed.

In order to cross the River Kelvin I detoured even further east and joined a good track that led me to Balmore. As I hobbled through the little village I was hailed by a man who must have noticed my distress.

'Going far?' he inquired.

'Milngavie,' I replied, expecting to be chastised for limping through the village sporting a bulky rucksack.

'Would you like to come and rest awhile?' the man asked solicitously. 'I live just round the corner.'

I was touched by the man's kind offer, but I refused on the grounds that I was already well behind schedule. I thanked him and made for another track that lay on the outskirts of the village. I found it without difficulty and enjoyed another three-quarters of a mile free of tarmac until I reached the tiny settlment of Flutcher.

From here it was all road walking, albeit quiet country ones and the strain really began to tell. I was eternally grateful that this was the final day of my walk, for I could not face further torment. Grass verges again came to my rescue as I craved relief from the hard surface of the road.

After a further painful mile I came upon a welcome stream and took the opportunity to soothe my feet. As I did so I kept a wary eye out for any irate farmers, recalling my previous experience when seeking release from my crawl across the plain to Strathaven. I checked the map. One and a half miles remained. Hopefully the soaking would enable my feet to last out. Thankfully the June evenings were long and plenty of light remained, which was just as well, for I was nearly done for.

I was reduced to counting each weary step as I followed the road that passed between a wood and a golf course. Each step counted signified one less to endure. The final leg of my day's journey took an hour, despite the fact that my night's accommodation was handily situated in Milngavie. When my host opened the door I staggered inside with a huge sigh of relief that my ordeal was finally over.

'You look whacked,' the man said.

I gave him a weary smile, unwilling to divulge the details of my over-ambitious route planning. In hindsight it would have been much easier to stay the night in Glasgow, but I suppose impatience got the better of me.

Despite my tribulations it had been a tremendously fulfilling experience to link two premier long-distance footpaths and, as I lay in the comfort of my bed later that evening, I counted myself the pioneer of a new route that would eventually be followed by countless long-distance walkers.

CHAPTER SEVEN

The West Highland Way

DAY SIXTY-FIVE : MILNGAVIE - BALMAHA

On my return home I began to write an account of my walk across the Borders, in the hope that it could be published. Imagine my chagrin a short time later when I passed a local bookshop and a new publication caught my eye. Unbelievably the book was entitled *Pennine Way to West Highland Way*. Desperately fighting the urge to heave a missile through the window, I pressed my face against the glass in order to discover the author of this dastardly work. It turned out to be Hamish Brown, author of *Hamish's Groats End Walk* and *Hamish's Mountain Walk*, the latter being an account of his non-stop traverse of all the Scottish Munro peaks. Cursing him for getting his latest book in first, I dashed into the shop, grabbed a copy and enviously scanned its pages. His route, I observed, varied significantly from mine, but this was of no consequence because he had already committed his account to print. From his viewpoint it would be merely an addition to his previous books, but to me it was a severe blow.

Eventually my annoyance turned to acceptance and I began to plan my next venture, the West Highland Way. I knew that there would be no purpose in writing an account of this particular walk, for many had already been published. The previous year I had acquired a walking friend named Maurice who I had met on Wainwright's Coast to Coast Walk and we agreed to tackle the ninety-five-mile long-distance route linking Milngavie and Fort William. We studied the Official Guide published by the Countryside Commission for Scotland that provides a detailed description of the route and relevent accommodation.

Our planning complete, we travelled to Milngavie full of anticipation and I took the opportunity to explore the former mill town that lies on the Allander Water. On my previous visit I had been only too glad to take the weight off of my blisters and get a night's rest. Much quieter than when its cotton mills, snuff mill and paper mill where running full pelt, the town has managed to retain some of its former personality and has a pleasant, unhurried air.

On the morning of our departure we posed for photographs in front of what is probably Milngavie's most prominent landmark, a dainty clocktower, before crossing the market-square to join the Way. The initial section offered easy walking amidst attractive surroundings as we followed the bank of Allander Water through wooded parkland. Eventually we climbed gradually to the upper part of Allander Park, a rough moorland of birch, broom and gorse. At the crest of the rise good views appeared of the suburban fringes of Glasgow to the south and the Kilpatrick Hills to the west.

We were soon walking through Mugdock Wood, noted for its flora, which includes the prolific yellow tormentil and others that decorate further sections of the Way, such as blue milkwort, pink lousewort and scabius. In the days when whisky distilling was officially regulated the thickets of the wood provided cover for several illicit stills and in 1818 there was an ugly skirmish between armed smugglers and a party of Excisemen and soldiers. On that occasion the smugglers won the day.

As we crossed a narrow road that traversed the wood a farmer pulled up his tractor and inquired if we were walking the West Highland Way. When we nodded he said, 'We get a lot of walkers

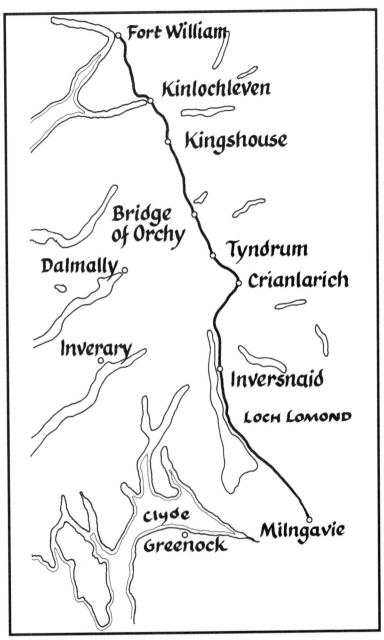

The West Highland Way

passing through. It must be a popular route.' It transpired that he was secretary of the local black-faced sheep breeder's association but he ommitted to reveal who had black faces, the sheep or the breeders. The farmer also indicated that he had helped to erect the Border fence across the Cheviots that provides a lifeline to Pennine Way walkers in bad weather.

Craigallian Loch appeared beneath retreating grey clouds as we emerged from Mugdock Wood. Its calm, ashen waters lay beneath an inspiring backdrop of the Campsie Fells with the knobbly, hunchbacked hill of Dumgoyne at their western end. This landmark dominates the Way as it passes through the valley of Strath Blane and remains visible for several miles. Beyond tiny Carbeth Loch we climbed to a crest at the head of what is known as the 'Tinker's Loan.' This forms an important watershed at the northern edge of the Glasgow basin and from this point the streams drain northwards and westwards into Loch Lomond. A fine vista opens up to the north, enclosed by the rolling Kilpatricks on the one hand and the rugged scarp of the Campsies on the other.

As Maurice and I descended into Strath Blane its slopes were ablaze with banks of vivid broom that came alive under the welcome glare of the sun. Beyond the site of Duntreath Castle the West Highland Way conveniently joins the line of the dismantled Blane Valley Railway that led us under the significant shadow of Dumgoyne whose craggy slopes I found fascinating. So much so that I took numerous camera shots of them, causing Maurice to remark that I had developed a fetish for the distinctive hill.

The lush farmland of Strath Blane surrounded us as we followed the old railway to the gentle hamlet of Gartness where it joins another dismantled line, the former Forth and Clyde Junction Railway. This was opened in 1856 to link Stirling and the Vale of Leven. A terrace of warm sandstone cottages overlooking the meandering River Endrick, which sweeps down from the Campsie Fells, caught our eye. None of the abodes were alike and they were all constructed from material hewn from the surrounding beds of old red sandstone.

When we reached the hilltop by Old Gartness an excellent panorama unfolded. It seemed the perfect spot to have lunch, with eight miles of our day's journey remaining. As we chewed sandwiches in the bright sunlight we looked northwards at the landscape that formed the final part of our day's itinerary. Amongst a rolling patchwork of farmland and hedgerow sat the compact village of Drymen and beyond, the distinctive hills surrounding Loch Lomond came into view. The most cheering sight amongst them was the dark hump of Conic Hill that overlooks our destination, Balmaha. What an invigorating prospect the scene provided with its promise of Highland scenery at its finest.

With eyes fixed on the approaching wilder country of moorland and forest we marched along a minor road to Gateside where we passed within half a mile of Drymen, which possesses a compact village green and has a population of less than 1,000. The Romans built a small fort hereabouts as part of a chain of frontier posts along the Highland edge. Unfortunately it has all but disappeared, but aerial photography revealed its existence on Drumquhassle Ridge.

Just beyond Gateside we were obliged to follow the A811 road for a short distance, which forms a natural dividing line between the rich farmland that we had been traversing and the forest and open moors to the north. On leaving the road we were soon immersed in the vast green carpet of Garadhban Forest and any views were temporarily suspended until we passed convenient gaps in the trees. We finally emerged over an hour later amidst the heather-clad, rolling hills that overlook the south-east corner of Loch Lomond.

The great bastion of Conic Hill drew nearer as we trod the peaty moorland paths beneath Moor Park and it completely obscured any views of the loch. From the shape of the landscape we could make out a natural barrier, of which Conic Hill is a part, which forms a distinct demarcation between the Lowlands and Highlands of Scotland. These hills comprise a section of the Highland Boundary Fault, a massive geological upthrust that stretches from near Helensburgh on the Clyde to Stonehaven on the east coast.

As though offering a strenuous finale to our day's walk we were required to climb the daunting slopes of Conic Hill. Our masochistic urge surfaced when, following a long pull up the hill we left the contouring path, which avoids the summit, and struck out up a steep slope to obtain a view from the top. Hot and breathless we arrived on what we thought was the summit only to be confronted by another two humps that lay between us and a view over Loch Lomond.

At last we achieved our goal and were rewarded by a panoramic view over the southern end of the loch. A line of islands, forming part of the Highland Boundary Fault, could be clearly seen protruding from its blue waters. Beyond, a band of hills stretched to the west coast. A celebratory drink of coffee was called for, but our commemoration seemed tame when we spied an empty champagne bottle nearby. Someone had obviously celebrated in style on attaining the summit of Conic Hill.

All that remained of our day's toil was to descend to Balmaha that nestled on the lochside beneath us. We negotiated the steep summit slope to rejoin the Way, which dropped sharply into a grassy corrie before descending a built-up staircase on slopes carpeted with bracken. At the foot of the hill we traversed a small remnant of Garadhban Forest to enter the car park in the village.

Balmaha is a small, but old-established settlement that is very popular with boating enthusiasts. When we reached the bay at the lochside it was flecked with a variety of craft, from motor-launches to dinghies, nodding gaily at their moorings.

After a hard day's foot-slogging, for over eighteen miles, Maurice and I were thankful for the comfortable sanctuary of a guesthouse run by an elderly couple who were very friendly and obliging. The husband knew the area exceedingly well, for he had been the Head Forest Warden of the Rowardennan area for many years. 'You'll pass through my patch tomorrow,' he told us, before describing much of the day's route. He then bemoaned the recent modernisation of the village. 'Balmaha had a timeless quality until they built a ghastly row of shops and a restaurant, which, in my opinion, destroyed the appeal of the place.'

We also learnt that Balmaha had not always been a quiet village. According to our host there was a factory in the vicinity at one time that produced 'wood vinegar,' a crude acetic acid, by distillation from oak trimmings and thinnings. The acid was used in the textile bleaching and dyeing industry in the Vale of Leven, but in the 1920's cheaper supplies were purchased from large-scale chemical producers and the factory closed. 'The Forestry Commission have a sawmill here,' he told us, 'but our mainstay now is catering for day visitors and tourists. Boat trips to Inchcailloch, the nearest of the islands in Loch Lomond, are very popular,' he added.

Maurice and I retired to our beds knowing a great deal about the district thanks to our knowledgeable host. It did not take long for us to drift off to sleep as the long day's hike and the fresh air took their effect.

DAY SIXTY-SIX : BALMAHA - INVERSNAID

Sunlight filtered through the bedroom curtains on the following morning as I lay pondering what lay in store for us that day. It would not be as strenuous as the previous one for we had only fourteen and a half miles to cover along the 'bonny' east bank of Loch Lomond. However, it is always dangerous to count your chickens and I prepared myself for any eventuality.

After a hearty breakfast our hosts waved farewell as we headed for the bay once more to rejoin the Way and walk beside the largest body of inland water in Britain. Loch Lomond is one of the longest Scottish lochs, at twenty-seven miles, but it is also one of the deepest and most beautiful. It comprises two distinct sections. In its southern reaches the loch is wide, relatively shallow and studded with islands that were once populated and cultivated. At Ross Point it begins to narrow and deepen and has fewer islands. Its deepest point, 623 feet, is south of Inversnaid and all but twenty-seven of those feet lie below sea level.

Although the line of the West Highland Way from Balmaha to the hotel at Rowardennan is never far from the shore of the loch it winds amiably up and down hill, into bays and round promontories, through open woodland and dense conifer plantations. This section of the way contains Scotland's largest remnant of oakwood and we were only allowed occasional glimpses of the loch as we forged through it.

At the bridge over the Blair Burn we entered the Queen Elizabeth Forest Park, which stretches from Loch Lomond eastwards through the Trossacks. The greater part of the oakwoods on the land, much of it formerly belonging to the Montrose estates, has been retained and is prudently managed in consultation with the Nature Conservancy Council.

Periodically the Way joins the road that hugs the shore of the loch as far as Rowardennan and I was glad that the stretches on tarmac were intermittent. On the approach to Ross Point, road and footpath diverge and the Way cuts across the promontory amidst the extensive foliage of Ross Wood. This adjoins the extensive Rowardennan Forest and unfortunately blots out views of the significant narrowing of the loch. However, there were occasions when the trees relented and we enjoyed the, albeit, cloudy view across the loch to the rugged range of hills topped by Beinn Bhreac at 2,074 feet.

We progressed to Coille Mhor where we crossed a burn amidst peaceful, secluded surroundings and were able to look across a sheltered bay to the site of Iron Age loch dwellings known as crannogs. These served the same defensive purpose as the islands in the loch did, in warlike times, and they were constructed in the shallow waters near the shore. Great oaken trunks were sunk into the bed of the loch, on top of which wooden platforms were laid to support rough dwellings made from wattle covered with clay.

Another mile of lochside walking brought us to Rowardennan, which is literally the end of the road, although there is four miles of track to Rowchoish. It boasts a good hotel, a pier and a delightfully situated Youth Hostel on the loch's edge.

As we were exactly halfway along our day's route Rowardennan appeared a good place for a lunch stop. We made for the lochside where the grey waters gently lapped the shore, which was almost deserted. There were several cars and a caravan in the distance and I spent the next few minutes watching a lone water-skier cavorting on the loch. Our gaze eventually turned to the broad shoulders of Ben Lomond, its head shrouded in cloud, rising majestically behind a cluster of ash and larch lining the lochside. It was disappointing to be unable to view the evocative mountain in all its glory. Other Scottish hills can claim greater height than Ben Lomond's 3,195 feet but, because of its commanding position amongst surrounding fells and its proximity to the rolling Lowland hills, it casts an aura of grandeur over a wide area. Rowardennan is the starting-point of the main path up the Ben, one of Scotland's most climbed peaks and how I would have loved to make that climb in good weather when views from its top must be spectacular.

We did have some companions, however, for nearby we noticed two walkers, one bandaging his colleague's foot. Inquisitive, Maurice and I joined them for a chat. It appeared that the sufferer, Reg, had acquired a blister on every toe, to which his friend, Tony had applied plasters. The careful bandaging of his feet enlarged them and we pointed out that the poor fellow would not be able to put his boots back on.

'That's okay,' Reg replied, grimacing with pain, 'I'm switching to trainers.'

I thought of my similar experience whilst walking through Glasgow.

'Are you walking far?' Maurice asked.

'We're doing the West Highland Way,' Tony answered.

'So are we,' I said. Considering they were only halfway through the second day of what is normally a six-day walk, Reg's chances didn't look good, but we kept our thoughts to ourselves and wished him luck.

'Thanks,' he replied, 'perhaps we'll meet again.'

Thinking that highly unlikely we left them to their first aid and rejoined the Way. As we did so we discussed poor Reg's prospects and concluded that if by some miracle he reached Fort William, God should reward him with a new pair of feet. Never having seen anyone plagued so badly by blisters I nicknamed him 'Red-raw of Rowardennan.'

From Rowardennan to the head of Loch Lomond the Way alternately runs close by the water's edge and well up the east shore. The initial section, to the hotel and road-end at Inversnaid, is a traverse through woodland under the steep flanks of Ben Lomond. We left the public road beyond the pier, passed the Youth Hostel and joined the forest track at Ptarmigan Lodge, named after the spur of Ben Lomond that towers above it. Swathes of brilliant-red rhododendron surrounded us, brightening a landscape dulled by gathering dark clouds as we took the high-level alternative route, by track through oak and birch, to Rowchoish bothy. The lochshore route is distinctly rough in places and can involve scrambling by the water's edge among boulders and broken crags, so we discounted it. This meant missing out on Rob Roy's Prison, as one of the larger crags is named, where, it is reputed, he kept hostages and kidnap victims in a natural rock cell close by the loch. This landmark signifies entry into Rob Roy Country. The lands of Craig Rostan, through which we were passing, to the head of the loch were his property before he was outlawed.

As we progressed through the woodland we were occasionally

rewarded with views to the west through the Arochar-Tarbet Gap to the hills above Loch Long. We could discern the dark, craggy profile of the Cobbler, otherwise known as Ben Arthur, the most distinctive of that range. The monotony of the forest track was relieved at this stage by overtaking two ladies and enjoying a chat with them. We discovered that they were very accommodating - no, not towards Maurice and me, if that's what you're thinking. They were also walking to Inversnaid where they were due to rendezvous with their husbands who were following them, not on the track, but along the loch in a boat, whilst indulging in their favourite pastime of fishing. This apparently was a common occurrence, the ladies being sent ahead to a pre-arranged meeting point whilst their husbands enjoyed themselves. I can think of many wives, who, when handed such a proposition would gladly throw their spouses in the loch. These particular ladies were completely unabashed and evidently enjoyed their enforced marches. Showing a remarkable interest in their husbands' antics they explained that their boat would be hugging the lochside, as close to the overhanging vegetation as possible. The reason for this strategy being that from the trees and bushes dropped succulent caterpillars and grubs, straight into the waiting mouths of the fish congregating beneath. The shoreline obviously provided rich pickings for their selfish husbands.

The ladies were taking their time so we bade them farewell and pressed on, secretly feeling that their wretched husbands deserved to drown. We were eager to reach Inversnaid, for a night of luxury in the hotel was in prospect, but our anticipatory bubble was about to burst. When we reached the Inversnaid Hotel a glassy stare greeted our arrival at reception. Did we detect a note of disdain in that searing look? This was far from the welcome we had anticipated, despite the fact that we had removed our boots before entering. Maurice and I wondered if the other guests also received a less than enthusiastic welcome. There were plenty of them and the hotel seemed busy. It was obviously a strategic halt on tours of the Trossacks and beyond.

Suitably cleaned and refreshed we entered the dining room, which was virtually full and the prevailing hum of conversation enveloped us. It resembled the buzz of an angry swarm of bees. The meal was an anticlimax; poor food complemented by slow and impersonal service. Our fellow diners seemed impervious to such annoyances, chattering excitedly about the day's events.

After dinner we studied the map of the West Highland Way to see what lay in store. Tracing our following day's route, we noted any points of interest until the current day's walk began to take its toll. We were soon in our beds savouring thoughts of exciting days ahead in the splendour of the Highlands. Sleep quickly overtook me and I dreamt of Rob Roy, whose supposed prison we had passed. I fought alongside him and his outlaw band against his arch-enemy the Duke of Montrose. How brave I seemed in my dream.

DAY SIXTY-SEVEN : INVERSNAID - CRIANLARICH

Prior to breakfast on a grey, overcast morning Maurice and I had the temerity to request packed lunches at the hotel reception desk. An embarrassing silence ensued. The receptionist was obviously disconcerted by such awkward guests. Eventually a grudging concession was made to investigate the possibiltiy and we were asked to inquire again after breakfast. During our meal we pronounced judgement on the hotel, whose ethos was clearly to attract as many coach parties as possible, serve them inferior food and get rid of them before they could cause trouble. Walkers were obviously an encumbrance, inconsiderately lumbering in with muddy boots and sweaty brows, lowering the tone of the place. It was doubly unfortunate that one of the most popular long-distance footpaths in the country happened to pass the door. For those about to leap up and cancel their booking at the Inversnaid Hotel, have no fear, it is now under new management and its ambience has greatly improved.

As we checked out of the hotel we were each handed a couple of sandwiches filled with slices of cold pork. Reasoning that we were lucky to get anything at all, we paid for them and made a quick exit before the staff could change their minds.

Departing hurriedly, we cast a hasty look across Loch Lomond. The view was unfortunately marred by an overflowing rubbish bin in the hotel forecourt. Maurice and I chuckled at the sight of this bulging container, which nicely summed up our opinion of the Inversnaid Hotel. Through the morning haze we could just discern

Wallace's Isle on the opposite side of the loch. It is named after Sir William Wallace, the great patriot and chieftan who led the Scottish armies against Edward I. He was captured in 1304, condemned for treason in London and executed at Smithfield. Slightly to the north lay Inveruglas Isle, the site of a castle once occupied by the MacFarlanes. They ruled the west shore of Loch Lomond north of Tarbet and like the MacGregors gained a reputation as raiders and cattle thieves.

Our day's journey began with a tramp through another band of woodland that hugs the east shore of the loch as far as Doune Farm. As we forged through a carpet of oak, birch, rowan and hazel we saw nothing of the wild goats, deer and grey squirrel that reputedly inhabit the area. Being 'townies,' our untrained eyes probably missed many tell-tale signs

Approximately twenty minutes of walking brought us to the site, indicated by the map, of Rob Roy's Cave. Much to our chagrin we spent half an hour scrambling over a jumble of massive boulders that litter the hillside and never found it. When we related this abortive tale in the guesthouse that evening, our embarrassment was complete. The object of our search, we were told, was not a cave at all, merely a deep crevice between two large rocks. It had, however, managed to shelter some of the MacGregors who met there before many of their raids and also Robert the Bruce, who reputedly spent a night there in 1306.

Abandoning our frustrating search we rejoined the path to find the hillsides scoured by numerous streams, which, during the heavy rains of previous years, had created landslips, some having gouged channels across our path. A party of Royal Engineers was helpfully erecting a temporary bridge over a newly created ravine. It was a scene of hard hats, squeeling winches and barking orders.

We emerged from the arboreal tunnel near the head of the loch and extensive views unfolded before us. White-walled Doune Farm, recently restored, nestled on the gently sloping lochside amidst welcome turf and stunted bracken that stretched to the water's edge. Under a brightening sky the upper extremity of the loch was clearly visible, encircled by an assortment of towering green hills. Ardlui lay at its northern tip alongside a cleft in the hills through which the River Falloch emerges to empty its waters into Loch Lomond.

Walking became easier as we progressed to Ardleish and onwards to the head of the loch where we stopped for some welcome refreshment. Maurice had worked up a fine lather in the humid conditions and stripped off his damp shirt, which he hung on a convenient tree branch to dry. He cautiously opened the sandwiches that had been provided at the hotel and gave them an exploratory sniff. Very cautious was our Maurice. His nose wrinkled, indicating his distaste, and they were returned to his rucksack. I was so hungry I recklessly ate mine and suffered later for my stupidity. By mid-afternoon I had rampant stomach-ache, which refused to subside until the late evening. More curses for the Inversnaid Hotel! Meanwhile, our pleasant lunchtime interlude was spent lazing on the lochside and watching energetic salmon leaping from the water, unfortunately beyond our reach. Oh for a rod and line!

After lunch we entered Glen Falloch, its lower reaches a deep trench scoured by a retreating glacier. During an exhilarating walk to Inverarnan the dark profile of the Crianlarich Hills appeared, huddling beneath a bank of dark, brooding cloud. We passed the remains of a canal, constructed in the mid-nineteenth century to link the Iverarnan Hotel with Loch Lomond. It was now a forlorn and overgrown channel, long disused. The hotel itself is a former drover's inn, strategically sited on the old drove route from Glen Fyne, in Argyll, to Glen Gyle. Beyond the Inverarnan Hotel the glen veers north-east towards Crianlarich. The beautiful valley was a revelation, particularly the Falls of Falloch where the lively river twists and swirls around myriad protruding rocks in a series of extremely attractive cascades. Conveniently the sun began to shine and remarkably, it was to remain a constant companion for the remainder of the West Highland Way.

A steady climb to the farms at Derrydaroch took us into open moorland and we had a clear view of the A82 Glasgow to Fort William road threading through the heart of the glen, accompanied by the West Highland Railway. They travel hand in hand through the narow valley on their journey to Fort William.

We crossed the river near the collection of farms at Derrydarroch - the 'oak grove.' One of the many distinct Way signs, bearing the Countryside Commission for Scotland's emblem of a thistle within a hexagon, directed us towards the road and railway. We kept both of them company for roughly three-quarters of a mile, listening to the roar of the traffic, before thankfully passing beneath the railway and crossing the busy road. The Way then struck across the moorland towards Keilator Farm, lying in the upper reaches of Glen Falloch.

As we contoured the fellside beneath Craw Knowe a splendid, rugged landscape basked in penetrating sunshine. At this point we joined a wide, grassy path that formed part of the military road network, constructed by General Wade and his successor, Major Caulfield, in response to the Jacobite uprisings of 1715 and 1745. The road system, consisting of gravelled tracks, was built to aid the movement of English troops through the Highlands in order to control the Jacobites. Some have been converted into modern metalled roads but the broad tracks and clear pathways that form the modern remnants of the road system were to guide us for most of our route to Fort William.

The rugged peak of Ben More, one of the impressive Crianlarich Hills, hove into view, thrusting into a sparkling-blue sky as we approached the head of the glen. On reaching a watershed above the village of Crianlarich we could see its scattering of buildings spread beneath us. The population of this tiny, but very popular tourist centre swells to many times its normal size during summertime.

The tantalising prospect of cooling drinks and a chance to refresh ourselves carried us rapidly down the Old Military Road and into the village. Here we mingled with a variety of visitors ranging from sightseers to hardened walkers sporting bushy beards and sweatbands. A party of youngsters bustled from the railway station full of excited chatter and expectant gazes. Crianlarich sported two stations when the line from Callander was still in use, but is now reliant on the busy West Highland Line.

Finding a convenient pub, we enjoyed a deliciously cool drink and struck up a conversation with three walkers, Don, Derek and Peter who were also tackling the West Highland Way. They had taken up walking later in life, as we had done. Like most novices they experienced some hairy moments at the outset. Their first walk of any distance was the Pennine Way, on which they embarked with no training or experience. They set out from Edale without any food, armed only with a map, which they couldn't read, and attempted to cross the notoriously featureless and boggy Kinder Plateau. Their map soon sank into one of the treacherous peat groughs, rendering them completely rudderless. After wandering aimlessly amidst the peat they eventually found their way from the plateau, unfortunately several miles from where they intended. Shades of the 'Brothers in Law'! Blundering onto a nearby road they sought directions at a pub and miraculously found the path to their next objective, Bleaklow Head, where they joined forces with a group of experienced walkers who guided them to their destination at Crowden Youth Hostel. They decided that from then on things could only get better and decided to persevere. Purchasing another map they completed the next day's walk successfully. Bolstered by this they progressed all the way to Byrness, without serious mishap, until ill fortune struck. Derek went down with a gastric infection and had to drop out. His companions ensured that arrangements were made to get him home before pushing on without him to complete the final lap across the Cheviots. We discovered that the three friends were also staying overnight in the village and arranged to meet them that evening for a meal.

After finding our guesthouse, which lay in a fine setting overlooking the imposing Crianlarich Hills, Maurice and I relaxed before cleaning ourselves and returning to the pub. We found the lounge bar heaving with an assortment of walkers and climbers. Finding Don, Derek and Peter tucked in a corner we squeezed in alongside them and were very surprised to find that their companions were none other than Reg and Tony. We discovered that Reg was coping manfully with his sore feet and was encouraged by the fact that Crianlarich lies halfway along the Way. 'I'm still determined to reach Fort William,' he told us with a broad smile.

Maurice and I concluded that the room should be re-named the 'Blister Bar,' for we met another party of West Highland Way walkers suffering their ravages. These abused feet belonged to six nurses from Glasgow who, bravely or foolishly, were walking the Way to raise money for their hospital's charity. Unused to covering great distances in debilitating boots their feet had rebelled. One of the young ladies was hobbling very badly and we reckoned she would be lucky to make it to journey's end.

Throughout the evening we chatted to many other walkers, swapping experiences and outlining ambitions for future walks. The pleasant interlude assured us that the West Highland Way was extremely popular and attracted a great variety of walkers.

DAY SIXTY-EIGHT : CRIANLARICH - ACHALLADER

The following morning Maurice and I enjoyed a hearty breakfast before bidding goodbye to Crianlarich. The sun beamed cheerily upon us and we were delighted at the prospect of another bright day. Tyndrum was our initial destination as we returned to the Way and followed the broad track that snakes to and fro across wide Strathfillan, as though uncertain which side of the River Fillan to follow. The river is spanned by Kirkton Bridge, from where the views along Strath Fillan are truly memorable, highlighted by a most pleasing aspect of the shapely Crianlarich Hills, with Ben More and Stob Binnien the most prominent.

A little further along the Way an intriguing reminder of one of Breadalbane's early religious influences appeared, in the shape of St Fillan's Chapel and graveyard. Unfortunately very little of the chapel remains, its sad ruins lying amidst a pleasant cluster of trees. The graveyard, its brooding headstones still intact, stands nearby, perched on a grassy knoll above the valley floor. It is a stark reminder of Breadalbane's troubled past.

St Fillan was the patron saint of Breadalbane and he was very active in the area during the seventh century. On a sign by the chapel are depicted two tokens of his mission and these were given to lay brothers for use in certain rites there, such as taking oaths or treating the sick. These tokens are currently housed in the National Museum of Antiquities, in Edinburgh. One is the head of St Fillan's crozier, or staff - an ornately carved piece of silver, inside which was found an older and simpler version. The other, which has humorous connotations, is a bell, supposedly used as a cure for insanity. Sufferers of this affliction were dipped in the Holy Pool in the River Fillan, then taken to the chapel and left overnight tied to a tombstone or the font, depending on the weather, with the bell over their head. The next morning, when the bell was removed they were reputedly found cured. Maurice had a good laugh over this, declaring that it would be a great test for anyone feigning insanity.

Our historic diversion provided an opportunity to cool down. We had already felt the effects of the unwavering sun and more perspiration was imminent as we rejoined the track that heads for the bridge at Auchtertyre Farm. Beyond the bridge an awe-inspiring vista of mountains appeared, vividly etched on a giant canvas. After re-crossing the A82 road we headed for Tyndrum and passed the point where the River Cononish tumbles into the valley, having flowed beneath several disused leadmines, which spatter the hill-slopes to the west. This once thriving industry originated the building of a crushing and smelting plant at Tyndrum that eliminated the dispatching of lead ore to Glasgow by way of Loch Lomond. The plant has long since gone but a few years ago a prospective gold mine in the locality was being probed.

A stretch of forest walking brought us to the outskirts of Tyndrum and as we broke from the ubiquitous trees we were treated to an extremely attractive view of white-walled buildings glistening in the sunshine beneath the grey mass of Beinn Odhar. Formerly one of the main halts on an important drove route that stretched as far north as Skye, and to Crieff, Falkirk and the English markets to the south, the village has succumbed to mass tourism.

The place was crowded as we entered. Eager visitors spewed from car and coach and the village store was awash with walkers replenishing supplies. Here was the last chance for backpackers to stock up, there being no shops on the Way until Kinlochleven, twenty-eight miles away. In the store we met the Glasgow nurses who seemed much more cheerful than on the previous evening. Evidently the splendid weather and scenery had rejuvenated them and even prompted jokes about their blisters.

On our way from the village we rejoined the Old Military Road that heads into the pass leading to Bridge of Orchy. It was to become our constant companion, apart from minor deviations, until we were within easy reach of Fort William. Beads of sweat stood out on our foreheads as we climbed the broad track that follows the Crom Allt into the hills. As we entered the pass the A82 road could be seen snaking along the opposite side of the valley, whose slopes were carpeted with familiar forests. A helicopter flew overhead, which, Maurice quipped, was on the lookout for exhausted West Highland Way walkers.

The pass narrowed to form a shapely valley, scoured by a glacier flowing south from Rannoch Moor. Above its forested base, mountains sweep upwards to create a dramatic, symmetrical semi-circle. Bolstered by a backdrop of distant Black Mount Hills, it formed one of my most memorable views. It is set in Campbell country, for this fearful clan were the hereditary keepers of the surrounding deer forest. The Campbells of Glenorchy, as they were known, were required to supply venison for royal feasts at the hunting lodge, which formerly stood a little way ahead at Auch. James IV in particular loved the area and was known to have spent a week at the lodge in 1506.

The character of the pass changed once more as we contoured the lower slopes of Beinn Odhar and were reunited with the West Highland Railway, which was heading for Bridge of Orchy. We were truly amidst some of the finest scenery of the Way, accentuated by the formidable bulk of Beinn Dorain that towered over the flat valley floor, making us feel minute and insignificant. Auch seemed a good place to rest and we discarded our rucksacks before perching on a low wall. Don, Derek and Peter came into view. Despite the heat they were also enjoying themselves, their route-finding difficulties now a thing of the past. Before continuing, Maurice led us to the river where we dangled our feet in the deliciously cool water. Life felt good.

Our friends joined us for the final stretch to Bridge of Orchy, which lay four miles away. Striding beneath Beinn Dorain we crossed numerous bubbling streams that poured from its flanks. Great gullies slashed the fellside above us but its craggy higher reaches, home to the abundant mountain saxifrage, remained tantalisingly out of view.

Tiring of the valley floor the Way crossed the railway and climbed above it. Maurice and I were full of anticipation as we struck a good pace, spurred on by our three friends who were anticipating a welcome drink at their destination, the Bridge of Orchy Hotel. They were conveniently staying there that night but we were not so lucky. I was about to lose several brownie points, for we had to leave the Way and cover a further four miles to the accommodation I had booked at Achallader Farm.

Bridge of Orchy station, a strategic halt on the West Highland Railway, shimmered in the afternoon sunlight as we approached, its slate-grey roof complementing a startling-red platform. It was fringed by a multi-coloured cluster of trees that contrasted sharply with the surrounding scrub, curiously peppered with stones. This miniature arboretum displayed a hint of softness against the harsher backdrop of the snow-tipped Black Mount Hills.

The hamlet of Bridge of Orchy is a tiny oasis of habitation lying on the fringe of some of the wildest country in Britain. A few dwellings cluster around the distinctive hotel, and the bridge from which the place takes its name was built by the military in 1751. Apart from this structure and the hotel, the other thing of note is the annual rainfall, which can reach 110 inches per year. Thankfully, Maurice and I were not subjected to any.

We bade farewell to Don, Derek and Peter outside the hotel and we had gone but a few yards when round a corner came Reg and Tony who were making remarkable progress, considering Reg's sore feet. We found that they were also staying at the hotel, which increased our envy. Wishing them well we headed along the A82 road towards Loch Tulla and Achallader. Sweat flowed and boots chafed in the heat, but the tremendous views over Loch Tulla took some of the sting out of our struggle. Young pine and spruce clothed the roadside but permitted views of the austere fringe of Rannoch Moor. Silent prayers were offered for the remarkable weather to continue until we had covered the most inhospitable section of the Way that lay over the desolate moor.

Three miles of road-walking seemed endless until the eagerly awaited track to Achallader appeared and we enjoyed a peaceful, traffic-free final stage of our day's journey. As we approached the farm I won back a few points from a begrudging Maurice for a breathtaking setting. The farmhouse of Achallader, looking bright as a button, huddled beneath the dramatic bulk of Beinn Achaladair, its sleek lower slopes transforming into the grey ruggedness of its indented crest. The snow-white walls of the farm rose to red gables above vivid-green lawns bedecked with multi-coloured rhododendron. Hosts of buttercups in the surrounding meadows added a further splash of colour to a scene, which, in my view completely vindicated my choice of accommodation. If Maurice agreed he did not concur, merely appearing grateful to take the weight off his feet.

An effusive welcome, probably born of relief, awaited us. The farmer's wife, Fiona, had become concerned about our late arrival. Piping-hot tea and delicious cakes were quickly forthcoming as we sank blissfully into cavernous armchairs. Fiona excused herself, explaining that the place was full and she had many mouths to feed. Resisting the strong urge to fall asleep we eventually stirred ourselves, not wishing to sit down to supper unkempt and unwashed.

Heads swivelled in our direction as we entered the dining room a little later, minus the dust and sweat and ravenously hungry, despite the cakes we had consumed earlier. Our fellow guests included a party of five affable West Highland Way walkers from Aberdeen, three of whom were lively teenagers. The chatter was unbroken as we recounted our respective adventures and they were obviously relishing their walk. A couple sitting nearby remarked that merely listening to our conversation made them feel tired. They indicated that four-wheeled travel was their preference and they were bound for Fort William, Ullapool and, eventually, Inverness.

Whilst busily keeping us supplied with splendid food, Fiona wickedly suggested that we all climbed Beinn Achalladair after supper, to round off our day in style. The touring couple visibly paled but the Aberdonians were enthusiastic until they learnt it is all of 3,404 feet. Another time perhaps, thought Maurice and I.

As an alternative Fiona recommended a stroll along nearby Water of Tulla that flows beneath the slopes of Beinn Achaladair, or, if our feet had already suffered sufficient punishment, an inspection of the adjacent ruined fortification. This, we learnt, had a chequered history, for in 1692 it housed a detachment of Campbells who marched from there to participate in the infamous massacre of the MacDonalds at Glen Coe.

Maurice and I plumped for the fort inspection after supper whilst the Aberdonians walked along Water of Tulla. We were keen to see our first manifestation of the massacre. Although little of the original fort remained it did evoke a sense of involvement in a notorious episode of Scottish history. Unfortunately, the charm of this relic was marred by an adjacent barn, topped with a gaudily painted corrugated roof.

As we strolled around the farm's perimeter the colour of the landscape softened in the mellow evening sunlight. The farmhouse looked even more stunning bathed in an orange glow and a photograph was imperative. Thus the final satisfying touch was added to an unforgettable day.

DAY SIXTY-NINE : ACHALLADER - KINGSHOUSE

Rannoch Moor awaited. The section that I had been quietly

dreading, which involved crossing one of Scotland's bleakest landscapes had to be faced. Luckily, the weather was on our side as it was another perfect morning. A study of the map revealed a convenient short cut. It was possible to rejoin the Way by means of a good track that hugs the north shore of Loch Tulla, but this produced a dilema. Should we take advantage of this time-saver, or should we trudge the four miles back to Bridge of Orchy and then circle the western end of the loch? Good boys, for a change, we decided to return to Bridge of Orchy, because the short cut missed out three miles of the Way and also a former drover's inn at Inveroran.

Our feet were in decent shape after a night's rest and the stretch of road-walking to Bridge of Orchy was completed without undue pain. Our fellow travellers had departed from the hotel where all was quiet, apart from a few guests enjoying a leisurely breakfast. We were evidently at the rear of the pack, with no one to turn to if misadventure struck.

We crossed the 250 year-old bridge and a climb from the river through a plantation on the lower slopes of Beinn Invereigh took us to a cairn at Mam Carraigh, a splendid viewpoint at 1,050 feet above Loch Tulla. The loch stretched beneath us, with the tiny island of Eilean Stalcair at its centre. This was probably another of the many such islands used for defence, for we learnt later that it had been shored up with timber and stone. The view northwards revealed one of the most dramatic panoramas on the West Highland Way, if not one of the finest in the Scottish Highlands. Its impression was one of vastness as we overlooked a massive basin, in which sat the Inveroran Hotel, dwarfed by its majestic surroundings. The hollow was rimmed by Black Mount Forest, a huge massif, topped with snow, overlooking the wild reaches of Rannoch Moor.

When we approached the inviting hotel it appeared a splendid halt for travellers. Bright and attractive, the place was a far cry from the eighteenth-century version that existed when William Wordsworth and his sister Dorothy stayed overnight. They found the food inedible and living conditions basic, but Dorothy was intrigued by the harmoniously pleasant atmosphere of the kitchen. The hotel probably furnished a dash of local colour during the Glen Coe to Bridge of Orchy section of their Scottish tour in 1803. For many years a droving stance, it provided a sheltered resting-place for cattle and sheep on their way to market. The Scottish Mountaineering Club met there in their early days, for it served as an ideal base for attacking the Black Mount Hills.

The old Glen Coe road, now a wide track, leads up the Black Mount Pass with our reliable friend, the Old Military Road running parallel on a slightly higher line. Feeling the heat and the effort we hauled ourselves up the dusty track with the fierce sun beating down on us. At the head of the pass we took a welcome lunchtime breather. Not only did sandwiches appear, but also Maurice's handkerchief, which he carefully knotted and placed on his head. His portrayal of the archetypical Englishman on holiday was not on as far as I was concerned. Despite my threats to abandon him he resolutely stuck to this headgear for several days. Whilst eating our sandwiches, caringly prepared by Fiona, we gazed over the placid expanse of Loch Tulla, lying far below us. In the far distance we could make out the faint outline of the Grampians.

John Hillaby likened Rannoch Moor to the opening scene of *Macbeth* - the meeting place of the three witches. He had joined the West Highland Way at Crianlarich and made his lone journey over the moor as evening was closing in, half-expecting to see the three sorcerers appear in the twilight. It was now our turn to venture into this expanse, which boasts sixty square miles of emptiness and a prodigious annual rainfall. The sodden heart of the moor displays more water than land. On a hot summer's day it is possible to swim across it and on a freezing winter's day achieve a crossing on skates. Maurice and I would have loved a swim on that scorching-hot day but nothing was likely to steer us from the lifeline of the track.

Walking became easier as the ground levelled out and we made steady progress for two miles until the Old Military Road rejoined us. A further mile brought us to Ba Bridge, the most remote spot on the Way. It proved less daunting than expected, affording admirable views over the lively River Ba whose gathering grounds are the slopes of Clach Leathad and Stob Gabhar, two of the most prominent Black Mount Hills. The river traces the course of a great glacier that retreated from these mountains and scoured the deep depression of Coire Ba, a gigantic corrie whose beauty is undeniable. Our eyes were drawn to its head where snow-dusted, purple peaks presided over the lush green hollow at their feet.

We were roughly halfway across what we had anticipated would be the most testing part of our walk and the Kingshouse Hotel lay only four miles away. Once again the actual event had proved much better than the imagined. Rannoch Moor was obviously on its best behaviour, but we realised that conditions would be very different in bad weather when it is imperative for all but the most experienced to keep to the Way, as shelter is non-existent.

With lighter hearts we climbed gradually to the ruins of Ba Cottage and onwards to a memorial cairn dedicated to Peter Fleming, the brother of Ian Fleming, author of the James Bond novels. Tragically, Peter died suddenly whilst shooting on the moor and his family and friends provided this simple monument in surroundings that he had loved. Less famous than his brother, he had nevertheless lived an accomplished and exciting life as an author, traveller, explorer and special correspondent for *The Times*. He visited many countries, in particular Central Asia, South America and, during service in the Second World War, Norway, Greece and Burma. In the latter three countries he made successful escapes from enemy-occupied territory. Maurice felt that such an interesting character deserved a 'lean,' as he was apt to do whenever he was being photographed, and thrust one hand against the cairn, which did not budge an inch.

The track persevered around the base of Meall a'Buiridh before easing gently into another wide basin through which the streams begin to drain into the River Etive. Our day's toil was nearly over as we coasted into this welcoming arena and obtained our first view of striking Buachaille Etive Mor. This group of granite peaks stands sentinel over the giant fissures of Glen Etive and Glen Coe. Its crags and crevices offer some of the most popular rock-climbing conditions in Scotland. The best known climb is the dramatic 700-foot ridge that plunges from Crowberry Tower, a projection just below the summit.

Maurice and I burst into celebratory song as we followed the downward track to the A82 road, which traverses the moor. Our lusty rendition of *The Road to the Isles*, a great favourite of Maurice's, was born of relief; an antidote to earlier fears of extinction on Rannoch Moor. The Kingshouse Hotel, the oldest in Scotland, beckoned from beneath Beinn a'Chrulaiste. It was the only evidence of habitation in the isolated and compelling amphitheatre, with the exception of nearby Blackrock Cottage. This lone hut, operated by the Ladies' Scottish Climbing Club, crouches beneath a chair-lift that serves the ski-slopes of Meall a'Buiridh.

Our pace quickened as we crossed the A82 road once more and began the final half-mile of our day's journey. The faithful Old Military Road led us conveniently to the door of the hotel and the place looked just as appealing at close quarters. Like the Inveroran Hotel, it is far removed from its original version of 200 years ago. Sampled by William and Dorothy Wordsworth during their tour, it received a damning write-up from Dorothy who described it as a miserable and wretched place. Maurice and I hurried inside to give it our own appraisal.

We were not disappointed and a little later we emerged from our comfortable rooms to seek the bar where we found many familiar faces. Don, Derek and Peter invited us to join them for an update on events. They had also experienced no problems in crossing Rannoch Moor and were anticipating a straightforward two-day journey to Fort William. We optimistically agreed to meet in a hotel there for a celebration. The team of nurses told us that although their blisters were still troublesome they were hopeful of finishing the walk. Also in attendance were Reg and Tony. Reg's feet were free of bandages, but he was apparently using plasters at an alarming rate. He joked that he now had blisters on his blisters.

I joined Maurice for a stroll outside the hotel before dinner. In the softening light of early evening the surroundings were spellbinding. The entrance to Glen Etive beckoned, a ten-mile defile cut by the River Etive, its brown waters flowing into the glen between the Buachaille and Clachet. In the distance lay the portals of Glen Coe, beyond the plantation at Altnafeadh, which marks the foot of the Devil's Staircase, a demanding climb to the highest point of the West Highland Way, at 1,800 feet. This would be our objective on the following morning and, if the weather held we also planned to explore Glen Coe and the scene of the historic massacre.

Dinner was an extremely pleasant affair, with good food and stimulating company. Maurice and I shared a table with a Scottish actor, Paul Young, and his wife Jean. They were spending a short holiday walking part of the Way. A friendly and modest man, Paul described himself as a jobbing actor who, unlike some better-known stars managed to keep in regular employment. His description was remarkably accurate, for I have frequently seen him on television since our meeting in a variety of roles. He has appeared alongside many notable performers, including Penelope Keith and Gregor Fisher, of *Rab C Nesbitt* fame. His portrayal of the devious owner of the indefatigable boat, 'The Vital Spark' in *Tales of Para Handy* proved an able foil to Gregor Fisher's wily captain. He also appeared as Hamish MacBoan in *The Crow Road*.

Whilst relaxing in the hotel lounge after a most agreeable meal we noticed an elderly man sitting nearby with a newspaper incongruously folded over the top of his head. He was engrossed in a television programme, seemingly oblivious to the puzzled glances from those around him. No one had the courage to ask him why he needed a newspaper over his head and he eventually left the room amidst sniggers and ribald comments. We thought no more about the incident until the following morning when we saw him depart, amidst a cloud of dust, in a battered Volkswagen.

Now that Rannoch Moor lay behind us there was no longer the nagging fear of losing our way. Consequently, I slipped into blissful semi-consciousness until I was shaken by Maurice and told that if I did not want to spend the night in the soporific lounge, I had best go to bed.

DAY SEVENTY : KINGSHOUSE - KINLOCHLEVEN

The ubiquitous sun beamed upon us as we left the hotel to rejoin the Old Military Road that runs to Altnafeadh and the head of Glen Coe. Our surroundings were dominated by the gaunt triangle of Stob Dearg, the most impressive peak of Buachaille Etive Mor, looking distinctly like a volcano with solidified lava spattering its wrinkled slopes. The distant hump of the iron bridge that carries the A82 road over the River Etive was dwarfed by its massive bulk and appeared out of keeping with the bare landscape.

Boots scuffed the track behind us and we turned to greet two young men who had seemingly appeared from nowhere. They were attempting to walk the Way in four days, which meant covering twenty-four miles each day, a formidable task. On target so far, they had set out from Bridge of Orchy that morning and covered the twelve miles to Kingshouse in a mere three hours. Maurice and I felt positively pedestrian as we watched them forge ahead at a punishing rate. Speed is all very well but at what price? Records boost the ego but allow no time for appreciating views or enjoying your surroundings. We pitied those high-speed walkers who charged from sight, heads down, with only the ground to contemplate.

Stimulated by the untamed environment we soon arrived at the tiny outpost of Altnafeadh, nestling by the A82 road where it enters Glen Coe. In a lay-by at the bottom of the Devil's Staircase stood the Volkswagen that had torn away from our hotel a little earlier. Its owner was nowhere to be seen but all his belongings were strewn over the car seats and covered with newspapers. Recalling the episode of the previous evening, Maurice and I joked that the man had to be a frustrated journalist.

The writhing track of the Devil's Staircase snaked above us, certain to demand sweat and toil. Brushing aside our anxiety we turned towards Glen Coe determined not to miss a golden opportunity. Its bold, granite peaks beckoned, inviting us to enter the 'Jaws of Death' as the entrance to the pass itself is known; another reminder of the carnage wreaked within it. We left the Old Military Road, to which we would return for our journey to Kinlochleven, and struck out across the fellside. Our path traversed the headwaters of the River Coe, passing sparkling streams that congregate in the valley floor for a journey to Loch Leven. Glen Coe exuded a distinct starkness and lack of vegetation as we approached the pass, where the mountains crowd in on either side, squeezing the road and infant river into an intimidating channel beneath them. Pausing at 'The Study,' a flat-topped rock, we had a grandstand view of the river plunging through the gorge beneath a high waterfall and flowing through a series of pools towards the Meeting of Three Waters.

From our vantage point the dramatic character of the pass was revealed. Formed by a massive ring fault, it is bounded by 3,000-foot mountains shaped by millions of years of subsequent erosion. Maurice and I had anticipated an eerie and atmospheric place, heavy with vibrations of evil slaughter, but this was far from the reality. Our perception was one of austere beauty, enhanced by benevolent sunshine.

Anxious to see as much of the pass as time would allow we

descended to the valley floor and hurried to the bridge at the Meeting of Three Waters where we gazed in admiration at the three streams tumbling from the granite corries of the Three Sisters. Now in the heart of the pass we stood beside the A82 road and watched it snaking through the great defile towards Glencoe village and, eventually, Ballachulish where it crosses Loch Leven. There was no proper road through the pass at the time of of the massacre, which took place in the early hours of a February morning in 1692. If there had been, the consequences could have been more dreadful, for it may have aided the Campbells in taking up their positions at either end of the pass, thereby rendering escape impossible for the MacDonalds

Few are unaware of the Massacre of Glen Coe, even though its butchery was often equalled in the strife-torn annals of Scottish history. What made this particular carnage unique and unforgivable was the associated political intrigue and the systematic arrangement of mass murder by responsible government figures, supported by the Hanoverian King. It all began when MacIan, chief of the MacDonalds, was late in swearing allegiance to King William, as all clan leaders were ordered to do. The Secretary of State for Scotland cunningly decided to take advantage of the hatred by other factions for the troublesome MacDonalds and make an example of them. He set the train of events in motion by ordering 120 men of the Argyll's regiment, consisting mainly of Campbells, to billet themselves with the unsuspecting MacDonalds. Led by Campbell of Glenlyon, who was related to MacIan by marriage, they were welcomed as friends. On the day before the massacre, other detachments were dispatched to cordon off the pass, but fortunately for the MacDonalds, they encountered blizzards and some arrived late. At five o'clock on the morning of the 13th of February, Glenlyon and his troops stealthily arose and put to the sword any poor victims they could lay their hands on. Forty of the MacDonalds were slain, including MacIan and his wife, and the remainder fled into the hills, under cover of a violent snowstorm, where many died from exposure. Some managed to escape through the unsecured end of the pass.

Keeping a wary eye peeled for marauding Campbells, Maurice and I beat a hasty retreat from the pass; only because we were short of time, you understand. We hurriedly returned to Altnafeadh where we were confronted by the untamed Devil's Staircase. As we began the tortuous climb our footsteps were dogged by a tourist who trained a Camcorder on us. Maurice flashed a broad smile at the cameraman from beneath his knotted handkerchief, now regular attire, realising that we were starring in the man's home video. We were haunted by him for quite a distance before the gradient forced him to return to his family. With a farewell wave, Maurice and I battled up the remorseless slope. It proved hot and demanding work and our sweat mingled with the dust of the track. We stopped several times, hands on knees, gulping air. Our torment proved worthwhile, however, for as we lurched over its crest to collapse onto the summit cairn, a superb panorama was revealed. Exhaustion was replaced by wide-eyed wonderment. To the north a Herculean range of mountains shimmered beyond the colourful green cleft of the Leven Valley. Wisps of feathery cloud lazed in a vibrant-blue backdrop above Mamore Forest and the distant Ben Nevis range. Weatherwise, very few days could match this, with air so clear that every detail stood out in stark relief. The snowy crown of Ben Nevis was sharply exposed and the Mamores carved a jagged imprint in the massive canvas.

Whilst enjoying revitalising drinks we watched other walkers struggling from the valleys on either side of us and several stopped to rest at the cairn and admire the view. Amongst them were two elderly ladies who were walking the Way in the opposite direction. Unlike Maurice and I, who had only a further one and a half days to its completion at Fort William, they had the majority of their traverse ahead of them. Both ladies were slightly built, very thin and seemed remarkably fit. They were relishing their walk and in very optimistic mood. As they disappeared down the Devil's Staircase I remarked to Maurice that neither would be of much use in a cannibal's stewpot.

Suitably recovered, we began the long descent to Kinlochleven by crossing an expanse of bleak moorland. Amidst the featureless terrain lies Blackwater Dam and its attendant reservoir, dominating the head of the Leven Valley. They were constructed between 1905 and 1909 to supply power to the large aluminium works in Kinlochleven.

Eventually the barren moorland receded and attractive birchwood coated the steepening valley sides. Across the defile the shapely mountains of Mamore Forest crowned a splendid scene. Beneath us a series of huge pipes hurtled down the valley, transporting innumerable gallons of water to the factory set in its heart. The massive British Aluminium Works dominates Kinlochleven that lies in otherwise delightful surroundings. The attractive azure waters of Loch Leven lap at its back door and steep, wooded slopes enclose it.

As the late afternoon shadows lengthened Maurice and I entered Kinlochleven and strolled through its outskirts searching for our accommodation. We discovered the pleasant house in a quiet, tree-lined road and expectantly approached the entrance porch to remove our dusty boots. Our welcome from the friendly mother of the family was warm, but her husband was much less forthcoming. He hardly uttered a word during our stay. Her children eyed us suspiciously as we entered. Luckily we had a couple of fellow guests, also walkers, for company at mealtimes, otherwise they would have been silent affairs. Flora, the mother, busied herself in the kitchen whilst her husband, James waited at table. The food was unceremoniously dumped in front of us in dead silence. Recalling the saying, 'If you see someone without a smile, give them one of yours,' I deliberately smiled pleasantly at him during one of his forays with our food, but his stern features never softened. This was very uncharacteristic of the hospitality that we normally enjoyed and I charitably imagined that a pleasant person must lurk behind the gruff exterior. I was reminded of the slamming hatch at Langdon Beck Youth Hostel.

After supper Maurice and I wandered around the village and I was kept busy photographing the splendid surrounding hills, which positively glowed in the soft evening light. The strees were deserted, reminiscent of a Western film where nothing moves apart from occasional brushwood rolling in the wind and the plaintive howl of a prairie dog shatters the eerie silence. Devoid of all but local traffic the place resembled a ghost town. It used to be busier before the bridge over Loch Leven was built at Ballachulish, which meant that traffic no longer passed through on its way to Fort William.

DAY SEVENTY-ONE : KINLOCHLEVEN - FORT WILLIAM

The hardest work of our final day on the West Highland Way came at the outset when we grappled with a demanding climb from the

Leven Valley. Maurice and I tackled this with determination knowing that only fourteen miles remained to Fort William. The sun kept up its remarkable record and accompanied us once again. Its searching rays filtered through birchwood and pine as we hauled ourselves, already hot and legs protesting, to the entrance of a gorge, through which jingled the lively Alt Nathrach. Here we joined a track that traverses the hillside from Mamore Lodge, a reminder of the sporting attraction of Mamore Forest, once a very popular deer-stalking area. Stopping to catch our breath we were treated to an invigorating view across Loch Leven. The magnificent pinnacled crest of the Aonach Eagach, the north wall of Glen Coe, towered above the slender sheet of blue water that stretches fiord-like towards the sea.

Progress was much easier as we headed through the gorge towards the Lairigmor Pass and the hillsides enveloped us, blotting out further views. To keep him amused, I told Maurice that we were now in the ancient province of Lochaber, which is mentioned in his beloved song, *The Road to the Isles*. This was a mistake, for I was immediately berated once more by the lusty strains of, 'By Tummel and Loch Rannoch and Lochaber I will go . . .!' Eventually his Kenneth MacKellar impression subsided as he sheepishly confessed that he had always believed Lochaber to be a loch, but could never find it on the map. My laughter was cut short when he burst into song once more and out came his knotted handkerchief. I suggested that he tied it over his mouth. Unabashed, his singing continued to reverberate from the surrounding hillsides as we followed the undulating track towards the head of the pass at Lairigmor, which proved to be nothing more than an abject ruin. Here the glen widened and our track skirted the foot of Meall a'Chaorainn. Rabbits scurried from sight and a skylark hovered at a safe distance like a feathered helicopter, joining Maurice in joyful song. The occasional grouse flew from the grass calling indignantly, 'Go back . . . go back . . .!' I assured Maurice that they were protesting at his raucous singing.

An extensive Forestry Commission plantation loomed, but Maurice was undeterred and strode on, confident that the Old Military Road would guide us unerringly through. It was hard to keep pace with him and he was evidently spurred on by the culmination of the West Highland Way lying tantalisingly within our grasp. We did spare the time to stop and talk to several passing walkers who were roughly halfway through their first day of a north to south traverse of the Way. They were all eager to know what conditions on Rannoch Moor were like.

Emerging from the forest we caught sight of the diminutive Lochan Lunn Da Bhra, its waters shining temptingly in the bright sunlight. Maurice and I would have loved a cooling dip in them, but we were mindful of the legend concerning the mythical 'waterbull' that supposedly emerges from its depths to drag in unsuspecting victims to drown. Being devout cowards we kept well out of reach.

A gate marked an unfortunate parting of the ways. The Old Military Road deserted us at this point and headed for Fort William, by an alternative route, in the form of a narrow metalled road. The Way, inflicting a final sting, lured us uphill. As a momentary respite from climbing our final gradient of the day I paused to take a photograph of the full extent of Lochan Lunn Da Bhra. We were surprised to see the Glasgow nurses, strung out in a long line below us, who were evidently going to complete their challenge and hopefully collect a significant amount of sponsorship. The leader approached with slow, but determined, steps and when she finally reached us she stopped to recover her breath and mop her dripping brow. She quipped that the fierce sun was keeping her weight down and we had to admire her tenacity and that of her companions. The Way is a stern test for novice walkers and they had come through with flying colours, despite the continual, intense heat. Suggesting that we carried on, she sat down to wait for the stragglers with a promise that their group would meet us that evening at our planned gathering. The jungle telegraph was obviously alive and well, for they had heard about it from several sources.

It was a relief when we began to descend, signifying that the most demanding part of the day's walk was over. We were eager for our first glimpse of Ben Nevis that we knew from the map lay beyond the deep furrow of Glen Nevis, but was obscured from view. In a clearing amidst relenting spruce our hopes were fulfilled when the massive khaki dome of the Ben appeared, thrusting all of 4,418 feet into the blue sky, its summit liberally carpeted with snow. As we gazed at its awesome presence we began to doubt the wisdom of scaling it on the following day. Trying to overcome our trepidation with flippancy, we joked that such a little hill would not defeat us. It just happens to be the highest little hill in Britain!

When we reached another clearing, a little farther on, we found Paul and Jean resting on tree-stumps. We chatted about Ben Nevis and the magnificent, but energy-sapping weather that showed no sign of abating. Paul was quite taken with Maurice's distinctive headgear. A knotted hanky, he reckoned would be just the thing, for he was constantly mopping his brow. Despite a ribbing from me he carefully knotted his own handkerchief and emulated Maurice who suggested I take a photograph of their sporty headgear. Jean, not to be outdone, also got in on the act and joined the 'Knotted Handkerchief Club,' as I dubbed them. Maurice was over the moon, convinced that his headgear had been completely exonerated by an accomplished actor.

Bidding farewell to the congenial couple we zigzagged through mature larches, pausing periodically to scrutinise Ben Nevis. Its rugged features were now discerible and great gashes, scoured by the elements, cleaved its enormous crest. A smooth thread could be seen, snaking up its tortuous slopes. This was the testing path, its intimidating gradient demonstrating what the mountain held in store.

Nevis Forest, through which we were walking, stretches to the mouth of Glen Nevis and almost to Fort William, but we joined a spur of the Way that took us from the trees and into the heart of the glen. The appealing valley seemed a very popular spot for holidaymakers and campers, its lush green floor providing a pleasant contrast to the miles of forest walking. We made for the Youth Hostel, which stands near the starting point of our next day's test, a path that climbs the lower slopes of Ben Nevis.

To avoid retreating into the forest once more Maurice and I followed the road through the glen for the final two miles to Fort William. Numerous campsites and picnic areas flecked the valley, through which scurries the River Nevis, eager to join Loch Linnhe during its journey to the sea. Amidst this sheltered setting nestles the town itself, bounded by disconcerting industrial sites. The suburbs of Fort William present an urban sprawl when compared to the smaller settlements found on the Way. At the junction of the Glen Nevis road and the ubiquitous A82, on the outskirts of town, the West Highland Way gracefully bows out, having completed its ninety-five mile journey. On reaching this goal, Maurice and I duly pumped each other's hand in celebration.

Seizing the opportunity to explore the historic town we arrived at its busy heart amidst bustling crowds. Its name originates from the fort that formerly stood where the River Nevis flows into Loch Linnhe. Built in 1654 by General Monck, it was strategically sited at the south-west end of the Great Glen. During the reign of Charles II the fort was allowed to decline, but it was repaired at the accession of William of Orange. Grateful townspeople gave it the name of Fort William, in honour of the Dutch king. The town was originally named Inverlochy, by Monck, after the nearby castle, which still stands in a beautiful setting two miles to the north-east and has been converted into a luxurious hotel.

After purchasing some momentos of our visit we hurried to the guesthouse where we were to spend the night and discovered to our delight that it offered superb views from its upper windows over the blue waters of Loch Linnhe as it curves towards Corpach. At supper we were entertained by a talkative American couple, who were enjoying a tour of the Highlands. They were captivated by their first visit to Scotland and inquired if the weather was always so wonderful. Maurice replied that it did have its moments. By the end of the meal we knew a great deal about their home city of Detroit where the husband, Floyd, was a senior lecturer. His wife, Jane, enthused over her daughter who was taking a break from college to tour Europe.

Begging the use of an iron, Maurice and I attacked our crumpled casual clothes that had suffered continual crushing in our rucksacks. Looking vaguely presentable we headed for our rendezvous in the cool of evening. On our arrival at the hotel we were delighted to see so many of our friends. Virtually everyone that we had come to know along the Way had turned up, together with other walkers. Everyone seemed determined to let their hair down and enjoy themselves. The nurses were in good form, cheekily moving through the throng demanding contributions to their charity. Reg, still hobbling, was delighted to be there, but had not yet been given a new pair of feet. Don, Derek and Peter were already planning their next long-distance challenge, considering themselves hardened veterans now that they had several successful completions under their belt. The celebratory mood was bolstered by a singsong accompanied by an enthusiastic accordianist. After many Scottish renditions, the Aberdeen lads demanded *Flower of Scotland,* which, I felt, was becoming excessively patriotic. English pride was at stake, so, after being subjected to, 'sending proud Edward's army homewards to think again,' I bribed the accordianist to play *On Ilkley Moor Bah't At.* Yorkshire's anthem was belted out with relish by the English contingent, which prompted a taunt that we Sassenachs might consider ourselves good singers, but we were hopeless at dancing. We were dared to participate in some eightsome reels; not in the hotel, but on the pavement outside in full view of passers-by. Undaunted, we took up the challenge, flinging ourselves into the fray, much to the amazement of open-mouthed onlookers.

The illicit dancing crowned a memorable evening that ended with *Auld Lang Syne* and a horde of weak-kneed walkers staggering away to their beds. A fine preparation for climbing Ben Nevis!

CHAPTER EIGHT

Fort William to John O'Groats

DAY SEVENTY-TWO : FORT WILLIAM - SPEAN BRIDGE

Ben Nevis marked the start of the second phase of our journey together, which would eventually take us to Shiel Bridge. Unsurprisingly, Maurice and I were not at our best on that morning. Throbbing heads and an inability to concentrate plagued us during breakfast. The American couple was full of lively chatter, in stark contrast to our occasional mumblings. What must they have thought of our surliness? Whilst they enthused over their plans for the day our thoughts were elsewere; on the forthcoming 4,418-foot climb, God help us!

Many walkers celebrate a successful completion of the West Highland Way by climbing Ben Nevis but how many live it up on the previous evening and jeopardise their chances? One thing worked in our favour, however, for Floyd helpfully offered to take our rucksacks to Spean Bridge, our day's destination. He and his wife were driving through the Great Glen and would pass our accommodation that lay on the main road through the village. This kind gesture relieved us of the burden of cumbersome rucksacks for a whole day and meant that we could attempt Ben Nevis unimpeded.

Despite the weather maintaining its incredible sequence we knew that conditions could easily turn nasty at high altitude. Accordingly we packed weatherproof clothing, along with our food, in a carrier bag. The roof of Ben Nevis, we had learnt, gets only two hours of sunshine per day on average, as atmospheric condensation often causes the summit to be shrouded in cloud when the remainder of the sky is clear.

In pensive mood we retraced our steps towards the Youth Hostel in Glen Nevis. Our movement was leaden in the glorious sunshine but eventually the fresh air began to clear our heads and dispel the lethargy. By the time we reached the steep path running up the hillside near the hostel we felt ready to rejoin the human race.

The severe gradient hit us with a vengeance, quickly making us breathless and tormenting our limbs. Several halts were needed to catch our breath and ease protesting muscles before meeting the pony track that ascends from Achintee Farm. This thoroughfare signifies the main route up the mountain and it was originally laid to serve an observatory, situated on the summit, which supplied meteorological data around the turn of the twentieth century. We gazed apprehensively along the rising track that climbed agonisingly up the steep south-west slope of Meall an t-Suidhe. Steeling ourselves we struck out along its rough surface, baked hard by the late spring sunshine.

A steady stream of people was climbing the track, in all kinds of attire ranging from light summer wear to full walking outfits. The sight of lightly clad sightseers pricked our consciences and made us pick up our pace; we did not wish to be seen toiling amidst people out for a jaunt. We made steady progress around the southern shoulder of Meall an t-Suidhe and met a friendly party of Americans who exchanged good-natured banter as we passed. They offered a race to the summit, with free cups of tea as the prize, which would be difficult to claim unless there was a newly built café on it.

The track steepened and clawed its way to the crest of a snug

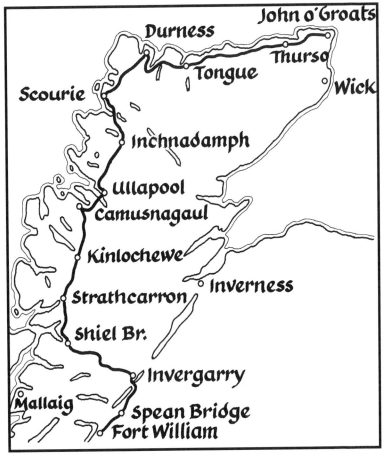

Fort William to John O'Groats

basin in which reclines tiny Lochan Meall an t-Suidhe. Welcome respite came with a short descent into this secluded valley and we were pleased to note that we had already climbed 2,000 feet, nearly half of the total ascent. This was soon forgotten as the ferocity of the gradient began to take its toll. The loose stones that littered the track were a hindrance, frequently causing us to glide backwards.

In intense heat, despite the altitude, we reached the first snowfield and our steps slowed as we negotiated the soft, white carpet that overlaid the shattered rock fragments strewn over the mountainside. All vegetation had disappeared. Pausing for breath we enjoyed a captivating view over Meall an t-Suidhe and its attendant lochan, whose rich-blue waters contrasted vividly with the snow beneath our feet. The wide sweep of Loch Linnhe was visible, with the miniscule buildings of Fort William and Corpach hugging its ponderous curve.

As Maurice and I completed the traverse of the snowfield, its virgin-white surface stained by a multitude of grey footprints, the jagged teeth of the Mamore summits appeared amidst distant haze. They looked even more majestic from this viewpoint. More tripping and skating over myriad stones brought us within sight of the summit ridge of Ben Nevis, heavily bedecked with snow. This had a galvanising effect as we summoned our remaining strength for the final push.

Conditions underfoot began to improve, the stones on the path having compacted, and Maurice forged ahead as I took a photograph of the approaching summit. He looked resolute, combating the heat with rolled up trouser legs and shirt sleeves, but the knotted handkerchief was conspicuously absent. Was he too embarrassed to wear it in the company of so many people, I wondered?

A final snowfield separated us from the summit plateau and as we plodded through it I was able to study several structures coming into view, all of which were built with the indigenous stones. The rather incongruous red roof of a shelter stood out above the largest configuration, which turned out to be the ruins of the observatory. After its demise in 1904 it was utilised as a hotel for a period. This seemed astounding. We thought of an eye-catching advertisement for such a lofty retreat. 'Situated in remote and quiet surroundings at an altitude of a mere 4,418 feet. Superb unimpeded views for two full hours per day. Guests should be physically fit and carry ice axes, ropes and survival kit. No car parking facilities!'

When we reached the summit plateau the hardest work was over. During our ascent the sun had resembled a giant toaster, under which we were roasted, wrung dry and finally ejected on to the roof of the mountain, where it was still amazingly warm. Surely we had no perspiration left as we made the final assault on the beckoning finger of the trig point, which was surrounded by an excited crowd. It perched on a broad, flat cairn, and as we approached many people reclined around us, enjoying the sunshine. Some were clad only in shorts and sweatshirts, despite the snowy surroundings, as they took respite on rocky outcrops. We passed a memorial cairn, which displayed a wreath of bright red poppies. It is Britain's highest and stands near the remains of the observatory.

Maurice, who had noticed a Union Jack fluttering proudly on top of the trig point, clambered onto its supporting cairn for a triumphant 'lean.' I obliged with a celebratory photograph and then joined him when a passer-by kindly offered to take a shot of both of us.

We eventually perched on rocks that overlook the sheer north-facing cliffs. The view is probably the most dramatic that the mountain offers, for the ground fell away beneath us for a staggering 2,000 feet to the head of the Allt a'Mhuilinn valley. A landscape of rugged mountains, penetrated by yawning valleys that were peppered with shining lochs, stretched as far as the eye could see. Whilst ravenously tearing at our sandwiches we noticed a walker sitting nearby. His name, we discovered, was Arthur and he had scaled Ben Nevis many times. He asked how long our ascent had taken and we sheepishly told him, three and a quarter hours. The average time, he told us, is a quarter of an hour longer, so we had not done badly, despite our slow start. As Maurice peered cautiously over the cliff edge, Arthur jokingly suggested that we took the quickest possible descent, down the precipice. That hazardous challenge was best left to skilled climbers, we reckoned, reeling at the thought.

Grudgingly we left the summit, for we hoped to reach Spean Bridge by early evening. Clouds were energetically scudding overhead, but posing no real threat, as we began a fairly rapid and occasionally heart-stopping descent. Many people were still toiling upwards, some anxiously inquiring how much farther it was to the summit.

In what seemed a remarkably short time we arrived at the junction of tracks near Lochan Meall an t-Suidhe, its placid waters seeming to welcome our return. Here we changed course, taking a track that contours the northern slopes of Carn Dearg to reach the Mountain Rescue hut at the head of the Allt a'Mhuilinn valley. The burn has cut a deep cleft between Carn Dearg and Carn Beag Dearg, gathering the waters of numerous rushing streams as it plunges towards its rendezvous with the River Lochy, far below. Maurice and I scrambled, as hastily as was prudent, down the valley, stopping occasionally to admire some arresting views over the Great Glen.

Descending to the western fringe of Leanachan Forest we deserted the Allt a'Mhuilinn to head into its restrictive confines on a dire forestry track. Landmarks were non-existent as we ploughed through a series of confusing arboreal tunnels, searching for tiny Creag Aoil secreted in the depths of the forest. From the freedom of the heights we had been plunged into an oppressive prison of never-ending trees, where all tracks looked identical. After some cursing and backtracking we eventually found our objective, whose link with the outside world is the narrow road to Torlundy. Just beyond this isolated outpost we were relieved to find the track that heads north to Tom na Brataich in the Great Glen.

On reaching the Glen the roar of traffic speeding along the nearby A82 road confronted us as we joined the line of General Wade's Road, which traverses the Great Glen, from Fort William to Inverness. The general embarked on this demanding venture with a 500 strong road-building squad in 1726.

Our strength was beginning to ebb away as we pushed towards Spean Bridge, with three miles still remaining. The combined effort of our mountain climb and the struggle through the forest was taking its toll. Tired legs and protesting bodies forced us to take a breather. Our condition was hardly surprising considering that we had already covered sixteen tough miles.

Afternoon dissolved into evening as we dragged ourselves over the final interminable mile and entered Spean Bridge with profound relief. We barely noticed the ancient stone bridge, straddling the River Spean, which gives the village its name. Our attention was rooted on our lodgings that lay beyond it; sightseeing could wait.

We were solicitously ushered into the lounge by Mary, who ran the place with her sister, Betty. She confirmed that our rucksacks had been delivered that morning by the helpful Floyd. As we sank gratefully into ample armchairs Mary bustled from the room, to return promptly with welcome tea and biscuits. A little later she led us up several flights of stairs, apologising for relegating us to the attic due to an overflow of guests. We entered a cramped attic bedroom, whose effect was claustrophobic. The sun had obviously beaten upon the single window of the sloping ceiling all day and the heat was stifling. Space was at a premium around the twin beds and it proved difficult to move about the room, the low, angled ceiling making it impossible to remain upright. Maurice escaped to the bathroom and returned with a broad grin on his face. The place, he said, was fit only for Quasimodo, the bathroom being even more cramped than the bedroom. He joked that he could not even sit upright in the bath. From then onwards, as we moved awkwardly around those deadly attic rooms, there were mutterings of 'The bells . . . the bells,' and 'Esmarelda!' We christened the place 'Notre Dame' and I told Maurice it was reminiscent of the tiny cottage where I stayed in Kington.

After a hearty supper we did a spot of sightseeing. Dusk was falling as we gazed over the broad stone parapet of the bridge and along the River Spean, its ripples dancing in the moonlight and casting silvery shimmers onto the surrounding pines. Feeling tired, but thankful that Ben Nevis was behind us, we needed no persuasion to return to our cramped garret. Hopes of sound sleep were unfortunately ruined by the hot and airless conditions; the solitary window refused to open. Bedclothes were flung off in desperation as we tossed and turned, until exhaustion mercifully overtook us in the early hours.

DAY SEVENTY-THREE : SPEAN BRIDGE - INVERGARRY

For the second morning running we were not at our best. Exhausted by fitful sleep we stumbled around the attic rooms in a semi-stupor. At breakfast we spoke little amidst a loud hum of conversation. On our departure the caring sisters handed us substantial packed lunches. Not having the heart to voice our complaints we viewed the previous night's discomfort as an amusing experience. It did provide some humorous interludes later, for in secluded places, away from prying eyes, we mimicked Quasimodo as we lurched along with rolling eyes and lolling tongues.

The initial section of our day's walk lay to the east along Glen Spean as my route-plan ignored the direct, but more hectic approach to Invergarry by way of the Great Glen. Seeking the sanctuary of quiet Glen Roy, which branches from Glen Spean at Roy Bridge, we set out on yet another sun-drenched morning.

An hour's walking brought us to the tiny village of Roy Bridge and, judging by the presence of numerous camping and caravan sites, many others had discovered the attractive surroundings. Beside the diminutive church a narrow road begins a twisting journey into Glen Roy, which runs north and parallel to the Great Glen. The good news was that this road would guide us to the head of the eight-mile-long glen. The downside was that it terminates at that point, thereby necessitating an unchartered route over encircling fells to Laggan that lies deep in the Great Glen. Thrusting this unsavoury prospect to the back of our minds, we embarked upon what proved to be a delightful exploration of the secluded glen, which was virtually devoid of traffic.

Its wide lower reaches revealed a quiet, unspoilt landscape of colourful meadows and variegated woodland. Having the area to ourselves rendered us free to perform Quasimodo impressions to our heart's content. The only annoyance in that idyllic setting was the searing heat, which became so intense that, despite my previous chastisement of Maurice's headgear, I relented and donned a knotted hankerchief. The laugh was now on me.

As the glen narrowed it acquired a vastly different aspect. The fells began to crowd in on either side and the lush green vegetation of the lower slopes ended abruptly and evenly, part-way up their flanks. This remarkable phenomenon stems from the time when spectacular glaciers covered this part of Lochaber. 10,000 years ago a huge glacier damned the entrance to Glen Roy and water flowing from the surrounding hills submerged the glen and formed a loch. As the great glacier in Glen Spean melted, the water level in Glen Roy dropped. New beaches formed in stages with a resulting series of demarcation lines, or 'roads,' indicating the various water levels as melting took place. These 'parallel roads,' as they became known, can be clearly seen scouring the mountainsides in dead-straight lines.

Through the narrowing valley flows the lively River Roy that rises in the foothills of the Corrieyairack Forest, the old country of the MacDonald's of Keppoch. Its bubbling waters beckoned with a promise of refreshing coolness in every ripple. This was too good an opportunity to miss so we hastened to its bank for a lunch-stop. The bliss of removing red-hot boots and plunging swollen feet into the soothing river was a highlight of our day. Beneath the shady foliage of an accommodating tree we enjoyed a relaxing lunch as our feet dangled in the swirling waters.

When we reached the head of the glen we found it deserted and the pervading silence was broken only by melodic birdsong; a reminder that the area is a Nature Reserve in the care of the Nature Conservancy Council. With only the birds for company Maurice and I began an exhausting climb over the mountainous barrier that encircled us. Initially, all went well as we ascended a gradually sloping path into the foothills, our knotted handkerchiefs thankfully discarded, for the heat was mercifully subsiding. Elation turned to anxiety, for the path was merely a false dawn. It swung, in the wrong direction, up a side-valley that had not been visible from the floor of the glen. We were forced to abandon it and clamber up a steep gully. Maurice and I grabbed the tussocky grass in order to haul ourselves up the fierce incline. His face was grim as we struggled and his expression said it all. Progress became painfully slow and our breathing became laboured as we forced ourselves to the head of the hostile cleft. At the top we were forced to rest and as we gasped for breath we threw off our rucksacks. The prospect before us was uninviting, for a steep, boggy slope led up to bleak moorland that forms the watershed between the Great Glen and Glen Roy. Leaden legs were dragged through clinging peat as we edged upwards towards the barren and windswept 2,000- foot crest. At last we mounted it with tortured limbs protesting and lungs heaving. As we began to recover and take in our surroundings there was the compensation of extensive views on either side of us. Ben Nevis and its satellites were clearly visible beyond Glen Spean but our attention was drawn to the beckoning Great Glen and our confidence soared at the sight of habitation directly beneath us. This signified we were dead on course for Laggan. Elated, I tried to reassure Maurice that the worst was over but I was to be proved wrong.

An obstacle appeared, during our descent, in the form of an ominous band of dense forest that coated the lower mountainside. Fixing our position on the map we hunted for signs of a track through the dark velvet curtain of trees. Taking a compass bearing towards one that began a little distance within the forest we climbed the perimeter fence and began to search for it, despite the possibility of incurring the wrath of the Forestry Commission, into whose territory we had trespassed. Several minutes of struggling through dense undergrowth wiped the smiles from our faces and reduced us to near exhaustion. Concealed tree roots added to our discomfort by tripping us and we narrowly escaped being sent sprawling. There was no sign of the track and after twenty minutes of toil and sweat I began to despair of finding one.

Eventually we came upon a stream that plunged through a rock-strewn gully and, reckoning that this channel would at least lead us to lower ground, we began to clamber over its mossy boulders. This did nothing for our tormented limbs but salvation suddenly appeared in the shape of a bridge that carried a track over our tortuous channel. Our delight evaporated at the sight of a dour-looking man leaning on the parapet and observing our antics with keen interest. Too tired to try and avoid him we lurched and stumbled over the remaining rocks to arrive at the bridge. Our worst fears were justified as we clambered onto it. 'What the blazes are you supposed to be doing?' The terse inquiry had us abjectly mumbling about being lost and our hearts sank even lower when we learnt that the man was employed by the Forestry Commission. He declared that his organisation did not take kindly to idiots roaming aimlessly over their property and despoiling it. I profusely apologised and explained that we were heading for Laggan, whereupon he gave us a lecture on irresponsible behaviour and the necessity of keeping to authorised routes. Having vented his ire the man indicated the direction to take and bade us a curt goodbye. We heaved a sigh of relief and although very tired, we scurried away, extremely glad to escape.

We emerged from cover into an area of recently felled trees and we were still at a sufficient height to enjoy good views along the Great Glen. The head of Loch Lochy lay below us with the tiny settlement of Laggan nestling nearby. In both directions, as far as the eye could see, sparkling blue water covered the valley floor, broken only by the short strip of land linking Loch Lochy and Loch Oich. A section of the Caledonian Canal was visible, its course followed closely by the A82 road, which we were shortly to cross for the last time.

Beautiful though the views were, Maurice and I were in no mood for hanging around. Our supply of liquid had run out and dust from the track was irritating our parched throats. Maurice declared that he could murder a pint, but wondered if he had the strength to find an inn. We were both nearly dead-beat and Maurice reckoned he couldn't go much further. I began to feel concerned for him; he certainly looked all-in and it was my fault as route-finder. Shepherding him down to the A82 road, I tried to encourage him with the promise of finding a convenient watering-hole. Too tired to search for a path we tottered along the roadside, our eyes peeled for a pub or café. Just as Maurice reached the end of his tether deliverance materialised in the form of a Watersports Centre just beyond Laggan. By our reckoning there would be a bar or cafeteria within the complex and we barged in, ignoring the possibility that admission may be for participants only. In no mood for tiresome restrictions we we found a bar and tumbled in. I sat Maurice down before he could fall down and quickly obtained two pints of beer from the barman who thankfully asked no questions. Maurice raised the glass to his dry lips and gulped . . . and gulped . . . and gulped, barely allowing the reviving nectar to touch the sides of his throat. I had barely sampled my drink before Maurice's glass was drained. Still worried about him I hurried to the bar for another pint, which he demolished with consummate ease. Immediately his empty glass touched the table it was whipped away and replenished. Although the cure was drastic it seemed to be working but there was a strong possibility that I would get him blind drunk. His third pint, lovingly savoured, was consumed more slowly and he began to talk between draughts. He had obviously been seriously dehydrated and I would not recommend my remedy as a normal cure. It would have been prudent to carry more liquid with us and nip any such problems in the bud.

We got into conversation with a young couple sitting nearby who watched Maurice's performance with awe. As he drained his third pint he declared his thirst well and truly quenched. 'If I have any more I won't be able to walk at all,' he joked. It was a relief to see his sense of humour returning. The man and his pregnant wife had a good chuckle and told us that they were travelling from Fort Augustus to Fort William by canal boat, hired for the week. The young lady declared that she was nearly exhausted due to her condition, but was nevertheless enjoying the trip. Her husband joked that she and Maurice would make good companions.

After allowing Maurice further time for recovery I suggested that we made the final push to Invergarry. Emerging into the bright sunlight we went in search of our destination, a farmhouse on the outskirts of the village. We rejoined the A82 road close to where it crosses the Caledonian Canal at Laggan Bridge. The construction of this significant waterway began during the age of sail and its completion in 1822 permitted a passage for ships through the breadth of the country from the Atlantic Ocean to the North Sea.

Beyond the bridge we passed the Well of Heads, a monument erected on the shore of Loch Oich in 1812 by the Chief of Glengarry. It carries a gruesome cluster of seven heads on its lichen-encrusted apex, which commemorate the vengeful action taken against seven local murderers. Their heads were presented to the outraged chief in Glengarry Castle, after being washed in what became known as the Well of the Heads, as reprisal for the slaying of two young members of the Keppoch family. The monument marks the site of the well, which is now buried under the A82 road. Anxious to reach the sanctuary of the farm, with its promise of a hot meal and a cool bed, we gave a mere cursory glance to this gory reminder of a local feud. Protesting limbs were dragged, as speedily as possible, towards Invergarry. Even the sight of Glengarry Castle on the flat ground between Loch Oich and the road could not distract us. The former mansion has been converted into a fashionable country house hotel and it stands in close proximity to the old Glen Garry Castle that sheltered Bonnie Prince Charlie before and after the debacle of Culloden.

The welcome was warm and friendly when we finally reached the farmhouse. Jean, the farmer's wife, remarked how tired we looked. How right she was. A soothing bath was followed by a typical farmhouse meal of gigantic proportions. Maurice and I ate what we could but we were too tired to do it real justice. I was worried that Maurice would fall asleep and bury his face in the main course.

It was late evening when our meal was completed, whereupon we immediately crawled upstairs to our beds. My weary brain prophesied that an earthquake would not keep me from sleeping that night as I sank into the blissful comfort of a soft mattress. However, fate had a cruel blow in store; an attack by rapacious Scottish midges that don't merely bite, they devour. The cool bed that I had been deliciously anticipating did not materialise, despite the open window, which unfortunately provided an invitation to the squadron of rampaging insects that invaded the room. I leapt out of bed and closed the window but it was too late. They attacked with a ferocity that had us writhing as they gleefully bit lumps out of us. Sleep became impossible, for we were stinging all over and the air was cloying.

DAY SEVENTY-FOUR : INVERGARRY - LOCH CLUANIE

Over breakfast Maurice and I were bemoaning the trial by midges that had ruined our night's sleep. Jean listened sympathetically and promised to rid our bedroom of those pests as soon as breakfast was over. I told her that we were aiming for the inn that stands at the west end of Loch Cluanie, near the entrance to Glen Shiel. Eager to help she suggested a convenient route, by quiet roads, which, in places, proved little more than tracks. We were advised to leave the A87 Invergarry to Glen Shiel road after three miles and take the older and much narrower version that follows the shore of Loch Garry. On reaching the hotel at Tomdoun we were to change course and walk across Loch Loyne. We found this prospect disconcerting, never having walked on water! Jean read our thoughts and laughingly indicated that there would be no problem, as the old road would carry us across the loch, which would be very shallow at that time of year. From thereon we could follow the partially overgrown road to Glen Shiel.

As promised, Jean went to our bedroom a little later, armed with a vacuum cleaner, fitted with a flexible hose. She ran the nozzle along the window ledges that were overlaid with ugly layers of midges. Maurice and I looked on in amazement as she performed a regular routine of sucking up writhing, black heaps. No wonder we had been whipped into a frenzy the previous night, there were masses of the beasts.

Jean wished us well as we departed and handed us provisions that could keep an army supplied for several days. As we followed the A87 road Glen Garry began to broaden and the long expanse of Loch Garry appeared, glistening in the resolute sunshine. Across the loch we could see the mountains of Glengarry Forest, presenting a vastly different perspective to when we had viewed them over the Great Glen.

Traffic was thankfully light as we tramped the main road to reach the point where the old road that Jean had recommended, branched from it. A road sign indicated that Tomdoun lay six miles along the now deserted road and that Kinloch Hourn could be reached at its termination, twenty-two miles away. Maurice remarked that he had fond memories of the secluded settlement of Kinloch Hourn, having explored the wild country that surrounds it many years before.

Our journey along the quiet backwater proved delightful, for the leafy lane that the road had become meanders along the north shore of Loch Garry, fringed by a splendid assortment of rowan and birch. Despite the warmth and blue sky, there were surprisingly no marauding midges. Maurice suggested they were having a lie-in that morning. It was pleasing to see him on form and he began to sing *Lochaber No More* with his usual gusto. It was a timely farewell to the ancient province that had so inspired us.

His singing was abruptly curtailed by the sudden arrival of a boisterous red setter that leapt upon him and rested its paws on his chest whilst playfully trying to lick his face. Narrowly avoiding being bowled over, Maurice managed to calm the animal with a few soothing words. Its curiosity satisfied, the dog bounded into the woods, disappearing as abruptly as it had appeared. The whereabouts of its owner remained a mystery, for we saw no other signs of life. As the friendly animal departed, Maurice donned his knotted hankerchief, a sign that we were in for another roasting.

This section of our journey, amidst agreeable lochside scenery, ended as we approached the ancient Tomdoun Hotel, conveniently at lunchtime. The ancient, red sandstone building possessed a porch that overlooked the loch and I sat in its shade on a convenient bench. Eager to repay me for reviving him on the previous day, Maurice disappeared inside, soon to reappear with welcome drinks. In his absence I chatted to a couple who were touring the north of Scotland and had eschewed the main road in order to explore Glen Garry. They asked how far we had travelled and as I explained, the thought struck me that Maurice and I were to part company within two days.

As we gazed over the narrowing loch the couple remarked upon the splendid profile of the mountains surrounding Loch Quoich, which dominate the view to the west. They had driven that morning to the point where the River Garry flows from that distant loch, which lies beneath the jagged mountain range that guards the western seaboard. That lonely area evoked memories of John Hillaby's journey through Scotland on his way to John O'Groats. He had skirted the west end of Loch Quoich as he headed for Kinloch Hourn. The track that he was following inconsiderately disappeared into the loch, which, along with its tributaries, had been converted into a large hydro electric scheme incorporating several dams and involving the submerging of much of the valley. During his traverse of the region Hillaby was existing on a diet of oatmeal and raisins, similar rations to those carried by the clans during the old campaigns.

Our lunch completed, it was time to strike north to Loch Loyne and, as we had twenty miles to cover that day there was no time to waste. The road, little wider than a track, squeezed between brutal wire fences that bordered forests of fledgling pines. When the trees relented we entered a large basin, devoid of cover, in which lay what can only be described as the dregs of Loch Loyne. Jean's prophecy was absolutely correct, for the water had shrunk to a mere quarter of its normal level, exposing great tracts of stony shoreline overlaid with mosses, lichen and soils of varying hues. Across the centre of the parched loch coursed the road, barely recognisable as such, its surface shattered by weather and erosion into little more than an embankment of fractured tarmac, edged with rubble. Despite its dereliction it would allow safe passage across the water. I happily took a photograph of Maurice, complete with knotted handkerchief, surveying the shrivelled loch from the crumbling walkway.

As we reached the far bank the road, now partially grass-covered, turned west, skirting the foothills of Bunloinn Forest, which separates Loch Loyne from Loch Cluanie. We toiled up a steady incline, with the sun's fiery heat hampering us, until we reached the pass between Bunloinn Forest and the mountains of Cluanie Forest. The view as we emerged from this rocky channel was a revelation. Loch Cluanie's seven miles of deep-blue water spread beneath us. Despite being fuller than Loch Loyne, it displayed a sandy fringe around its curvaceous perimeter that glowed in the sunshine. The panorama was resplendent in the clear conditions with the encircling mountains carving a magnificent skyline.

Striding down the gentle slope to the lochside we were treated to a splendid backdrop of mountains that guard the entrance to Glen Shiel. On the far side of the loch a steady stream of people, cocooned in their cars, hastened along the A87 road. At this point we met a farmer, who, with the aid of an energetic dog, was trying to round up some sheep. The dog was dashing hither and thither but the sheep weren't having any of it and darted in all directions. Despite our interrruption the farmer didn't complain and joked about the weather, which, he declared, was remarkable. He added a warning that the forecast was not good and rain was on its way. 'Aye, we get a lot of it in these parts. The 'Cluanie Curtain' we call it.'

The farmer raised the familiar query as to where we had walked from and where we were heading. His eyes widened as we explained our route and it was soon evident that he had spent his entire life in the glen. Inheriting the farm from his father, he had left the area only on rare occasions and had never ventured further than Fort William. 'All I ever wanted is here,' he explained. As we gazed around the inspiring landscape, it was easy to see why.

When we mentioned that we were staying at the Cluanie Inn he replied that we could do a lot worse. 'It's a very popular place,' he told us. 'An excellent base for shooting, fishing and fell-walking.'

The sheep had taken advantage of the farmer's distraction by galloping away and searching for juicy vegetation. His faithful dog, which had been called to heel, sat patiently beside him during our conversation, with a pleading look in its eyes. If the animal could speak it would have expressed annoyance at having its work disrupted. The farmer declared that he must chase his flock or he would be out there until nightfall.

At last the inn came into view. There was no doubting its strategic position at the head of Glen Shiel. It has long been a halt on the route to the Isles, for the glen splits the mountain barrier that stands between the traveller and the romantic Isle of Skye.

The farmer's weather prediction came true remarkably quickly and with a vengeance. Menacing clouds rolled across the sky as we crossed the bridge at the west end of Loch Cluanie. The glen was plunged into dark shadow and warning drops of rain were already falling as we made a dash for the sanctuary of the inn. Welcoming lights beamed from its windows, as they would have done in the days when travel-weary passengers tumbled from coaches and tired drovers brought their herds to a thankful halt. We rushed into the entrance porch and hastily removed our rucksacks and boots as the grey, sweeping rain got into its stride. It formed an impenetrable curtain, just as the farmer had described. Maurice echoed my relief at not being caught in open country during the deluge. Our hearts went out to the poor farmer who would still be out there bearing the brunt of the storm with only his tweed jacket for protection.

A very pleasant receptionist greeted us, remarking on the sudden change in the weather. She smiled when we told her we couldn't complain after enjoying nearly ten days of continuous sunshine. As she guided us to our room, rain lashed the windows, but the receptionist comforted us with the news that according to the local forecast the heavy rain would abate by morning.

Emerging later from our comfortable quarters we made a beeline for the dining room, appetites honed by the sweet Highland air. Our expectations were well founded, for the food was delicious and the service admirable. However, one note of sadness did prevail during the meal, caused by the realisation that the following day would see the culmination of our walk together. We agreed that even if the last day proved to be a washout, we would still have enjoyed an unforgettable journey through some of the finest scenery that Britain has to offer.

There was no shortage of company in the lounge after supper and we struck up what turned out to be a rather one-sided conversation with three friendly Scotsmen whose very broad accents were difficult to decipher. We nodded our heads in reply as we grappled with their thick brogue. Apparently they were keen fishermen who came frequently to fish the loch, which, according to them, was well stocked with brown trout. They enthusiastically related what we took to be shaggy fish stories about the monsters they had captured.

DAY SEVENTY-FIVE : LOCH CLUANIE - SHIEL BRIDGE

Breakfast was a time for reflection and anticipation. We recalled some highlights of our journey, such as humbling Ben Nevis and dancing in Fort William. The debacles of Rob Roy's Cave and floundering through the forest above Laggan were omitted. Having greatly enjoyed travelling more than 140 miles together we were poised to embark on separate adventures. At Shiel Bridge Maurice planned to travel westwards and head for the Isle of Skye, via Glenelg, whilst I would steer to the north through Wester Ross and Sutherland. I reminded him that a treat lay in store that morning. Following his earlier expedition to Kinloch Hourn and Knoydart, Maurice had completed the superb ridge walk over the Five Sisters of Kintail. They overlook Glen Shiel and his wish to see them again, albeit from ground level, was about to be granted. An added bonus, I remarked, was the fact that we would be walking downhill for the whole of the day's journey, courtesy of Glen Shiel, which descends gradually, between 3,000-foot mountains, to Shiel Bridge.

Stepping from the inn into a fresh morning breeze and light drizzle we said farewell to Loch Cluanie and went in search of a footpath through Glen Shiel. We were obliged to follow the A87 road, which passes the Cluanie Inn, for a quarter of a mile before we found one. It was, in fact, the remains of another Old Military Road. This one is attributed to Major Caulfield, the unsung hero and successor to General Wade. He built the road between 1750 and 1784 to link Fort Augustus with the military barracks at Bernera on the west coast.

The irksome drizzle melted away and the cloud began to lift. Stately mountain ranges that border the glen began to reveal themselves, minus their peaks, which remained buried in cloud. A quick burst of song was called for as we ventured into the open arms of Glen Shiel at a lively pace. The head of the glen lies just below 900 feet and heralds the gathering grounds of the River Shiel, which ultimately expends itself into Loch Duich.

Time was plentiful as we had only twelve miles to cover, which allowed us to relax, take stock of our surroundings and to admire the wild flowers that flourish in the valley. Particularly colourful were the tall hollyhocks that swayed rythmically in the breeze. As we rested beneath a small outcrop of trees we were attacked by a posse of midges. Recalling the voracity of their relatives at the farm near Invergarry we beat a hasty retreat.

Roughly halfway through the glen its narrow floor begins to widen and here stands the Bridge of Shiel, which transfers the A87 road to the opposite side of the River Shiel and also denotes the entrance to Kintail. Nearby we found a tiny sign marking the site of the Battle of Glen Shiel that took place in 1719. This conflict was one of many between Jacobite sympathisers and Hanoverian troops. Immediately prior to the battle, exiled Jacobite leaders of the 1715 rebellion had returned from Spain and their forces had taken Eilean Donan Castle, the proud fortress that still stands on a promontory where Loch Alsh, Loch Duich and Loch Long meet. They were, however, soon ousted by the crews of three English frigates that sailed into Loch Alsh. The castle was reduced to ruins and the embattled Jacobites, together with their companions, a company of Spaniards, fled. They took up positions on the hill-slopes to either side of the Bridge of Shiel in order to defend themselves and were joined by a party of MacGregors that included the ubiquitous Rob Roy. In the ensuing battle the Hanoverians won the day and many Jacobites were slain as they tried to flee into the mountains. The name of the mountain that looms over the battle site is Sgurr nan Spainteach - 'The Peak of the Spaniards.' This is the most eastern peak of the Five Sisters and its name relates to the Spaniards who took part in the battle.

Some years later, in 1746, Bonnie Prince Charlie passed this way during his flight from Cumberland's forces. The fugitive lay hidden behind a boulder throughout a long, hot summer's day. He had slipped from Loch Hourn over the Bealach Duib Leac, a 2,400-foot pass, into Glen Shiel before heading up the glen for a well-earned respite beyond Conbhairean.

The Military Road petered out, so Maurice and I crossed the bridge to see if conditions were better underfoot on the other side of the river. As we did so a car crawled towards us, travelling so slowly it seemed to be free-wheeling. However, the throb of its engine could be heard as it approached and the man and woman inside, sporting voluminous sun hats, gazed around as though mesmerised. The driver was jerked from his reverie as the bridge loomed before him and they waved to us as they passed. We could see them staring at their suroundings once more as they disappeared from view. Some people never learn.

The temperature was rising steadily and the clouds fragmented, exposing patches of pale-blue sky. Courtesy of the improving weather we got our first good view of the Five Sisters. Protruding above their indented ridge were three ragged peaks, including the tallest of the range, Sgurr Fhuaran at just over 3,500 feet. Maurice was thrilled to see the scene of his high-level traverse once more. The views on that occasion, he indicated, were magnificent and encompassed much of the western seaboard and the Hebridean Islands.

We spent the next part of our walk meandering along the floor of the glen, alternating between spells of road-walking and hugging the riverbank. During frequent stops we scoured the River Shiel for signs of fish, particularly the elusive salmon, without success. A pleasant interlude of unpressured walking was very welcome after several hard days.

As we neared the mouth of the glen the river widened into a tiny lochan. On its banks a splendid display of yellow, slender leafed flags lit up the glen's lower reaches. Despite our leisurely pace we had worked up quite a sweat and Maurice stopped to dry himself as I took in our invigorating surroundings.

The River Shiel narrows once more for the last half-mile of its journey and as it prepares to enter Loch Duich it passes under rustic Shiel Bridge that gives the adjacent village its name. Here we encountered a backdrop of grey, furrowed hills with tentacles of vegetation creeping into the corries of their upper reaches. The historic high-arched stone bridge appeared almost indistinguishable from the exposed rugged slopes that overlook it.

We strolled from the bridge and passed a caravan site squatting on the outskirts of the village. Here we found a convenient café and spent a relaxing half-hour over some welcome refreshment, which made a pleasant change from the strenuous episodes of some afternoons. Maurice kept me entertained with stories of his previous visit to Kintail, adding that he was happy to pay his respects to the Five Sisters once more. He was eagerly anticipating his visit to Skye, where he planned to stay for two nights to allow a trip to the Black Cuillin. His intention was merely to view the dramatic horseshoe of the Cuillin Ridge, not to traverse it!

Eventually we found the farm, where we were due to spend the night, tucked beneath the hills that overlook Loch Duich. As we approached the farmhouse we were set upon by two lively Border collies that leapt at us spiritedly. Fortunately they were friendly and only wished to lick our hands and faces. A curt command from the farmer's wife, who had appeared in the doorway, sent them scampering towards her. Their excited yelps virtually drowned the straight-faced welcome from Margaret, our host. 'I hope you don't mind the dogs,' she said as she dispatched them to the barn. We were invited into her kitchen and treated to a huge pot of tea and a mouth-watering assortment of home-made cakes, despite our protestations that we had been in the nearby café. Margaret seemed friendly, but rather stern; a person not to be argued with. Whilst Maurice and I munched the delicious cakes I got my first sight of a salmon, albeit a dead one. A man entered clutching a monster of a fish that he had obviously just pulled from the loch. It transpired that he was a helpful neighbour who had brought the massive salmon for our meal that evening.

Bathed and changed, we reported to the dining room, as instructed, at just before seven o'clock, not wishing to incur Margaret's wrath. Seated obediently at the table were a middle-aged couple who whispered that they dared not be late for one of Margaret's meals. As we awaited the first course our whispered conversation revealed that the couple lived in Bradford, not far from my home village, and were using the farm as a base for touring the area by car. They were full of praise for Plockton, which lies at the south-west tip of Loch Carron, declaring it to be the highlight of their visit so far. Maurice and I should not miss it, they declared, and we had to explain that we were parting company the next morning. Loch Carron lay on my route through Wester Ross, I told them, but unfortunately, not Plockton.

On the stroke of seven o'clock Margaret entered with a gigantic dish of soup. We each had several helpings, reluctant to offend her by leaving some uneaten. The main course, when placed in front of us, was a revelation. On each of our large, oval plates lay a quarter of the enormous salmon, surrounded by a jungle of salad that left virtually no space for the mounds of potatoes and vegetables heaped in expansive dishes in the centre of the table. We wrestled manfully with our intimidating portions and everyone but Maurice managed to make significant in-roads into them. He was ruing the cakes and other goodies we had eaten earlier, and failed miserably. When Margaret came to collect our plates he looked crestfallen as she snatched his away, and tight-lipped, slammed a huge slice of fresh cream gateau in front of him. This proved too much for my friend who humbly declared that he could not eat another thing. Margaret stared incredulously at him and demanded to know what was wrong with her food. His apology was met with a cold stare as she grabbed his plate and stormed out of the room amidst an embarrassed silence.

Conversation was understandably sparse for the remainder of the meal but when we were back in the privacy of our room, Maurice brightened and even managed to joke about the incident. He christened our angry host, Dawn, because, he said, she had come up like thunder when he rejected her prized gateau.

DAY SEVENTY-SIX : SHIEL BRIDGE - STRATHCARRON

Maurice and I parted with a handshake at the farm entrance and I watched him set out for Glenelg, his eye-catching red socks unmissable as he marched along the road. At one point he turned and waved, whilst I vigorously waved back, realising with some trepidation that I was on my own with much wild country ahead of me. The day would not be easy, as it involved an eighteen-mile crossing of outer Kintail, which stretches north from Loch Duich and is bounded by Loch Long to the west and Strath Croe to the east. Much of it is mountainous, riven by deep valleys, scoured by fast-flowing rivers. My intention was to aim for Attadale that lies near the head of Loch Carron. When that outpost was reached the hardest part of my journey would be over, for only two miles of level walking separate it from Strathcarron.

My journey began by circling the east end of Loch Duich and heading along its north shore towards the village of Inverinate. My spirits were dampened by the weather that was turning decidedly nasty. Angry clouds marshalled themselves for a downpour and I donned waterproofs in anticipation of a soaking. I had been very lucky with the weather so far, but, unbeknown to me, nature had wickedly decided to redress the balance. The impending storm was a prelude to the vile conditions that I would suffer during several of the remaining days of my walk.

I turned for a final view of the Five Sisters before the weather closed in but their magnificent outline disappeared in the mist that was insidiously rolling towards me. Rain began to fall with a vengeance and I was loath to leave the security of the A87 road that had guided me from Shiel Bridge.

Trudging apprehensively past the string of gloomy roadside buildings that lay beyond Inverinate, I was keeping my eyes peeled for the valley of the Choire Dhuinnid that cleaves a gap between Uillt Tharsuinn and Boc Beag. Its entrance finally appeared out of the murk and I joined a path that snaked upwards alongside the tumbling burn and soon vanished into a thickening mist. I climbed past several small cascades that frothed and churned in a frenzy of activity. A couple of miles of squelching along the sodden path brought me to a more daunting one that rose sharply into the hills of Inverinate Forest. Only the sound of my laboured breathing broke the eerie silence as I struggled upwards, cocooned in swirling mist. As the path was indistinct I followed its line with the aid of my compass and I was frequently startled by the appearance of ghostly sheep and the angry calls of grouse as they took flight. An anxious hour was spent with my head down, eyes straining for signs of the fickle path.

As many walkers know, if you are alone and isolated by mist from the outside world, your imagination can go into overdrive. To dispel thoughts of my rigid corpse being found sometime later by a local shepherd, my mind conjured up the tantalising image of scaling a challenging mountain in perfect conditions with superb views all around me.

I was jolted back to reality with the sudden realisation that the mist was clearing, for I had begun to descend into a valley. Beneath me nestled the hamlet of Killilan, which confirmed that I was overlooking Glen Elchaig and was directly on course. Despite being barely visible through the rain and gloom it was a reassuring sight. Eagerly I dropped down towards the scattering of buildings and reached the River Elchaig, which was conveniently spanned by a wooden bridge. I cast a glance up the grey and sombre glen. Tucked away in its upper reaches lies the offshoot valley of the Allt a'Glomaich through which tumble the magnificent Falls of Glomach. Known as the 'Hidden Falls', because of their inaccessibility, they draw many would-be visitors, but few actually reach this remarkable spectacle. It is not the highest waterfall in Britain, but at its head is one of the longest drops, at 350 feet.

The only splash of colour in the bleak landscape was provided by bright yellow flowers on the thickets of broom that sheltered by the bridge. Crossing the river, I passed a school on the outskirts of

Killilan and turned north into Glen Ling. Here I coincided with John Hillaby's route for a few miles. He, apparently, had not enjoyed a good day by the time he reached this point. Setting out that particular morning from Glenelg he had travelled by boat, chartered from a local boatman, up the Sound of Sleat and across Loch Alsh to Ardelve. Part way through the voyage the boatman treacherously demanded double the agreed payment, which nearly resulted in a fight on board. After another violent argument on the quayside at Ardelve he paid an inflated fee before setting out along the shore of Loch Long. When he reached Nonach, near Killilan, he was bitten on the calf by a dog. Things went from bad to worse as he entered Glen Ling and found that his map had fallen from a torn pocket of his jacket. As a consequence he blindly followed the River Ling for miles, in thick mist, before ending up in a quagmire of peat at its remote source. My worries were as nothing when compared to his.

Determined not to make the same mistake as he had, I kept a sharp lookout for a path that diverges from the main one about a mile up the glen and climbs into the Attadale Hills. According to the map this path would eventually reach Attadale and the shore of Loch Carron. I found the path in question and began to climb from the glen, pausing as I did so to survey the upper reaches of the River Ling that had lured John Hillaby into difficulties. The sinister river wound, beneath tentacles of mist, through a scene of pure desolation; the kind that scares the pants off you in a horror film. You are always treated to such a spectacle just before the blood-curdling baying of a werewolf rivets you to your seat. My heart went out to John Hillaby.

I ascended into the pea-soup of a mist once more, which returned me to my eerie and disturbingly silent world. Somewhere on those shrouded hills I lost the path and all my attempts to re-locate it failed. I was forced to blunder through inhospitable terrain with only my compass to guide me and to make matters worse I twisted my ankle in a bog. Feeling sorry for myself I tottered over the rough ground until a forest loomed out of the mist. This cheered me a little, for I knew that one lay on my route, but there was no track at the point of entry, as there should have been. Thankfully there were frequent breaks in the tree cover, but I still spent an uncomfortable half-hour lumbering through it.

When I finally escaped from the forest the ground began to plunge sharply downwards and I was soon extracted from the mist, to find Loch Carron lying 1,000 feet below. What a joyous sight it was, with the Kyle of Lochalsh to Inverness railway line hugging its south-east shore and Attadale lying beside it. Elation turned to frustration, for despite being able to see my goal, I had great difficulty in attaining it, as I had when above Laggan. My descent was halted by a steep gorge, which demanded a detour and I then had to tangle with dense bracken, frustrating woodland and numerous fences. I was nearly exhausted when I finally reached the lochside road.

Loch Carron marks the demarcation between the softer country to the south, which is more open to the Atlantic Drift, and the harder land to the north. It lay calmly beside me, as I approached Attadale, enfolded by hills, which give way to gaunt mountains that surround its head. All around were ash, alder and conifer plantations, whose dark sprawl was punctuated with bright-green meadows. Loch Carron and its environs exuded a tranquil beauty.

The most notable building in the small settlement of Attadale is Attadale House that stands in a lovely situation not far from the loch. It hosts the annual Lochcarron Highland Games in its grounds - not on the same scale as those at Braemar, but nevertheless a splendid source of entertainment. The skirl of pipes and the thrill of competition are guaranteed to delight whatever the setting.

As I passed Attadale House I was feeling the effects of tussling with the Attadale Hills and was eager to put my feet up. The realisation dawned that, up to that point, I hadn't met a soul that day. The countryside was hardly buzzing with walkers and I was learning that Wester Ross is empty, apart from occasional pockets of habitation.

During the final two miles of my day's journey I had a close companion; the impressive railway that I had observed from my high-level vantage point above Attadale. I passed Attadale station, which lies on the line and could have been built for the convenience of the residents of Attadale House, for they stand adjacent to each other.

The broad head of Loch Carron fragments into a series of watery tentacles that intrude into the surrounding pastureland as though striving to swamp Strathcarron that lies a mere half-mile beyond.

Into this lacerated shoreline squirms the River Carron, which is immediately confronted by two small islands that threaten to block its mouth. This watery scene provided an introduction to Glen Carron, which would form the early part of my following day's walk.

I passed through Achintee, a near neighbour of Strathcarron and was relieved when Strathcarron station came into view, signifying that journey's end was near. A short search amongst nearby cottages lying in the shadow of Carn Mor, a great dome that towers over the village, resulted in a very cordial welcome at the home of Jimmy and Jennifer, with whom I had booked accommodation. It was a great relief to remove my boots and enter that most hospitable household, where everyone chatted like old friends from the outset.

At supper the conversation was lively, particularly from Jimmy who possessed a fund of anecdotes. He kept me and my fellow guest, a pianist who was holidaying in the area, entertained throughout the meal and for several hours afterwards. The young piano player, I discovered, had visited many parts of the world with the small orchestra to which he belonged. He related numerous adventures, which made mine seem mundane by comparison. Unlike him and other members of his orchestra I have not had to endure extremes of climate and geography, for many of their venues were in far-flung locations, remote from the more grandiose facilities on the major concert circuit.

My walking exploits were made to appear even more trivial when Jimmy mentioned his accomplished neighbour, Martin Moran, a formidable mountain guide who is equally at home in the Himalayas, the Alps, or the Scottish Highlands. One of his outstanding achievements is conquering all the Scottish Munros in one continuous circuit, in the depths of winter. It took him eighty-three days to complete this marathon, a remarkable length of time when you consider that it takes many fell-walkers the best part of their lives. Another of his feats, which I find incredible, is crossing the Cuillin Ridge on Skye in three hours and thirty-three minutes. This is all the more amazing when you learn that it includes eleven Munros.

I was quite overcome with such tales of derring-do and crept up to bed feeling decidedly inferior. My night's sleep was invaded by a recurring nightmare in which I was hauling a piano across the Cuillin Ridge.

DAY SEVENTY-SEVEN : STRATHCARRON - KINLOCHEWE

My fitful slumber was broken by the drumming of rain on the bedroom window. I yawned and tumbled from my bed. Not a good start to the day, which promised 'more of the same,' weatherwise. When I went downstairs the wet clothes that Jennifer had taken away to dry were laid out for me, ready to wear. My shirt had been washed and ironed. What wonderful service, I thought, so typical of the warm Scottish hospitality.

During breakfast Jimmy inquired where I was heading that day. When I told him Kinlochewe, by way of the Coulin Pass, he said that I had made a wise choice. In his opinion, a walk through the pass was essential, for it epitomises the true character of Wester Ross. All I needed, he reckoned, was a break in the weather.

The young pianist outlined his plan for the day, which involved driving to Kyle of Lochalsh and crossing to Skye for a tour of the island. Walking, he said, was not for him. I suggested that he kept a lookout for Maurice who should be on his expedition to the Cuillins. It reminded me that I must ring my friend that evening to discover how he had fared.

I hauled myself from Strathcarron, uneager to attack the mist and rain that permeated the glen. Not a glimmer of brightness did Glen Carron reveal for the whole of my six-mile journey through it to Achnashellach. Crossing the River Carron near New Kelso Farm I joined a track that accompanies the languidly meandering river through the wide valley floor, but was forced to abandon it after one mile as it was fenced off. Forced onto the A890 road for a period, I crossed a burn, which funnelled through a deep cleft in the grey hills, before I passed under the railway and was able to return to the riverside.

A little farther on I came upon Loch Dughaill that gradually widened and filled the valley bottom, forcing the road and railway to squeeze side by side along its shore. The low-lying land was saturated with the incessant rain and I endured a boot-filling mile before I was obliged to rejoin the A890 road and follow it to Achnashellach. The loch looked gloomy as rain lashed its surface and I strode along with head down, occasionally leaping aside to avoid a drenching from passing vehicles.

Arriving in the hamlet I searched for shelter, for the rain had intensified and was bouncing gleefully from the ground. Eventually I found refuge at the lonely station that housed a tiny brick-built shelter, which had no door but at least provided some respite. The deluge beat ferociously on the roof as I gazed through the doorway at a solid sheet of water. There I cowered for twenty minutes before the torrent abated slightly but showed no signs of stopping.

Steeling myself, I vacated my refuge and climbed through an extensive plantation, trusting it would provide a little shelter from the rain. Remarkably, when I emerged from the trees the rain suddenly stopped as though someone had turned off a giant tap. To my delight the sun appeared and shone on a series of tiny, frothing waterfalls that punctuated a passing burn. In a remarkable transformation the sky turned a startling blue and I was surrounded by vivid colour. Out came my camera to capture a mosaic of heather, rusty-hued bracken and velvet grassland, bounded by tightly packed spruce.

Now that Glen Carron was relieved of its mantle I could look back across the valley to the distant Attadale Hills, emerging from a retreating bank of cloud. It aroused memories of struggling through those fells in the mist.

With lighter heart I climbed to the crest of the hill in glorious sunshine. Here I enjoyed a panoramic view over Coulin Forest, which, in common with many others in Scotland is a deer, not a tree forest. It stretches to Glen Torridon that lies eight miles to the north of Glen Carron and is an area of unrivalled appeal. Jimmy's promise of an outstanding walk was no exaggeration. Surrounded by majestic mountains, the Coulin Pass steers through a stark landscape, typifying the unique character of Wester Ross. I stood spellbound, for it was so different to all that had gone before. Here was another world, where heather and heath hugged the land like a giant brown carpet beneath an array of purple mountains, their slopes remorsefully exposed.

As I gazed at this empty panorama I found it difficult to comprehend the origins of its age-old rocks, amongst the oldest in Britain. It appeared deserted to my untrained eye, which could only pick out the occasional bird, but to a naturalist there is intriguing activity on even the most bare and exposed ground. John Hillaby passed this way during his journey and discovered an infinite variety of tiny plants and insects that frequent such wastelands. How I envied his powers of observation and recognition.

I entered the Coulin Pass determined to be more vigilant but my resolution soon waned as I became infatuated with the magnificent views. The majestic summits of Sgurr Ruadh and Beinn Liath Mhor lay to the west, which was home territory to Martin Moran. I recalled a photograph that Jimmy had shown to me of Martin's wife Joy on a winter expedition in those mountains, courageously carrying their young child in a harness on her back.

Pangs of hunger demanded a lunch-stop in the heart of the pass at the opportune point where the Eason Dorcha Burn and the Allt Doire Bheithe converge to form the River Coulin. The tributaries rippled over stony beds through a scene of sheer delight as I eagerly removed my rucksack and found a convenient viewpoint. Life felt much sweeter now that I was bathed in sunshine amidst an oasis of tranquillity. The prospect upstream, where the burn emerged from a scattering of graceful trees was rivetting. Reflections in the water gave it a soft-purple hue, which blended subtly with the backdrop of gnarled peaks. The crests of the mountains of the Coulin Forest were presided over by the distant crown of mighty Liatach.

It was a short journey to Loch Coulin and its neighbour Loch Clair that occupy the north end of the Coulin Valley. The ashen surface of Loch Coulin was gently rippled by a taunting breeze that rustled the leaves of colourful shrubs and a cluster of stately birches that clothed its bank. An occasional decapitated tree added austerity to the scene, its trunk standing erect like a gaunt flag-pole.

Progress was good as I followed a wide bridle-path along the shores of the lochs. It was overlaid with shale, scoured from the surrounding hillsides. The slate-grey surface complemented an attractive archway of silver birch that enclosed it. Emerging from the tree-lined tunnel I saw the massive bulk of Beinn Eighe thrusting skywards beyond Loch Clair. The mountain oozed character, from its long and dramatically indented summit ridges to the vivid quartzite outcrops on its angular slopes that glinted like silver in the sunshine. Determined not to be overshadowed, the giant arrowhead of Sgurr Dubh beckoned from across the loch.

The track became a metalled private road as I passed Coulin Lodge and I marched at a good pace until I met the A896 road that traverses Glen Torridon and heads for Kinlochewe. No convenient paths were evident so I struggled along the stony bank of the

A'Ghairbhe River that flows parallel to the road. The riverside scenery was splendid, but short-lived, for I was beaten back by thickets of broom and an impenetrable wood that stood in my way. Accepting defeat, I rested on a rock and enjoyed a lingering view of the river. It was pleasing to watch the occasional coot and moorhen, with their distinctively coloured foreheads, gracefully skim the water. The river looked inviting for travel-weary feet, but the water felt ice-cold, so I lazed in the sunshine.

As I rejoined the A896 road for the two-mile final push to Kinlochewe I had a clear view of Beinn Eighe protruding from undulating moorland that comprises a National Nature Reserve. In the care of the Nature Conservancy Concil, the reserve encompasses 10,500 acres and includes a mountain trail on Bienn Eighe itself.

The stately mountain occupied my thoughts until I reached a road junction on the outskirts of Kinlochewe. Here the A896 road meets the A832, which links Gairloch on the west coast with Fortrose that lies on the Moray Firth. The junction is overlooked by the mountain wall of the Letterewe Ridge, which guards the north-east flank of Loch Maree and forms the southern boundary of Letterewe Forest. A dash of colour was added to this grey canvas of grizzled rock by the brightly-flowering broom that flourishes in the valley beneath.

I entered the small settlement of Kinlochewe and easily found the bungalow in which I was to spend the night. The home of the local district nurse, Ivy and her husband Brian, it was the ideal place for walkers suffering with aches and pains or troublesome blisters. Brian talked enthusiastically about the area whilst I enjoyed some refreshment and he told me that the village had been an important staging post on the old packhorse routes. If the Kyle of Lochalsh to Inverness railway had not avoided Kinlochewe in favour of Achnasheen, he indicated, it could well have grown in prominence. However, he reckoned that it was currently doing very nicely as a halt for tourists, many of whom visited Gairloch or Inverewe Gardens. Admittedly not a climber or walker, he said that mountaineering opportunities were limitless in the surrounding heights and one could walk for miles through uncluttered territory without meeting a soul. I could attest to that, I told him, having walked for the previous two days in virtual isolation.

After supper I wandered from the village towards Loch Maree

along the Letterewe track that traverses its north-east shore. This splendid loch is one of the most highly-rated in Scotland, surrounded as it is by magnificent wild country for the whole of its twelve-mile length. Long before Wainwright devised his English Coast to Coast Walk and prior to the advent of the Inverness to Lochalsh Railway, postmen carried mail on a Scottish cross-country route between Dingwall on the east coast and Poolewe on the west. This remarkable postal round took a week to complete on foot, and the track on which I was walking formed a section of it. Mail for the Outer Isles was carried along the shore of Loch Maree, beneath the Letterewe Ridge; an apt name. In the glow of a fine evening I enjoyed a close inspection of the ridge's towering mountain chain that once yielded many veins of iron ore from its lower slopes. As I looked along the blue expanse of Kinlochewe River, the pointed peak of Slioch protruded above its neighbours into a perfect evening sky. Completing the unforgettable picture was the ubiquitous broom that lined the riverbank as far as Loch Maree.

Returning to the bungalow, I rang Maurice who had thoughtfully given me the telephone number of his lodgings on Skye. His surprisingly disgruntled voice greeted me, but it brightened when he realised who his caller was. Apparently he had not had a good day. His journey to Broadford on the previous day had gone smoothly, but his attempt to get within viewing distance of the Cuillins had been a disaster. He was defeated by the bus service to Elgol that failed to materialise and was forced to be content with a visit to Portree.

DAY SEVENTY-EIGHT : KINLOCHEWE - CAM'NAGAUL

Another long day was in prospect. Twenty-four hard miles lay ahead before I could reach Camusnagaul, a scattering of dwellings on the shore of Little Loch Broom. The sea-loch is one of many that bite into the ravaged coastline, which borders a Designated Area of Natural Beauty that encompasses much of Wester Ross. That day I planned to cross the wild, desolate region of austere mountains and rampant peat that is sandwiched between Loch Maree and Little Loch Broom.

Things appear rosier when you are fortified with a good breakfast and so it was on that challenging morning. With enough colesterol to block every artery I looked from the dining room window at a garden bathed in subshine. Emboldened by the favourable weather I felt ready to tackle whatever nature threw at me.

I was thankful for excellent visibility as I followed the valley of the Abhainn Bruachaig towards Kinlochewe Forest. Walking was easy along a good level track that wound alongside the burn. All was at peace as I covered the three miles to the Heights of Kinlochewe at a good pace. The occasional warning cry of a protective curlew floated on the breeze and rabbits scurried to their burrows. I turned periodically to enjoy a splendid retrospective view of snow-spattered Beinn Eighe attractively framed by the foothills of Carn a' Ghlinne and Kinlochewe Forest. Consisting of dwellings you can count on one hand, tiny Heights of Kinlochewe appeared to be no higher than Kinlochewe itself. Where were the dramatic rocks that its name suggests? All around were lush meadows in which shaggy Highland cattle quietly grazed; a serene amphitheatre, ringed by steep, heather-clad hillsides with not a formidable rock formation in sight.

I swung north into the valley of the Gleann na Muice. Here I passed a daunting notice indicating that deer are shot in the surrounding hills from mid-August to February, for sport meat, in accordance with government control policy. It advised walkers not to venture onto high ground during the stalking season as the area is rich with red deer, around four percent of their number being culled to maintain a balance. As it was June there was mercifully no fear of my being stalked.

Sweat and toil was imminent, for I could see an extensive track unravelling before me as it twisted through the steepening valley in search of lonely Lochan Fada. Gritting my teeth I began a four-mile ascent to the loch that lay hidden 1,000 feet above me. I climbed steadily until the stark features of approaching mountains appeared beyond the head of the valley. They beckoned me towards isolation rarely experienced. When I emerged from the valley to gaze over the serene indigo waters of Lochan Fada, they heralded a scene of untamed splendour; a veritable undisturbed and deserted haven. The loch lies in a long, narrow basin surrounded by a galaxy of impressive peaks, its south shore overlooked by the furrowed north face of the Letterewe Ridge. Slioch's distinctively sharp peak dominated once again, overshadowing the more rounded summits of Beinn Lair and Meall Mheinnidh. It is a mountain that impresses from all angles. The north shore of Lochan Fada rises gracefully to the foothills of a softer mountain range whose pinnacle is Mullach Coir Mhic Fhearchair.

From hereon I had to rely on map and compass, for there would be no paths until I reached Lochan Nid that lay four miles to the north-west. Searching for a landmark on the map I identified tiny Loch Meallan an Fhudair as an initial objective. Secreted a mile above me in the hills it has a stream issuing from it that tumbles almost exactly to the point where I was standing.

I began a stiff climb up the rough fellside, guided by the lively stream. Perversely it soon disappeared underground, much to my consternation. However, it remained close to the surface, for I could hear it gurgling merrily and I was able to follow its sound as I renewed my struggle up the testing slope. Keeping one ear as close to the ground as possible I staggered up the incline, lurching from side to side. My antics were reminiscent of Maurice and our Quasimodo impressions as we stumbled around the attic rooms in Spean Bridge. How I wished that he were with me now, his sense of humour would have been a great asset.

With back aching and ears straining I reached the crest of the hill and found the secluded loch that is nothing more than a large pond. The garland of hills that encompass it resembled the rolling waves of a jade ocean and they compelled me to pause and enjoy the stimulation of the vast emptiness. I turned towards distant Torridon, beyond Slioch, which now exhibited pockets of snow that glistened in the afternoon sunshine. Beinn Eighe and Liatach shimmered in a far-off haze, bidding me a final farewell.

On the move once more, my admiration for the appealing wilderness began to wane. How fickle I became when faced with that savage adversary, cloying peat. All romantic thoughts vanished as I leapt in and out of peat groughs that would severely test the metal of an Olympic steeplechaser. Having conquered the glutinous peat bogs of Kinder Scout and the Cheviots that threaten to swallow Pennine Way walkers, I reckoned that I could deal with any kind of terrain. However, nothing had prepared me for this hostile country, which made Kinder pale into insignificance. The quivering mass of peat threatened to engulf me and I was convinced that I was about to disappear without trace.

As I struggled an eagle floated effortlessly above me. I fervently hoped that it wasn't hungry and I wished it would miraculously metamorphose into a helicopter and pluck me from the mass of brown treacle. Sadly, I could only gaze upwards and wonder what it thought of my antics. Could it be a sea eagle? I knew that ten pairs had recently been released from the Western Isles where they were bred as part of a regeneration project. This was much to the chagrin of many Highland farmers, who report incidents of these predators picking up lambs and carrying them to their nests. I hoped that I was not about to suffer the same fate!

I ploughed through the mire, my spirits flagging and understanding exactly how the combatants had fared in the Battle of the Somme. My compass was gripped tightly and my eyes were glued to it lest I lost my bearing. I was soon confronted with a selection of valleys and, concealed beyond one of them was Loch an Nid. Mercifully the going became easier as I descended the selected valley, hoping that I had chosen correctly. The surroundings appeared dull and featureless in its confines when compared to the broad canvas that I had recently enjoyed. As the hills on either side began to recede I kept my eyes peeled for a path that crosses the mouth of the valley. Eventually it appeared and I heaved a sigh of relief. My heart sang as Loch an Nid appeared, directly on cue. A study of the map confirmed that the path formed the beginning of a straightforward route to Little Loch Broom.

The sun beamed upon the grassy shore of Loch an Nid, imparting a subtle yellow tone to its sheep-cropped covering. My eye was drawn to the lustrous gleam of Cambrian quartzite that coats the lower slopes of Meallan an Laoigh, which soar from the west shore of the loch. I had not seen this bright rock at such close quarters and its dazzle made the attendant mountains appear extremely sombre by comparison. There was, however, nothing undramatic about the magnificent outline of the famous An Teallach Ridge that filled the horizon to the north. The huge bulk of the mountain covers a wide area and its northern slopes career almost down to the sea beyond Camusnagaul. I could not take my eyes from it as I progressed through the valley, alongside a lively burn. Eventually my strength began to ebb and I rested beside a small, foaming waterfall. My rations had gone apart from some biscuits and milk that I carried in case of emergency. As I leisurely chewed on custard creams, shaded by the bright foliage of some welcome larches, I realised they were the first trees I had seen since leaving the Heights of Kinlochewe.

When I restarted it was a struggle to regain my momentum and my feet began to protest. Thankfully I had not been seriously troubled with blisters, but patches of hard skin were beginning to develop. I made a mental note to attend to them when I reached my destination.

Eventually the path joined a stony track, which I could see stretching for several miles ahead. At least I no longer needed to scratch my head over map and compass; merely keep moving. The great mass of An Teallach drew closer and I noticed its fickle colour, which had turned a chocolate brown. My eyes ranged along its massive spine, the vertebrae transforming from rounded humps at its lower end into ragged teeth on its higher reaches. What a thrill, I thought, to walk along that remarkable backbone to its 3,484-foot summit.

The track steepens as it skirts the base of the mountain, revealing the distant peaks of Inverleal Forest that lie to the east. This spiky range is crowned by mighty Beinn Dearg, which rises to over 3,500 feet. During the Ice Age it was one of several mountains in the locality that were covered by an ice-cap, thousands of feet thick, from which glaciers flowed to the Atlantic Ocean.

I trudged wearily to the brow of the hill, where I removed my rucksack and took a breather as I surveyed the final descent of the day, into the Dundonnel Valley. The distinctive grey of the track was clearly visible as it squirmed through a sepia landscape, given a lustrous veneer by the early-evening sun.

As I tottered down the track I was on automatic pilot, a state many walkers find themselves in towards the end of a gruelling day. Even the sight of waterfalls dancing in the nearby Gleann Chaorachain failed to lure me from the track. Another feast of views was unfolding before my tired eyes and, although I was unable to see Little Loch Broom, the mountains of the Cailleach Head peninsula, that separates it from Loch Broom, were clearly visible. The shadows were lengthening on their rugged flanks, an indication that time was slipping away.

My spirits received a boost when I met the first walkers that I had seen since leaving Shiel Bridge. I was approaching the Dundonnel River when I saw two sprightly, middle-aged ladies coming towards me, accompanied by a splendid golden Labrador. They obviously believed in sharing their load, for in addition to their own rucksacks, the dog had one strapped to its back. When I laughingly commented on this I was told that the animal was regularly made to carry its food and blanket.

I soon joined 'Destitution Road,' as the local section of the A832 road is known, which led me down to Little Loch Broom. Its name is a reference to its construction during the potato famine of 1851, thus providing work for destitute and starving men.

At last Little Loch Broom appeared, stretching serenely towards the open sea, signifying that I had a further two miles to complete. Desperately tired, I summoned my remaining strength and passed the Dundonnel Hotel, reposing by the south-east corner of the loch. Aching limbs were dragged along the pleasant lochside road as the sun was waning, until I finally reached my objective, an attractive dormer bungalow overlooking the water's edge.

My first remark to my host as she opened the door concerned my anxiety about supper. I need not have worried, for after a hurried shower I was treated to an admirable meal. Considerately, she made no mention of my late arrival nor did she complain that the other guests had already eaten. These, I discovered, were four young men, all doctors, who were staying for a few nights. I was very interested to learn that they had scaled the An Teallach Ridge that day and I eagerly asked how they had fared. Exhilarating and exhausting was their judgement. In fact they were so tired they were in bed by nine o'clock and I wasn't far behind them.

What a night! I was dragged from my bed in order to lead a rescue party onto the An Teallach Ridge in pitch darkness. Delighted to call upon the services of a seasoned traveller and heroic mountaineer, the local mountain rescue team had begged me to mastermind the daring recovery of four young doctors who were at that very moment clinging for dear life to one of the pinnacles of the mountain's great backbone. Realising that the request was deadly serious, I agreed to accompany them with the proviso that I could take my faithful Labrador, which would carry the necessary ropes and equipment in a rucksack strapped to its back. After a record-breaking night-time ascent of the ridge, the piercing beam of my torch revealed the four protagonists who were reduced to jibbering wretches. Their white knuckles were radiant in the shaft of light; glowing fingers clung to slivers of rock poised above the black void that separated rescuers and potential victims. Their agonising cries rose to a crescendo as I reached for the nearest petrified figure. My outstretched hand clutched the air a taunting foot away from him. Summoning every ounce of courage and strength I stretched as far across the terrifying chasm as I dared and flung out my hand once more. I was straining . . . straining with every ounce of my being . . . then I woke up and realised it was all a dream!

DAY SEVENTY-NINE : CAMUSNAGAUL - ULLAPOOL

My agenda on the following morning was far more mundane than the fantasy I had experienced during the night. I was about to treat myself to a seven-mile stroll to Ullapool, provided things went according to plan. Success hinged on the small ferry that crosses Loch Broom from Allt na h-Airbhe. If it was operating, my day would be easy; if it wasn't, a seventeen-mile walk around the head of that loch was in prospect, something I did not relish after three long days in the hills. I had no wish to suffer the same fate as John Hillaby when he tried to cross Loch Broom. He reached Allt na h-Airbhe at dusk to discover that the ferry was not operating, but he was helpfully put up for the night in a partly completed house that a man was building for his sick wife. The following morning he managed to cross the loch in a boat that carried the workmen, who were building the house, from Ullapool.

My concern over the ferry was the sole cloud on the horizon as I joined the doctors for breakfast. They were greatly amused when I mentioned my dream. They swore that they would not go near An Teallach again and showed me their knuckles, which were far from white. Whilst they were finishing their breakfast I rang the inn at Allt na h-Airbhe and inquired as to the availability of the ferry. A cheerful male voice told me that he would take me across and asked what time I would arrive. We settled on a rendezvous at one o'clock, much to my relief. I returned to give the news to the doctors who were preparing to spend the day in the mountains of Inverleal Forest. Now there was no need to hurry I had another cup of coffee to celabrate.

Retracing my steps along the shore of Little Loch Broom I felt quite fit and took the opportunity to study the locality, which I had barely noticed the previous evening. The loch seemed aptly named, for its banks were ablaze with colourful broom, brilliant yellow in the morning sunshine. Visibility was as clear as a bell and a backward glance down the placid loch revealed the profile of distant Cailleach Head jutting into the open sea. As I passed the Dundonnel Hotel I found it worth a second look. Its attractive façade had a style that is often lacking in modern hotels and its pristine-white walls were in keeping with the buildings of Camusnagaul.

I left the road at the hamlet of Dundonnel and joined a track that led me, through verdant meadows, around the head of the loch. Leaving the comfort of the valley at Eilean Darach I began an 800-foot climb onto the Cailleach Head peninsula along a narrow, unfenced road that initially traversed a pine forest. It was a hard pull to the peninsula's crest and I did not spare myself, despite the heat, for I was concerned about missing the boat, as it were. At the top of the incline the road turns abruptly and heads west to the isolated settlement of Badrallach and a brief stop was taken to have a last look over Little Loch Broom to the mountains beyond. The white oases of Camusnagaul and Dundonnel looked miniscule beneath the towering slopes of An Teallach, but it was an indelible scene, crowned by a vault of unclouded blue.

I was obliged to transfer to a rough track, which continues north and provides the only access by land to Allt na h-Airbhe. Residents and guests at the inn can only reach it by four-wheel-drive vehicle, or boat. After a short respite beside a secluded lochan that relieved the monotony of undulating moorland, I strode along the now descending track, eager for my first glimpse of Ullapool. The ground soon began to decline sharply and suddenly a wide expanse of water lay below me with a sprawling landscape beyond. Ullapool seemed close enough to reach out and touch as it beckoned from the far side of the mile-wide Loch Broom. Its pier and harbour, clearly visible, formed the focal point of the popular village that appeared a bustling metropolis when compared to the isolation of the previous three days. It shelters beneath rolling hills that surge north towards the distant rock formations of Inverpolly Forest and the Cromalt Hills. What a thrill it was to see the next stage of my journey spread before me like a giant relief map.

It was mid-day when I arrived at the lochside, one hour ahead of schedule; my impatience earning me a long wait. A small launch was moored at a nearby narrow jetty and this, I assumed, was the ferry. Ullapool was frustratingly close at hand and its cluster of buildings, all of which were coloured the indigenous white, looked appealing, even from a mile away. The white paint manufacturers have a field-day in this part of Wester Ross and they have adopted and slightly modified the Henry Ford edict - you can have any colour you like, providing it is white!

Sitting down on the jetty I removed my boots and socks and dangled my feet in the deliciously cool water as I sat eating my lunch. The hour passed sluggishly as I waited, breathing the remarkably pure air, typical of the sub-arctic lands of the Western Isles. I continually checked my watch until the ferryman appeared at one o'clock and told me that I was his only passenger. He cast off and the tiny craft chugged from the shore towards the flesh-pots of Ullapool. The water, which had appeared calm from the jetty, became quite choppy and we were soon bobbing to and fro like a cork. The boatman chatted merrily, oblivious to the conditions, but I became quite concerned, for I didn't fancy a swim. I struggled to concentrate on the emerging features of the harbour to keep my worries at bay. The wooden ramparts of the pier were clearly visible and several anglers were perched on them, lines dangling expectantly into the loch. Behind the harbour a line of bright, unblemished buildings overlooked a shingle beach and their white walls positively gleamed.

Immediately after depositing me on the harbour jetty, the boatman sped away with a friendly wave, leaving me to enjoy the view of the mountains that encircle the head of Loch Broom. Above the ragged contours of Inverleal Forest I caught sight of Beinn Dearg once more and I visualised the doctors dangling from its challenging summit!

The afternoon was spent enjoying the delights of Ullapool and I could appreciate why it is such a popular resort and an important halt on Highland excursions. There was a bustling, yet carefree air to the place and visitors are assured of a friendly welcome, for it is heavily reliant on tourism. Originally the village was a busy fishing port, which owed its prosperity to herring. In recent times fishing has sadly declined, a fact cruelly demonstrated when I returned to the harbour to watch the boats landing their catches. How meagre they looked; the sad remnants of a once-thriving industry.

A cheerful greeting awaited me at the Tourist Information Centre where I inquired about accommodation beyond Kylesku. I had, in fact, rung the centre some months earlier and they were unsuccessful in this regard. The helpful lady made several abortive telephone calls before suggesting that I made further inquiries on reaching Kylesku.

Around five o'clock I arrived at the Youth Hostel where I was staying that night. It was bulging with people of many nationalities and appeared more like a cosmopolitan hotel than a hostel. Conditions were fully acceptable but I longed for that special atmosphere of smaller and more traditional hostels. The warden was friendly and had a sense of humour, for on the reception desk he had placed a cryptic notice that read, 'Ring TWICE for slow service.'

Whilst enjoying supper in the crowded dining room I met an agreeable young couple who, I discovered, had recently graduated from strollers to the local pub into keen long-distance walkers. Ullapool was their current base for exploring the wilder areas of Wester Ross and like me, they were drawn to its remote and sometimes intimidating landscape. Away from its sparse network of roads, they indicated, you could walk all day in complete isolation, with which I heartily concurred. Our mutual feelings included the cordiality shown by other walkers and we agreed that their greeting often depended on where you encounter them. The lonelier the meeting-place, the more friendly the reaction.

After supper I joined my two acquaintances for a walk around the still-busy streets and we were treated to the most glorious sunset over the Summer Isles. Such fiery evening skies are apparently a regular occurrence and evening cruises will take you to Outer Loch Broom to view them at close quarters.

DAY EIGHTY : ULLAPOOL - ELPHIN

The day began poorly and went downhill. I left an Ullapool that scowled under heavy skies and spitting rain, cursing the weather pendulum for swinging once more. As I followed the road out of the village I was seeking a path that would lead me into the hills overlooking Strath Kanaird. This particular thoroughfare looked promising on the map, for it cuts out a broad loop in the only road running north from Ullapool, the A835.

I found the path about a mile from the village, which was a signal for the rain to switch to overdrive, and a thick pea-souper to obliterate any landmarks. In a few minutes I was wet through and annoyingly, was to remain so all day. With visibility down to a few yards I struggled to keep sight of the inconspicuous path, frequently resorting to the compass in order to stay on its line. I suffered some anxious moments until I met the track for which I was aiming. Relief flooded through me, for I now had a lifeline and would soon be in Strath Kanaird, or so I thought. My pace quickened as I ventured through a silent, ethereal world, but imagine my shock and dismay when the track abruptly disappeared into an expanse of water that lay across my path. I anxiously scanned the map to pin-point my position, only to find that I had walked off one map and nearly onto the next one, which unfortunately did not exactly correspond. Two miles of my route were missing and I had no idea what lay directly ahead. How far the water extended was impossible to assess, due to the murk, and it seemed risky to try and walk round the obstruction, for I might lose my bearings in the fog. The only sensible solution was to backtrack several miles to the A835 road and take the longer route to Strath Kanaird. Angrily, I turned on my heel and did just that, seething with frustration.

I rejoined the road a mere mile farther on than where I had left it over two hours previously. A double disappointment was that John Hillaby had successfully negotiated a cross-country route to Strath Kanaird and I had failed. The A835 road is far from sedate as it cavorts and bounces into the Moine Thrust, which extends north to the long ridge of Breabag. It is a land where limestone intrudes into the indigenous sandstone and schists, revealing caves, potholes and vanishing streams. During its passage the road weaves through Strath Kanaird and onwards to Drumrunie and Elphin, my day's destination. As I trudged along it I became acquainted with a strategic tourist corridor that extends for over sixty miles to Durness that lies on the north coast. It searches out gaps in the hills and glides over a rocky bed through the arid desert that is Sutherland. A scourge of modern society is beginning to disfigure the corridor; litter thrown from passing cars or discarded at roadside picnic-spots. I followed a trail of drink cans, plastic containers and waste paper all the way to Durness, by which time I had become well versed in the eating and drinking habits of uncaring visitors.

Eight miles of tarmac-crunching brought me to Drumrunie and almost to the border of Britain's farthest-flung county that boasts over three hundred lochs and to the casual observer, consists merely of water interspersed with deserts of barren gneiss. Closer inspection, however, reveals that despite its solitude there is organisation and management; demonstrated by deer estates and regimented forests. Drumrunie nestles between Coigach and the Cromalt Hills. It is a tiny settlement that clusters round a road junction where an animated unfenced road leaves the A835 and circles the mountains of Coigach. This lonely thoroughfare provides the only link with the Rhuba Mor peninsula and isolated outposts, such as Achiltibuie that looks out over Badentarbat Bay to the Summer Isles. It also skirts the southern fringe of Iverpolly Forest and delivers you to the foot of Stac Pollaidh, or 'Stac Polly,' as it is commonly known.

I was thoroughly drenched and not in the best of moods as I tramped through Drumrunie in an incessant downpour. As I squelched from the hamlet through a gap in the hills towards Sasunnaich I relieved the drudgery of rain-soaked miles by giving free reign to my imagination. I became immersed in the exciting world depicted in *Reach for the Sky*, its well-thumbed pages being one of my favourite reads. The life-story of Sir Douglas Bader, the legless air ace of the Battle of Britain, it enthralls me each time I read of his struggle to overcome horrendous injuries sustained in a reckless bout of low-level aerobatics. What courage and sheer guts the man possessed to walk on artificial legs unaided by sticks and to eventually become one of the heroes of the Second World War. He drove a car, played golf and squash with boundless enthusiasm and tackled many other activities that the able-bodied take for granted. I was proud to see him from afar when he paid a brief visit to RAF Duxford whilst I was stationed there during my National Service. It was the wartime aerodrome where he cut his teeth as a fighter pilot. His natural leadership blossomed with the responsibility of leading squadrons of the renowned Duxford Wing into battle with the

Luftwaffe. He instigated air-battle tactics that became invaluable against superior enemy numbers.

I was mentally flailing around the skies, shooting down enemy aircraft with reckless courage, as Bader had done, when I was jerked from my day-dream by a screech of brakes. A landrover lurched to a stop beside me and a cheery young farmer shouted through the open window to inquire if I wanted a lift. What a temptation! Here was a golden opportunity to speed through the murk and gobble up the remaining miles. Then I thought of Bader. He would not have taken the soft option. Stoically I declined the man's invitation, which prompted a retort that I must be mad; a logical conclusion when your kindness is rebuffed by a bedraggled walker dripping water from every pore. He roared away in a cloud of spray leaving me to savour a solitary crumb of comfort; Bader would have been proud of me.

I laboured through the defile, its floor peppered with a multitude of tiny lochans. Only the roadside ones were visible; iron-grey expanses that provided a chilling reminder of my earlier misfortune in the hills. How I longed for the tenacious clouds to depart, for I was heartily fed up with staring at a cheerless landscape.

On the wettest ground the road coasts over embankments and hovers on concrete rafts that prevent it becoming submerged. Drumrunie Forest was merely a lingering smudge on an ashen canvas as I passed its south-east fringe oblivious to its crowning glory, Cul Mor, whose craggy faces guard its 2,785-foot quartzite summit. At tiny Sasunnaich I entered Sutherland and found myself wishing the remaining miles away; a futile pastime, for it makes a journey more tiresome.

Sutherland looked no different to Wester Ross under its mantle of mist. The weather was hardly conducive to a clear-cut impresion of this wild, untamed land. The remaining miles steadily dwindled beneath my feet and I was soon following the lurching road into Knochan, a neighbour of Elphin. The rain was finally easing as I passed a sprinkling of buildings that shelter at the foot of the Cromalt Hills. In the retreating mist the landscape came into sharper focus and I could see the bridge over the Abhainn a'Chrocain Burn that links Knochan with the first of the scattered dwellings of Elphin. They dotted the surrounding hillsides as I galloped over the bridge, their white walls prominent beneath a pall of persistent grey cloud that hovered over their rooftops like a giant wad of soiled cotton wool. The painters of Ullapool had obviously been active in the area with their mega-litres of white paint.

My destination, Birchbank Holiday Lodge, turned out to be a brand new building, rising amidst surrounding rubble and debris that normally litters a building site. Some of the exterior paintwork remained unfinished and the solid front door had yet to be varnished. Carefully avoiding obstacles left by the builders I reached the entrance and rang the bell. A harassed-looking man opened the door and seemed surprised to see a walker on his doorstep. I introduced myself, indicating that I had made a reservation by telephone with Tom Strang. With a sharp intake of breath he replied that he was Tom and had completely forgotten I was coming. He invited me inside and apologised for the turmoil. He was fighting to get the place ready for his first group of guests who were due the following week. It transpired that, as proprietor of Assynt Guided Holidays, his aim was to entertain parties of walkers, climbers and anglers who could enjoy their particular pursuits, with Tom acting as guide and instructor. I later discovered that he is a well-known walker and mountaineer, a fact he modestly omitted to mention, and is also an accomplished author.

His worries temporarily thrust aside by the intervention of a tired and hungry walker, Tom promptly arranged for someone to come and prepare supper for me and make up a bed. He insisted that I made myself at home, indicating that the television and his collection of CD's were at my disposal.

Supper was well in hand when I had showered and changed and I was soon enjoying a splendid meal with personal service by a helpful lady who obligingly promised to come again the following morning and cook breakfast for me.

A little later Tom and the lady departed leaving me to enjoy a superbly relaxing evening. I was serenaded by Pavarotti and soothed by the strings of Mantovani until fatigue overtook me and I retired contentedly to bed.

DAY EIGHTY-ONE : ELPHIN - KYLESKU

The layer of cotton wool cloud hovered stubbornly over the landscape as I peered anxiously through the bedroom curtains for a quick weather check. Thankfully it was dry and I reasoned that the sun might eventually destroy the fruits of the cloud factory that had annoyingly been working overtime. I entered the dining room to find everything laid out for breakfast and the tempting smell of bacon wafting from the kitchen. Despite Tom's predicament I could not fault the hospitality and service.

Tom arrived whilst I was finishing my third cup of coffee and remarked that I seemed very relaxed. His harassed expression had not faded with a night's rest and he clearly didn't relish another day fighting with contractors. He inquired if I had been comfortable and slept well. I assured him that things had been first-class and once he was over his teething problems his guests would agree. It brought the first smile I had seen, to his lips.

Back on the road once more I came upon another group of dwellings that comprise the remainder of straggling Elphin, where, I assumed, life was not easy for the small crofting community. A sign at a roadside farm indicated that it had been put to more lucrative use as the Scottish Farm Animal Visitor Centre, which offers displays of animals as an attraction to passing tourists. According to the sign it features 'over 300 breeds, ancient and modern, to see, stroke and feed.'

The road swung east, skirting the shore of Cam Loch, the gateway to Assynt, which, although only fourteen miles by twelve miles, displays a remarkable geological structure. Terminating at Kylesku, its indigenous bedrock of Lewisian gneiss is overlaid in places by virtually horizontal layers of Torridonian sandstone. Great masses of this ancient rock, such as Suilven and Canisp bulge from the choppy expanse of gneiss and should be visible if the cloud would only lift. Unfortunately it persisted, at around 500 feet, and ensured that I saw very little of them. The wooded island of Eilean na Gartaig squatted in Cam Loch, its rich vegetation seemingly out of place amongst a denuded landscape. Habitation disappeared as I strode through the silent valley, occupied only by a Bronze Age burial cairn, one of several I was to pass on my way to Inchnadamph.

A further two miles brought me to Ledmore Junction where I joined the A837 road that heads north to Inchnadamph, turns west at Loch Assynt and provides the only main road link with the coastal village of Lochinver. The countryside remained bleak and uninviting as I pushed on towards Inchnadamph. Decapitated Canisp rose to the north-west beyond the placid waters of Loch Awe and I passed some wild ponies grazing nearby. Apart from the occasional vehicle, the isolated crofts of Ledbeg and Lyne were the sole signs of life, their presence marked by crude wooden post-boxes standing by the roadside.

It was a lonely walk that morning and, from the few vehicles that passed, eyes stared incredulously at me, their owners amazed that anyone would choose to make such a solitary journey on foot.

As I approached the hamlet of Inchnadamph, a collection of crofts at the head of Loch Assynt, I noticed the Inchnadamph Hotel standing in dignified seclusion. A magnet for visitors, judging by its bulging car park, it offers the only accommodation of any magnitude in Assynt. Lying near the foot of Ben More Assynt, Sutherland's highest mountain at 3,273 feet, it provides an ideal base for sportsmen and geologists. Nearby Loch Assynt bristles with salmon and brown trout and the Cambrian limestone of Ben More Assynt's lower reaches, now a National Nature Reserve, abounds with caves and underground streams.

The hotel looked enticing and I ventured inside for a drink. I struck up a conversation with two elderly, distinguished-looking gents who, similar to the pair I met later amongst the Clwydian Hills, believed that walking should not be rushed. Their route usually covered seven or eight miles and, wherever possible, passed a convenient watering-hole where they could enjoy a good meal, washed down with copious amounts of gin and tonic. I suggested such places might be a little thin on the ground in Sutherland.

Their morning had been a disappointment, for after a comfortable night in the hotel and fortified with a good breakfast they had taken the arduous path that winds for six miles through bleak mountains to the head of Eas Coul Aulin waterfall. Their objective, Britain's highest cascade, proved elusive. Severely tested by the harsh terrain, they were defeated by the steep climb to the pass that separates Glas Bheinn and Beinn Uidhe. Sensibly they turned back, realising that such a hard twelve-mile walk was beyond their capabilities.

John Hillaby's name arose in conversation and I mentioned my fascination with his journey through Britain. Neville, the elder of the pair, had read several of his books and warned me not to make the same mistake that Hillaby had when he left Inchnadamph. Striking across country in a quest to reach Strathnaver, a deep valley that intrudes into the north coast at Bettyhill, he completely lost his bearings. His plan was to follow an appropriate line between the Inchnadamph Hotel and the north-west corner of Loch Shin, a distance of around nine miles, with few landmarks to guide him. What little identification there was disappeared in thick mist shortly after his departure and a few hours of floundering brought him to the south-east tip of Loch Glencoul, many miles off course. It took three more hours of anxious toil before he finally reached Loch Shin.

I assured Neville and his partner Harry that I would be keeping to the road, certainly as far as Kylesku. The thought of following John Hillaby's cross-country route had previously crossed my mind, but was discounted after remembering an episode of *Wainwright in Scotland* on television in which Wainwright and his companion Eric Robson gazed from Kylesku Bridge along Loch Cairnbawn. The scene was captivating and I vowed not to miss it. I told Neville and Harry that when I reached Kylesku I would decide wether or not to cut across country.

I left the hotel and approached Loch Assynt, searching for a pleasant spot to eat my lunch-time sandwiches. At the entrance to the churchyard that nestles on the shore of the loch, I found one and sat on the base of a stone memorial that is a poignant reminder of the Second World War. It was erected in memory of the crew of a RAF aircraft that crashed on Ben More Assynt in 1941.

After lunch I began to skirt the north-east shore of Loch Assynt and enjoyed an extensive view along its six-mile length. Dark hills encompassed it, but beyond, the overhanging cloud was at last relenting. The outlook was bright over the coast, a familiar situation where the sky is clear over the sea whilst the mountains attract the clouds inland. The road unwound before me, hugging the indented lochside as it heads for Lochinver. I was puzzled to see a woman walking, a hundred yards ahead of me, in the same direction. A quick glance at the map revealed that, apart from an isolated farm, there was no habitation for six miles. Surely she wasn't walking the twelve miles to Lochinver. I soon overtook her and she asked where I was headed. She smiled when I replied that I was about to ask her the same question. It transpired that she was returning to Calda

House, a ruin that stands beside the loch, a mile farther on. Apparently it was the venue for a clay-pigeon shoot in which her husband was participating. I learnt that he often took his wife to such events and then left her to amuse herself. The neglected lady had wandered into Inchnadamph to kill an hour or two, having no inclination to watch the menfolk shoot at hurtling black discs for a whole day.

I said goodbye to the woman and pressed on. Finally the sun had broken through but cloud lingered over the mountains. A short distance past the remnants of Calda House, built in 1660 for the third Earl of Seaforth, I came upon the shooting party and the remains of tiny Ardvreck Castle. Little more than a gnarled, fortified tower, the castle perches on a headland that juts forcefully into the loch. It is a former stronghold of the MacLeods of Assynt, erected in the late sixteenth century. The Marquess of Montrose, a distinguished general, victorious in many battles against the Covenanters, was imprisoned there by Neil MacLeod, after his defeat at Bonar Bridge. MacLeod reputedly gave up Montrose, who was taken to Edinburgh and hanged, for £20,000, which was never actually paid, plus a consignment of sub-standard meat. The first occurrence of BSE?

At Skiag Bridge I abandoned the A837 road and turned north along the A894 towards Kylesku. This road rises sharply from Loch Assynt to the pass between Glas Bheinn and Quinag. It proved a strenuous ascent, relieved only by the vivid-yellow broom lining the roadside. Quinag, its seven tops lurking under retreating cloud revealed slopes of smooth pipe-rock and quartzite. As I crested the hill I rested by Loch na Gainmhich which snuggles in a rocky amphitheatre, with weather-beaten boulders lining its banks. As I enjoyed a reviving drink my evocative surroundings seemed to encapsulate the very nature of Sutherland - wild, barren and beautiful. The view towards Kylesku is formidable, its centrepiece being the writhing band of tarmac that winds towards Loch Glencoul. Seemingly stretching to infinity, it is flanked by bare countryside, speckled with numerous pockets of water. Streams tumble from several tiny lochans towards Loch Glencoul and Loch Cairnbawn, the main sea-loch that runs inland from Eddrachillis Bay. East of Kylesku it forks into Loch Glendhu and Loch Glencoul, which are only accessible through a confined straight, which is crossed by Kylesku Bridge.

It seemed to take an age to cover the remaining miles to Kylesku. I breathed a sigh of relief when I eventually reached the Kylesku Hotel and turned to see the rugged dome of Sail Garbh, the highest of the seven tops of Quinag, reveal itself. It appeared through strands of feathery cloud dancing around its head; an inspiring sight. A welcoming sign outside the hotel advertised bar meals and a restaurant that serves local sea food, conveniently obtained from the nearby tiny harbour. A row of small fishing boats lined the jetty in this sheltered inlet and their paintwork was the only thing of brightness as wretched drizzle began to draw a veil over the scene.

I received an enthusiastic welcome at my accommodation from Joan who provided a wholesome meal and some lively conversation. She was keen to know my plans for the next stage of my walk. I told her of my desire to see Kylesku Bridge, with its impressive view over Loch Cairnbawn, before heading across country, weather permitting, to Loch More. Eventually, I indicated, I hoped to reach Strath More, which would lead me to the north coast. Joan suggested it would be wise to wait until morning to see what the weather held in store. If it looked promising she would telephone some friends who lived by Loch More to ask if they could arrange accommodation for me on the following night.

DAY EIGHTY-TWO : KYLESKU - DURNESS

I received the bad news as I sat down for breakfast. Joan had telephoned her friends at Loch More and apparently they could not see a hand in front of them. A thick mist had rolled over the loch and appeared to be inconsiderately heading in the direction of Kylesku. Rubbing salt into the wound they added that there was no accommodation, there being only estate cottages in the area. No point in venturing there in such conditions, was their advice. That ruled out the cross-country route. I had no option but to keep to the road.

The enjoyment of my breakfast ebbed away, for just as predicted, a pea-souper blotted out the view from the window. Nothing to see today, I thought. The road was definitely a wise choice.

Back in my room I checked the map and investigated the A984 road, which snakes through tracts of rock and gigantic puddles to Laxford Bridge. Here the A838 takes over for the journey to Rhiconich, and eventually Durness. The teaser was to find accommodation along this sprightly band of tarmac. I took the easy option and did nothing, choosing merely to head for Scourie, the first settlement of any size and see what developed.

I left the house, with Joan's good wishes and extra rations, and ventured into the grey clamminess of an atrocious morning. A chill breeze wafted over Loch Cairnbawn as I approached the bridge I was most anxious to see. It was undetectable until I was almost upon it, merely a black smudge on a steel-grey background. A dampening squall hit me as I stood on its shapely concrete span staring into nothingness. Visibility was barely thirty yards and the stunning view that I had been eagerly awaiting was non-existent. What an anti-climax!

Thoroughly disappointed I crossed the bridge and stormed past Kylesku's neighbour Kylestrome and entered Reay country, uninhabited apart from its coastline, which is indented by two sea-lochs, Laxford and Inchard, each four miles long. It has a wildly dissipated appearance on the map, as though shredded by a giant harrow to form a colander. Through innumerable holes, water has intruded, resulting in fearsome looking terrain. I felt comforted that I would have solid tarmac beneath my feet as it negotiates a path between searching coastal inlets and frolics amidst pock-marked Reay.

I soon became enclosed by the conifers of Duartmore Forest; quite a rarity in that rocky desert. When these retreated I was confronted by dark, heather moorland interspersed with leathery outcrops of gneiss. The only sign of life was forlorn, newly shorn sheep that appeared like ghosts from the misty morass. They sported brightly-painted numbers on their backs, looking accusingly at me as though I was responsible for purloining their warm coats.

Eventually I descended into the hamlet of Badcall that lies about three miles south of Scourie and overlooks Badcall Bay, normally one of the most attractive on the north-west coast. As I gazed over the rocky inlet all that was visible were black mounds lying in an expanse of tar. These dreary shapes were some of the islands that adorn the bay, a great place for lobster fishing.

A further hour of twists and turns brought me to the coastal village of Scourie, which, compared to Kylesku was a metropolis, boasting a store and a Post Office. It was Sunday and consequently the place was quiet. Perhaps it was always quiet. I tried the store and found it open, seizing the opportunity to obtain more supplies in case I became stranded overnight. As I scanned the shelves the proprietor approached and declared brusquely that the shop was closed. This seemed strange, as the door was clearly open. Sunday was closing day, I was informed and they were only open for stock-taking. This I found even more difficult to grasp. I explained my predicament and asked if an exception could be made in my case, but the man was adamant, suggesting I try the nearest shop. My heart lifted. 'How far is that?' I asked. 'Twenty-four miles,' was the astonishing reply. My jaw dropped and I left, disconsolate and lost for words.

Laxford Bridge seemed the next outpost to aim for and I hastily left uncooperative Scourie, making a mental note to cross it off my list of holiday destinations. The road bounced merrily over ripples of gneiss and lurched round innumerable curves as though unsure of its ultimate direction. Two hours passed on the roller-coaster of a highway before Laxford Bridge materialised from the murk. It stands at an important road junction, but you have the distinct feeling of being in the middle of nowhere, for the place is so tiny. Blink and you have missed it. Strategically placed on the south-east tip of Loch Laxford, it marks the end of the line, as it were, for the A 984 road. There was no sign of accommodation in the vicinity so I transferred my affections to the A838 and set full steam ahead for Rhiconich, the next pocket of habitation, five miles to the north. The feeling of isolation returned as I followed the differently numbered, but equally contorted road. No walkers had been encountered. None were really expected in the wild conditions that only an idiot would tolerate.

The only visible relief from monotony was the occasional cluster of roadside flowers. Splashes of flag irises and bog myrtle were nectar to a man figuratively dying of thirst. Suddenly the silence was broken by the sound of an approaching vehicle and a car pulled up beside me. Its occupants were Japanese and the driver, who spoke perfect English, politely inquired if I would like a lift.

Wouldn't I just! Then Bader took control once more and I heard myself refusing his generous offer. This caused a stir amongst the car's passengers, who gabbled animatedly in Japanese, throwing disbelieving glances in my direction. They obviously could not comprehend this crazy Englishman who chose to walk through the middle of nowhere in such weather. With a shrug of his shoulders the driver pulled away, bent on discovering more of Scotland in impenetrable mist. As the sound of the engine drifted away the door of my murky prison slammed shut once more and I began to doubt my purism. A golden opportunity to reach civilisation in comfort had been exchanged for the uncertainty of finding a bed for the night. The prospect of sleeping under the stars seemed far from appealing as I headed for Rhiconich that lies at the head of Loch Inchard.

As I approached the Rhiconich Hotel, its whitewashed walls beckoning through the gloom, I was denied the beauty of its superb lochside location. Apart from a few cottages strung out along the leaden lochside it stood in splendid isolation beneath a rocky buttress that loomed angrily above the sheltered bay. Surprisingly the hotel bar was quite busy, probably due to the awful weather. I took my drink to an unoccupied table and gratefully sat down. I had a decision to make and it had to be done promptly. As I mulled over my options, the strident tones of a man rose above the general conversation. He was leaning on the bar holding court with a group of tourists clustered around him, hanging on his every word. Dressed in designer walking gear that looked too immaculate to be well-used, he was bragging about his Munro-bagging prowess. Names, such as Suilven, Canisp and Ben More Assynt tripped off his tongue, as though indicating they had been easily conquered and he seemed blissfully unaware that the first two were not high enough to be Munro's. The paunch he displayed beneath his open fleece jacket convinced me that he had probably never been near a Munro.

It would have been enjoyable listening to his entertaining rubbish had I not to decide wether to seek accommodation at the hotel or move on. Move on to where? There was no habitation until Durness, which lay fourteen miles away. A quick check of my watch revealed that it was only three-fifteen, despite the fact that I had already covered twenty miles. My early start and brisk pace had put me in a quandary. It was possible to reach Durness by late evening, with the alternative of killing time for the rest of the day at Rhiconich. Reach Durness that evening? I must be mad. Thirty-four miles in a day was a tall order.

I certainly was mad, for I didn't linger over my drink and took to the road once more, steadily climbing through Achriesgill Glen to a watershed lying 600 feet above sea level. Here stands remote Gaulin House, once a hotel, now a shooting lodge, its gaunt features etched eerily on a blank canvas. Thankfully it marked the end of the last climb of the day, for acording to the map it was a straight and gradual descent to the Kyle of Durness. Gone were the twists and turns to which I had grown accustomed. It was as though a giant iron had removed the wrinkles from the A838 road.

The protracted and ultimately boring descent became almost a blur. Mile upon mile of resilient mist caused my automatic pilot to take over. What little I could see of the landscape took on a different character. No longer was I bouncing over ripples of gneiss; the ground was flatter with a good coating of grass. The road also appeared to be tiring as it led me, arrow-straight, across the neck of Cape Wrath's protruding headland that is bounded by Loch Inchard and the Kyle of Durness.

My long-suffering limbs began to rebel and I reluctantly stopped before I seized up. I slumped on the roadside verge and searched my rucksack for sustenance. The only nourishment I found was a few biscuits and the lukewarm dregs of coffee in my flask. These were soon disposed of and I grimaced as the foul-tasting liquid was forced down my throat. As I did so, a car suddenly floated past, its engine barely audible, and the occupants stared in amazement at the pathetic creature reclining at the roadside pulling disgusting faces.

Hauling myself to my feet I trudged wearily beside the Kyle of Durness, unsettled by the nagging prospect of scouring the village for a night's lodgings; if indeed I got that far. I was compelled to take frequent stops as the interminable miles dragged on. My limbs felt like dead weights and my tired brain ceased to function. Chafing with every step my abused feet complained bitterly and time was slipping away. It was well past seven o'clock before the Kyle retreated into the mist and I began the final two miles of my journey that seemed like six.

At eight-thirty I staggered into Durness and by a minor miracle I soon discovered a small hotel, tottered in and found they had a spare room. Relief engulfed me when I was told that a meal would be provided when I had showered and changed. I rushed to my room with as much strength as I could muster, but dared not throw myself on the bed for fear of falling straight to sleep and going without food until morning. It was impossible to throw myself anywhere in the cramped room, but I was past caring. There was a bed and somewhere to hang my clothes, which was all I needed.

A little later I ate a solitary meal, comforted by the luxurious feeling of reaching Durness against all the odds. Contentment washed over me as I demolished the last vestiges of a satisfying meal and retired to my garret. I quickly fell asleep, with the consoling thought that the hardest section of my journey was over.

DAY EIGHTY-THREE : DURNESS - TONGUE

I was jerked from a deep sleep by the fall-out from a battle royal being waged in an adjoining bedroom. The thin dividing wall reverberated with the blast of angry voices. A humdinger of an argument seemed well underway between what I assumed were husband and wife. They were going at it hammer and tongue as I tried to clear my befogged brain. Still drowsy, I checked my watch - seven forty-five. That cleared my head. I was late. Normally I was up and doing by this time. As the insults rose to a crescendo in the next room I rushed to the window for a weather check. The heartening sight of blue sky greeted me. There was some fibrous cloud, but the sun was working hard to demolish it. The mist had conveniently vanished.

Whilst I was dressing, the warring couple ran out of steam. Strangled tones lapsed into silence. Then I heard a door slam, which indicated they were probably heading for the dining room. Having covered so much ground the previous day I found it hard to motivate myself. I had no time to mess around, for the day's walk would be no pushover if I was to reach Tongue.

When I entered the dining room it was nearly full. I surveyed the array of faces, intrigued as to which was the fighting couple from the adjoining bedroom. It was impossible to identify them.

Everyone seemed to be chatting amicably, apart from a man sitting alone at a corner table. I noticed he was wearing walking gear so I approached his table and asked if I could join him. He introduced himself as Jamie from Edinburgh, who often visited the Cape Wrath peninsula, a firm favourite of his. A place of wild, unfettered charm was his glowing description. Apparently he had made several trips to the Cape itself, which involve crossing the Kyle of Durness by ferry and following the unfenced road that runs for ten miles across the Moor of Parph to the lighthouse. From there, he indicated, you have to walk to the tip of the Cape.

My sketchy knowledge of Cape Wrath, I admitted, was gleaned from books that put considerable emphasis on the birds that populate the great cliffs that surround it. I had been amused to discover that migrating gannets use the Cape as a landmark and staging post. One could imagine their leader calling, 'Right hand down for the Orkneys,' or, 'Left hand down for St Kilda.'

Jamie smilingly admitted that he owned a trig point on the peninsula; the most northerly in Scotland over 1,000 feet, to be precise. He had apparently acquired it under the 'Adopt a Trig Point' scheme, which enables enthusiasts to own and maintain their own ordnance column. Jamie had experienced great difficulty in finding his adoptive piece of concrete on his first visit as it was obscured by deep snow!

I could have happily carried on talking to Jamie but another demanding schedule loomed. The unknown factor was, once again, the availability of a ferry, this time across Loch Eriboll, a long sea-loch that intrudes deep into the coastline. A pier was indicated on the map at Portnancon that lies roughly at the mid-point of the loch. If I could get a boat from there across to Ard Neackie on the east bank I would save twelve miles. If not, thirty daunting miles lay ahead, courtesy of a long journey around Loch Eriboll.

Jamie told me he was off to do some bird-watching as we said goodbye outside the hotel. Nearby, a party of overnight guests was boarding a coach to continue their Highland tour. Their next port of call, we learnt, was Portree, on Skye, which evoked thoughts of Maurice. There was an excited air about them as they began what looked like being a perfect day for sightseeing. Many of them gave a friendly wave and wished us well.

It was great to have clear views once more and to be able to take in my surroundings. Durness is set on a limestone headland overlooking expanses of silver sand that circle the bays of Sango and Balnakeil. Rarely had I seen a more enticing beach as I walked above Sango Bay, but it it was deserted. I was to encounter many such tempting sands, washed by the remarkably blue waters of the Atlantic, and equally devoid of people. The keen wind that sweeps in from the sea must be the culprit.

The plan for my journey to John O'Groats was to remain as close to the coast as possible, keeping to the road in the absence of convenient footpaths. My limbs seemed to have recovered from their battering of the previous day, which augered well for reaching that goal. No protests were forthcoming from my feet, which had almost purred the previous evening when I smothered them in soothing cream.

A premier attraction of Durness is Smoo Cave, which lies at the head of a narrow cove that slices into the coastline beyond Sango Bay. As I gazed into this deep gash in the limestone cliffs it appeared an ideal haunt for smugglers - convenient shelter from the open sea, concealment and an enormous cave in which to store loot. I eagerly descended to the cave, a massive, dark cavity, scoured by thousands of years of erosion. A slender river flows into it through a hole in the roof but, unless it is in spate, you can explore the cave without fear of a drenching.

Emerging from its dark recesses I rejoined the road, and beyond the tiny settlement of Leirinmore, which overlooks another inviting bay, I took a track that climbs into the hills, as a short cut to Portnancon. As I ascended the hillside, the vegetation lay in wave-like formation due to its exposure to searching north-west winds. Small shrubs of heather, barberry and crowberry, their branches nearly horizontal, leaned away from the wind and, in the shelter that these provide, mosses and lichens flourished. How different the landscape appeared to the expanse of inhospitable rock that characterises much of Sutherland.

The path I was following petered out and as I carefully descended a tussocky slope to rejoin the A838 road, I could see the extensive blue band of Loch Eriboll stretching into the distance like a giant tongue licking its way inland. A short distance remained to Portnancon where I found an immaculate, recently extended house standing by the loch. In the tiny front garden, tables and chairs were arranged, indicating the likelihood of refreshment. A smart dinghy, which looked promising, rested on a nearby trolley. However, the adjacent pier was a disaster. Most of it had disappeared and the feeble remnants of the wooden structure appeared on the verge of collapse.

As I stood staring in disbelief the owner of the house emerged to inform me he had only recently acquired the 200-year-old building, which had undergone immediate improvement. I inquired about refreshment and was pleased to find it forthcoming. I sat down at one of the tables and gazed over the sapphire waters of the loch. When the man reappeared with tea and sandwiches I plucked up courage to ask about the dinghy. Could he take me across the loch? Disappointingly he replied that he was still in the process of renovating it, which was surprising considering its condition. Pointing to a tiny one-man boat bobbing by the jetty, he said that this was his only craft for the time being. He explained that he used it for fishing in the loch and visiting a small lighthouse that he looked after. Apparently the latter task would soon be unnecessary, for solar panels were about to be fitted and the light would no longer require regular maintenance. When I inquired about the rotting pier he indicated that it had been disused since the Second World War.

The extra twelve miles were now a reality and a frustrating trek around the head of Loch Eriboll faced me. This was greatly annoying as I could see the A838 road across the loch. It was returning along the opposite bank and passing Ard Neackie, bound for Tongue. I felt a ridiculous urge to swim across to it. Time had once again become an enemy. It was nearly lunchtime and only seven miles were completed. I would just have to knuckle down and walk around the loch as quickly as I could.

Thud, thud, went my boots on the tarmac. Drip, drip, went the sweat from my brow on that scorching afternoon. So intent was I on eating up the miles that I paid little heed to the loch. If I had I may have caught sight of playful seals that are particularly noticeable in their breeding season, which runs from September to November. Ignoring the heat and passing vehicles I walked like a man possessed, adrenalin pumping in great spurts. I was convinced that the man had lied about his dinghy and sentenced me to this route march. Fortunately my anger was acting as a spur.

When I finally reached Ard Neackie I had not let up, despite risking dehydration. I felt pleased with myself and checked my watch. It was three-thirty, which showed I had made good time. Tongue was still eleven miles away but with a little luck I might reach it by seven o'clock. I forced myself to take a breather and have a drink. It would be foolish to push myself to the limit.

Feeling refreshed I pounded the hot tarmac once more until I stopped to bathe my feet in a small lochan, taking more nourishment as I did so. This sufficed until I neared another vast stretch of water, the Kyle of Tongue that slashes the north coast almost as deeply as Loch Eriboll. Thankfully, a ferry was not required, having been replaced some years previously by a magnificent causeway and bridge that carries the road over the mile-wide inlet. It was a great feeling to walk across the attractively indented Kyle, lined with purple hills and a patchwork of verdant meadows and copses. The finest view was towards its head; a sunlit vista dominated by the shapely outline of Ben Loyal. Despite its modest height of 2,506 feet, it appears much grander because it rises, in splendid isolation, from a spread-eagled landscape. Its five pinnacles resemble a line of jagged teeth, similar to those of An Teallach, and from my vantage point their effect was stunning.

Mustard-coloured gorse surrounded Tongue Lodge that greeted me as I reached the far side of the estuary. It stands sentinel on a headland, beckoning visitors towards the village. Tongue seemed quiet, but appealing as I strolled into it and the first building to catch my eye was the white-walled kirk, typical of many such well-kept churches in Scotland. Despite its importance as a staging post in one of the most sparsely populated areas of the country, Tongue remains unspoiled and peaceful. I came across two inns and saw numerous 'B and B' signs at the gates of well-tended gardens. It was pleasing to find such a wide choice of accommodation, for I had to find a bed for the night. I struck gold at the second attempt and was invited into a small, but neat cottage, home to an elderly couple who seemed genuinely pleased to see me. They had a free room but could not provide supper, which was not unreasonable, for it was past seven o'clock. I apologised for turning up so late, explaining that I had walked from Durness. This caused Monica and Angus, lifelong residents of the village, to raise their eyebrows and look at me with some concern. I assured them I was fine and hurriedly switched the conversation to their peculiarly lilting accents. 'Aye,' said Angus, 'many visitors find it unusual.' To me it appeared more Welsh-sounding than Scottish and Angus found this observation quite amusing.

'You'll be wanting to freshen up and have some food,' said Monica and she whisked me to my room. It was simply, but tastefully furnished and my eyes lit up at the sight of an inviting double bed. She suggested that I sought the nearby inn, which provided good food at a reasonable price. 'After I had soaked away my fatigue,' she added.

Monica's recommendation proved to be sound, for I had an enjoyable and inexpensive meal at the inn. When I emerged into the cool of a lovely late evening the sun was still shining; perfect conditions for a walk. What a ridiculous idea, I thought. Hadn't I had enough punishment that day? Then I recalled noticing a tower perched on a hilltop overlooking the Kyle, not far from the village. My curiosity whetted, I decided to pay it a visit. If nothing else, the view would be worth a walk and I did feel reasonably fit.

As I left the village a narrow footbridge took me across a burn and deposited me on a path that soon climbed a punishing slope and entered a wood. As I battled through impeding foliage and shadowy overhanging branches I was made to pay for my impetuousness. I battled with the vicious gradient and semi-darkness until I finally broke cover to see the ruined tower tantalisingly poised a hundred feet above me. The light was rapidly fading as I scrambled towards the Pictish fort, its ghostly outline silhouetted against a cobalt-tinted sky.

A few strenuous moments later I clung to the gnarled stones at the base of Castle Varrich, as the tower is known, whilst I gathered my strength. I realised why it had been built in such an inaccessible spot. Enjoying a commanding view over the Kyle of Tongue, it ensured that potential attackers could be spotted before they could do much mischief. By the time they had scaled the abrupt hillside the element of surprise would be long gone and they would probably be as shattered as I was.

Ben Loyal basked in the diminishing light. Shadows filled its corries and crevices, accentuating the cragginess of its five steeples. To the north I could see along the Kyle to Tongue Bay that lies at its mouth; a memorable view, for the setting sun cast a sheen of burnished gold over this shapely inlet. My foolhardy venture had been vindicated.

DAY EIGHTY-FOUR : TONGUE - MELVICH

All was quiet when I awoke, in distinct contrast to the uproar of the previous morning. The idyllic warmth and softness of the great bed made me reluctant to face the day. I lazed in its seductive folds and was almost lulled back to sleep. I had to force myself into action with the thought of being late for breakfast.

All was ready and waiting when I got downstairs. Monica scurried attentively to and from the kitchen during the meal. Angus wandered into the dining room, ostensibly to inquire if everything was satisfactory. I reckoned he wanted a chat. As a passing stranger I probably represented the highlight of his day. Our conversation blossomed and Angus spoke with an authority born of a lifetime's experience of the locality. He told me that the castle I had visited the previous evening was of tenth-century origin and it overlooked water and grazing land, as did the brochs, those Pictish defensive towers so familiar to the north of Scotland. The remains of one such tower, he indicated, stand at the head of the Kyle of Tongue, amongst other relics of ancient habitation. Since mesolithic times people had inhabited the estuaries and green straths of that area of Sutherland. He added that the relics around the Kyle's head are typical of their influence. Cairns and stones, engraved with cup and ring markings, litter the slopes where the early hunters, and later the Bronze and Iron Age people settled.

Regretfully, life had changed dramatically in Tongue in recent years, according to Angus. Crofting, the mainstay of the area's economy for centuries, was dying out and the young people were drifting away to work in the oilfields or the industrial cities. Those that remained were virtually reliant on tourism or casual work.

I felt a pang of regret as I stepped into the chill morning air and thanked the couple for their kindness. It was my last day in Sutherland and it appeared that my meagre ration of sunshine in that corner of Scotland was over. I pulled the hood of my jacket over my head to keep penetrating drizzle at bay as I climbed steadily from the village to reach a strategic road junction where the A838 road meets the A836 that has travelled from Lairg. Here I was obliged to change numbers once again and follow the A836 for the remainder of my journey to John O'Groats. Shortly after joining forces we parted company for a couple of miles whilst I threaded, by track and path, around Ben Tongue and Cnoc an Fhreiceadain to avoid a pronounced loop in the highway. Visibility was poor but at least I gained relief from tarmac. Engrossed with thoughts of the ancient settlements around the Kyle of Tongue I mechanically followed the track through the gloom until it narrowed into an indistinct path. At this point I had to abandon my reverie and concentrate on my route. A tiny lochan suddenly appeared out of the mist. I had developed an aversion to confrontations with murky stretches of water, but on this occasion there was no problem.

When I rejoined the road we headed east together, bound for Bettyhill, which stands at the mouth of Strathnaver. The cotton wool blanket that obscured the landscape ensured that we stuck together like glue. After several miles, a farmer on a tractor overtook me and inquired if I needed a rest. He invited me to his nearby farm for a drink and was soon ushering me into a snug kitchen with a stone-flagged floor and whitewashed walls. My head nearly touched the gnarled beams of the low ceiling as the farmer, Calum, shouted for his wife. A stout ruddy-faced woman bustled in and bade me a pleasant, 'Good morning.' Calum introduced us and suggested a welcoming cup of tea. His wife, May, busied herself as Calum asked where I was headed. She produced a mouth-watering fruit-cake as I launched into a short account of my walk. Calum's eyebrows leapt in surprise and May, obviously taking pity on me, handed over an enormous slice of cake, adding that I needed to keep up my strength. My heart warmed to the hospitable couple and I told them about Angus and his mention of the ancient remains around the Kyle of Tongue. As May poured boiling water into a massive teapot she explained that there was a wealth of history in their locality. I was recommended to take a short detour on my approach to Bettyhill and visit the tiny hamlet of Invernaver. A mere half-mile from this collection of farms, she revealed, I would find the remains of a broch and a Bronze Age colony lying on the fringe of Torrisdale Bay.

The cake was sumptuous and I sipped scalding tea as I listened to May's account of the infamous clearance of Strathnaver, which, she said, was only three miles from their farm. 'It is a beautiful, but lonely valley with numerous brochs and cairns lining the banks of the River Naver,' she added. The village of Bettyhill, she informed me, was named after the wife of the hated Duke of Sutherland who was responsible for burning the crofts in the strath and driving their inhabitants to the coast. 'His personal fortune leapt when the land was converted to grazing for sheep,' she said

Declining the kind offer to refill my mug, I explained that I still had many miles to cover that day. As I left I was struck once again by the kindness that seemed to be the hallmark of this remote corner of Scotland - Scourie excepted!

After an hour's purposeful walking I entered evocative Strathnaver and could not rid my mind of the infamy that made it famous. Luckily, I was able to gain access to the ancient settlement, courtesy of the farmer who owned the land, who advised care in skirting the tidal water in the bay. I soon reached the remains of the broch perched on a fine vantage point overlooking the hut circles beneath, which were arranged on mounds of sand. Loose stones formed the rings and their centres were slightly hollow.

My curiosity satisfied I returned to the farm to find its owner waiting for me. I thanked him for his help, which prompted him to supply more information about Strathnaver and its clearance. Apparently, at the time of the torching of the crofts a blanket of smoke obliterated the valley, extending right down to Torrisdale Bay that lies at the mouth of the river. Near the modern bridge, which carries the A836 over the Naver, is a gap in the vegetation that formed a demarcation line across the valley, immediately following the clearance. The evicted crofters, many of whom had lost most of their possessions in the fires, were not allowed to venture up the valley beyond this point.

Time had stolen by during my detour and I was well behind schedule as I rejoined the road and stepped up my pace. I ploughed past Bettyhill's extensively scattered buildings and even ignored the Museum of Strathnaver that beckoned from the roadside. The afternoon wore on as I progressed, in incessant drizzle, along the contorted road that squirmed at every opportunity. In order to maintain an interest in the surrounding countryside, of which very little was visible, I studied my map closely, searching for any distinctive features. As I walked in the lee of the Strathy headland that lay to the north, I could see that it protrudes from the jagged coastline to terminate at the rocky finger of Strathy Point. Here stands a modern lighthouse, completed as recently as 1958, to keep wayward ships at bay. Towering cliffs line the east shore of this rocky peninsula, providing shelter to Strathy Bay, which huddles at its south-east corner. The bay is ringed by the straggling village of Strathy, where the A836 road almost touches the golden sands of its splendid beach as it crosses the mouth of the River Strathy. A grey pall of mist hung over the village but I caught a glimpse of the silken sands, so typical of the cruelly exposed north coast.

As I tackled the remaining three miles to Melvich, the prospect of finding accommodation loomed and I hoped that a protracted search would not be required. Another scan of the map revealed that I needn't wander far from the road when I reached the village, for its buildings were conveniently strung out alongside it.

My legs were just beginning to send disconcerting messages as I reached my destination. A metropolis, consisting of a hotel, a monument and public toilets signified my arrival at Melvich. Its dwellings form another of the numerous settlements that cluster around the foot of the great straths that intrude into the north coast. Melvich shelters at the entrance to extensive Strath Halladale. A main road runs through the strath to reach the east coast at Helmsdale and effectively divides the north-east corner of Scotland from the remainder of the country.

I spotted a 'B and B' sign in the garden of an inviting bungalow and hurried up the path to see if a room was available. Luck was with me. The door was opened by a congenial woman who said she had a spare room. She introduced herself as Janet and invited me in. The interior of her home was very pleasing and included a wonderful array of ornaments. She asked the usual questions. How far had I come? Where was I heading? As I answered I waited for the usual amazed response, but Janet took it in her stride, remarking that many of her guests were walkers.

When I was shown my room I found it just as delightful as the living quarters, with stylish décor and packed with bric-a-brac. As I took a bath in the adjoining bathroom I was surrounded by a multitude of perfumes, toiletries and knick-knacks. Only the rubber duck was missing.

At supper I was greeted by four fellow guests. Not the doctors of

Camusnagaul, but two married couples who were touring Scotland by car. Janet had obviously told them about me, for I received the usual probing questions relating to my lone journey. I steered the conversation away from my endeavours and asked them about their holiday. The men, I discovered, were teachers who liked to tour together each year with their wives. They elaborated on the many countries they had visited and by the end of the meal my mind was reeling with ceaseless accounts of their world travels. I felt quite mundane amongst people so clearly out to impress.

I spent the remainder of the evening in their company and found the wives very pleasant and retiring, whilst their husbands monopolised the conversation. It was quite a relief to escape to my room. The thought that my exploits had been completely overshadowed by the overwhelming pair raised a wry smile. It was their poor wives I felt sorry for. They must have suffered in silence for years.

DAY EIGHTY-FIVE : MELVICH - THURSO

The first thought that entered my head as I dragged myself sleepily from my bed was a comforting one. I had a comparatively short distance to cover that day; a mere seventeen miles. The realisation that I had only two more days before reaching John O'Groats added to my well-being.

I had the dining room to myself at breakfast. My fellow guests were evidently not early risers. I took the opportunity to chat to Jane about my previous day's walk, expressing disappointment at having to forego a five-mile detour to Strathy Point. 'Most of the land in that area, is owned by the Ministry of Agriculture and Fisheries,' she informed me. The Ministry had apparently offered the local residents, mainly crofters, ownership of their properties. Despite their current amicable sharing of common grazing and peat-cutting rights, disagreements had arisen over such a far-reaching proposal. It was surprising to learn that peat was still burnt on such a large scale. The wind of change, I gathered, was obviously unsettling some of these resourceful people, many of whom supplemented their inadequate earnings by working at the Nuclear Power Establishment at Dounreay.

Janet said that had I walked to Strathy Point I would have seen fishing nets hanging out to dry at the Salmon Station overlooking the cliffs, which drop sharply down to Strathy Bay. The nets are suspended on long poles whilst drying and they have to be raised from the shore by winch. The solitary fishing boat, Janet indicated, has to be taken to Melvich for launching each spring as the cliffs are too sheer for hauling it up to and lowering it down from the Station.

Noises from the direction of the bedrooms indicated the imminent arrival of the self-satisfied teachers. Not wishing to endure another verbal battering I beat a hasty retreat, thanking Janet for her cordiality.

The invigorating freshness of a windy and cloudy morning hit me as I left the bungalow and struck out for the Caithness border that lay temptingly four miles to the east. I was thankful for respite from the drizzle of the previous day and visibility, though not brilliant, had also improved. A greater extent of featureless moorland was detectable, which only induced a yearning for some shapely mountains.

There seemed little relief from my diet of heather and grey sky until I rounded a sharp bend in the road at Drum Holliston and several miles of rugged coastline suddenly presented itself. The centrepiece of this welcome view was the sprawl of the nuclear power plant at Dounreay. Controversy has surrounded this distinctive site since its erection in the 1950's. At odds with its admirable backdrop of indented coastline, it appeared vulnerable to attack from the breakers that scour the adjacent shore. The Dounreay Nuclear Power Development Establishment, to use its full title, probably represents a necessary evil to the inhabitants of the northern fringe of Scotland. At one time it employed 5,000 people, from all points along the north coast. Despite its activities being scaled down in recent years, it still provides a good source of employment.

Beyond this questionable site lay the leaden waters of the Pentland Firth. A dark smudge on the horizon was all that was visible of Hoy, the most westerly of the Orkney Islands. Closer to hand I could trace the next two miles of my journey to the village of Reay, which clusters around the band of tarmac snaking across ever-present heathland.

My entry into Caithness would have gone undetected but for two prominent signs by the roadside. The first welcomed me to the final county on my route, inducing a stab of excitement. This was tempered by the second sign that invited the traveller to visit the Caithness Glassworks at Wick. Considering that this town is the most easterly one in Caithness, it did not augur well for what lay in between. Surely the county must possess other delights? If it did, I reckoned, it was not letting on. However, I was soon to discover that there was far more to Caithness than the glassworks.

Golfers would be tempted by the next sign that caught my eye, as I approached Reay. It advertised the nearby testing links that overlook Sandside Bay. No good for a rabbit like me, I reckoned. The ball would most likely end up in the sea if I was let loose on the course. As I entered the compact village it semed an ideal place for holidaymakers who prefer the freedom of camping, or caravanning, as ample facilities for both activities were evident.

Lunchtime was approaching but I decided to walk on and after a further hour I was within reach of Bridge of Forss. Postponing lunch for a little longer I hurried towards it, reckoning that a place with such an intriguing name must be of interest. My expectations were not misplaced; Bridge of Forss was a delight. The hamlet nestles around the winding Forss Water and pride of place amongst its shapely, rustic buildings is given to stately Forss House. An array of tall chimneys sprout from the roof of this splendid three-storey mansion and protrude from the surrounding trees like watchtowers. Now converted into a tasteful hotel, it is built of the warm, eye-catching stone that characterises the neighbouring cottages and barns.

I found a convenient spot, by a preserved watermill, in which to eat my belated lunch. The tranquil river tumbled lazily over the nearby waterfall that formerly provided power for the picturesque mill. This silent, three-storey building stood impassively amidst a wreath of rowan, ash and beach, epitomising an earlier, gentler age.

Blessing my good fortune in finding such an endearing retreat, I enjoyed a restful interlude and recharged my batteries. The realisation that a mere five miles of my day's journey remained, presented a golden opportunity to abandon tarmac and explore at my leisure. A check of the map revealed a convenient cliff-top route to Scrabster, a neighbour of Thurso. I took a quiet road that winds seawards, squeezing between thick hedgerows on its pleasant approach to the hamlet of Crosskirk. A sign indicated a field path leading to St Mary's Chapel that lay slightly off my intended route. Having no time restrictions I made a short detour to the ruins of the twelfth-century chapel, one of the oldest places of worship in Scotland. The view out to sea was still overcast but the features of the extensive hump of Hoy were more discernible. I could make out ranging sea cliffs on the island, their sandy-coloured expanses rising from the agitated ocean like enormous battlements.

Returning to Crosskirk I peered over the rocky amphitheatre of Crosskirk Bay where the restless sea tore at rocks distorted and folded by geological upheaval before man was even thought of. A faint path guided me along cliff-tops that skirt lush pastures, resplendent with buttercup, milkwort and primrose. At Brims Nest, with its adjacent ruined castle and tiny harbour, the ocean swirls around the rocks in a confusion of hazardous currents.

My eyes lit up at the sight of the remnants of a Pictish hill-fort suspended high above the waves on a rocky promontory whose only tenuous link with the nearby cliffs is a slender ridge. The setting said a great deal for the defensive aptitude of its early inhabitants, I reckoned, as I marvelled at their ingenuity, my hair tousled by the wind and the sweet coastal air tantalising my nostrils. I scanned the ocean for shipping, knowing that I was near Scrabster, from which a ferry operates to Stromness on Orkney. Numerous fishing boats were visible, some probably carrying sea-anglers hunting the famous giant halibut that inhabits the Pentland Firth.

I followed the cliff-tops around Holborn Head that guards the entrance to Thurso Bay, and obtained my first view of the urban sprawl of Thurso that surrounds the bay's south shore. Stately Holborn Head lighthouse heralded my arrival at the fishing port of Scrabster lying a hundred feet below in the lee of ranging cliffs. Its harbour nestles beneath this towering wall of rock that provides ideal shelter.

A careful descent brought me to the busy road that serves the port and the fearsome draught from passing juggernauts nearly flung me to the ground. Massive container-loads of fish were being whisked away to far-flung markets. Oil tankers scurried to and fro, quenching their thirst at the austere tanks of a storage depot. Despite the activity in the thriving fish market being past its zenith, vehicles were were still busily swallowing the catches and scurrying from the docks.

I walked amidst the buzz and excitement of the energetic port, passing a variety of sheds, which house everything from ships' chandlers and riggers to an intriguing 'Wee Shop.' Craft of varying sizes gently bobbed at their moorings. Tiny launches vied for dockside space alongside tall-masted yachts and fishing boats. Most eye-catching of all was the brightly-painted RNLB lifeboat, the 'Queen Mother,' a colourful reminder of its namesake who loved Castle of Mey that stands not far from John O'Groats.

The remaining distance to Thurso was covered along a path that skirts the bay and permits elevated views of the jagged rocks and firm sands below. Amongst the rolling breakers expending themselves on the shore, skimmed several surfers. As in Cornwall, surfing championships take place amidst the mighty swells that pound the beaches and apparently, autumn is the best time of the year, when high rollers sweep in from the Atlantic.

My entry into Thurso coincided with the appearance of a veil of sea-mist. Greyness was all-pervading and its streets had a dispirited look. Two statues adorning St John's Square were reduced to nondescript, shadowy forms. The impressive Parish Church that overlooks the square fared little better, its tall tower, sporting shapely Gothic windows, was a disappointing blur.

When I reached my accommodation I met June and Raymond, the lively and affable proprietors. June asked what I thought of the town. Diplomatically I replied that I had been unable to see much of it, but I was particularly anxious to explore the castle and Harold's Tower, the burial place of the Sinclairs of Lybster. I remembered that one of the murky statues in St John's Square was in memory of Sir John Sinclair who was the architect of the herring industry in Thurso and a pioneer of the Agrarian Revolution. Raymond asked if I had seen Princes Street, the town's main thoroughfare. When I nodded he explained that it was named after its counterpart in Edinburgh. Thurso, he said, was designed on a similar grid pattern to that great city.

Suitably scrubbed and changed I had a meal in town and the mist was still lurking as I left the restaurant and walked towards the river. Thurso Bridge was a dark hump spanning its inky waters as I crossed and went in search of the castle. A long walk transpired before I inspected its hollow shell and once-proud towers that presided over a gloomy Thurso Bay. How grand it must have been in its prime when it commanded the entrance to Thurso harbour. Visitors are unfortunately prohibited from entering the ruin but I did discover within the seaward facing wall the protruding barrels of cannon that had not been fired in anger for centuries.

My enthusiasm for further investigation waned in the murky light. I decided to give Harold's Tower a miss, so, fanned by a stiff breeze I retraced my steps into town, passing the former home of Robert Dick, one of the outstanding naturalists of the nineteenth century. Unaware of their proximity to greatness, a posse of starlings gossiped on nearby telephone wires. In towns and cities these gregarious birds can be a problem when they leave their trademark on buildings and pavements and deafen the populace with their raucous clammer.

As I returned to my lodgings the sound of my footsteps reverberated through the silent, empty streets. Where had all the people gone? Thurso resembled a ghost town.

DAY EIGHTY-SIX : THURSO - JOHN O'GROATS

The big day had dawned. Absurdity ruled, as I lay semi-conscious, reluctant to stir. I was in Billy Liar-cum-Walter Mitty mode; my imagination running riot. Convinced that news of my imminent arrival would set John O'Groats aflame, I pictured my triumphal entry that coming afternoon. Flags fluttered, brass bands played their hearts out and the village was packed with ecstatically cheering crowds. I was barely able to reach journey's end at the famous signpost that points to Lands End. Battered by back-slapping and hands aching from continuous pumping, I was pushing through the milling throng of admirers . . . when the call for breakfast rang out!

The meal was a hurried affair, for I was eager to be on my way, but not before I had thanked my hosts for their hospitality. Stepping into the cool morning air I gratefully noted that the mist had retreated. My route that day would be the most direct one and a tarmac trail beckoned, to allow the maximum rate of knots. The A836 road seemed ideal for my purpose. It aims in a dead-straight line for the only village of any significant size between Thurso and

John O'Groats. This is Castletown that straddles the road as it prepares to sweep round the broad curve of Dunnet Bay.

The four miles to Castletown were covered at a rapid pace and I was soon marching past shops and an inviting café that line the main street of the village. I was stopped in my tracks by a sign indicating a notable quarry at nearby Castle Hill. Forcing myself to stop my reckless race to the finish, I went to investigate and discovered the Flagstone Trail, which is set in the cradle of the Caithness flagstone industry, on the shore of Dunnet Bay. Amongst the sand dunes runs a path leading to the derelict remains of the quarry buildings and the sandstone quarry itself. The decaying shells of a windmill and quarrymen's cottages huddle in the dunes near Castle Hill House that was partially destroyed by fire in the 1960's. These remains are a potent reminder of the once-thriving industry that blossomed here in the early nineteenth century. To illustrate the quality of material, elegant Devonian sandstone flags border the path leading to the site. From the quarry, Caithness flags were transported worldwide and paved much of the nineteenth-century confines of Edinburgh, London, Sydney and other major cities.

The road skirts Dunnet Bay, flanked by mountainous dunes that guard the golden sands. Dunnet Forest creeps remorselessly to the fringe of the bay, enveloping the road as it approaches the hamlet of Dunnet. Before reaching the forest I clambered over intimidating, grass-cloaked dunes to scan the great sweep of the bay. Energetic waves licked the luxurious expanse of sand. A flock of predatory gulls, undaunted by my presence, stalked the beach, bathed in sparkling rivulets, or teetered ponderously on mossy boulders. A handful of families dotted the bay and several hardy, vociferous children splashed in the chilly-looking ocean. Their excited cries reverberated around the great inlet that is protected on its eastern flank by the massive bulk of Dunnet Head.

At Dunnet a minor road branches north to traverse Dunnet Head and terminate at the lighthouse and viewpoint that mark the most northerly point of mainland Britain. A prominent roadsign invites motorists to undertake this journey across the significant landmark that juts like a giant nose from the splintered coastline.

The A836 road straightens once more between Dunnet and the village of Mey, whose main attraction, apart from the nearby castle, is the Castle Arms, a prominent roadside inn. I pressed my nose inquisitively to its windows hoping to catch sight of the collection of photographs of the Royal Family that is supposedly displayed within. Luckily the place seemed empty, so my intrusive face was unlikely to put any drinkers off their beer. Of the photographs there was annoyingly no sign.

Since noticing the conspicuous stacks on the roof of Forss House I had been conscious of an abundance of tall chimneys in the area. Mey proved no exception. A glance along its main street revealed clusters of them on the roofs of the surrounding houses. I wondered if they were a prerequisite for the burning of peat. One thing was certain, Caithness chimney sweeps would never want for work. Accommodation signs sprouted everywhere, as they frequently had since entering the county. Caithness would do well to transplant some of these signs in the more remote parts of Wester Ross and Sutherland, where they are sorely needed!

Less than a mile from the village I passed the entrance to Castle of Mey, the residence often visited by the Queen Mother. Sadly the castle is not open to the public, but on certain days in summer its gardens are made available to visitors. I had to be content with a long-range view of the castle from a minor road that winds towards the coast near East Mey.

The cries of inquisitive gulls accompanied my steps towards the furrowed outline of Gills Bay from where there is an exciting view across the Pentland Firth to the island of Stroma that lies a mere two miles from the mainland. A ruptured swirl of coastline circles the bay, which is battered by the fastest sea current in Britain. The Atlantic Ocean and the North Sea meet head on in the narrow confines of the Firth, creating a notorious tide-race known as the 'Merry Men of Mey'. Far from merry, it induces a maelstrom of wicked inshore currents that threaten to drag unsuspecting ships onto the treacherous rocks.

Evocative Canisbay Kirk overlooks the eastern flank of Gills Bay and its adjoining churchyard displays a rich assortment of elegant memorials. Proud headstones and graceful pillars sprout from the earth like an ornate forest, where marble compliments skilfully-carved stone. The kirk has its origins in medieval times and the most notable inhabitant of its graveyard is Jan de Groot, whose uniquely inscribed tombstone dates from 1568. He gained immortality by giving his name to the village of John O'Groats. The story runs thus: In the late fifteenth century Orkney came under Scottish rule and James IV of Scotland instigated a ferry to the mainland in order to embrace the islands into his kingdom. He enlisted three young Dutch brothers, by the name of de Groot, to operate the ferry. They were granted land, by the Earl of Caithness, where John O'Groats now stands. The family multiplied as the years passed and by the mid-sixteenth century there were eight different ferry proprietors with the name of de Groot. They held an annual feast to celebrate their landing in Scotland and unfortunately at one of these functions a dispute arose over precedence in the family. This manifested itself in an argument over who should sit at the head of the table. Jan, older and wiser than his relatives, foresaw a bitter fued erupting. He called a truce for a year and assured his family that by the next anniversary celebration he would find a solution. During the intervening year Jan built a symmetrical eight-sided house with eight doors and an eight-sided table inside. At the following annual feast he and the other seven family members could enter by their own door and sit at their own side of the table. As there was no head to the table, further argument was eliminated. This unusual building became known as Jan de Groot's House and the name was soon applied to the whole village. The ferry service was run by the de Groot family for 250 years and the name of the village eventually evolved into John O'Groats.

Throughout my journey along Scotland's north coast I could not avoid noticing the significant number of hollow, deserted crofts, and the area through which I was passing was no exception. These sad harbingers of change reflect the transition affecting much of the region. Old industries are receding and many young people are leaving to find regular employment elsewhere, as Angus had highlighted at Tongue.

Excitement growing by the minute, I strode past the huddle of crofts at Huna, acutely aware that only two miles remained. The suspense was agonising as I imagined John O'Groats appearing round each bend in the road. At last it lay before me, a scattering of farms and whitewashed cottages with a cluster of houses at its centre. Rolling, fertile farmland stretched from the sea to the distant moorland, where cultivation yielded to sombre emptiness. Sheep and cattle flecked rich pastures that mingled with fields of waving wheat and barley.

I covered the remaining dregs of my journey as I approached the hub of the village. Only the sound of a keen wind greeted my arrival. Where were the imagined crowds? Waving flags and blaring music were conspicuous by their absence. Life went quietly on around the Post Office and village store. No one gave me a second glance and I felt a tremendous urge to kick a nearby pile of peat in frustration. Then I saw the sign indicating the John O'Groats House Hotel, craft shops and museum that lie half a mile away by the harbour. What a fool I was. I hadn't reached the finishing point. That was where I would receive a tumultuous welcome.

I galloped to the shore to find the crowd I was seeking, but the throng of visitors had souvenirs and gifts in mind rather than welcoming exultant walkers. They flitted around a swathe of tarmac and disappeared into the John O'Groats Craft Workshop or nearby souvenir shops. The inanimate figure of Eric the Viking beckoned at the entrance to the workshop complex, which offered unlimited goods ranging from glassware and knitwear to satin-craft and furniture. Had he been alive, poor Eric would have reeled at the startling transformation of his surroundings since the arrival of his ancestors many centuries ago

The sight of a traditional fisherman's whitewashed cottage on the periphery of the swarm raised my dented spirits. A prominent sign at its door broadcast that the building is the famous Last House and it contains a folk museum. Faithfully portraying the original character of the village, it brought home to me that I had reached the end of the road. Wishing to share my accomplishment I realised there was no one to slap me on the back and pump my hand in celebration.

My eye wandered to the nearby John O'Groats House Hotel, which some believe is the true emblem of the village. It has dominated the grassy cliff-top since its opening by the Prince of Wales in 1874. Little-changed over the years it still boasts the original tower built on the style of Jan de Groot's House. A tiny oasis of permanence amidst a desert of change, it caused a public outcry when one of its purchasers, Peter de Savary, unveiled an abortive scheme to demolish the establishment and rebuild it as the flagship hotel of the northern Highlands.

I hurried to the celebrated signpost that perches on a hill overlooking the harbour and the Pentland Firth. It was a tremendous thrill to touch the post where countless completions of the cross-country marathon have been recorded. No one paid me any heed. Local inhabitants are all too familiar with the regular stream of arrivals from, or departures to Land's End and visitors were busily taking photographs for the family album. I was left to bask alone in the thrill of my achievement. The wise words of Wainwright echoed through my mind. 'You didn't tackle the walk to please other people. You did it because it was a challenge and you wanted to see if you could do it. You wanted to test yourself. You have learned not to give up.'

Appendix

NOTE FOR WALKERS

Reference is made in this book to certain walks and long-distance footpaths, such as the Pennine Way and the West Highland Way. The descriptions of these are not intended as definitive guides. If any of the walks mentioned are undertaken, it is advisable to make use of the relevant Ordnance Survey maps and guide books. The use of weatherproof clothing, boots, or sturdy shoes, is also recommended.

Index

Spean, River 273,274
Stac Pollaidh 309
Staffordshire 123
Stanbury Moor 157,158
Standedge Cutting 152
Standedge Edge 153
Stanegate 190,192
Stanley, James 124
Staple Tors 35
Steart 61
Steps Bridge 45,46
Stephenson, Tom 206
Stevenson, Robert Louis 220
Stert Point 60
Stirling 237
Stob Gabhar 256
Stockland Reach 60
Stockport 139
Stone House 102
Stone of Lamentations 119
Stonehaven 238
Stoodley Pike 154,156
Strang, Tom 311
Strange Meeting 105
Stranraer 214
Strath Blane 237
Strath Halladale 331
Strath Kanaird 308,309
Strath More 316
Strathcarron 289,293,294
Strathaven 225,226,227,228,229,230,233
Strathfillan 249
Srathnaver 314,328,329,330
Strathy 330
Strathy Bay 330
Strathy Point 330,332
Street 62,64,65,66
Stroma 339
Stromness 335
Stuarts, the 125,219
Suilven 313,320
Summer Isles 308,309
Sutherland 285,311,314,324,328
Sutherland, Duke of 329
Sutton Mallet 64
Swale Gorge 172,177
Swale, River 172
Swaledale 139,170,171,173
Sydney 338

Tales of Para Handy 258
Talla Reservoir 221
Tamar, River 32
Tamar valley 31,32,34
Tan Hill 173
Tan Hill Inn 139,173,174
Tarbet 245
Tattenhall 129
Taunton 56,57,58,59,62
Taunton Deane 57
Tavey, River 46

Tavistock 32,33,34,35,37,43
Tavistock Abbey 33
Taylor, John 2
Tebris 89
Teign, River 44,45
Teign Valley 43
Teignmouth 46
Telford, Thomas 106
Teme, River 98
Tees, River 176,177
Teesdale 177,178,179
Teeside, Vale of 178
The Crow Road 258
The Rivulet 122
The Road to the Isles 257,263
The Schil 202,203
The Study 260
The Thirty-Nine Steps 221
The Times 256
Thirlwall Castle 190
Thorney 61
Thornton in Craven 162
Thorverton 49,52
Three Brethren, the 217
Three Sisters, the 260
Thrushcross Grange 159
Thurso 332,334,335,336,337
Thurso Bay 335,336
Thurso Castle 336
Thwaite 171
Tibbie Shiels Inn 220
Tijou 124
Tinkers Loan 237
Tinney, William 19
Tintern Abbey 83
Tiverton 48,52,53,55,130
Todmorden 154,155
Tom na Brataich 273
Tone, River 56,57,58
Tongue 321,325,326,327,328,340
Too Long a Winter 175
Top Withens 158,159
Torridon 300
Torrisdale Bay 329,330
Torside Clough 149
Towan Beach 20
Town Yetholm 206
Traqair 214,217,218,219
Traquair House 218
Tregaswith 21
Tregawne 23
Tregolls Farm 22,23,27
Tregustick 23
Trelogan 118,119
Trelystan 102
Trent and Mersey Canal 133
Trethevy quoit 29,30
Trevaunance Cove 14,16
Trevemper 19
Trevithick 21
Trevithick, Richard 15